THE JEWS OF NEWARK AND METROWEST The Enduring Community

William B. Helmreich

THE JEWS
OF NEWARK
AND METROWEST
The
Enduring
Community

William B. Helmreich

Transaction Publishers

New Brunswick (U.S.A.) and London (U.K.)

Library of Congress Catalog Number: 98–34368
ISBN: 1–56000–392–8 (cloth); 0–7658–0493–X (paper)
Printed in the United States of America

Library of Congress Cataloging-in-Publication Data

Helmreich, William B.
    The enduring community : the Jews of Newark and MetroWest /
William B. Helmreich.
        p.   cm.
    Includes bibliographical references and index.
        ISBN 1–56000–392–8 (hardcover : alk. paper). —
ISBN 0–7658–0493–X (pbk.)
        1. Jews—New Jersey—Newark—History.   2. Newark (N.J.)—Ethnic
relations.   I. Title.
F144.N69J54   1998
974.9'32004924—dc21   98–34368
                                                                        CIP

This book is dedicated to all of the lay and professional leaders
of the MetroWest community, and, in particular, to
Michael H. Stavitsky and Herman M. Pekarsky.

Contents

Illustrations follow page 179

Introduction

To look at the lives of the Jews of Newark and the surrounding communities is to take a trip through American Jewish history. Their dreams, hopes, aspirations, and the lives they led typify the experiences of Jews in cities throughout this country. In the same way that every human being is unique by definition, there were aspects to the community that were special, but when all is said and done, the similarities to Jews elsewhere outweigh the distinctions. For this reason, students of American Jewish life in general, can benefit from an understanding of Newark Jewry's history.

Naturally, to those who lived out their lives in this community, it is special, very special. When they reminisce about their lives, they think in specific terms. They recall walking through parks, attending community schools, praying in their neighborhood synagogues, eating in certain restaurants, and frequenting different movie houses and theaters. And most of all, they see their lives in terms of their friends, relatives, and even acquaintances, those who were with them when they did all of these things.

This popular social history seeks to explore how all this happened and what it means. By allowing the people to speak for themselves it tries to bring to life the essence of what it meant to live in Newark, but it also makes use of documents, correspondence, newspaper articles, and novels about the community in order to understand it better.

As elsewhere in the Eastern United States, Sephardic Jews were among the earliest settlers in the Newark area. However, unlike New York City or Newport, Rhode Island, they left behind almost no trace of their sojourn here—no synagogues, no written records of communal life, and no descendants able to speak about the lives of their ancestors. The real beginnings of the Jewish community emerged in the 1840s when German Jews settled here. It was they who began the process of building the synagogues, schools, and communities that have become part of the collective memories of Newark Jewry.

The process was continued and significantly expanded upon by the large Eastern European migration that entered Newark starting in the 1880s. Together, these two groups made Newark and its nearby suburbs into a vibrant center of Jewish life. As one indicator, we have only to look at the many well-known people for whom Newark was home in the formative years of their lives: Philip Roth, Edward Koch, Jerome Kern, Fanny Brice, Jerry Lewis, Dore Schary, Leslie Fiedler, and many, many more. In industry and business too, Newark made its mark: Bamberger's, Ronson Lighter Company, Pathmark, Home Depot, Alpine Lace, and so on.

Newark faced a particular challenge in establishing itself as a community—the fact that New York City lay just across the Hudson River. How could it carve out its own identity in the shadow of the Big Apple? That it succeeded in doing so for more than 100 years is perhaps due more to the leadership of its community and those who chose it, than to anything else. How and why Newark avoided becoming merely another bedroom community is a fascinating story. It is one of the things that makes Newark stand out from many other places.

In the end, however, Newark's Jewish community was unable to survive, and in this sense it resembled the urban patterns of cities across America. The trek to the suburbs and the desire for a house with a little bit of green in front of it overcame the strongest bonds of communal life. As the tax base eroded, services deteriorated, accelerating the movement outward. By 1967, the year Newark's riots occurred, the Jewish community was already largely gone.

Gone, but far from dead. Newark remained alive in the minds of those who had spent their youth there. A substantial number of former Newarkers stayed in the same general area, joining other Jews to build new communities. They settled in places like West Orange, South Orange, Maplewood, and Livingston, towns in Essex County. And in the last two decades that westward pattern has extended further into Morris and Sussex Counties, and beyond.

The desire to be rooted in a community is present in most human beings, in large part, because of the security and meaning it gives to their lives. Because the Jewish community in Newark was so strong, the breakup had a powerful effect upon its former residents and left a real vacuum. The suburban communities, with their synagogues, parks, and restaurants, offered a pleasant way of life, but, somehow, possibly because of their size, it was not enough. What was missing was a sense that those who lived in them were tied to a larger whole.

The attempt to fill that need was made by the Federation. Every Jewish community of any size has one, but the difference here was the extent to which it tried to become a central address for Jews in the entire area. The name it gave itself, MetroWest, symbolized that goal, standing as it did for a community that encompassed metropolitan Essex County and the more countrylike areas of Morris, Sussex, and Warren Counties. That is why it chose Whippany as a site, a place accessible to Jews from the entire area. If anything distinguishes this Federation from others, it is the strong degree of centralization and the credo of operating by consensus, both carryovers from the Newark days.

The activities sponsored and run by MetroWest—lectures, cultural programs, social services, and leisure-time activities, served to bind Jews of the area together. Through them, people from different communities met and interacted, and out of that came a sense of belonging to a larger community. And the Jews of Newark, with their acute sensitivity to the importance of such ties and their own experiences, were an integral part of the process by which all of this came to be. This too, is an important part of our story.

The effort to paint a portrait of Newark's Jewish community was approached in a variety of ways. Interviews were done with eighty-two people. These ranged from leaders of various organizations and rabbis, to more anonymous residents from every walk of life. The time span in which these respondents lived in Newark went from the turn of the century to the present. In addition, there were many oral histories recorded by the Jewish Historical Society of MetroWest, which were made available.

All of the minutes of the MetroWest Federation, from its inception in Newark in 1923, to the present era, were reviewed. The same was done with local Jewish community newspapers which began publishing, on a weekly basis, back in 1922. General newspapers, such as the *Newark Star-Ledger* and the *Newark Evening News*, were also evaluated in terms of what had been written about Newark Jewry. Letters, circulars, documents pertaining to the Jewish community, caseworker files, synagogue histories, and many other sources were also perused. Finally, general books and articles about Newark were consulted in order to properly locate the Jewish community within a larger historical framework.

Notwithstanding these efforts, this book can only be regarded as an introduction to the subject. Much more can be written and the thousands of pages of gathered notes and information that were not ultimately used, testify to that reality. Each chapter, be it on the social life of Newark Jewry, the history of its economic development, or its religious institutions, could easily be the subject of an entire book. It is hoped that this volume will encourage others to delve more deeply into the topic.

A writer rarely stands alone and this case is no exception. I want to first thank the people who worked most closely with me on this book— Alan Lowenstein, Saul Schwarz, Ruth Fien, and Joe Settanni. Their help was invaluable.

I am further indebted to the following people and organizations whose financial assistance made this project possible: the Janet Memorial Philanthropic Foundation, the Alan V. and Amy Lowenstein Foundation, the Jewish Community Foundation of MetroWest, Stella Goldstein, the KSM Foundation, the Lautenberg Philanthropic Foundation, the Herman M. Pekarsky Memorial Fund, Eric and Lore Ross, Rita and Jerome Waldor, Wallace and Barbara Weininger, Morris and Lillian Grunt, Dorothy and Duby Cohen, and the Harold M. Goldberg Memorial Fund.

I am also very grateful to the members of the MetroWest Jewish History Committee of the MetroWest Jewish Historical Society for their careful and insightful reading of the manuscript, which resulted in more than 950 changes and corrections being made. They are, in addition to Saul Schwarz and Ruth Fien: Arthur Bernstein, Martin S. Fox, Warren Grover, Anita Hannoch, Max Kleinman, Marilyn Kussick, Janet Lowenstein, Victor Parsonnet, David Schechner, James Schwarz, Joseph A. Settanni, Stanley Strauss, Jerome Waldor, and Leo Yanoff. Naturally, whatever deficiencies remain are solely my responsibility.

Others who helped in a variety of ways, reading chapters, providing guided tours of Newark, and rendering other forms of vital assistance, were: Nat Dunetz, Jerry Lehman, Amy Lowenstein, Murray Laulicht, Howard Charish, Rabbi Joseph H. Ehrenkrantz, Charles F. Cummings,

Ronald L. Becker, Seth Jerchower, Daniel Drench, Stephen Levitt, Ed Brody, Laurie Pine, Peter Skolnik, Irving Louis Horowitz, Jeffrey Gurock, Steven Goldberg, Jeffrey and Alan Helmreich, Chaim Lauer, Paul Marcus, Jerome Fien, Wallace Greene, Joe Berger, and Lois Schlar.

Special thanks goes to all of those who allowed me to interview them. Besides speaking with me, many of them were very hospitable and gracious and I truly appreciate it. Last, but far from least, I want to thank my wife of twenty-eight years, Helaine, who read every word of this manuscript and willingly shared her wisdom and insights with me. As constructive critic, true friend, and life partner, who could ask for more?

1

Newark: From Earliest Times to the Present

To its Jewish residents, Newark has always been something of a paradox. For many, if not most, it is a city they think of with affection, love, and reverence. Its schools, parks, theaters, restaurants, and synagogues are often described as places that were truly special to those who experienced them. Most of all, perhaps, the collective memories of its people seem focused on the *sense of community* that characterized Newark, one that they assert was unique and impossible to duplicate elsewhere.

At the same time, Newarkers are acutely aware that others do not necessarily share these perceptions about their beloved city. An old vaudeville joke characterized Newark as "the place where the Pullman porter comes in to brush you off for New York." Moreover, New Jersey itself is often viewed in similar terms. Benjamin Franklin is reported to have described it as "a beer keg tapped at both ends," meaning, of course, Pennsylvania and New York.

In modern times, Newark has suffered greatly from the 1967 riots that gave it an image of chaos and urban decay from which it has never quite recovered. In a 1977 *Jewish News* article, Benjamin Kluger summed up the frustration felt by many former residents about their city and the stereotypes it has engendered:

> Of late, Newark has not been awarded any prizes as a model American city. But as one who grew up there, I resent the slurs against it in newspaper articles, or on radio or television. It is pictured as a hideous example of an urban swamp, fallen into a state of irretrievable decay. Some people shudder at the thought of passing through it. "Newark? I never go there." . . .Certainly some sections bear out their opinions. . . .It is my hope that enlightened leaders and vigorous action will stem its decline, open up its opportunities. . . .and make it once again the shining city on the hill I knew. For the Newark in which I grew up was a beautiful city.[1]

7

In reality, both images are correct because each speaks to a different time. But for many who lived in the Newark of old its disappearance makes them feel that they have somehow failed. There are no real monuments to a once vibrant way of Jewish life, no old neighborhoods to revisit, no remaining restaurants, only two functioning synagogues. Did we do something wrong, they ask?

And then there is the "New York Problem." The great city across the Hudson has always cast a long shadow over Newark, as it has over the entire metropolitan area. Thousands of Newarkers worked in New York City, enjoyed its Broadway theaters and fine eating establishments, as well as its elegant shops and boutiques. And yet, Newark was different from so many other smaller towns in the region. Listening to its denizens as they reminisce about the Mosque Theater or Proctor's, or shopping at Bamberger's and Kresge's, or eating at the Tavern or the Weequahic Diner, one realizes the fierce loyalties associated with Newark.

The real question then, is: How was Newark able to carve out a social living space for its residents? How, in the face of a large booming metropolis a mere fifteen minute ride away, a world-class city, was Newark able to grow and flourish? What prevented it from becoming merely another, albeit larger, bedroom community?

The answers to these questions are many and complex. To understand the vitality of the city we need to know a great deal about its history, its economic growth, its social, cultural, religious, and educational institutions, and the people who made them all happen. And to do that, we need to start at the beginning.

A Brief History

The origins of Newark can be traced to one of its most fabled landmarks—the intersection of Broad and Market Streets, otherwise known as the "Four Corners." It was here that a group of Puritans from New England, led by Robert Treat, first settled, in 1666. They hailed from four Connecticut towns—Branford, Guilford, Milford, and New Haven. Members from those towns took up residence at each of the corners, forming a new town, Newark, so named because Reverend Abraham Pierson of Branford had previously preached at the church in Newark-on-Trent, in England.

Treat was no invader. He and his followers bought Essex County from the Lenape Indians. They selected Newark, in part, because they feared the hostile tribes whose territory lay further inland and because New York had already been settled by the Dutch. No doubt, Biblical imagery affected them too, for they viewed the area to which they had come, by way of the Passaic River, as a sort of promised land.[2]

The group of Puritans who had left Connecticut were literally purists. They felt that the outside world was encroaching upon their community and were determined to build a truly religious society in their new homeland. As matters turned out, however, Newark became the last theocracy in America and by 1776 full religious freedom had been granted to all of its residents.[3] The only exception was the right to hold office, which remained under the exclusive control of Protestants. Amazingly, it took almost seventy years and many protests before that privilege was ended.

Newark was buffeted by the winds of the American Revolution in much the same manner as the rest of the East Coast, and its residents fought with bravery and distinction in the Revolutionary War. One of its most famous citizens was Aaron Burr, vice president of the United States under Thomas Jefferson. Alas, Burr's reputation was tarnished by his duel with Alexander Hamilton, whom he killed in nearby Weehawken, in 1804.

Until 1820, Newark was a sleepy little town, with small houses and farms bisected by meandering dirt roads that became small rivers of mud whenever it rained. Its main claim to fame was as a way station between New York City and Philadelphia. The hub of activity centered around the local religious institutions, such as Trinity Episcopal Church and the First Presbyterian Church, as well as some of the more popular taverns in the area. The uniformity of its population was fertile soil for the prejudices of its inhabitants who looked upon Catholics and other non-Protestant groups with a mixture of scorn and hostility. The days of the melting pot had not even appeared on the horizon.

Soon, however, everything began to change as the Industrial Revolution that was sweeping through Europe and the United States, came to Newark. Industry, shipping, railroads, inventions, immigration, all these and more, transformed Newark from a backwater town to a leading city. Instead of cows, chickens, and goats, the city became a place where everything from leather, hats, and jewelry, to iron, steam engines, and copper, was manufactured. It was here that Seth Boyden invented a process for making malleable iron, as well as one for patent leather, and built the city's first steam engine. Inventions, both large and small, proliferated in the surrounding towns as well. Out of Belleville came the copper wire for the world's first telegraph, a machine for engraving bank notes was invented in Irvington, and Nutley became known as the place that gave birth to the ice cream soda.[4]

To remain informed, many Newarkers read the *Daily Advertiser* which, after several name changes, became the *Newark Star-Ledger*. By 1836, Newark had become incorporated as a city and in 1840 its population numbered some 17,000 souls. For those who wished to travel to New York City there was one train a day (excepting Sundays) and a steamer twice a day. At night, darkness enveloped a city where evening lamps were nonexistent. There were no drainage or sewage systems and many of the wells were polluted. As a result, disease and epidemics were not uncommon. In some years up to a quarter of the population died from illnesses such as cholera and scarlet fever. And this was New Jersey's most important city!

Slowly, however, things improved. Gas lamps were introduced, cobbled streets replaced dirt roads, homes made of brick or sandstone were built, and schools were started. Naturally, the Civil War disrupted Newark's industrial growth. It may come as a surprise to those who think that geography determined loyalty, but Newark voted heavily against Abraham Lincoln, for most of its products were shipped to the South.

After the war, Newark continued to grow. Irish and German immigrants had been coming to Newark since the 1830s and they changed the face of the city's social landscape with their own churches, beer gardens, newspapers, and music, supplying much of the labor for Newark's burgeoning factories and stores. By 1870, the city had 105,059 inhabitants and, in 1872, the Newark Industrial Exposition had attracted an estimated 130,000 visitors. The local products displayed included leather, silver, shoes, beer, hardware, paint, cotton, chemicals, and much more.[5]

Those who believe that the growth of the suburbs and neighboring communities was a phenomenon of later times are mistaken. Orange, for example, was created as a separate municipality in 1806. It was followed by Bloomfield in 1812, Livingston in 1813 and many others. The reasons for doing so varied, from squabbles over railway service and taxes to a simple desire to forge a separate identity. Regardless, the failure of Newark to keep these municipalities within its boundaries was to have a severe effect on the city's financial health in later years.[6]

By the dawn of the twentieth century, Newark had become one of the most important industrial cities in the U.S. Its restaurants and theaters were crowded, its stores filled with shoppers, and everywhere, new buildings were going up. With a population of 240,000, Newark required new schools, community centers, and houses of worship. The Yankees, Irish, and Germans were now joined by immigrants from other lands—Italians, Hungarians, Poles, Jews, Portuguese, and, internally, African-Americans. Assisting the new arrivals presented Newark with a new challenge, one faced by cities across America, and it responded with enthusiasm, creating both organizations and agencies designed to acculturate the new arrivals.

The town fathers decided that the city deserved a world-class library as well as a first-rate museum. And so it did. John Cotton Dana was recruited and he turned the Newark library into an outstanding center for learning. Dana paid particular attention to the immigrants, stocking the shelves with many books in foreign languages. And in 1926, the great philanthropist, Louis Bamberger, donated a $750,000 building to the city as a home for its museum, one which was to become world renowned.

For decades Newark had attracted industry because it was centrally located and had an ample labor supply. Among the major corporations and industries that made their homes there were Ronson, Tiffany, Ballantine, Westinghouse, Mennen, Waterman, and General Electric. And, of course, there was the insurance industry—Prudential, Firemen's, Merchants, Mutual Benefit, and others.

Nevertheless, like the rest of America, Newark suffered through the vicissitudes of the Depression. The WPA (Works Progress Administration) helped tide thousands through the hard years, and the local churches and private agencies did their share too. It took years, however, for the city to recover. And then, World War II created an economic boom as Newark's factories hummed with activity, producing tents, uniforms, military instruments, and countless other items.

With war's end came the belated realization that Newark had been losing its economic dominance for at least two decades before the war, as other cities stepped up to challenge it. Highways were being built, housing starts were down, industry was leaving, and the quality of life was sinking rapidly as crime, slums, and family dislocation became major social issues. All of this was accompanied by racial polarization that had accelerated as the city's tax base eroded, and which, in turn, affected the quality of services offered to its residents. As the exodus to the suburbs picked up speed it was only a matter of time before the once proud city became a shadow of its former self.

The Beginnings of Newark's Jewish Community

The Sephardic connection to Newark's Jewish community remains somewhat shrouded in mystery, but it definitely exists. German and Bohemian Jews, it should be stated at the onset, were, no doubt, the real founders of the community. In terms of individuals, however, there is evidence suggesting that Sephardic Jews may have preceded them by at least sixty-eight years, for the records show that a Rachel Gomez died in Newark in 1776.[7]

Who was Rachel Gomez? A member of a prominent Sephardic family that was affiliated with Congregation Shearith Israel, she was the wife of Mattathias Gomez, one of those New York Sephardic Jews who joined the American Revolutionary forces in Philadelphia in early 1776.[8] Though no one can say for certain, it would seem possible that his wife died while she and her family were traveling between New York and Philadelphia.

Benjamin Gomez, son of Rachel, married Charlotte Hendricks (another prominent Sephardic family name), in 1797. Did they live in the Newark area? We don't know, but, in 1813, Charlotte's brother, Harmon Hendricks founded the Belleville or Soho Copper Works in nearby Belleville. From here on in, the Sephardic presence becomes much more definite. Solomon Isaacs was the foreman in charge of the mill and lived in Belleville, as did Aaron Gomez and Montague Hendricks, Harmon's nephew.[9]

The mill was well situated since the Passaic River provided it with easy transportation access to markets everywhere. It was located near the busiest networks of canals and rivers in the East, and benefited greatly from its proximity to the Morris Canal which was completed in 1825. The steamboat industry, engineering companies, and merchant vessels depended heavily upon copper and the business flourished, producing, in its heyday, 350 tons of copper a year. It was also considered one of the best equipped engineering plants in the country and its customers included people such as Paul Revere and Robert Fuller.[10]

When Harmon Hendricks died, his estate was worth over $1,000,000. Moreover, the family became an integral part of the Belleville community, deeding 200 acres to the town in 1924 for use as a public park. This was done in appreciation of the fact that "the Hendrickses, the Gomezes, and the Nathans, had lived [in Belleville] for more than a century."[11] We know that the Sephardic Jews who ran the mill were part of New York City's Spanish-Portuguese community and that they traveled regularly between New York and Belleville. Moreover, a good number of them were permanent residents of Belleville. But did they function as a Jewish community? Did they, for example, conduct religious services in Belleville or did they engage in such activities only in Shearith Israel? The rapid growth of the mill had made it necessary for the owners to build a spacious residence on the property. The home looked out over the Passaic River and was situated near what eventually became the Forest Hill section of Newark. Did it serve as a center for Jewish life, perhaps?

Not enough information is available to allow for any conclusions, but one thing is clear—the residents were proud of their heritage and clearly identified with it. One writer familiar with Belleville's history described the Jewish atmosphere there as follows:

> The merchants of New York had no doubt about his [Harmon Hendricks'] religious principles. It was a matter of firm religious conviction not to charge usurious rates of interest; no merchant could tempt Hendricks to do business on the Sabbath; and the mill at Belleville was closed to all on the Sabbaths and Jewish holidays.[12]

Unfortunately, there are no records that could prove the existence of organized Jewish life in Belleville and the minutes of Shearith Israel (many of which are, alas, missing from the period under discussion) do not shed any light on this question. They do, incidentally, make note of Newark on two occasions: The first pertains to a request by one Henry Settaz (clearly a Sephardic name) in 1847 for help in purchasing a cemetery. The matter was tabled without comment.[13] The second entry merely notes that, in 1898, Shearith Israel donated to Congregation B'nai Abraham the chandeliers that had hung over the president and vice president's seats in its 19th Street location, as well as some candlesticks that had been used for a brief period at the 70th Street site.[14] This was actually part of a pattern adopted by Shearith Israel to assist Ashkenazic congregations around the country whenever they requested it.[15]

And what of Ashkenazic Jewry during this early period? Again, there are isolated references to individuals such as Jacob Stern who reportedly came to Newark in 1837, as well as some early Jewish Newark residents who may have converted to Christianity, but nothing definitive. In addition, there were surely Jews who sold provisions to the Revolutionary Army.[16] Nonetheless, like the Sephardic settlers, they cannot be viewed as founders of today's Newark Jewish community for they left behind no known descendants, no synagogues, and no Jewish organizations. Credit for that clearly belongs, by all accounts, to Louis Trier, who arrived in Newark in 1844. Coincidentally, in that same year, the State of New Jersey abolished all religious tests as qualifications for holding public office.

The great wave of German Jewish immigration to America began in 1836 and lasted until the end of the nineteenth century. Like many other groups, these Jews were seeking to improve their lives economically and they also wanted a more tolerant environment. They chose Newark, in part, because Christian German-speakers already lived there, thereby making communication easier, and because it was close to a large Jewish community, New York City. Of course, the early settlers created a snowball effect, as the growth of the community made it increasingly attractive to yet more newcomers.

Most of these German immigrants came from small towns and farming communities, not from places like Berlin or Frankfurt. Their backgrounds had equipped them to meet the needs of local residents by working as tanners, butchers, and the like. Nevertheless, they progressed quickly in their new environments. Trier typified the upwardly mobile pattern of many Jews. A leather tanner in Germany, he soon became a manufacturer after arriving on these shores. He also raised six children, among them Abraham, who, in 1845, became the first Jewish child to be officially registered as born in Newark.[17] Initially, these new arrivals settled in the Down Neck section or in downtown Newark and then moved up South Orange and Springfield Avenues.

One of Newark's oldest families was the Kussy-Schwarz family, One of its members, Gustav Kussy, started out as a peddler and eventually became a butcher, a common pattern. These early Newark Jews were intent upon putting down roots and building a community, thus creating a need for butchers, tailors, dry goods stores, and the like, to provide for its residents' needs.[18]

Another important early family was that of the Newman brothers.

Isaac operated a boarding house on River Street which also served as a meeting place for the immigrants. His brother, Abraham, became a successful merchant, and was also instrumental in the founding of Congregation B'nai Abraham, named after him.

Isaac S. Cohen was one of the few prominent non-German immigrants. He came, in 1847, from England, and was the organizer and first president of Congregation B'nai Jeshurun. Other early arrivals of note included Bernard Hauser, Henry Weill, Moses Gans, Louis Adler, Wolf Bergstrasser, Bernhard Lowy, and Moses Schlosser. By 1855, the community numbered some 200 souls.

The Jews who settled in Newark were deeply religious and the founding of a synagogue was a very important matter to them. In 1847, B'nai Jeshurun, New Jersey's first Jewish congregation, was incorporated and began holding services in an attic on Arlington Street. Soon, however, in a pattern duplicated in Jewish communities everywhere, a dispute erupted, leading to a lawsuit, and Isaac Cohen departed for New York, taking the Torah scroll with him, which he had originally loaned to the congregation.

Realizing belatedly that no synagogue could function without a Torah, a delegation visited Cohen in New York and persuaded him to return. Cohen agreed, on one condition—that the congregation's name of B'nai Jeshurun never be changed. However, the synagogue was still missing another essential element, a leader, and so, in 1854 Rabbi Isaac Schwarz (of the Kussy-Schwarz family) was engaged as its spiritual head, serving in that capacity until 1860.

Meanwhile, a second house of worship was about to open. As difficult as life was for German Jewish immigrants, it was even harder for a small group of Polish Jews who had also chosen Newark as their promised land. Unable to communicate with anyone except those belonging to their tiny community, they lived in abject poverty in the area around Mulberry and Canal Streets, eking out a bare living as peddlers. Their one good fortune was a German Jew named Abraham Newman, a man who, moved by their plight, invited them to worship at his home. Little did they know that their tiny synagogue would someday become one of Newark's foremost temples, home to Rabbi Joachim Prinz, the city's most illustrious and best-known rabbinical leader.

Although peace reigned for a few years, disagreements again broke out at B'nai Jeshurun and this time the rupture was permanent. In 1860, after a close election, in which Rabbi Schwarz' bid for reappointment was defeated by one vote, a group of congregants walked out of the temple, never to return, founding their own synagogue, Newark's third, Congregation Oheb Shalom. Among those who left were Bernard Hauser, Philip Holzner, Leopold Lang, Henry Weiss, and Leopold Weill.

Through the years, literally hundreds of synagogues have come and gone, but throughout, it is these three, and Adas Israel and Mishnayes, all now located in the suburbs, that have symbolized the continuity of Newark. They were the first, they were large in size, and they are still there. The first, B'nai Jeshurun, eventually became Reform and the other two, B'nai Abraham and Oheb Shalom, followed the Conservative ritual, although formally, B'nai Abraham is unaffiliated with any movement. Originally, however, all were Orthodox, with separate seating for men and women, daily services, where men donned phylacteries, and there was no organ or choir. The members were deeply religious and, like the Puritans of Robert Treat's day, their faith pervaded their daily existence. Nathan Kussy, a chronicler of the era, has provided a glimpse of just what that meant:

> Bernard Hauser stumbles and falls down the front steps of the Oheb Shalom synagogue, as he emerges after Sabbath services. He cuts his head severely, is confined to bed for several weeks, vows to God that if he recovers he will remain standing throughout the Yom Kippur services for the rest of his life. Therafter, on every Yom Kippur day, the patriarchal figure of the old man, weak from fasting, dominates the congregation as he stands before his seat from early morning until dusk reciting his prayers.
>
> When Friday evening draws near [Gustav Kussy] folds up his butcher apron, leaves his shop, and devotes the evening to a study of the Scriptures. After a time, he familiarizes himself with the Hebrew language, entertains visitors from Jerusalem, converses with them in that tongue, and commits to memory almost the entire Scriptures in the original Hebrew so that one may open the Hebrew Bible at any page and he will proceed to quote its text word for word from memory.[19]

It was not merely a matter of being ritually observant that characterized these men. The moral principles that permeated their way of life was intertwined with their religion. As Kussy observes:

> It is felt that the synagogue is a democratic institution, and that in the House of God the poorest must be on an equality with the wealthiest. In order to perpetuate this democratic spirit the bylaws provide that every year, at a meeting held during Passover week, lots shall be drawn to determine the ownership of seats or pews during the ensuing year.[20]

In the beginning, life was difficult as the settlers struggled to earn a living, but, after a time they prospered. The peddlers learned the language, managed to save a few dollars, and bought stores, which grew in direct proportion to the industriousness of those who labored in them. At first these stores were quite modest in the scope of their operations. We have, for example, a description of how Hirsch May, a butcher, whose shop was located at the intersection of Prince Street and South Orange Ave, did his bookkeeping:

> He kept no books of account, but noted down the sales on scraps of paper which he hung on the tender hooks besides the hulks of beef in his shop. . . .[On them he noted] such descriptive items as, "the Woman with the Crooked Neck, 15c"; "The Shiksa with the Green Shawl, 22c"; "The Red Headed Woman with Pimples, 20c"; And these constituted his record of sales on credit![21]

By 1860, a remarkably short span of a decade, Jews owned some of the leading dry goods stores in the city—Ullman & Isaacs, Klein & Thalheimer, and Hart & Dettelbach. Another very important industry was trunk manufacturing, especially Edward Simon and Company, and Lagowitz and Company. R.G. Salomon and Abraham Rothschild each founded major leather firms and, in retailing, there was L.S. Plaut and Company, later called, the Bee Hive.

Until now we have focused on the men, but this was not an immigration of men only. Women came from the old country too, either with the men or in groups of two or three. Those who married here had simple weddings with a few friends from the neighborhood who joined them for a simple repast in a bare, sparsely furnished room. The presents fit the Spartan surroundings. When Gustav Kussy and Bella Bloch married in 1858, their presents included a broken stove, one of whose legs was missing and a wash tub. After the wedding had been paid for, they were left with $2.00.[22]

These were hardy women and they made their mark upon the society in which they lived through the organizations they formed. One of the earliest was the *Frauenverein Naechstenliebe* (Friendly Sisters) set up in 1852 to help the poor and the sick. Listening to the following description of one of their meetings to which husbands were invited does not exactly conjure up the image of obedient housewives working day and night to please their spouses. Rather, it reveals the sentiments of a group of women whose solidarity and fierce independence would put them in the front ranks of the contemporary feminist movement. It also suggests that communal life in those days, was vibrant and dynamic:

> For some unknown reason the participation of the men . . .arouses the ire of their hostesses. Perhaps the women feel that the presence of the men robs the meeting of that mystery and secrecy so characteristic of women's organizations. Perhaps the men, instead of being silent spectators, open their lips, like Balaam's ass, and speak. Or perhaps—who knows?—the startled husbands, beholding the unwonted spectacle of dutiful wives and mothers cultivating the art of public speaking, are suddenly confronted with the vague but gruesome spectre of female emancipation, glimpsed through the mist of years, and, having come to scoff, remain to bray.
>
> Whatever the cause, the dutiful wives became of a sudden undutiful, fiery, incensed, as though determined to repel the plebian mob of husbands that has ventured to invade, as it were, the sacred Temple of Diana. Breathing defiance to the trembling males, the outraged women decide that never, never, never thereafter shall men be invited to meetings of the organization.[23]

The feistiness of the organization's members was, nonetheless, guided by a sense of realism. Notwithstanding their vow, the women concluded after a year that their organization would be better off financially under a new finance committee made up of men and they invited, however reluctantly, G. Cohen, Samuel Meyer, and David Marx to run it.

Women did play a role, it should be mentioned, in their husband's businesses, helping them to run their affairs but they were not, as a rule, equal partners. The Newark Directory of 1853–54, did, however, list a woman, Hester Goldstein, as a dressmaker. She was perhaps the first Jewish woman, and woman in general, to run her own business in Newark.[24]

Naturally, the Civil War roiled the Jewish community as it did Newark's population in general. Not surprisingly, however, given Jewish sensibilities, there was a strong moral component that attached itself to the issues surrounding the war. Thus, we learn of B'nai Jeshurun's Daniel Webster Society and its debate on "Ought Slavery to be Abolished?"[25]

Like Newark businessmen in general, Newark's Jews were beneficiaries of their trade with the South. Still, there was a strong identification with Abraham Lincoln and his moral message. Jews were fond of telling the story of little Daniel Hauser, "the boy who shook hands with the President," when he passed through the city. Most significantly, there was a tremendous, spontaneous outpouring of grief after Lincoln's assassination. They saw in him a latter-day reincarnation of the Biblical figures who preached justice in the Bible and, in fact, had fondly called him, *"Unser Avrohom"* (Our Abraham).[26]

Given their worldview, it is not surprising that, despite their own penurious circumstances when they arrived, Jews immediately became active in charitable causes. In 1861, The Hebrew Benevolent and Orphan Society was founded, with Isador Lehmann as its president. The synagogues too, were active in this area, starting relief aid societies in which women played a prominent role.

Education has always been a priority for Jews and the Newark community was no exception. Typically, during this period, children attended public school, usually completing the elementary grades. An exception to this pattern were the children of B'nai Jeshurun, who, by and large, attended the synagogue's own day school. A good number of youngsters also attended synagogue-run Hebrew schools in the afternoon. Occasionally, gifted students went further. One such example was Henry Lowy who entered Newark High School (later renamed Barringer High School) at the age of ten and finished in 1860, at age twelve, the youngest graduate in that institution's history. At the time he was also the only Jewish student in the school and his commitment was such that after a long day of studying, he also attended Hebrew classes for two hours, finishing up at 6:00 PM[27]

For entertainment, people gathered in taverns, boarding houses, at each other's homes, and in the parks that dotted the areas in which they lived, discussing the issues of the day as well as exchanging gossip and general information. Interestingly, the main highlights of the year were the annual picnics sponsored by the Hebrew schools. Led by bands playing marching music, the children would parade through the streets to Caledonia Park on Springfield Avenue, to Doelger's Park, near Morris Avenue, and other favorite locations. And in the evening, the adults came and danced until the wee hours of the morning.[28]

For the emerging elite of the city there was the Progress Club, founded in 1872 by seventeen young men, whose ranks included Samuel Froehlich, Leopold Simon Plaut, Simon Weil, Leopold Fox, Uri Dannenberg, and Morris Cohn. They appeared to have a good instinct for public relations, initially naming the organization the No Name Club, to, as they put it, "arouse the inquisitiveness of non-members . . .make them wonder as to its purpose and thus make them anxious to apply for admission."[29] Judging from the response, the approach worked as young men from around the city vied for membership. Its well-appointed facilities included a beautiful dining hall, meeting rooms, and a lounge. There were also picnics, Purim and Simchat Torah balls, and excursions, but its main function was as a meeting place for the financial and political leadership class of Newark. The Club's existence had a dampening effect on the growth of the Y, which was also in operation at the time.

Of course, Jews as a group suffered the pain of prejudice and discrimination in those days. This was true economically, residentially, and socially. In this sense, their treatment was no different from that meted out to Jews across the United States. At the same time, Jews and gentiles interacted in a variety of ways as individuals. For example, German Jews and gentiles often met in the Greisenheim Park, where they would chat with their German friends over coffee and cake. Coming from the same country, speaking the same native language, belonging to the middle class, and having a history of shared cultural experiences, they felt a sense of kinship that frequently tended to overshadow religious differences.[30]

Newark Becomes a Major Center for Jewish Life

Starting in 1881–82, a great wave of Jewish immigration from Eastern Europe began to make its way toward the United States. By the time it was over in 1924, about 2,000,000 Jews had come here, with about 45,000 of them settling in Newark, the "Workshop of the Nation," as it was popularly known. Their reasons for coming varied, but for most it was a combination of persecution in their native lands and the firm belief that America was the land of opportunity.

When these Jews arrived, they came face to face with fellow Jews whose culture differed in many respects, whether it was language, philosophical and religious outlooks, or economic level and occupational patterns. In most instances the Eastern Europeans had lived in towns and villages where they had formed the majority of the population. Consequently, they had little interaction with non-Jews, with the result being that their level of identification as well as knowledge of Jewish traditions was quite high. Moreover, the Enlightenment in Europe had affected them differently. While in Germany it resulted in Reform Judaism, the outcome in Eastern Europe led in the direction of radical proletarian movements and Zionism. These ideologies naturally accompanied the immigrants and affected mightily the rate at which they were absorbed into the dominant German Jewish culture, one which looked upon these newcomers and their seemingly strange beliefs with a mixture of condescension and noblesse oblige.

All of this affected the course of Jewish history in Newark as it did that of Jews elsewhere in the land. Still, it would be an oversimplification to assume that the distinctions between the earlier and later groups were so clear and sharply defined. While B'nai Jeshurun became Reform and Oheb Shalom and B'nai Abraham embraced the Conservative pattern of worship, all started out as Orthodox congregations and were influenced by that fact. And while it is true that many of the Orthodox-raised Jews from Russia and Poland became Conservative over time, there was at least some movement in the other direction as well. The historian, Jonathan Sarna, has argued quite cogently that more Orthodox viewpoints had already appeared in the 1870s, especially in Philadelphia and New York, and that it was not simply a matter of traditional East European Jewry colliding with their more assimilationist German-Jewish coreligionists. In addition, the growth of Y's, which began in the 1870s, tremendously enhanced Jewish identity well before the Eastern European Jews made their appearance on the American scene.[31]

Nevertheless, pride in Jewish culture was by no means universal among the new immigrants. Reminiscing about her family, Elaine Menkes, a Morristown resident, recalled:

> I didn't find out till much later that my mother was born in Europe. They didn't want to be known as greenhorns. In those days, to be born in Europe, it was a *shanda* [shame]. You didn't say.[32]

Parallel to such discomfort there was a real sense of pride in being an American, almost as if a conscious effort was being made to drown out the past. Muriel Bloom of West Orange, remembered how:

> My father wanted to be a real Yankee. When they played the Star Spangled Banner, he was the first one to stand up. He came here by himself in 1900 at age twelve.[33]

Conflict was not limited to German and East European Jewry. Distinctions were made within the groups too, whether it was the Bohemians and the Bavarians or the Galicianers and the Litvaks. Bernard Bloom, Muriel's husband, noted, with a twinkle in his eye:

My father used to think I was cursed, that I married a *Galitz*. But he was crazy about her. And my brother married a girl from a very old desiccated, German-Jewish family.[34]

Notwithstanding the humorous tone accompanying such recollections, the rancor and animosity often ran deep, with predictably negative consequences. As Saul Schwarz, one of the most astute and knowledgeable observers of Newark's Jewish history, has pointed out, the hostility led to a great deal of duplication of services and unnecessary fund-raising. There were many organizations, all competing for the same funds. Nevertheless, there was one positive outcome—the establishment, in 1923, of one central Jewish communal organization, the Conference of Jewish Charities, today known as the United Federation of MetroWest. As a result, it became possible for the various fund-raising efforts to be combined, in 1926, into one general campaign, under the heading of the United Jewish Appeal of Essex County. This development fundamentally changed the character of the Newark Jewish community and it is a topic about which much more will be said later on.[35]

For the Eastern European Jews, Prince Street was the hub of activity. As they moved in, the German and Irish population, which had originally come there from the Ironbound section, moved out. Jews lived and shopped there, as well as on Springfield Avenue and Broome Street. They lived lives of poverty, but what attracted them most was the abundant supply of jobs. Newark in those days had more than 2,000 factories and a variety of public works projects—parks, trolley lines, and a tunnel to be built under the Hudson River.

Above all, there was a palpable sense of movement, a feeling that the city was dynamic and that one could get ahead if only one worked hard enough. Prince Street was Newark's answer to New York's Orchard Street. Filled with pushcarts, it was paved with wooden blocks and its stench blended with the foul odor that came from the nearby Passaic River. There were live carp swimming in big glass tanks, corned beef, pastrami, pickles, herring, St. John's Bread, sugar cane, fruits, and vegetables. Colorful scarves, dresses, suits, clothing of every description, hung from the racks. Vendors grabbed passers-by and shouted: "Mister, just take a look." Saul Schwarz called it "Baghdad on the Passaic."

Whenever people talk about their pasts they use the shops they frequented as markers. For Jewish Newarkers in the early part of the twentieth century, that meant Springfield Avenue, and the stores that come to mind included Graubard's Childrens' Clothes, Daddy Rich's Pawn Shop, Schottenfeld's (now Dean's) Carpets, Hausman Shoes, and the West Side Trust Company (the first Jewish-owned bank). And for those familiar with the Ironbound Jewish section, here is the following loving portrait by Benjamin Kluger:

> My father had a shoe store at the corner of Ferry and Congress and we lived in the back. We were mostly poor people. The Italians swung their pickaxes or repaired shoes; the Germans sweated in their breweries; the Poles worked in foundries; the Irish built the factories and the bridges or worked for the city, and the Jews owned the stores strung out along Ferry Street. Phantom-like, the old businesses rise in my mind. The Rivoli Theater, that dim beatific manufactory of dreams. Reuben's Sweet Shoppe next door where we sipped our sodas after watching the passionate eye-rollings of John Gilbert and Vilma Banky. Further up, the Ironbound Theater, where the Westerns galloped across the screen. Weintraub's Women's Wear, Jaffe's Grocery Store, Shulman's Hardware.[36]

The Jews did not stay any longer than they had to in these neighborhoods. As soon as they had saved up enough money, they moved on. In the early 1920s, Jews settled in Clinton Hill and from there it was on to Weequahic. Along the way, Jewish professionals opened offices on previously gentile High Street. Many physicians moved into one of two major office sites, an apartment building on Clinton Avenue and in the Medical Towers near Lincoln Park. Others moved to Roseville, to North Newark, and to the suburbs that lay beyond the city line.

New organizations also sprang up at this time to accomodate the changing needs of the Jewish community. The newcomers needed assistance in acclimating to life in the U.S. and the National Council of Jewish Women, formed in 1912, provided it. Out of that organization came the Reciprocity Club, headed by Jennie Danzis, which gave Americanization lessons to the immigrants. The Hebrew Free Loan Society gave financial assistance to those who required it and the Daughters of Israel Home for the Aged (now known as the Daughters of Israel Geriatric Center) ministered to the elderly.

While all this was going on, Newark's philanthropists were making contributions to the city at large that not only benefited the city's residents in general, but the immigrants as well. As mentioned earlier, Louis Bamberger not only donated the building for the museum but also the structure that was to house the New Jersey Historical Society on Broadway. The cherry blossoms that so beautified Branch Brook

Park were a present from Mrs. Felix Fuld. Not to be omitted is Leonard Dreyfus who gave the planetarium to the Newark Museum. Dreyfus may have become an Episcopalian but in life perception is often everything. Evidence for that can be seen from the comment made by one of his coreligionists to Samuel Kessler, the well-known Jewish community leader: "One of your fellow Jews is a member of my church."[37] Whatever the case, these gifts clearly helped raised the stature of all Jews in the eyes of Newarkers in general.

One of the most significant achievements was the founding, in 1901, of Newark Beth Israel Hospital. The decision to do so was based, not only on need, but on the fact that Jewish doctors were often barred from other hospitals. As Saul Schwarz put it, "A world treatment center was born out of an act of discrimination and prejudice."[38] At the time it had a capacity of twenty-one beds. In 1906, it inaugurated a new building at the corner of Kinney and High Streets. By 1929, it had moved again to Lyons Avenue where it had a capacity of 300 beds and was known throughout the country as an outstanding institution, where a top-notch staff incorporated the latest techniques into the treatment of its patients.

Jewish education for most of the immigrants consisted of late afternoon study a few days a week, sometimes in private schools, called *heders* and, in other cases, at synagogue-affiliated centers. The hapless teachers who taught in these schools were often underpaid and ill-treated, by both students and parents. To remedy the situation, the Hebrew Educational Society organized a school in 1888 with the help of several prominent German Jews, including Meyer Hood, Isaac Schwarz, Moses Strauss, and the Reverend Joseph Leucht. The building, on the corner of Prince and Spruce Streets, was a gift of the Plaut family and the school was named after it.

At the time, the Plaut Memorial Hebrew Free School was probably the best such institution of its kind. Nevertheless, it was looked upon with some suspicion by the Eastern Europeans who saw in its creation more than a trace of condescension. Saul Schwarz recalled his own brief experience there:

> I enrolled at age five in 1919. A week later my father noticed the dedication plaque on the wall outside the building, saying the school had been established to "bring the civilizing influences of American democracy to our Eastern European brethren." And that was the last I attended the school.[39]

Eleven years later, in 1899, a new school, the Talmud Torah of Newark, was established by Eastern European Jews to meet the growing demand for such education. At first, it was situated on Broome Street, the heart of the Third Ward. Later, it moved to the Clinton Hill section and grew to more than 700 students. Like the Plaut School it enjoyed an excellent reputation and contributed greatly to ensuring the continued identification of Newark's Jews with their traditions.

In terms of the larger Jewish community, Newark became an important center of support for Zionism. There were many Zionist clubs and organizations devoted to the idea of a Jewish homeland, among them Hatehiya, Young Judea, Mizrachi, and Poale Zion. The *Jewish Chronicle* reported in its September 15, 1922 edition, how more than 8,000 Jews marched up Broad Street to celebrate the ratification of the Palestine Mandate. The Parade featured a float depicting the gates of Jerusalem, where a high priest was standing. England was shown opening the gates to the Jews (How unprophetic, in view of later developments!). Every major Zionist figure, from Chaim Weizmann, to Nahum Sokolow, to Ze'ev Jabotinsky, spoke there.[40]

In 1924, Nathan Kussy, one of Newark's most prominent Jewish leaders, declared at a dinner held in Schary Manor, that "The Zionist Movement will bring the Jews back to Judaism. Even we," he continued, "feel as outcasts, although the spirit of America is preserved by aliens who come here because of persecution overseas."[41] Kussy came from an old-line German-Jewish family that had settled in Newark in the mid-nineteenth century and that was, by 1924, thoroughly Americanized. That he, of all people, made these comments, speaks volumes about the insecurity of many Newark Jews at that time.

To really understand such apprehensions it might be helpful to look at the newspapers of the period, which were filled with articles about anti-Semitism, not only throughout the world, but in the U.S. as well. To take just two examples, the *Jewish Chronicle* reported, in its July 11, 1930 issue, on a Troy, New York man who was ordered to remove a sign that hung outside his service station, proclaiming: "No Jews or dogs allowed." Closer to home, in the July 18, 1930 issue, an Irvington man complained about the refusal to rent him a cottage at Morris Harbor, a resort development on the Raritan River, because he was Jewish.

Jews responded in kind too. It is probably difficult for those who did not live through these times to imagine the Jewish community's antipathy towards the vicious and constant anti-Semitic attacks by Henry Ford. Many of his articles were translated into Yiddish and reprinted in Jewish newspapers. While not everyone reacted in the same way as did Jacob Scarr, they certainly shared his abhorrence for the man and what he stood for:

> I drove the three Ford trucks that I owned to a junk yard and was offered $150.00 for them. I had paid more than $1,000.00 for them, but I said, "Well, all right, but I want those trucks to be destroyed so they will never be on the road again.
> The man looked at me and said, "I am Jewish too. In that case, I will give you the same deal we gave to L. Bamberger & Company. That is $10.00 per truck, and you stay and see the bolts loosened, the body lifted up and carried away, and the chassis smashed to bits. By now we have acres and acres of [Ford] bodies stored away, one on top of another, three high. We hope that another chassis manufacturer, but not Ford, will make a half-ton chassis, and we will be able to sell those bodies. And then we will get rich." I accepted the man's offer . . .and have never gone near a Ford since.[42]

Many of Newark's Jews considered themselves Zionists in varying degrees, but such sentiments were by no means universal, not even amongst Jewish leaders. The most vociferous such opponent was B'nai Jeshurun's rabbi, Solomon Foster, and while it was not the dominant view, it reportedly had some impact on his congregants.[43] In a 1932 article that appeared in the *Jewish Chronicle*, the well-known Zionist leader, Rabbi Stephen S. Wise, asserted that "Newark Jews had an inferiority complex" that was the cause of opposition to Zionism in that city. From the article, it can easily be seen that the focus of his ire was Rabbi Foster.[44]

Proletarian movements also found support in Newark. And small wonder. All of the ingredients were there—poverty, conflict between labor and management, Jewish intellectualism, and the well-known Jewish passion for social justice. They were an integral part of the cultural baggage that the Eastern European Jews brought with them. There were secular socialists and Zionist socialists, Bundists and members of the Workmen's Circle. Even German Jews, albeit few in number, were drawn in. Bella Milmed, daughter of Meyer Kussy, joined the Socialist Party in 1936. She credited her teacher at West Side High School, Max Katzen, with having influenced her to join:

> I gave a report in his class, on political party platforms and, after reading them all, I decided socialism was the best one. I felt it stood for greater equality and not so much for making a profit at the expense of poor people.[45]

Many Jews did not make a clear distinction between socialism and religion. It was not unusual for a Jew in Newark to be a staunch proponent of socialism, even as he or she attended synagogue on a regular basis, particularly if the person was a union member. For many, such coexistence was made easier because belonging to or sympathizing with such movements was simply part of the culture of being Jewish.

To others, however, the separation was quite clear. Jerry Ben-Asher, music critic for the *Jewish News* and a retired chemist, always saw himself as a secular Jew interested in Jewish culture and history. In his youth he was a member of YPSL (Young Peoples Socialist League) and became a paid union organizer for the Perth Amboy-based Mine, Mill, and Smelters Union, in 1934, at the ripe old age of seventeen. YPSL had many Jewish members as did the Communist Party and its dissident Trotskyites and the Student League for Industrial Democracy. In fact, Ben-Asher met and became friends with the writer Irving Howe through his involvement with the Student League.

For most young people in the 1930s, the heyday of the socialist movement, the impetus for such involvement came from the family, but other factors also played a role, depending on the case. For one person it might be a film, for another a speech given at a rally, for a third, a book or article, for yet a fourth, a teacher or friend. As Ben-Asher observed:

> I remember reading a book by John M. Work, *What's So and What Isn't*. It offered me an outlet for my idealism. And my family was always very socially conscious. One of my uncles was very active in the Labor Zionists and my aunt, Naomi Ben-Asher, eventually became National Director of Education for Hadassah. I went to South Side High School, but nobody there encouraged me.[46]

Newark Jewry also achieved importance in another area and that was the bootleg industry. After all, the New Jersey coast was known as "Rum Row" and Jews contributed their fair share to its reputation. The route began in England and, to a lesser extent, France, and then went to the islands of St. Pierre and Miquelon, off of the Canadian Coast. There, the Bronfmans took over and arranged for the liquor to be shipped to the U.S. And the biggest name was the mobster, Abner "Longy" Zwillman, nicknamed in Yiddish, *"Der Langer"* (literally, "The Long One"). He, Joe Reinfeld, and others turned Newark into the central location for the illegal liquor trade. Millions were both made and spent and this had an effect on the economic structure of the local Jewish community. Just how many jobs it created through the warehouses and how the money was spent, would make a very interesting dissertation topic.

The Jewish community may not be especially proud of the fact that one of America's biggest gangsters was a Newark product, but it's a fact. Alan Block, in *East Side, West Side*, a study of organized crime generally, has documented the extensive power of the Zwillman-Reinfeld group in the liquor industry,[47] as well as in Florida and in the Nevada gaming industry. Maybe it was his *yiddishe kopf* but Zwillman made sure to diversify, investing his money in steel mills, real estate, railroads, and even a General Motors truck dealership.[48]

One should avoid stereotyping, however. While there was crime in the Jewish community, most Jews were uninvolved. Looking at the Newark city records in the 1920s one finds the following: between 1923 and 1926, the height of the same Prohibition Era, there were 2,356 reported cases of juvenile delinquency. Jews, who were certainly not well-to-do in those days, constituted but seventy-three cases of the total. And that says it all.

Newarkers also found time for relaxation, especially once they had become "established." Newark was an important center for Jewish culture. Elving's Metropolitan Yiddish Theater was a popular local center and the Y was one of the best in the United States. In part, Newark's importance in this arena was that it often served as a proving ground for many who went on to achieve national fame. Examples are Dore Schary, Pulitzer Prize winners Moss Hart and Mark Silver, Norman Tokar, and many others. Credit for nurturing these individuals and for giving them a forum goes largely to George Kahn of the Y who created its famous "Bits of Hits" shows. Some of those who performed in Newark had grown up in the city; others chose Newark because it was the nearest place to New York City that would give them a break.

When the residents of Newark ventured elsewhere for fun they generally stayed within the state, traveling to places like Bradley Beach or Mount Freedom, or sailing up the Hudson River on the Day Line. Some of the more adventurous went to the Catskills while others rented beach houses in Coney Island. Closer to home there were picnics in the parks of neighboring Irvington and Union, or Olympic and Dreamland Parks. There were fights at Laurel Garden and bicycle races at the Velodrome, as well as baseball games at Bears Stadium on Wilson Avenue. And when they wanted a good meal, there was the Tavern, not to mention the adjacent bakery with its delicious desserts, as noted by Ruth Fien, the founding president of the MetroWest Jewish Historical Society.

Even as Newark began to climb out of the Depression, the gathering clouds of war began to intrude on the community's collective consciousness. As a result, economic preoccupations were soon replaced by alarm over the rise of Nazi Germany and the threat it posed, not only to the country they loved but to their Jewish brethren as well. Actually, the Nazis had been a concern of Jews here as early as 1933. In March of that year more than 2,000 people had filled the Y's Fuld Hall to protest Nazi persecution of Jews. And on that same evening, Prince Street merchants had closed their stores five hours early, at 5:00 P.M., in protest, after a day of fasting and prayer in sympathy for Germany's Jews. Across the river, 22,000 more Jews jammed into Madison Square Garden to register their dismay over Hitler's actions.[49]

The first direct influence in Newark was felt in the mid-1930s as refugees from Germany began arriving, just as they did in other cities with major Jewish populations. Social workers were sympathetic to these newcomers but their colorful case entries did, at times, betray a certain subjectivity:

> She is about 5'3 inches tall, stocky, looks like a peasant girl. Has a large face and wears her hair in a very old-fashioned way; wears unbecoming clothes.
>
> Has a large face, kind grey eyes, a ready smile, and charming manners.[50]

Many of these refugees adapted quickly, finding both employment and a social place in the community. Learning from past experience, Jewish organizations moved decisively to aid them in the adjustment process, creating social environments like the Jewish Unity Club, where they could meet other immigrants and socialize with them.

People made desperate attempts to enter the U.S. right up until the beginning of the war. The case files tell of a particularly heartbreaking instance in which a woman arrived from Poland, right before the war, to visit the World's Fair. She returned in August on the *S.S. Pilsudski* and, after being on the ocean for three days, she learned that Poland had been invaded by the Nazis. As a result, the Polish vessel was not allowed to land anywhere for six weeks until finally given permission to do so in Newcastle, England. The woman knew that returning to Poland was folly, so she sold her belongings and returned to the U.S. on her visitor's visa. After a brief stint operating a button-hole machine, she took a job in a Brooklyn pillow factory. In her meetings with her social worker, she spoke of "fantasies" in which "I saw my husband and family mutilated by the Nazis." Alas, they were not fantasies. She never saw them again.[51]

In the early 1940s, the Nazis' mistreatment of Jews continued to dominate the headlines of the Jewish papers. And, as the awful truth about the genocidal policies and practices of the Nazi war machine became better known, the fear and near panic of Newark's Jews mounted. At the same time, Jews flocked to Army, Navy, and Air Force recruiting stations to enlist in the war effort, anxious to do something concrete, as well as to demonstrate their patriotism.

Even Newark itself found a place in the demented mindset of the Nazis. There was the bizarre story reported in the *Newark Evening News*, courtesy of the Associated Press, regarding the Newark Jew whose book was blamed for the expulsion of the entire Jewish community of Hannover, Germany! The action was attributed by the city's mayor to the publication of a book by Theodore N. Kaufman of Newark, called, *Germany Must Perish*. The book, it was alleged, "demands sterilization of all Germans and employment of German soldiers as coolies in foreign lands." Kaufman, a graduate of South Side High School, responded as follows:

> The Nazis are merely finding a scapegoat for their barbarities. They have hounded the Jews from the beginning . . .and I am sure anything I have written could not make their atrocities worse. In July the Nazis claimed that President Roosevelt wrote my book, although I have never met Mr. Roosevelt. Now the Nazis claim they are evacuating the Jews from Hannover because of my book. . . .But perhaps the RAF is writing an even better story with its bombs over Hannover.[52]

The Postwar Era

In 1948, Newark had the seventh largest Jewish population among cities in the U.S. About 56,800 people lived within its boundaries, about 12 percent of the city's total population, mostly in the Weequahic and Clinton Hill sections, and an additional 29,500 resided in neighboring communities such as Irvington, Hillside, Maplewood, the Oranges, Bloomfield, Millburn, and Verona. Newark's Jews followed the national pattern of leaving the cities in favor of the suburbs, although they differed in that the process had begun earlier, well before World War I. In part, this was because the boundaries of Newark were so small to begin with, compared to other cities.

In the mid to late 1940s, Newark Jewry's attention turned to helping the refugees and to the founding of the Jewish State. The National Council of Jewish Women played a major role in assisting Holocaust survivors who came to Newark find apartments, jobs, and, in general, rebuild their shattered lives. The Jewish Community Council of Essex Country, founded, in 1923, as the Conference of Jewish Charities, which was the umbrella organization for a variety of Jewish agencies, became heavily involved at this time in supporting the establishment of Israel. Funds were desperately needed to smuggle Jews from the DP camps to Palestine and the UJA of Essex County responded dramatically, raising more than $2,000,000 in its 1946 campaign.

In a process that began in the 1920s, Jews were becoming more and more like other Americans, perhaps more so, as the political scientist, Seymour Martin Lipset, once observed. Their values and lifestyles became more middle class and the Jewish working class that had been so integral to the community in the 1920s and 1930s was gradually replaced by a business and professional class. Postwar prosperity had a good deal to do with this development and the net effect was to create a more homogeneous community. The trend was accelerated by increased college attendance as well as rising numbers of synagogue members. In this last regard, Jews were simply following the dominant trend of rising church membership that characterized the 1950s, a pattern which, in itself, was linked to the desire for middle-class respectability. And for Jews there were the additional motivators for Jewish identity of the Holocaust and Israel.

Jewish families also became more heavily committed to their childrens' Jewish education. The Jewish Education Association (JEA) had already been formed in 1937 for the express purpose of coordinating such efforts, offering courses, and licensing teachers. In 1943, the Hebrew Academy of Essex County became the second all-day school in the area. By the 1950s, Jewish education of some sort, be it afternoon school or study in a yeshiva, was becoming very much accepted in the community. All told, 6,500 children were attending Jewish schools in 1954.[53] In 1952, an alternative Jewish school was founded. Called the Bet Yeled Jewish Folk School, it was supported by the

Labor Zionist organization and emphasized a Jewish education that taught Jewish history, literature, and values but which did not place any emphasis on religion, per se.

Newark's Beth Israel Hospital also continued to expand during this period, developing outstanding departments in a number of areas. In 1949, Alan Lowenstein spearheaded an effort to establish a home-care program, thus helping to make Newark a leader in providing for the needs of the chronically ill. Of course, the hospital was considered a superior institution before then. Former New York City mayor, Edward Koch, a Newark resident during the 1930s, credited it with having performed an operation requiring 150 stitches, that saved his left hand.[54] It also had an excellent nursing school, one of whose most famous students was Paula Ben-Gurion, wife of Israel's former prime minister.

Although few realized it at the time, Newark's viability as a Jewish community was nearing its end. By the 1960s, however, there was little doubt as to where things were heading. Nevertheless, Jews did not simply sit back and do nothing. For example, the Weequahic Area Committee was formed to deal with crime, housing, and social action, and to establish closer Jewish organizational linkages with the surrounding suburbs. In the end, however, the larger economic and demographic forces that were eroding the city overwhelmed it. In 1972, five years after the Newark riots, there were 6,000 Jews remaining in Newark out of a total of 100,000 Jewish residents in Essex County.

In the 1930s, Newark was not really in the mainstream of Federations in this country. This was due to several factors. First, there was the proximity of New York and many people, especially those who worked there, identified strongly with the Empire State. Second, people began moving to the suburbs and they took their businesses with them to their new communities. Third, the Community Chest in Newark (now known as the United Way), when compared to other cities, did not give much money to Newark's Jewish community. Finally, the fact that so many national Jewish organizations were headquartered in New York, weakened, or dwarfed, if you will, the nearby Newark chapters.

Organizationally, the critical period in the history of Newark's Jewish community was the 1940s. It was in those, and later, years that Newark became an important community at the national level. In a pattern that began then and which has continued into the present,

Newark's Jewish community has produced more than its fair share of people who have led national organizations. These include: Michael A. "Mike" Stavitsky, founder and first president of the American Association for Jewish Education (today known as the Jewish Education Service of North America [JESNA]); Herbert Abeles and Louis Stern, both of whom served as president of the Council of Jewish Federations (CJF); Alan Lowenstein, vice president of CJF; Philip Hoffman, president of the American Jewish Committee; Jacqueline Levine, chairperson of the National Jewish Community Relations Advisory Council (NJCRAC); Ralph Wechsler, honorary president of Poale Zion (National United Labor Zionist Organization of America) and board member of the Jewish Agency; Martin Fox, president of the Jewish Telegraphic Agency; Arthur Brody, president of JESNA and president of the Jerusalem Foundation; Martin Kesselhaut, president of United Hebrew Immigrant Aid Society; and Philip Lax, vice president of International B'nai Brith. The most famous Essex County resident to attain a national leadership role is Senator Frank Lautenberg, who served as both the national and local chairman of the United Jewish Appeal Campaign.

Led by Herman Pekarsky, the dynamic executive director of the Jewish Community Council of Essex County, and assisted by Stavitsky, Samuel Kessler, and Alan Lowenstein, the leadership succeeded in uniting the various groups into one fund-raising and organizational entity for local, national, and overseas functions. They brought together the community chest, those active in community relations councils and the welfare fund, as well as those who worked on Israel-related issues. A rump group, led by Joel Gross, a Newark attorney, opposed the merger, but its efforts to prevent it from happening were unsuccessful.

While the idea of linking them originated with the national CJF, the mechanics of doing so were made possible by the vision of Pekarsky and Essex County was the first to actually use it. Although there were other great Federation executives like Isidore Sobeloff of Detroit and Henry "Hank" Zucker of Cleveland, Pekarsky was probably unequaled as a planner. He also brought in good people like Charles Miller (planning director) and Morris "Marchy" Schwartz (fund-raiser). His main objectives, according to Saul Schwarz, were to professionalize and unify the different agencies and to increase services to the community.[55]

Even as it struggled mightily not to do so, Newark always perceived itself as living in New York's shadow. In looking at the community, however, it becomes clear that great leadership can, as happened here, overcome structural/geographical limitations. That is an important lesson which Newark can impart to other communities that exist in similar circumstances.

In 1945, a committee, chaired by Alan Lowenstein, restructured the Essex County Council of Jewish Agencies, creating the Jewish Community Council of Essex County. Prior to that the community was weak, a blessing in disguise because it meant that the different groups within it were unable to sustain any real opposition to a reorganization that ultimately proved to be the best approach. It also resulted in the emergence of a democratic structure that encompassed within it all of the Jewish organizations—synagogues, women's groups, Jewish education, and so on. Parenthetically, Lowenstein accomplished the same objective later on in reorganizing Newark's civic structure.[56]

Eventually, Newark, as a Jewish community, came to receive very little support from the Community Chest.[57] It became, in 1945, the only city in the country with this form of operation.[58] In this sense, Newark's contribution as a model of communal integration was singular, if not unique. And, in fact, its example was followed thereafter by Los Angeles, San Francisco, Boston, Philadelphia, and many other cities.

If the fifties were characterized by steady growth, the sixties were the embodiment of social change. The children of both Federation professionals and volunteers became enamored of the hippies, political activists, antiwar protesters, and feminists. The establishment was "out" and the counterculture was "in." While the Federation could certainly not wrap itself in the mantle of vanguard radicalism, it could and did become an agent for social causes. The agency sponsored civil rights marches and demonstrations and linked up with the black community to protest on behalf of social justice. Towards the end of this period, the Six Day War galvanized the Jewish community into action and, again, the Federation served as a central rallying point for Jewish activism on behalf of Israel.

Between the founding of Newark's first three synagogues—B'nai Jeshurun, B'nai Abraham, and Oheb Shalom and the post-World War II period, many other synagogues were established. Some, like Congregation Adas Israel and Mishnayes and Anshe Russia, flourished, while others languished in obscurity. Many were nothing more than tiny rooms, with perhaps ten to twenty congregants, but to those who worshipped in them, they were everything. All told, Newark was graced by more than forty synagogues in 1948. Today, there are two left. Among the best known rabbis throughout these years were Joachim Prinz, Solomon Foster, Charles Hoffman, Hyman Brodsky, Joseph Konvitz, Julius Silberfeld, Ely Pilchik, and Louis Levitsky. Prinz was also president of both the American Jewish Congress and the World Jewish Congress. Famous cantors performed in Newark, including Yossele Rosenblatt and Berele Chagy, both of whom sang in Congregation Adas Israel.

Architecturally, a good number of the temples were impressive structures, but, they were generally, as Ruth Dolinko, an expert on the topic, has observed, distinguished by an emphasis on "functionalism." Unlike, say, Atlanta or San Francisco, they did not reflect specific cultural or regional antecedents. Rather, the purpose was utilitarian—to provide the population with a place that was economical, spacious, and reasonably edifying. Exceptions were Millburn's B'nai Israel and Springfield's Beth Am. Percival Goodman was the architect in both cases and he became, in 1951, the first such individual to have complete independence in designing a synagogue. As part of his efforts at B'nai Israel, Robert Motherwell was commissioned to produce a work of art for the synagogue. Naturally, worshippers developed fierce loyalties to their synagogues and temples irrespective of design or motif, but this was due primarily to the sense of community and belonging that characterized such institutions.

For most Newarkers, it is the culture of the city that touches them most deeply. When they reminisce they think about how it was a cultural beacon for thousands of Jews. The Newark Library, under the guidance of the great John Cotton Dana, gave inspiration to all who ascended its marble staircase. But to the "people of the book," it possessed a special resonance. And as they left it at sunset they could see the throngs of people shopping at Hahne's, Kresge's, Bamberger's ("Bam's"); socializing at the Robert Treat, the Douglas, and the Essex House. For good food and company it was the Chanticler, the Weequahic Diner, the Tavern, of course; Achtel-Stetters, Simonson's, Childs, Schrafft's, Zig's, and so many more. And what about the movie marquees—Proctor's, the Paramount, the Branford, the Goodwin, the Rialto, the Loew's, the Mosque, and the Little?

Whether it is the places themselves or *who* the people were when they went to these places, or both, matters little. What counts is the central role they played in their lives. It was at the Mosque that they first heard Yehudi Menuhin or Rudolf Serkin perform. The Newark Museum provided the setting for poetry readings and art exhibitions of high caliber. And then there was the Y.

The Y was different because, unlike the restaurants, museum, and library, it provided culture in a Jewish setting. Only the Yiddish theater and some of the temple programs could also lay claim to that distinction. Saul Schwarz recalled the Y as the place "where I discovered the Jewish world and it was one of the few places where my friends and I, poor, from an East European heritage, were truly welcomed."[59]

From 1924 to 1954, the Y had been situated on High Street. Tens of thousands of people used its facilities. There were concerts, Broadway shows, choral societies, and, most important, an environment where young Jews could meet, socialize and, as often happened, find a marriage partner. In the early 1950s, membership was about 8,000, with slightly more than half coming from Newark. In addition, the Y had satellite locations in Weequahic, Hillside, South Orange, and Irvington. It also supervised programs located in synagogues in Belleville, Nutley, Kearny, Bloomfield, Montclair, and elsewhere.

The main Y moved to Weequahic and then to West Orange and its migration, so to speak, mirrored what was happening to Newark Jewry. Similarly, the theaters, department stores, and restaurants began to close, one by one, with some enjoying a reincarnation in the suburbs. By 1967, the year of the riots, there was very little left to speak of.

The Demise of the Jewish Community

Discussions of how Newark collapsed as a viable Jewish community seem to inevitably lead to the question of black-Jewish relations in Newark. Such a connection is, to say the least, a gross oversimplification. Nevertheless, it is a crucial issue and while there were unique aspects to it in the city, it can only be properly understood when placed in the larger context of black-Jewish relations in the U.S. The two groups have both positive and negative feelings toward each other and one thing is certain——they are almost always strongly held views.

Jews have tended, for a variety of historical, cultural, and economic reasons, to find themselves in roles where they were immediately ahead of African Americans or where African Americans were dependent on them. Examples are the teacher-student and principal-teacher relationships; the landlord-tenant and merchant-customer relations. Since one has power over the other, resentment and conflict are bound to occur, and they did, both in Newark and elsewhere. In fact, by a curious coincidence, Imamu Amiri Baraka (aka LeRoi Jones) is a nationally known black leader but, as a native of Newark, he wrote about such tensions with specific reference to the city.

In many neighborhoods across America, African Americans and Jews often found themselves occupying the same residential space. This is no accident. The knowledge and awareness of blacks that Jews are traditionally liberal made them feel more comfortable about moving into predominantly Jewish neighborhoods. In addition, the often violent reactions that greeted blacks who moved into Italian or Irish areas, made Jewish neighborhoods seem much more attractive.[60] The vigilante activities of Anthony Imperiale as head of the North Ward Citizens' Committee are a textbook case of such responses. In fact, Max Geltman, recounted the following story in, *The Confrontation*, a work that deals extensively with black-Jewish relations in Newark:

> A friend who has worked as a newspaperman in Newark for a generation and who lives in the Italian community there told me: "Nobody really cared. It was a war between the Negroes and the Jews. And many Italians just sat back and laughed, saying the Jews had it coming, especially the civil-rights rabbi [Rabbi Joachim Prinz] . . .it is the Italians whom the Negroes have the most difficult time dislodging from their homes. They do not run. . . .They never establish committees to defend this or that civil-rights cause.[61]

The anti-Semitic legacy that was part of Christianity in general, was also present in the black community. The great writer, Richard Wright, observed in *Black Boy* that the children in his town disliked Jews, not so much because they exploited them economically but because they had been taught at home and in Sunday school that the Jews had killed Christ. Wright cites the following poem that he used to sing together with his friends outside a local Jew's store in Arkansas:

> Bloody Christ Killers
> Never trust a Jew
> Bloody Christ Killers
> What won't a Jew do?[62]

Jews often say: "We worked so hard for blacks and look at how ungrateful they are." Notwithstanding the tendency on the part of some

Jews to be patronizing, the fact is that Jews as whites were very much involved in Civil Rights causes and were overrepresented in the movement, at least until the late 1960s. In part, this was because their tradition emphasized helping disadvantaged groups and because at least some of them believed that reducing prejudice benefited all minorities, including themselves. It may also have come about because, as a marginal people, Jews hoped that by being in the forefront of successful social movements, they might finally gain the acceptance that seemed always to be just beyond their grasp. In fact, this last explanation could account for the disproportionate involvement of Jews in many social causes, from the Russian Revolution to the antiwar movement.[63]

Jews have experienced a good deal of discrimination in this country, but nowhere near as much as African-Americans. They have been and continue to be substantially better off as a group than most blacks and it has created a good deal of envy in the black community. Nor are such feelings necessarily limited to the economic sphere. Conversations with blacks suggest that they are acutely aware of Israel's importance to Jews and to their collective identity. How are they supposed to feel when they see how easily Jews relate to Israel, a new-old nation whose waves of immigrants began coming to that country only in this century?[64] As though, all this were not enough, there was the rise of black nationalism during the 1960s, with its accompanying identification with the overwhelmingly anti-Israel (and, by extension, anti-Jewish) Third World.

Looking at Newark itself, we see a black community whose roots go back quite far. The first formal black church was founded in 1822, on Academy Street, by Christopher Rush, a black Methodist. The Anti-Slavery Society was started in 1834 and there were 112 black males listed in the 1849 Newark Directory. There were carpenters, barbers, blacksmiths, and restaurateurs and a number of black homeowners, all indications of a thriving, if small, community.[64]

The real growth in the community began in the early twentieth century as blacks migrated northward from the Deep South in search of jobs. Part of the problem was that, while the factories offered employment, adequate housing and schools were sorely lacking. The common folk wisdom is that Mayor Meyer Ellenstein, Newark's first and only Jewish mayor, encouraged blacks to come to Newark by placing advertisements in southern newspapers announcing the availability of work in the city. In so doing, the argument goes, he "ruined" Newark by creating a large population of poor and resentful people and this led eventually to the devastating riots that destroyed the city's viability.

In fact, there is no evidence that Ellenstein did anything of the sort. What is known is that, in the 1920s, well before Ellenstein became mayor, the Newark Chamber of Commerce advertised on billboards in an effort to attract blacks to the city. As the great sociologist, Gunnar Myrdal, noted in his landmark work, *An American Dilemma*, trying to persuade African Americans to come to the North was a *regional phenomenon*, and not limited to Newark. Black newspapers not only printed advertisements for jobs in the area but editorialized that conditions in the North were better for their people. And Northern industries sent out agents, both black and white, to recruit workers. It is also worth mentioning that migration to Newark from the South began in the early part of the century, long before Ellenstein became mayor.

Larger economic conditions were a factor as well. Ellenstein became mayor in 1933 and was reelected in 1937. But that very year, as Myrdal reports, unemployment for blacks had reached a whopping 39 percent. And that was the problem. With no jobs, many African Americans were forced to go on welfare and they knew that it was much easier to become eligible for relief in the North than was the case in the South and they knew it without Ellenstein's encouragement. Eventually, under Louis Danzig, the Newark Housing Authority built 17,000 units of public housing, to accommodate the needs of the poor, many of whom were black.[65]

It is easy for outsiders to think of Newark as a city where black-Jewish relations were poor but, in fact, this was only true in the years immediately preceding the riots. In reality, Newark was seen as a relatively peaceful city in that respect, with no more than the usual tensions that characterized race relations in the North during the pre-Civil Rights Movement era. Many Jews report having positive personal contacts and even some friendships with members of the black community. Milton Konvitz, a prominent professor of law at Cornell University and the son of Joseph Konvitz, past rabbi of Congregation Anshe Russia, was the vice president of the Urban League in those days:

> In 1943, I became Assistant Counsel for the NAACP to Thurgood Marshall and worked closely with him. He was a very congenial, jolly, and optimistic person. He liked to live well. I socialized with blacks in those days. There were no problems then.[66]

Konvitz was a person with extensive contacts in the black community, both here and abroad. From 1952 until 1980, he was a close adviser to the Liberian government. This was atypical, however; few Jews were as involved as was Konvitz with the black community.

As Jews began moving out of the Third Ward towards Clinton Hill and Weequahic, African Americans established a presence in the Third Ward. There they lived together with Jews.[67] The same held true later on in Weequahic. Yes, there was blockbusting in Weequahic and Jews fled,[68] but many others remained and tried to work things out. A front-page story in the *Newark Evening News* reported on an integrated welcoming party for John and Montez Loney, who had bought a home on Weequahic's Lehigh Avenue.

The Y, which had moved, in 1959, from High and Kinney Streets, to Chancellor Avenue and Aldine Street in Weequahic, sponsored many programs during the 1960s aimed at fostering racial harmony. Unfortunately, these efforts were not successful as mistrust, fueled by politicians and community leaders with agendas of their own, built up in the years immediately preceding the riots, causing more and more Jews to depart for the suburbs.[69] As we have already seen, the historical relations between the two communities had always been problematic despite the lofty principles of tolerance and a common history of oppression so often expressed by leaders on both sides.

July 12, 1967 marks for many the end of Newark as a livable city. The arrest and harsh treatment of a taxi driver on that date sparked five days of rioting in the Central and South Wards with an estimated $8,000,000 worth of looting and close to $2,000,000 in damage to property. By the time it was over, twenty-three people, almost all of them black, had died. In the wake of the riots, militants on both sides gained a more prominent role in the city's political life and culture. Baraka founded the United Brothers while Imperiale gained control of the North Ward. Further evidence of the changing times can be found in the South Ward where black residents organized a recall election for a city councilman that replaced a Jewish landlord with a black minister. And Ed Brody remembers what happened when, in the post-riot period, he offered to help a black fellow merchant with his problems:

"You (whitey) don't understand our (black) problems." We, the white merchants were told: "You are exploiting the neighborhood, as you earn your living here but spend your money living in big houses, in the suburbs." The parallel was made of our situation and of colonialism.[70]

Jews suffered disproportionately in the riots, but only because so many of them owned stores in the affected area. The rioters did not distinguish between Jews and Christians as they burned and looted shops. Nevertheless, the fact that so many of the proprietors were, in fact, Jewish, did not go unnoticed. Bigots need identifiable scapegoats and Jews have played that role for centuries.

As Clement Price has noted, the riots "symbolized for many Americans the death of Newark."[71] For Jews and blacks, however, reality was different. To blacks, the riots represented a victory by the oppressed and an opportunity to take control of the city and reshape it according to their vision. For Jews, the death of Newark represented the destruction of the inner core of their community. Jeffrey Brody, a journalism professor who wrote his master's thesis on the riots, observed:

> Walking along the former business section, it seems inopportune to recall the names of former shops (Blaustein's Furs, Kartzman's Deli, Kaye's Drugs, Manhoff's Fishery, Masur's Furs, and Tabatchnick's the herring king, for example). Repeating their names is like reciting Kaddish, the Jewish prayer for the dead.[72]

In the outer core, however, the suburbs and nearby towns, life continued to flourish and memories of the "old Newark" refused to fade. Some, such as Edith Kay, owner of a furniture department store, opted to remain, at least for a while:

> We decided to remain for one reason—we owned all the buildings. We had five buildings. We had them torn down after they burned us out in 1979. . . .Today, there are town houses on [what used to be] our property.[73]

The fear radiated outward too, beyond the immediate affected area, though not as intensely. Betty Lipman reflected on the atmosphere at the time in Maplewood's Columbia High School:

> There were blacks in the school system but everyone was walking on tiptoes, not to offend anyone else. As far as I can see, the only effect was the fear of the kids about going into Newark, or whether the rioters would come up [to Maplewood].[74]

The idea of responsibility for others certainly fell out of favor within the Jewish community. Those victimized spoke often of the hatred and hostility that was directed at Jews by many African Americans, especially some of their most outspoken leaders. In the end, however, nothing helped. Even Rabbi Joachim Prinz, Newark Jewry's most famous champion of black-Jewish cooperation, was forced to admit, as he stared gloomily at the many empty seats in his temple on Clinton Avenue: "Jews had been here for many generations. I felt they belonged here. But I was wrong. It was a European romanticism that was ill-placed."[75]

Sidney Spector, a former federal housing official, once character-ized American cities as "doughnuts,"—nothing in the middle and all the dough on the outside.[76] That would aptly describe Newark in the aftermath of the riots. But why and how did it happen? Did the Jewish community die simply because of the riots? Absolutely not. Yes, the riots were a contributing factor, but only one of many.

The demise of Newark's Jewish community can only be understood against the backdrop of the larger forces that operated to shape it, forces that affected this country as a whole. It was America's love affair with the suburbs, with the idea of a backyard, a little green grass, and a private home that they could call their own, that provided the impetus for the outward movement of Newark's Jews. In truth, when this movement, which had begun, on a small scale, as early as the 1870s, began to gather steam, in the early twentieth century, the Jews, and other whites as well, were not running away from blacks. Rather than being pushed out of Newark, they were being pulled to the outlying areas which had experienced a tremendous upsurge in home building. Added to this was the fact that Newark's size, twenty-four square miles, was very small compared to that of other urban centers. The surrounding communities, not wishing to be burdened with Newark's poverty, fiercely and successfully resisted efforts to be in-corporated by Newark, thus making it a less attractive place to live in in terms of resources.

The movement gained added momentum after World War II, when G.I. mortgages became available and the economy was strong. A key factor throughout was the development of the automobile and the construction of highways designed to provide easy access to the new communities. The decrease in prejudice against Jews opened up more communities and resulted in a diverse movement to a variety of towns and villages, with those locations where Jews had settled early gaining the most numbers. And the fact that Jews were more upwardly mobile to begin with, also played a role in both their ability and willingness to leave the areas of first settlement. Finally, the continuing relocation of industry to the "Essex County sunbelt" and to Morris County in the post-World War II era, served to further stimulate such movement among Jews and non-Jews. People wanted to be where the jobs were.[77]

Not to be ignored is the collective psychology of Jews in America. When faced with the choice of leaving or staying and fighting, they leave. In part, this is related to their history as a marginal, often persecuted minority but it is also due to their greater financial resources. Their generally higher socioeconomic status makes it easier for them to recoup the financial setbacks associated with selling a house and moving to a new community. Once the pattern takes hold, it snowballs, making it untenable even for those who would rather stay, to remain. As a result, the entire community eventually dies out. Contrast this with the Portuguese, who snapped up cheap land after the riots and rebuilt the Ironbound section into a viable community, or the Italians, who fought the entry of blacks into North Newark, just as they have done in other cities throughout the U.S.

In all fairness, it must be pointed out that the Jewish community, owing largely to its liberal attitudes, took a chance on integration, hoping it would work. It didn't, but in welcoming blacks initially into their neighborhoods, the Jews created apprehension that the neighborhood would "turn." The departure of those who felt this way resulted in a self-fulfilling prophecy, one augmented by block-busting. The outcome obviously does not mean that the Jews did something wrong, but that does not change what happened. In other white neighborhoods, where integration was strongly resisted, white residents saw no reason to leave.[78]

The departure of Newark's Jewish population both caused and was caused by a decline in city services that accelerated as the city's tax base eroded. The quality of education deteriorated and Jews, for whom education has always been a priority, were particularly concerned. Rising crime, illegal drugs, political corruption, poorer sanitation, inferior transportation, and higher insurance rates, all contributed to the growth of a generalized belief that Newark had had it, that the future lay elsewhere. To be sure, the business community, especially under Mayor Leo Carlin, made a valiant attempt to reverse the trend, but, in the end, it was like trying to put a finger in the proverbial dike.[79]

Given all of these problems, it was hardly surprising that the riots were seen as the denouement. But they were indicative, not causative. There were 400 riots in the U.S. between 1964 and 1968. What made this one different for Newark's Jews, was that for them Springfield

Avenue was the neighborhood they themselves remembered shopping in. The riots in Harlem or Watts occurred in neighborhoods that Jews worked in but were not committed to residentially. Jews had been out of Harlem for at least sixty years. For Newark Jews the memories were still fresh. In addition, because of Newark's small size, the riots could not be treated as something that happened in a far off corner of the city. Weequahic was minutes away and Millburn and Short Hills not much further.

Explaining why Newark fell apart as a Jewish community and became a power base for the African-American community is difficult, in large part, because the truth does not serve the interests of either community. The most insightful analysis of this reality was succinctly stated by David Mallach, executive director of the Federation's Jewish Community Relations Committee:

> You have all these myths. You have Jews saying the riots brought about Newark's destruction. Why? Because to say the community ended because we got up and left, that's not a very energizing thing. And for the blacks to say, we came to power because the Jews or Italians left, that's not very energizing either. So you have the Jewish need to blame the riots for the destruction of the Jewish community meshing with the black need to create an empowerment myth. How did we [the blacks] do that? We fought and took over the city.[80]

When all is said and done, the main reason for Newark's decline as a Jewish community was that, for many reasons, Jews wanted to move to the suburbs. And the primary cause for the ascension to power of Newark's black community was that by the time it all ended they were the largest group left. Paradoxically, it may be that the closeness which so many Jews feel for the Newark of their youth makes it even harder for them to acknowledge having rejected it for any reason. For African Americans, the intense need and desire of a subjugated minority to control its own destiny makes it very difficult for them to admit that control of a city was acquired by default rather than by struggle and victory.

Notes

1. Benjamin Kluger, "Growing Up in Newark," *Jewish News*, September 8, 1977,B1.
2. Frank J. Urquhart, *A Short History of Newark* (Newark, N.J.: Baker Printing Company, 1910),8,11–13.
3. John T. Cunningham, *Newark* (Newark: The New Jersey Historical Society, 1988, revised edition),8.

4. Mary Travis Arny, *Red Lion Rampant: An Informal History of Essex County, New Jersey* (no publisher, 1965),106.

5. Barbara Lipton, "Newark Long Ago: 19th Century Photographs From the Museum's Collections," *The Newark Museum Quarterly*, 26, No. 4 (Fall 1975),2.

6. Arny, *Red Lion Rampant*, 104–05. Jacob Stern was a forebear of the genealogist, Malcolm Stern. See Stephen Birmingham, *The Grandees*.

7. I am indebted to Stephen Levitt for suggesting this line of inquiry. See David De Sola Pool, *Portraits Etched in Stone: Early Jewish Settlers, 1682–1831* (New York: Columbia University Press, 1952),319,432.

8. David and Tamar De Sola Pool, *An Old Faith in the New World: Portraits of Shearith Israel, 1654–1954* (New York: Columbia University Press, 1955),329.

9. Alan Crisp, "Belleville's Historical Past: The Hendricks Family: Copper For America 1755–1939." Belleville Historical Society, Belleville Public Library, un- dated.,21–24. Available records suggest that all of these individuals were related. Correspondence between Joseph Settanni and Stephen Levitt, March 21, 1995.

10. Max Whiteman, *Copper For America* (New Brunswick, N.J.: Rutgers University Press, 1971), 144–145.

11. Ibid., 232.

12. Crisp, "Belleville's Historical Past,"26.

13. Minutes of Congregation Shearith Israel, January 17, 1847.

14. Minutes of Congregation Shearith Israel, July 1, 1898.

15. De Sola Pool, *An Old Faith*, 1955,433.

16. Stephen Birmingham, *The Grandees: Americas Sephardic Elite* (New York: Harper & Row, 1971),3. Stephen Levitt has identified on an old map of Newark the names Lyons and Rose, which he believes belong to Jews who converted.

17. Abner R.Gold, "Pilgrims in a New Land," *Jewish News*, July 15, 1949,12.

18. Another member of the family who came at this time was Victor Lowenstein, grandfather of Alan Lowenstein, prominent community leader in the twentieth century.

19. Nathan Kussy, "Early History of the Jews of Newark," in *The Jewish Community Blue Book of Newark* (Newark, N.J.: Jewish Community Blue Book Publishing Company, 1925),37.

20. Ibid.,36.

21. Nathan Kussy, "Early Jewish Settlers Helped Build Newark," *Jewish Chronicle*, Twentieth Anniversary Issue, June 20, 1941,41.

22. Kussy, "Early History,"34.

23. Ibid.,30–31.

24. "Newark," *Universal Jewish Encyclopedia*,206–09.

25. Kussy, "Early History,"31; Amy Lowenstein, *One Hundred Years of the "Y," 1877–1977: History and Guide for the "Y" Centennial Exhibition*, September 18 to November 28, 1977 (West Orange: YM-YWHA of Metropolitan New Jersey, 1977, unpaged).

26. Kussy, "Early Jewish Settlers," 41.

27. Kussy, "Early History," 25,35.

28. Kussy, "Early Jewish Settlers," 44.

29. "Progress Club's Long History is Monument of Achievements That Stand Aloft in Splendor," *Jewish Chronicle*, January 27, 1922,1.

30. Alan Lowenstein, interview, October 26, 1994 and December 11, 1996.

31. Ibid.,interview, October 26, 1994.

32. Elaine Menkes, interview, August 5, 1996.

33. Muriel Bloom, interview, August 5, 1996.

34. Bernard Bloom, interview, August 5, 1996.
35. Saul Schwarz, talk given at Charles Bierman Home, June 9, 1994.
36. Kluger, "Growing Up in Newark," B1.
37. Correspondence from Stanley Winters to Alan Lowenstein, September 12, 1990.
38. Comments made on *A Taste of Honey TV Program*, 1986, "Images of MetroWest, with Saul Schwarz and Ruth Fien.
39. Ibid.
40. "Newark's Zionists, 8,000 Strong, Stage Big Demonstration in Celebration of Ratification of Palestine Mandate," *Jewish Chronicle*, September 15, 1922, 1.
41. "Zionism Seen as Move Back to Judaism by Nathan Kussy," *Jewish Chronicle*, February 1, 1924, 1.
42. Jacob Scarr, *Listen, My Children: A Grandfather's Legacy* (Philadelphia, Pa.: Dorrance, 1972), 243–44.
43. "Majority of Jews are Anti-Zionists, Says Rabbi Foster," *Jewish Chronicle*, August 14, 1925, 1.
44. "Newark Jews Have Inferiority Complex, Claims Rabbi Wise," *Jewish Chronicle*, January 8, 1932, 1.
45. Bella Milmed, interview, August 14, 1996.
46. Jerry Ben Asher, interview, May 26, 1997.
47. Alan Block, *East Side-West Side: Organizing Crime in New York*, 1930–1950 (New Brunswick, N.J.: Transaction Publishers, 1995),132–41.
48. Mark Stuart, *Gangster #2: Longy Zwillman, the Man Who Invented Organized Crime* (Secaucus, N.J.: Lyle Stuart, 1985),13,76.
49. "Nazi Attacks on Jews Draw Protests Here," *Newark Evening News*, March 28, 1933,1. Newark's Jews were certainly patriotic and participated actively in America's wars, both before and after the Holocaust. Its Jewish War Veteran's group was founded in 1931 and, a mere five years later, it was the largest in the nation. For more on the organization, see "War Veterans Lead Fight for Principles," *Jewish Chronicle*. Fifteenth Anniversary Issue. April 24, 1936,73. They served in all divisions. Some, like Sam Convissor, were Marines; others, like Eugene Marder, were in the Cavalry Division. Many received medals for heroism, such as Eliezer Schulman, who earned a Bronze Star and Purple Heart in World War II, and Jacob Birnholz, who was awarded a Bronze Star in Korea. Private First Class, Louis Schleifer, was the first Newark soldier to be killed at Pearl Harbor and a park on Elizabeth Avenue was dedicated in his memory. For more on those who defended their country, see Gershon Gelbart, Sylvan H. Kohn, and David Rudavsky, *The Essex Story: A History of the Jewish Community in Essex County, New Jersey* (Newark, N.J.: Jewish Education Association of Essex County, 1955),61–65. An estimated 8,500 Jewish men and women were in the Armed Forces during World War II.
50. Jewish Family Service Files, Rutgers University,Box 68.
51. Ibid.
52. "Book of Newarker is Blamed: Germans Retaliate in Hanover." *Newark Evening News*, September 8, 1941,1. Kaufman was the son of Anton Kaufman, publisher of the *Jewish Chronicle*.
53. See, Gershon Gelbart et al., "The Essex Story,"36.
54. Edward I. Koch, with Daniel Paisner, *Citizen Koch: An Autobiography* (New York: St. Martin's Press, 1992),19–20.
55. Saul Schwarz, interview, December 6, 1994.
56. Alan Lowenstein, interview, October 26, 1994.
57. Harry Lurie, *A Heritage Affirmed: The Jewish Federation Movement in America* (Philadelphia, Pa.: Jewish Publication Society, 1961),288.

58. Daniel Shiman, "Newark Sets Up Joint Council," *The Jewish Community*, January 1947,5–7.
59. Saul Schwarz, interview, December 6, 1994.
60. See Jonathan Reider, *Canarsie: The Jews and Italians of Brooklyn Against Liberalism* (London: Cambridge University Press, 1985) and Hillel Levine & Lawrence Harmon, *The Death of an American Jewish Community:A Tragedy of Good Intentions* (New York: The Free Press, 1992).
61. Max Geltman, *The Confrontation: Black Power, Anti-Semitism, and the Myth of Integration* (Englewood Cliffs, N.J.: Prentice-Hall, 1970),61. See also, Robert G. Weisbord and Arthur Stein, *Bittersweet Encounter: The Afro-American and the American Jew* (New York: Schocken, 1970),123.
62. Richard Wright, *Black Boy* (New York: Harper & Row, 1966),70.
63. William B. Helmreich, "Jewish Marginality and the Struggle for Equality," *Journal of Intergroup Relations*, 5, No. 3, 1976, 37–40.
64. John T. Cunningham, *Newark* (Newark, N.J.: The New Jersey Historical Society, 1988, revised ed.),117, 131–32.
65. Gunnar Myrdal, *An American Dilemma: The Negro Problem and Modern Democracy* (New York: Harper Torchbooks Edition, 1969),191–97.
66. Milton Konvitz,interview, April 8, 1997. Clement Price has observed that black-Jewish relations were often "affairs of elites between the two groups." See "The Twilight of Optimism: Black-Jewish Relations in Newark During the Sixties." Paper delivered at the Conference on Politics, Law, and the Jewish Community in Greater Newark, Whippany, New Jersey, September 21, 1997.
67. Clement Price, "Blacks and Jews in the City of Opportunity: Newark, New Jersey, 1900–1967," Paper presented at the Meeting of the MetroWest Jewish Historical Society, Whippany, New Jersey, June 1994,4.
68. Ruth Fien, interview, November 24, 1996.
69. Correspondence from Saul Schwarz to Ed Brody, August 23, 1995.
70. Ed Brody, "The Neighborhood Merchants Associations in Newark, N.J.:A Personal Recollection," August 30, 1995,24. Unpublished manuscript. See also, Fred Siegel, "The Mental Ruins of the Newark Riot," *New York Post*, July 27, 1997,47. Siegel writes that the riots were an awakening of "black collective consciousness," not simply a destructive act. He concludes: "Much of the physical ruin from the riots still clutters Newark. Worse yet, much of the mental rubble of the riots still forms the architecture of our thinking about race."
71. Clement Price, "Blacks and Jews," 13.
72. Jeffrey H. Brody, "Bergen Street Ten Years After the Newark Riot" (MA thesis, Columbia University School of Journalism, 1977),1.
73. Edith Kay, interview, November 2, 1995, Jewish Historical Society of MetroWest.
74. Betty Lipman, interview, March 1, 1994, Jewish Historical Society of MetroWest.
75. Anthony DePalma, "Exodus," *New Jersey Monthly*, September 1985,93.
76. Correspondence from Saul Schwarz to Ed Brody, August 23, 1995.
77. Sam Convissor, interview, January 10, 1997, Jewish Historical Society of MetroWest.
78. Bruce Dunn, "The Jews of Newark, 1955–1970." Paper written for Newark history class at New Jersey Institute of Technology.
79. Dorothy M. Guyot, "Newark: Crime and Politics in a Declining City," in Anne Heinz, Herbert Jacob, and Robert L. Lineberry (eds.), *Crime in City Politics* (New York: Longman, 1983),31–45.
80. David Mallach, interview, January 21, 1997.

2

Where They Went and How They Lived

"Our house was in the midst of a semi-rural setting. There were small stores on Spring-field Avenue, which was an unpaved country road that led westward across the mountains. Small houses, void of architectural preten-sions—surrounded by fenced-in gardens—lined the side streets. A rustic bridge spanned a rip-pling brook at Springfield Avenue and Bedford Street. Empty lots covered with weeds, hills and woods, farmland and orchards, walnut, hickory, and chestnut trees, all could be found within the radius of a few blocks from my par-ents' home."[1]

It should not be surprising that any Newarker reading these pages would have difficulty reconciling this description with his or her own memories of Springfield Avenue. Most would recall it as a bustling street filled with stores of every variety catering to the needs of Jews and others living in the city. But these words, written by Sarah Kussy, an early German-Jewish immigrant to Newark, depict the avenue as it appeared in the second half of the nineteenth century. No one had any idea then that Springfield Avenue would become a hub of the Jewish community. And to understand the community better we need to know more about how that process took place.

The first group of Jewish arrivals, mostly from Germany, settled in the Canal Street area from Hunterdon Street to the west to Adams Street to the east and from Clay Street to the north to Clinton Avenue to the south. By the turn of the century they had moved into the

ɔr Third Ward, replacing the Irish and Germans who had
re from the Ironbound section of the city.

ɔir economic situation improved, Jews settled in the Clinton
Hill and Weequahic sections, living there through the 1920s, 1930s,
and 1940s. This was the golden age, so to speak, of Newark Jewry. It
was the era that Philip Roth, Edward Koch, and others remember with
fondness and it was the period during which the greatest number of
Jews lived in the city proper.

Parallel to this movement a smaller, outward flow to the suburbs
had begun in the 1870s, with people settling in the Oranges and other
nearby communities. They were joined, starting in the 1920s, by people
who had decided that there were greener pastures beyond Clinton Hill
and Weequahic. What began as a trickle eventually became a wave in
the post-World War II era. In addition, there were those who moved
into communities further away from the immediate area, such as
Morristown. This pattern was not only similar to the suburban trek of
Jews around the country but it mimicked the trend among other white
groups in Newark. For example, The Irish moved into the Vailsburg-
Roseville section and the Italians put down roots in the northern end
of the city, centered around the old First Ward. These areas, it may be
noted, also contained pockets of Jewish settlement.

Life in the Third Ward

A 1911 map of the Third or Central Ward identified an area in
which Jews lived in close proximity to a number of ethnic groups,
including Greeks, Italians, Chinese, blacks, Irish, and Germans. The
Jews settled around Prince Street. Living conditions were difficult
during this period—wooden tenement houses in which families had
their own coal bins and the coal had to be dragged from the basement
to the apartment and put into the stove. Very few apartments had heat,
electricity, or toilets, although ten years later the situation had improved considerably. In the winter, people undressed in the kitchen
and then raced to their bedrooms and jumped under the covers to keep
from freezing to death.[2] They worked long hours in factories in miserable circumstances, and infant mortality rates were high.

Nevertheless, people still found ways to enjoy life. Children gathered in the streets in the late afternoon to play games, hang around the
shops that lined the crowded streets, or swim in nearby bodies of

water that, while refreshing, were invariably polluted. They went to
the theater and ate in restaurants—George's, The Paradise Dairy, The
Royal Dairy, Reinfeld's Delicatessen, and many more. And as they
walked to these establishments, they could smell the aromas of fresh
baked bread, pastrami, herring, coffee, and vegetables.

One aspect of life that seems to stand out in the memories of many
who grew up then was the bathhouse or "*schvitz.*" Here are some
evocative descriptions which demonstrate how the schvitz was not only
a place for recreation but also a bonding experience for the family:

> There were baths on Broome Street, Charlton, and Mercer. They were all over the
> place. A father would take his sons there on a Saturday night. They'd get a
> rubdown in a room and then have a steak dinner and maybe sleep overnight there.
> It was like Silver's in Coney Island. The Third Ward in those days had just about
> anything you could ever want in a Jewish neighborhood.
>
> —Len Kurland[3]

> My father went to the schvitz on Friday night. Sometimes he took me. I have vivid
> memories of corned beef and sauerkraut, which they served, and sleeping over-
> night in the schvitz house. There was a wet steam room, massages, and cots to lie
> down on. There was a general room where you could lounge around in. You stayed
> until about eight the next morning. My dad went about every six weeks.

> There were regulars who went every week. You have to remember, many people
> didn't even have bathrooms or refrigerators in their apartments. The man brought
> us ice. To wash up, I went to the public bathhouse every Saturday. It cost us five
> cents.
>
> —Saul Schwarz[4]

> People went to the Morton Street or Howard Avenue baths, usually once a week.
> You got a towel, a hunk of soap, and a wooden shower stall. At the end of four
> minutes, they opened the latch with a long stick and out they went."
>
> —Jerry Lehman[5]

There were unusual events, too, that broke the monotony of daily
life. In his loving memoir , *For Special Occasions*, the producer, Dore
Schary, wrote about one such happening:

Occasionally, the Orthodox population that was clustered around
Prince Street would have a parade. These processions, in celebration
of a Jewish festival or in honor of the dedication of a new Hebrew
school or synagogue, seldom included more than two or three hundred
people. The marchers usually took the same route, a square bordered
by Prince, Kinney, High, and Court streets. A small band always
preceded the marchers and most of the songs had Jewish themes,

interspersed with American marches. It was incongruous, but lovely, to see bearded elderly Jews striding along to "The Stars and Stripes Forever." As the men marched, carefully avoiding the souvenirs left by horses, they would wave and call out "*Mazeltov*," "*Vus machst du?*" (How are you?). In turn, the spectators would be shouting, "Hello, Moishe," "Hey, Maxie," "*Mazeltov*, Reb Brodsky."[6]

The major center for social and cultural life was the Y, which opened its doors in May of 1924 at the intersection of High and Kinney Streets. Prodded by Mike Stavitsky, the Y was built by German Jews, most notably Louis Bamberger, Felix Fuld, Abe Dimond, and Milton Adler, but it served a largely East European population. A report by the Jewish Welfare Board expressed the rationale for its founding in the following terms:

> Within the [Third] Ward there are at least 20,000 Jews. Of these, 3,600 are between the ages of ten and nineteen. These young people live in one of the most congested parts of the city. Some of them live above and behind stores or in tenements. There is no organized community effort concerned with their problems. There are boys and girls with immense possibilities who are caught in the complexes of different languages, customs, ideas; who are cramped in dingy homes; who, unacquainted with the beautiful presentation of Judaism, are disinherited from the spiritual wealth that is rightly theirs.[7]

The Y was to be all of that and more. There were dramatic clubs, glee clubs, literary clubs, theater, lectures, extensive sports facilities, and, above all, a place the immigrants could feel welcome in. Without it, the social dislocation that was the fate of so many other immigrant groups who lived out their unhappy lives in grinding poverty, would have been inestimably higher. Here, they could socialize with one another and catch a glimpse of a brighter and happier life.

Had they journeyed (and some did) a few blocks away, these Eastern European Jews would have seen ample evidence that such a life already belonged to the German Jews who came before them and even a few of their own more successful brethren. High Street was perhaps most representative of those who had made it. It was widely regarded as the most exclusive residential street in Newark, as well as the address for the best doctors and lawyers. The names of its residents, both Jewish and non-Jewish—Krueger, Hollander, Frelinghuysen, read like a "Who's Who" of Newark society. The changeover from a gentile to a Jewish street was perhaps most clearly defined when Newark's best-known temples, such as B'nai Abraham and Oheb Shalom, relocated there.

Former New York City mayor, Edward Koch, moved to Newark in 1931 after his father, a furrier, went into bankruptcy. Home was a two bedroom apartment at 90 Spruce Street and eight family members occupied its cramped quarters:

> Harold and I slept in a double, pull-out cot in the dining room; we pushed the table and chairs to the wall every night after dinner. The one substantial piece of furniture we didn't move was our old Emerson radio. That radio dominated the room. It had a beautiful cabinet, supported by long, carved legs. Harold and I used to lie under it for hours, playing tick-tack-toe on the underside of the cabinet with a piece of chalk.[8]

Clinton Hill and Weequahic

As soon as they could, Jews left the Central Ward for Clinton Hill and Weequahic. While these are ingrained in the minds of Newarkers as Jewish neighborhoods, it was not always so. An editorial in the March 17, 1922 issue of the *Jewish Chronicle* decried the bigotry of Clinton Hill's residents, complaining that on at least four occasions in one week the *Newark Evening News* had printed blatantly discriminatory advertisements in its pages for apartments. The following sample advertisement was reprinted in the *Chronicle*:

> Six large, cheerful rooms; all improvements except heat; third floor; Clinton Hill; vacant May 1; rent $45; Gentiles only.

"How can rooms be cheerful that are owned or controlled by people whose hearts are hardened against their fellow beings?" asked the paper.[9]

Despite such attitudes, by the 1930s, Clinton Hill was firmly established as a Jewish center. It definitely possessed a strong appeal for those who lived in the teeming slums around Prince Street:

> Unlike Prince Street, Clinton Avenue had dignity. The houses were principally fashioned in brick, were well-maintained and housed many communal institutions . . .Faige enjoyed strolling on Clinton Ave with Moshe and Leah, gazing at the elegant homes and tilting her chin upwards when passing someone on the street, as if to say, "I live here, too." Whenever anyone asked Kalman or Joshua where they lived, they would always reply "off Clinton Avenue" and then wait for the ever so subtle lift of the eyebrows they inevitably received.[10]

Clinton Hill was actually a mixed area economically. The eastern section, close to the Third Ward, was lower middle class, but the upper section, west of Bergen Street, to the Irvington line, tended to be middle class. There were also plenty of "down on their luck" cases interspersed throughout. One former resident remembers living in fourteen different apartments as a child. He and his six siblings were constantly on the move because, as he put it, "We didn't pay the rent." Moreover, it was never as Jewish as Weequahic. Generally speaking, the pattern of Jewish movement was divided, with German Jews residing in Clinton Hill for a short period of time on their way to the suburbs and with Eastern European Jews living in Clinton Hill en route to Weequahic.

Mary Mapes Dodge, author of *Hans Brinker, or the Silver Skates*, was perhaps Weequahic's most famous resident in the nineteenth century, but to the Jews that settled there, it is undoubtedly Philip Roth who put Newark and, in particular, the Weequahic section, on the map. Whether or not they liked what he had to say, few could deny that his writings gave a portrayal of the city that greatly enhanced its significance in American Jewish literature. His descriptions of Weequahic and its people demonstrated how that community was, in many ways, a microcosm of the changes in Jewish life that began in the early twentieth century and which continued through midcentury. Roth calls Newark "as safe and peaceful a haven for me as his rural community would have been for an Indiana farm boy."[11] He is fiercely loyal to it and that which it is a part of:

> Ordinarily nobody more disquieting ever appeared there than the bearded old Jew who sometimes tapped on our door around dinnertime; to me an unnerving specter from the harsh and distant European past, he stood silently in the dim hallway while I went to get a quarter to drop into his collection can for the Jewish National Fund (a name that never sank all the way in: the only nation for Jews, as I saw it, was the democracy to which I was so loyally—and lyrically—bound, regardless of the unjust bias of the so-called best and the violent hatred of some of the worst.)[12]

The name "Weequahic" referred to a subgroup of Indians affiliated with the Lenape tribe but, historically, the neighborhood was part of the Lyon's Farm area. For Newark's Jews in the 1930s and 1940s, it meant a better place in which to live and raise one's children and what could be more important than that? Many of the homes, especially above Bergen Street and Osborne Terrace, were 2 1/2 family houses—two full apartments on each of the first two floors and a small three-room apartment on the top floor. Near Weequahic Park were luxury apartment buildings and beyond Lyons and Chancellor Avenues, near the Hillside border, as well as on Wilbur, Chancellor, Elizabeth, Pomona, Weequahic, and Hansbury Avenues, were many stately homes.

Bergen Street was the main business thoroughfare. It was a place one went to for necessities, but it also had upscale clothing stores and fur shops, not to mention fine bakeries.[13] Meanwhile, the Y opened up in a succession of interim locations in the Weequahic area in order to better serve the burgeoning population. Later, in 1959, the Y would move from High St. to Chancellor Avenue and Aldine Street.[14] And, of course, there was Weequahic High School, but more about that later.

Other Newark Neighborhoods

Jews also lived in the Down Neck or Ironbound part of Newark. The main drag that ran through the neighborhood was Ferry Street. Benjamin Kluger tells what it was like to live there:

> The street was surrounded by powerful attractions for a little boy: the forbidden tracks of the New Jersey Central Railroad, the fire engines charging out of Engine #5 and Hook and Ladder #4, East Side Park, Keisch's yard, the river and the docks, the boys diving off near the Jackson Street Bridge, bellywhopping on Flexible Flyers down the snowy incline of Congress Street, baseball in the summer, playing on and on tirelessly until there was hardly a flicker of light, and coming home to be scolded (mildly) and washed and fed. Out front, the organ grinder came along to play his wistful melodies.[15]

It was a close-knit community and its center was the synagogue on Jefferson Street, Congregation Toras Emes, all the more important as a focal point of identity because of the polyglot neighborhood in which it was situated. The geographical separation of Down Neck from the rest of Newark has given those who grew up there a special feeling of esprit des corps even greater than those who came from greater Newark.

Jews also settled in Vailsburg, Sanford Heights, and in the West Ward around 16th Avenue, where they shared the local turf with Italians and a smattering of Poles, Czechs, Russians, and even some blacks. Ed Brody, in an article called "Mother's Shtetl," has sketched a loving portrait of the shops that were located on 16th Avenue from 11th to 14th Streets and the items they stocked:

> Butter was cut into pie-like shapes from a large tub and wrapped in wax paper. The concept of self-service was foreign to these entrepreneurs. . . . When you asked the butcher for a specific cut of meat, he would cut and trim the piece. . . . Periodically an odoriferous truck would arrive to purchase the fat that was trimmed off of the

> meat. . . .Ice for the icebox was ordered by placing a square sign, with one numeral on top (10,15, 20, or 25) of each side, in the window facing the street. This informed the iceman just how big a piece to deliver . . .. During the heat of the summer we would renew our friendships with all the neighbors, as the oppressive heat of our apartments would drive all of us onto the sidewalks in front of our building . . ..The secret was to live in an apartment that had "cross" ventilation. This meant that there would be windows on opposite walls. The big disadvantage to this was the fact that you were able to hear what was going on in your neighbor's house. But, then again, who listened?[16]

One of the loveliest neighborhoods in Newark was Forest Hill, in the northern part of the city. It was an upper-middle-class enclave and a good number of successful Jews, many of German origin, owned homes there. There they mingled with the WASPs who had not yet departed for the suburban hinterlands. The area bordering Branch Brook Park, where the cherry blossoms made their appearance every year, was especially beautiful.

Nearby was the mostly Christian section of Roseville, named after James Rowe, an Irishman who sold his land to the city only after someone hit upon the idea of naming the neighborhood after him. One of its most famous Jewish residents was the spy, intellectual, and baseball player, Moe Berg.[17] As the following account by another resident, Rose Katz, indicates, life there was different for Jews than in Weequahic:

> We were the only Jewish family on the block. The women at times would come close to our fence and would want to make friends with me. They would occasionally start with the now well-known remark "you are different from other Jews." Then I would explain that I am not different and that they were merely misinformed about the Jewish people. That is how we became very good neighbors indeed.[18]

For those who were not so economically fortunate, there was Seth Boyden Housing Project, one of Newark's first efforts at providing public housing. At one time, the area had a sizeable Jewish population and the Federation was involved in providing various services. Situated on Frelinghuysen Avenue, on the site of what was once Dreamland Park, the project was an attempt to create a sense of community for the Jewish urban poor, or the not yet rich. As time went on, however, a rising crime rate, coupled with generally deteriorating conditions in Newark, made living there untenable.[19]

The Move to the Suburbs

The trend towards suburbia was irreversible and seemingly final. It had begun even before Newark deteriorated, but the erosion of the city's infrastructure caused it to accelerate even more.[20] The unaffiliated and those who belonged to the Conservative and Reform temples were the first to depart. Unlike the Orthodox, they did not need to be within walking distance of a synagogue. Eventually, however, the Orthodox left too, creating new enclaves in places like Livingston, West Orange, and Springfield.

Paradoxically, perhaps, Jews found an even greater need to identify ethnically and religiously in their newly adopted communities. What follows are some typical views on this subject:

> When you live in a suburban community like we do, you have to identify yourself with the Jewish organizations. How else can you show you are a Jew?"
>
> The only way you can achieve anything is through united action. As Jews, we have to stand together just like the non-Jews do. This is life in a suburb. In the city, we don't worry about things, we have plenty of Jews around.[21]

It was not simply a question of Jewishness, but also an adaptation to life in general. The suburbs regarded organizational affiliation as a sign of conformity to a lifestyle, one which emphasized duty, responsibility, and the acceptance of the idea that one lived in a community. In a very real sense these organizations became a vehicle for creating intimacy and a sense of common purpose:

> Since I moved here some five years ago, I joined a number of the Jewish and non-Jewish organizations. Somehow they pressure you into joining something, or otherwise you're made to feel like a stranger or an outsider in town. In Newark, where I was born, I could have lived out my life without joining a thing. But in this town, somehow, I get the feeling you have to join these organizations or you are not part of the community.[22]

What this meant in concrete terms was joining a synagogue, one or more Jewish organizations, and increasing one's observance of Jewish customs and traditions. In doing so, the suburbanites were following the same lifestyle that their Christian counterparts had embraced. In fact, Jews discovered that afffilation with a temple won them greater respect from their non-Jewish neighbors because it meant they too had values and believed in the efficacy of religion in general.

There were several communities bordering Newark, such as

Belleville, Nutley, Harrison, Kearny, and Arlington. These did not have the glamour or glitz of Short Hills or South Orange. They did, nonetheless, attract people from Newark, though they were also settled by people who came from elsewhere. The first Jew to arrive in Kearny, for example, was Jack Goldstein, who came there from Lithuania in 1879. He opened a dry goods store and was joined two years later by his brother, Israel.

Perhaps the most prominent man to take up residence in Kearny was Ephraim Deinard. Born in Sasmakken, Latvia, Deinard was a bibliographer and author, writing over fifty books and pamphlets in Hebrew. A polemicist, he attacked Hasidism, Reform Judaism, and Christianity. His first rate Judaica collections formed the basis for the Library of Congress and Harvard University's Widener Library collections. Deinard lived in Palestine for some time and also tried, without success, to start an agricultural settlement in Nevada. In 1892, he moved from Newark to Kearny and built a home on Windsor Street, thereby becoming the first property-owning Jew in the town.[23]

Kearny's synagogue, Congregation B'nai Israel, was founded by local residents but, not long thereafter, they were joined by Jews from neighboring Arlington. Together, at their peak, in 1950, these two communities had about 600 residents, with approximately 220 children attending the temple's Hebrew school. The principal at the time was Nathan Winter, later to become chairman of the Hebrew Culture and Education Department at New York University.

Certainly, the community had advantages. It was conveniently located, about a half hour by bus from New York City, the housing stock was decent, and the area was relatively crime free. So what prevented it from taking off? The answer is instructive for quite a few communities in the area. Put simply, it lacked snob appeal. Its homes weren't fancy enough and it acquired a reputation as a transition community, one that served people who were "on the way up" but who hadn't quite gotten there yet. Edith Saletan, a resident there from 1923 until today, summed it up best:

> As soon as Jews made more money they moved to a fancier neighborhood. We weren't grand enough for them. The neighborhood wasn't Jewish enough for them; we didn't have enough Jewish stores. It had originally been settled by Scottish people and Jews were always a small minority there. There was only one Jewish appetizing store. When I was a child there were two butcher shops but nobody remembers that.[24]

The same was true for Nutley, Belleville, and Harrison. When Jews in Newark decided that they wanted to live in a higher-status community, they looked elsewhere. As a result, most of those who lived in these communities came either from New York or from other New Jersey communities such as Hoboken, Weehawken, Bayonne, or Jersey City.

Today, most of Kearny's original residents are gone and their children have moved away. The last remaining symbol, the synagogue, has been sold to a Portuguese church. And a similar fate has befallen nearby Nutley. Among the first Jews to settle there was Harry Steinlauf, a dairy farmer:

> My father came from Austria and had originally been in the dairy business in Maspeth, Queens. But one day he saw two ads in the *New York Times* for farms, one in Nutley and one in Irvington. So he figured it was either go into competition with the Borinskys of Tuscan Farms in Irvington or go to Nutley, where he started Nutley Dairy Farm.[25]

The Nutley Hebrew Congregation, founded by the Steinlaufs and others, had opened in 1927, holding services at first in the Steinlauf home. In a not unusual pattern where the Jewish community was small, the residents had assiduously cultivated ties with their non-Jewish neighbors to demonstrate their desire to be accepted. For example, the rabbi was not only an honorary chaplain of the police and fire departments, but a member of the Rotary and Lions clubs. The congregation recently closed due to lack of funds, merging with a congregation in Bloomfield. The new owner is a Korean church. As for the Steinlauf farm, only the house remains. Part of the pasture is now Route 21, which runs from Newark to Passaic.

Another early community was Belleville. Aside from the Sephardic residents discussed earlier, one of the earliest settlers there was Nathan Schwartz who arrived from Manhattan in 1907. Schwartz had run food concessions for theaters in New York and was persuaded to move to Belleville by some friends who were opening the Hillside Amusement Park there and wanted a partner with experience in the food service business. Other early residents were the Lempert, Becker, and Paul families.

The Jews of Belleville worked hard at becoming Americans. Irving Berkowitz recalled how his grandfather, Nathan Schwartz, told the immigrants who, upon first arriving from Romania, stayed with him for a while: "You speak English in this house. If you continue to speak Romanian you'll never get anywhere in America." Belleville was a predominantly Scotch-Irish, English, and German community in those days and Berkowitz recalls little anti-Semitism then: "The worst that happened was when they put a matzo in my Uncle Max's desk in school as a joke around Passover." The uncle later became a star second baseman for the high school team and was fully accepted by his classmates.

As with all of these communities Jewish cultural life revolved around the synagogue. Ahavas Achim Anshe Belleville was founded in 1924 and at its height there were several hundred families and a Hebrew school with 115 children. The need for a synagogue became clear as a result of a rather humorous incident that occurred several years earlier:

> From about 1919 on we used a room given to us by the town fathers. It was right next to the fire and police departments. Then, one year, I remember that we were blowing the shofar and suddenly we heard some guys laughing. It was the fire department fellas. So we asked them—"What's so funny?" "Well," they said: "we heard you guys blowing the bugle and we thought, hey, you're supposed to be praying. So we thought it was pretty funny." Then we realized we just had to have our own place.[26]

A much smaller neighboring community was Harrison. One of the first residents there was Max Jacobs, who moved there in the early 1900s to establish a furniture business. His daughter, Florence Lax, was born and raised in Harrison. There were only two or three Jews in her classes at school but she apparently got along quite well with her gentile classmates: "The only thing I remember was that when we passed the Holy Cross school, the kids would sometimes yell: 'You killed our Lord.'" While there was a kosher butcher in town, the Jewish community never had more than 100 or so residents and the synagogue was forced to close in the 1940s.[27]

There were also restrictive communities that made Jews feel most unwelcome. The best known example was Llewellyn Park, where Thomas Edison had a home. Llewellyn Park was America's first gated suburb and it had been established in the nineteenth century as a white Protestant community that excluded all others. When Harold Grotta moved into the area in 1969, there was only one other Jewish family in Llewellyn Park. Today, many Jews make their homes there.[28]

One of the larger communities on Newark's borders was Irvington. Jews settled in two areas there, one close to the center of town, near

Springfield Avenue, and the other along Chancellor Avenue, having come there, for the most part, from Weequahic. The first synagogue, B'nai Israel, had been founded in 1922, with Ahavas Achim-Bikur Cholim following suit a decade later, in 1932. The latter had been started by Jerry Lewis' grandfather.

The real growth of the community came in the late 1940s after the war ended. An estimated 7,388 Jews lived within its environs in 1948. Irvington had acquired a reputation during the war as a hotbed of Nazi Bund activities. But not even that could dissuade Jews who, desperate for homes during the postwar period, eagerly snapped up the apartments that had been built there. To alleviate the housing shortage, developers were granted the right to build garden apartments on large tracts of vacant land with the government guaranteeing the mortgages for almost the entire cost. Servicemen were given extremely favorable terms—4 percent mortgages and almost no down payment required.

In Irvington/Union, Stuyvesant Village, built by George and Maurice Levin, was one of the favorite choices for young Jewish families looking for inexpensive apartments. In the evening, after the children had been put to bed, the parents would sit outside and talk and laugh, dreaming all the while of the private homes they would one day purchase, dreams which many of them eventually realized. East Orange was another popular location, especially the high rises on Harrison Street and Munn Avenue. Nearby was an excellent shopping center on Central Avenue containing several fine stores—B. Altman's, Franklin Simon, and the exclusive Doops. East Orange was also home to the first suburban temple in the Newark area, Sharey Tefilo, established in 1874.

Although it was close to Newark, very few Jews moved to Montclair. Those who did tended to see it as a beautiful place to live in but not especially friendly to Jews. One woman, Molly Rosenberg, spoke of her reception when she moved there from Newark in 1939.

> I encountered anti-Semitism when using a party line phone. She said something like "You Jews. You are always taking over." The second time was when we tried to buy a house in Upper Montclair . . ..When we left, the owner of the house called and asked us if we were Jewish. We said we were and asked what difference it made. She said it did not make any difference to her but that she could not possibly sell her house to Jews. Her neighbors would not like it.[29]

Still, there was Jewish life in Montclair. The first synagogue, Shomrei Emunah, had been founded in 1905 by eighteen residents. It served the small community and Jews did form friendships with each other through the years. But it in no way resembled the life that developed in the more heavily Jewish suburbs. Molly Rosenberg lived there in the 1940s and when her daughter graduated from high school, there were only four Jewish children in the entire graduating class of some three hundred students. Today, of course, Montclair is simply another suburb with a substantial number of Jews living in it. Reflecting the upscale and intellectual values of the town, it has added a Reconstructionist synagogue (B'nai Keshet) and also has the distinction of having appointed the first female rabbi in the Reconstructionist Movement, Joy Levitt.

Neighboring Bloomfield was also serviced by Shomrei Emunah, which was originally located in Glen Ridge, halfway between Bloomfield and Montclair. In addition, there was another synagogue in Bloomfield itself, B'nai Zion. By the 1950s the synagogue's Hebrew school, drawing from Bloomfield, Caldwell, Verona, and Montclair, had some 200 students. Today, the main center is at Temple Ner Tamid, the result of an unusual merger between the Conservative B'nai Zion and the Reform Temple Menorah. As Julius Fisher, a past congregation president, put it:

> The Conservatives didn't like bingo and wanted a kosher kitchen. The Reform wanted their prayer book. There was give and take on both sides. We wanted people to feel comfortable in their new home.[30]

Demographics have changed too as the always small community has recently begun integrating Russian Jews into its own cultural life and activities.

This instance of cooperation between the Conservative and Reform congregations was not unique. It existed wherever the Jews were few in number and, at times, extended even to the Christian community. One case in point was nearby Cedar Grove. In 1953, thirty-five members founded a temple called The Jewish Community of Cedar Grove. At the time they had no place in which to hold services and were grateful when the Reverend Donald Frazier of the Community Church allowed them to worship in the parish house until their own synagogue was completed.[31] As Jerome Fien recalled:

> In 1947, we moved to an apartment in Caldwell. At that time, my father-in-law, Sam Klein, said: "Caldwell—it's the end of the world. It'll take you forty minutes

to get to Newark." And then, just as a matter of interest, three months later, he and eighteen other guys bought the Green Brook Country Club in North Caldwell and then it wasn't so far away anymore.[32]

Caldwell really began to grow as a Jewish community in the 1950s, but its origins go back even further. In 1919, Harry Goodwin came to Caldwell from Brooklyn because his son had asthma and he wanted him to live "in the country." In 1920, due to his efforts and those of a handful of other Jews, the first High Holiday services were held in the local Masonic temple. A year later, a Hebrew school was founded and housed temporarily in a real estate office and the community was on its way. As for Harry Goodwin, his influence on Jews was felt far beyond Caldwell's borders because, among other things, he was the founder of Mother's Gefilte Fish Company.[33]

In 1953, there were approximately 350 Jewish families in the Caldwells. The spurt of growth was due to the general building boom that had taken place in the suburbs following the end of World War II. A new synagogue structure had been erected, at a cost of $100,000, to house Congregation Agudath Israel. Central Hebrew High School, an after-school institution, was established and it served the children of Essex County. Most of the people hailed from Newark and New York City, but there were also a number of families from nearby Pine Brook.[34]

In nearby Verona, a synagogue was incorporated in 1936, although some Jews were already living there before that time. In the beginning, the community depended on Newark and Caldwell for help in running its religious services at the Jewish Center of Verona. Fifteen years later, however, more than 300 families lived in the town and it was necessary to build a separate Hebrew school to accommodate them.[35]

On the other side of Essex County, Hillside was a popular area for Jews looking to purchase affordable homes. Located in Union County, it bordered the Weequahic section of Newark and that part of the town identified strongly with the Newark Federation. Residents of the other part of Hillside tended to view themselves as tied into the Elizabeth Jewish community. The first synagogue, the Sinai Congregation, built in 1925, followed the Orthodox tradition. Later on, Shomrei Torah, a Conservative temple, was established and attracted quite a few new families with young children. In reality, Hillside was seen by many as an extension of Weequahic, especially with its Jewishly oriented shopping area along Maple Avenue, where there were Jewish butcher shops, appetizing stores, and the like. Hillside still has a Jewish community, mostly in the area near Elizabeth, while the section near Weequahic has become predominantly black. Sinai Congregation still exists today, while Shomrei Emunah has become a Lubavitch synagogue. Edith Pascal is one of the few remaining Jews in the area near Weequahic. Although she gets along very well with her African-American neighbors, she remembers well the militant roots of the ethnic transformation that took place where she lived:

> In the sixties Imamu Amiri Baraka came and said: "We're going to break the white Jewish monopoly in Hillside." And he did. Once you went beyond Chancellor and Lyons Avenues to the Hillside border, you had people in Weequahic that were living in magnificent homes. After the riots though, they were giving these homes away for $25,000 and $29,000. They were brick homes with all the amenities and middle-class blacks bought them.[36]

Millburn was one of the older Jewish communities that developed in the suburbs. Religious services were held in the village as early as 1910. In 1923, the local pastor, Reverend H.W. Dickinson, allowed the members of the newly formed Congregation B'nai Israel to worship in the parish house of St. Stephen's Church until they could find permanent quarters. In 1946, the well-known German rabbi, Max Gruenewald, assumed the leadership of the temple, and five years later, a new structure, designed by the prominent architect, Percival Goodman, was dedicated. The earlier kindness of the local Christian community was repaid in 1956 when the members of B'nai Israel offered assistance to the local Wyoming Presbyterian Church after a fire in their building.

It is impossible to overstate the importance of the role played by the synagogues in the suburban communities, particularly those with small Jewish populations. Reflecting on this, Evelyn Goodstein, a long-time resident of the community, observed:

> In 1944, we moved to Millburn. B'nai Israel gave the kids the social opportunities that would otherwise have been denied them as minority members. When we first moved to Millburn there were no Jewish children in the schools. That's why we became involved in the temple, for our children.[37]

One section of Millburn, Short Hills, was notorious for hostility to Jews, yet Jews still moved there. Norbert Gaelen who has lived there for many years, explained why and what Jews went through when they tried to move in:

Jews were actually steered within Millburn to the South Mountain Estates area. That was sort of the Jewish ghetto. Some Jews moved in during the early 1950s, but they had to move out because their children had a lot of problems being accepted in the junior high schools. Millburn High School was not a problem because it was mixed. In the late 1950s, Jews who bought in Short Hills began staying there, with the newer parts becoming settled first. Despite not feeling wanted, Jews went because the homes were nicer, the area was quieter, with pretty streets that had no sidewalks. Today, Short Hills is probably at least one quarter Jewish.[38]

Short Hills is also the permanent home today of the venerable Temple B'nai Jeshurun, Newark's oldest synagogue.

The big Jewish movement to South Orange, a beautiful community renowned for its stately homes and tall trees, began in the 1950s. Short Hills was still fairly closed to Jews and so those who could afford bigger houses gravitated to South Orange.[39] In an earlier period, South Orange had also been restricted, with the prime case in point being the Orange Lawn Tennis Club which allowed no Jews to join. Today, the club is mostly Jewish. In addition, there were three prominent temples there—Temple Beth El, which was Conservative, Temple Israel, affiliated with the Reform Movement, and Oheb Shalom, which had relocated to South Orange from Newark.

Maplewood, which lay adjacent to South Orange, was equally popular with the more affluent Jews. Many were attracted to the area by the outstanding school system, especially Columbia High School, which served students from both communities. In 1948, there were 2,240 Jews living in Maplewood, but most of that growth took place in the 1940s. And it was a different Maplewood from the one that Harry Aidekman, whose son, Alex, was a founder of the Pathmark Supermarket chain, knew in 1910, when he arrived there at his brother's three-acre dairy farm. In those days, Maplewood was an overwhelmingly gentile (mostly German) community of farms and rolling hills, with almost no cars or trucks to be seen on its small country roads. Moreover, Alex Aidekman remembers his non-Jewish neighbors as friendly, welcoming people:

In 1918 or 1919, all of us came down with the flu, so our house was put in quarantine. Worried that we would not have enough to eat, our neighbors came and left bowls of delicious steaming soup and baskets of fresh-baked bread on our window sill. Of course, my mother was worried about our eating meat that was *traif* [not kosher], but we were all terribly grateful for our neighbors' concern. It typified the kind of people they were.[40]

West Orange's Jewish community dates itself back to 1930, when about thirty families lived there. At that time, private homes served as houses of worship for the community, with a small bungalow being purchased in 1933 for use as a synagogue. By 1948, about 125 families had joined the Jewish Center of West Orange, now known as B'nai Shalom, and, by 1955, membership had jumped to over 400 families.[41]

Overall, however, Jews were very much a minority in the 1950s and were seen as interlopers trying to gain power by the mostly Italian gentile community and the old-line Protestants. But the area was beautiful and the school system was regarded as one of the best in the area. Jacqueline Levine recalled what it was like in those early days:

> I ran for president of the local school board then and lost to a write-in candidate. That was the only time I ever lost and it was due to a whispering campaign. West Orange was very conservative in those days and they thought I was a communist because I was against bomb shelters.[42]

Today, West Orange has a very large Jewish presence, part of which consists of the largest Orthodox community in Essex County. The town's largest Orthodox synagogue is Congregation Ahawas Achim B'nai Jacob, headed by Rabbi Alvin Marcus. In addition, it is home to the Jewish Community Center of Metropolitan New Jersey.

Jews first began arriving in Livingston in the 1920s. and the community remained small for quite some time. During World War II, out of a population of 6,000, about fifteen families were Jewish. By 1951, encouraged by affordable housing built by Martin Levin and his brother-in-law, Alan Sagner, that number had grown to about 200 and it was then that the community began to take off. A group of fifty families got together and held a meeting in the home of Abe Goldberg, son of the first Jewish settler in Livingston. Rabbi Samuel Cohen became the spiritual leader of the newly formed Conservative congregation. By 1954, there were over 300 children enrolled in the synagogue's Hebrew school. The following year saw the founding of Temple Emanuel, a Reform temple which today has a membership of several hundred families. Eventually, B'nai Abraham, one of Newark's first temples, moved to Livingston too.

In more recent times, Livingston has witnessed the growth of a vibrant Orthodox community, led by Rabbi Moshe Kasinetz of the Suburban Torah Center. The synagogue was founded in 1969 by Miriam

Greenberg who had come to Livingston from the Brownsville section of Brooklyn, New York. As she described it:

> When I first moved to Livingston, it was Jewish but the people didn't really identify. I remember when I was washing the windows of my house, a Jewish woman came up to me and said: 'You ought to be ashamed of yourself. We don't do that here.' Well, in Brooklyn, Jewish women do that. They wash the windows of their homes before *Pesach*.
> I belonged to Beth Shalom, the Conservative temple, but my background was much more traditional and when they started giving women *aliyahs*, I left. Several Orthodox rabbis with whom I was friendly urged me to start a *shul* and I did, renting out a place in Livingston. I was always in sales and I guess this was my biggest sales job.[43]

Today, Livingston is a center of Jewish life, with synagogues and kosher restaurants, and a population that is active in many Jewish causes. The newly developed Bel Air section has its own synagogue, Etz Chaim, which is Orthodox.[44]

When Helen Freedman came to Springfield from nearby Hillside in 1942, there were only five Jewish families there out of a total of 3,000 residents. Anti-Semitism, while not overt, existed as an undercurrent, as was the case in many suburban communities back then. Interested in making those few Jews who lived in Springfield feel welcome, Freedman hosted monthly social gatherings in her own home. It was a popular move and within a few years, as Jews kept moving in from Newark, Elizabeth, Irvington, and elsewhere, close to 100 people were showing up at the house on Milltown Avenue.

In 1951, the first synagogue in Springfield, Temple Beth Ahm, was founded, followed six years later, by the Suburban Reform Temple, known today as Temple Sha'arey Sholom. Incidentially, the temple's first rabbi, Israel Dresner, is believed to have been the first rabbi arrested for civil rights activities in this country. In 1971, the Young Israel of Springfield opened. Several years later it merged with the remnants of sixteen Orthodox synagogues that were originally in Newark and the new group became known as Congregation Israel of Springfield, whose rabbi is Alan Yuter. The earliest antecedent of this synagogue is Congregation Adas Israel & Mishnayes. Today, Springfield is a thriving community, boasting a Jewish population of 6,000 Jews out of a total of 13,500 residents. Among the amenities available are a bakery, and a bagel and deli store, both kosher, and a new post-high school yeshiva.[45]

This then, is the story of how and where Jews decided to live in the areas surrounding Newark. It is a story of an upwardly mobile community whose members wanted a better life, but it is also a story of people who had lived in a Newark that was teeming with Jewish life and culture. And wherever these people went they took with them a piece of Newark. Thus, when they formed new synagogues and local Jewish community centers, they did so with a distinct memory of life in the "old city." The restaurants, delicatessens, bakeries, and other stores that sprang up to meet their needs resembled those of Newark in certain ways because those who came from there wanted it that way. And those who administered the schools in the suburbs heard from parents who wanted an emphasis upon education similar to that which characterized their own experiences in the Newark school system. In short, while Newark as a city may have been left behind, the idea of Newark was not.

Before, and even during the years when Newark was enjoying its heyday, Jewish communities were emerging in Morris and Sussex Counties. In some of these places, Newark residents were among the earliest settlers, but, for the most part, it was not direct migration from there that fueled the growth. Jews came from all over, from many cities in New Jersey as well as from New York and elsewhere in the U.S., not to mention, directly from Europe.

Some of the towns were major centers, such as Morristown, while others, such as Newton, were much smaller. Still others were resort villages, such as Mount Freedom and White Meadow Lake, and there were also those, like Pine Brook, founded by Jews more than a century ago, that were farming communities. In any case, the development of Morris and Sussex as centers of Jewish life is a phenomenon of the last two or three decades and will therefore be dealt with in the last chapter of this book.

Notes

1. Sarah S. Kussy, "Reminiscences of Jewish Life in Newark, N.J.," *Yivo Bletter* 29 (1947), 14.
2. Arthur Bernstein, interview, January 21, 1994, Jewish Historical Society of MetroWest.
3. Leonard Kurland, interview, December 26, 1994, Jewish Historical Society of MetroWest.
4. Saul Schwarz, interview, December 6, 1994.
5. Jerry Lehman, interview, June 27, 1996.

6. Dore Schary, *For Special Occasions* (New York: Random House, 1961), 83-84.

7. Amy Lowenstein, *One Hundred Years of the "Y," 1877-1977: History and Guide for the "Y" Centennial Exhibition*, September 18 to November 28, 1977 (West Orange: YM-YWHA of Metropolitan New Jersey, 1977), 10.

8. Edward I. Koch, with Daniel Paisner, *Citizen Koch: An Autobiography* (New York: St. Martin's Press, 1992), 11.

9. "Cheerless Rooms for Churlish People." *Jewish Chronicle*, editorial, March 17, 1922, 4.

10. Sidney R. Lewitter, *American Dreams: The Story of a Jewish Immigrant Family* (Lakewood, N.J.: Bristol, Rhein & Englander, 1994), 159-60.

11. Philip Roth, *The Facts: A Novelist's Autobiography* (New York: Farrar, Straus & Giroux, 1988), 30.

12. Ibid., 30.

13. Edith Pascal,interview, March 28, 1995.

14. Amy Lowenstein, *One Hundred Years*, 18,21-22.

15. Benjamin Kluger, "Growing Up in Newark," *Jewish News*, September 8, 1977, B1.

16. Ed Brody, "Mother's Shtetl," unpublished manuscript.

17. Nicholas Dawidoff, *The Catcher was a Spy: The Mysterious Life of Moe Berg* (New York: Pantheon Books, 1994), 22, 303. Moe's brother, Sam, was a highly respected physician.

18. Rose D. Katz, *Golden Memories* (no publisher, no date), 42-3.

19. "Meeting Religious Needs of Jewry in Housing Project," *Jewish Chronicle*, April 4, 1941, 1.

20. "Newark and the Suburbs," *Jewish News*, editorial, September 5, 1958, 10; Letters on "Newark and the Suburbs" editorial, *Jewish News*, September 26, 1958, 11; Letters on "Newark and the Suburbs" editorial, *Jewish News*, October 3, 1958, 11.

21. Morris R. Werb, *Jewish Suburbia: An Historical and Comparative Study of Jewish Communities in Three New Jersey Suburbs*. Ph.D. dissertation, New York University, 1959, 232.

22. Ibid.

23. Jacob Romm, *History of Jewish Community of Kearny and North Arlington*, (no publisher, no date), 5.

24. Edith Saletan, interview, June 24, 1997.

25. Frances Teichholz, interview, June 26, 1997.

26. Information on Belleville is based largely on an interview with Irving Berkowitz, June 27, 1997.

27. Florence Lax, interview, June 27, 1997.

28. Harold Grotta, interview, August 29, 1996.

29. Molly Rosenberg, interview, September 26, 1996, Jewish Historical Society of MetroWest.

30. Marion Kwartler, "Synagogue Central Address for Bloomfield Jews," *MetroWest Jewish News*, April 20, 1995, 16.

31. *Temple Sholom of West Essex: A Handbook for our Members*. Pamphlet, Rutgers University Archives: Synagogue Collection.

32. Jerry Fien, interview, November 24, 1996.

33. Harry Goodwin, interview, July 22, 1954, with Haim Gould.

34. Morris Werb, *Jewish Suburbia*, 92-97.

35. Ibid.,97-99.

36. Edith Pascal, interview, June 27, 1997; Jules Terry, interview, June 30, 1997.

37. Evelyn Goodstein, interview, August 8, 1996.
38. Norbert Gaelen, interview, June 27, 1997.
39. There was a development, Newstead, at the top of First Mountain. Its attractive homes were, in most instances, owned by younger Jewish families.
40. Lynne S. Dumas, *Elephants in my Backyard: Alex Aidekman's Own Story of Founding the Pathmark Supermarket Powerhouse* (New York: Vantage Press, 1988), 6.
41. Morris Werb, *Jewish Suburbia*, 99-101.
42. Jacqueline Levine, interview, August 29, 1996.
43. Miriam Greenberg, interview, June 29, 1997.
44. David Safir and Herman Safir, interview, June 29, 1997.
45. Cheryl L. Kornfeld, "Jewish Community's Diversity Called 'Tribute to Springfield's Pluralism,'" *MetroWest Jewish News*, June 15, 1995, 15.

3

Striving Towards the American Dream

As the Jews of Europe traveled across the Atlantic Ocean, their thoughts turned often to what lay ahead in their lives. For many, the crowded and uncomfortable journey, the poor food, the cramped quarters, were but a foretaste of what was to come. For them, the welcoming words emblazoned on the Statue of Liberty—"Give me your tired, your poor, your huddled masses yearning to breathe free . . . " would take on an almost mocking quality as they struggled in America's dust-choked sweatshops to earn their daily bread.

At the same time, their situation was in no way comparable to that of their Biblical forebears who, as they wandered through the desert, were known to have yearned nostalgically for "the fleshpots of Egypt." For these travelers had, in most cases, left behind a life of grinding poverty where their existence was not much more than that and where they were at best tolerated and far more often viewed with suspicion and hatred. And this was especially true of the masses who had embarked for Newark and other American cities from the Russian Pale, from Poland, and from Romania and Hungary.

Given these circumstances, it was not surprising that they plunged into their new lives with a vigor and enthusiasm unmatched by most other immigrant groups. Unlike the Italians, Irish, Greeks, Scandinavians, and Germans, the Jews really had no country to which they could return if they failed in America, certainly not a place that would welcome them back in any way, and this fact made succeeding in America almost an imperative. They were, in that sense, here for good and they knew it.

Moreover, America was truly a land of opportunity. Despite the need to learn a new language, new skills, and adapt to a new way of life, the immigrants sensed that there was a point to overcoming these problems. They glimpsed, even as they struggled to somehow get through each day, a brighter vision of a future that could one day be theirs if only they would not give up. The sense of dynamism and forward movement that had already infused the United States since the heady days of independence a century earlier was palpable even in the darkest corners of America's ghettoes, where the teeming masses lived in filthy and crowded tenements and worked in unsanitary and unsafe factories.

Newark's Jews who came from Eastern Europe between 1881 and 1920, already had a Jewish model of success to emulate, that of their German and Bohemian coreligionists who had preceded them in the mid-nineteenth century. These Jews had invariably started out, not as factory laborers, but as peddlers and small shopkeepers. One early arrival, Sarah Kussy, recalled her parents' struggle to make it in the New World:

> He began life, as so many Jewish immigrants did, by walking the streets of Newark and suburbs—with the peddler's pack on his back, filled with dry-goods and notions. Peddling gave him a chance to refrain from business on the Sabbath. Probably some kind-hearted "Landsman" provided an initial loan of five or ten dollars for the purchase of goods. The "greenhorns" helped each other; organized philanthropy did not yet exist. . . . Mother, having disposed of her millinery business, waited on customers in the butcher shop; cooked, washed, sewed for her family, while every drop of water had to be carried into the house from the pump which stood in the yard, close to the privy—for conditions were primitive in those days.[1]

Eventually, through hard work and struggle, Gustav and Bella Kussy achieved a level of economic success to the point where they bought property and were able to live reasonably well. But the true measure of accomplishment can best be discerned from what happened to their children. One became a banker, another a lawyer, a third a dentist, a fourth a teacher, and a fifth a successful wholesaler. And all this in one generation!

While the German-Jewish emigres were carving out a niche for themselves, Newark was beginning its tremendous growth as a city and one of the main engines that drove the locomotive of financial progress in Newark was the insurance industry. It was during this period that the giant Prudential Insurance Company was founded (1873) and, along with it, the Mutual Benefit Insurance Company (1845). In addition to the availability of cheap labor, a chief attraction of New Jersey at the time was its looser system of financial controls relative to New York. While insurance was never a "Jewish" industry, it was important for the community because, perhaps even more than banking, industry profits helped finance much of Newark's business expansion, whether Jewish owned or otherwise.

Jews were active from the start in a number of industries, among them leather, trunk, and harness manufacturing, jewelry, dry-goods, and retail department stores. In general, the industrial process was one where home industries were replaced by small stores, which then gradually became factories. Beginning in the mid-1800s, Newark entered a period of tremendous growth and expansion, a key element of which was its degree of diversification. Besides the above-mentioned areas, there were breweries, malleable iron, clocks and watches, hats, and precision instruments of every kind. These products were all showcased in the Newark Industrial Expositions that took place between 1872 and 1875, and which greatly enhanced Newark's reputation as a national industrial center.

In that sense Newark was also a magnet to both Jews and non-Jews already in America who, for one reason or another, were looking for new places in which to start. Immigrants to New York City were one such resource. In some cases, people moved because they felt it would be easier to start up a business in a locale that was less crowded than New York. In other instances relatives already living in Newark served as he impetus for relocation. Sometimes the reasons were idiosyncrat c but all too real nonetheless:

My father was in the wholesale coal business in New York when, one day, he got a note shortly after he started in business: "You'll find your truck in the river and next it'll be your family." It must have been mob troubles. But it scared him enough to get out.[2]

The bulk of immigrants to Newark in the early years were, of course, not manufacturers, real estate tycoons, large-scale retailers, or professionals. They were members of the working class or proprietors of small stores, people who were simply eking out a living. They rose early in the morning and worked far into the night, falling into bed exhausted, dreaming, no doubt, of a better life for their children. Education beyond elementary school was often out of the question, though

for their children, nothing was out of reach. These aspirations reflected the quintessential Jewish values—family and education. Ultimately, they prevailed. A 1946 survey conducted on behalf of the
United Jewish Appeal reported that among businessmen and professionals, almost half were making at least $10,000 a year, and about 7
percent reported incomes of more than $30,000 annually. These were
impressive figures for that time, especially given the propensity of
people to understate their earnings in surveys of any kind.[3]

Helping others is an integral part of Jewish tradition and the role of
the community in the adaptation of the newcomers to the workplace
was often critical. While in the beginning, philanthropy was either
private or the result of efforts by small Jewish groups, it soon became
a major facet of Jewish organizational life. The National Council of
Jewish Women sponsored Americanization classes and the Jewish Vocational Service (JVS) (originally called the Jewish Employment Service) helped applicants find jobs commensurate with their skills while
the Hebrew Free Loan Society provided financial aid. The JVS, through
its job counseling service, also matched employers with available workers. Between 1939 and 1954, a total of 5,000 jobs were found for its
applicants.[4] The following ads that appeared in the July 28, 1950 issue
of the *Jewish News* were typical of the placements made:

POCKETBOOK MAKER, age 25. Five and a half years European and American
experience on ladies handbags, cutting, assembling, framing, art work. Good English.

PHOTOGRAPHER - FINISHER, age 42, eighteen years European experience and
four months in U.S. as a retoucher, colorist. Fair English.

And another ad for someone equally in need but with less to offer:

TRAINEE, age 38. Alert, intelligent young man. Forced labor in concentration
camps. Seeks training opportunity in skilled trade. Fair English.

The ads were accompanied by an appeal from George Sagan, then
Chairman of JVS' Advisory Committee on Employment of Refugees,
who exhorted readers to help:

Remember that when a newcomer finds a job it is a threefold "mitzvah:" the
employer gets a qualified worker; the newcomer starts on the road to personal
rehabilitation; and the community reduces relief costs.[5]

The community's needs ebbed and flowed with the changing times. Naturally, during the Depression, Jews were affected in the same way as other Americans, with small businesses and factory workers among the hardest hit. One Jewish journalist poignantly described what it was like for both Jews and non-Jews:

> Random scenes flicker in my memory: whole families sitting disconsolately amid their furniture dumped into the street: men selling apples out of baskets at the Four Corners: a long line of mendicants stretching across Military Park, moving slowly toward a soup kitchen where food was being doled out: a huge crowd of job-seekers gathered in front of the *Newark Evening News* building on Market Street, waiting for the first edition, snapping up the papers when the newsboys appeared with them and then breaking in all directions with the Help Wanted sections flying in their hands: Oh for a job at the "Pru," New Jersey Bell or Public Service!
>
> The [Jewish] storekeepers of Ferry Street suffered along with the rest, my father and mother among them. Customers who had always paid in cash pleaded for shoes for their children on credit and got them. Others wore their old shoes to a pulp. The tenants who lived in the building my father owned could no longer pay their rent.[6]

And later on, each succeeding wave of Jewish refugees—Holocaust survivors, Hungarian refugees, and, more recently, Russian immigrants, was to find itself similarly grateful that the community was supportive of their needs, for that was, and is, the Jewish way.

Although America was the land of opportunity, Jews faced prejudice and discrimination throughout, whether it was on the employment line, in the corporate boardroom, or at the country club, where so much of America's business was done. In the poorer neighborhoods, like the Central Ward, such prejudice was far more common:

> A block away, the trouble is swirling in from Montgomery and from Broome. Thin, acne-scarred Irish youngsters from 18th Street and 5th Avenue are engaged in a favorite caper: raiding the peddlers of pushcart row. They're not interested in stealing the pitiful wares on sale. There's more fun in plain, safe Jew-baiting—pulling beards and snatching skullcaps.[7]

Frieda Mayers, whose maiden name was Samberg, recalled how, in 1932, as a single woman, she and a German friend named Mueller applied for a position at the RCA plant in nearby Harrison. Her friend received a job offer by telegram and she did not. Suspecting anti-Semitism she applied again the next day, using the name of "Frances Smith." That night she received a telegram informing her that she had been hired.[8] Similarly, in education, Jews seemed able to get jobs in

Newark, but only with great difficulty in nearby Union or Irvington, where prejudice against them was quite strong.[9]

In the end, Jews in Newark prevailed, succeeding despite the odds, just as they were to do well elsewhere in the country. The combination of their social and cultural backgrounds, coupled with sheer determination and will, made the difference. Where they encountered discrimination, their response, more often than not, was simply to do better than others. Knowing they started out with two strikes against them often served as an additional incentive. And where the field was open, they often entered in such numbers that they came to dominate the industry, thereby making Jewishness an irrelevant issue. And if they did not achieve at the level that they had hoped to reach, their children invariably did. Now let's take a closer look at how Jews fared in the specific occupations and professions in which they were concentrated.

Industry and Business

It is symbolically significant that the first permanent Jewish resident in Newark was Louis Trier, for he operated a tannery, which was to become a dominant industry in the city. In fact, a mere twenty-five years after Trier's arrival, 90 percent of all patent leather produced in the U.S. came from Newark, the adopted home of its inventor, Seth Boyden. R.G. Salomon, who pioneered in the manufacture of cordovan leather in the 1880s, was also the country's leading tanner of alligator skins. Among the most important people in the industry were T.P. Howell, Daniel Kaufherr, and Martin Dennis.[10] And in trunk manufacturing, also related to leather, the most influential Jewish name was probably that of Jacob Lagowitz. Leather was one of two flourishing industries in Newark, the other beer brewing, whose success depended on the soft water that coursed through the Passaic River.

Jews were much in evidence in the leather industry and some had been active in this area in Europe before arriving here. In the early twentieth century, two individuals in particular were prominently associated with it—Abraham Lichtman and Joseph Kaltenbacher. It was difficult work and most of those who toiled in the foul-smelling factories were Irish, Slavic, and Italian immigrants, with a few Jews here and there. Philip Roth, in his 1997 novel, *American Pastoral*, provides an evocative and richly textured description of what it was like to work in the tanneries:

The son Lou—Swede Levov's father—went to work in the tannery after leaving school at fourteen to help support the family of nine and became adept not only at dyeing buckskin by laying on the clay dye with a flat, stiff brush but also at sorting and grading skins. The tannery that stank of both the slaughterhouse and the chemical plant from the soaking of flesh and the cooking of flesh and the dehairing and pickling and degreasing of hides, where round the clock in the summertime the blowers drying the thousands and thousands of hanging skins raised the temperature in the low-ceilinged dry room to a hundred and twenty degrees, where the vast vat rooms were as dark as caves and flooded with swill, where brutish workingmen, heavily aproned, armed with hooks and staves, dragging and pushing overloaded wagons, wringing and hanging waterlogged skins, were driven like animals through the laborious storm that was a twelve-hour shift—a filthy, stinking place awash with water dyed red and black and blue and green, with hunks of skin all over the floor, everywhere pits of grease, hills of salt, barrels of solvent . . . [11]

Another allied industry in which Jews had a major role was fur. The most important firm was A. Hollander and Sons and the story of how it grew was a prototype of the Horatio Alger stories that typified those Jews who made it big in America. Adolph Hollander, the company's founder, came to this country in 1883 and, together with his brother, began operations in a tiny building on Polk Street with a capital fund of $200. The machinery was driven by a mule-pulled treadmill. By 1936, the company had become the largest fur dressing and dyeing operation in the world and had introduced all sorts of major innovations into the field. It advertised everywhere in the U.S. using both radio and fashion magazines as its mediums. By 1941, its capital and surplus was estimated in excess of $3,500,000 and it employed 2,500 workers in ten plants around the country.[12]

Newark was a jewelry manufacturing center from early on and its beginnings can be traced to Ephraim Hinsdale, who opened a jewelry-making store in 1792. In the years before the Civil War, Southern planters often came to the city to buy their jewelry. Its reputation was greatly enhanced by James Madison Durand, who developed innovative methods for producing jewelry in his factory. More than 800 people worked in twenty-seven jewelry factories between 1840 and 1860.

Eventually, Newark came to be seen as an international center for jewelry (this was in the days before New York's 47th Street, of course), attracting not only foreign customers, but also craftsmen from Italy and Germany who came in search of employment opportunities. In addition to jewelry, Newark also became a gold and silver refining center. As evidence of its importance, Tiffany's built a plant in 1896 in North Newark for its sterling silver operation.

Jews became involved in this industry at the turn of the century. Among the leading firms in those days were Shiman and Company, Jabel Ring Company, Henry Blank and S. Fischer, F.A. Schlosstein, Arch Crown, Meyer and Gross, Franklin Jewelry (later Capitol Ring), and Krementz, the only jewelry manufacturer still left in Newark. A number of these companies no longer exist and others, like Jabel, which is now in Irvington, pulled up stakes and left Newark. Most of these companies had their special niches. Thus, Arch Crown made labels for the industry. Franklin Jewelry, which was founded by Sol Goodman, specialized in childrens' rings, and Meyer and Gross created mountings for engagement rings. Today, however, jewelry is no longer a real presence in Newark, with most of the factories either out of business or located elsewhere in the state.[13]

These were, by far, not the only industries in which Jews played a role. In fact, they were present in hundreds of different areas, and an entire book could easily be written about the contributions made by Jews to Newark's business and industrial life. Roth's description in his book gives a sense of the variety:

> There was a factory where somebody was making something in every side street. . . . when my father bought the [glove] factory, a stone's throw away Kiler made watercoolers, Fortgang made fire alarms, Lasky made corsets, Robbins made pillows, Honig made pen points, . . . 'The joint's jumpin,' he used to say.[14]

Two of the most prominent businessmen in the community were Louis Aronson and William Schiffenhaus. Aronson built the Ronson Lighter Company into one of the largest such firms in the world and there is no doubt that among the millions of people who used them, probably few were aware that the company was Jewish owned. As for Schiffenhaus, he established a very large and successful corrugated box company. But what distinguished these and other Jewish businessmen in Newark was their often singular devotion to the Jewish community. Aronson, for example, who was active in B'nai Abraham, enjoyed taking orphans from the Jewish Childrens' Home on outings aboard his yacht and Schiffenhaus was active in numerous Jewish organizations, including B'nai Brith, Oheb Shalom, and the Newark Talmud Torah.[15]

What is also interesting is the combination of intellectual and business interests that coexisted within so many families. Many of the immigrants were attracted to books and learning, but they were also guided by a pragmatic realization that scholarship would not necessarily put bread on the table. Bernard Bloom's family started a paper business in 1918 and although his father expected him to enter it, he also encouraged him to attend Columbia University, which the younger Bloom did. Perhaps not surprisingly, Bernard's own son followed the same pattern, attending Princeton as an undergraduate and then the Harvard Business School. Upon graduation he worked for a time at the World Bank but then, in 1977, he too entered the family business. When the company was sold, in 1993, to International Paper, it had annual sales of 75 million dollars.[16]

Quite a few successful businessmen became presidents of the Essex County Jewish Federation. One such individual was Clarence Reisen whose family manifested the same combination of scholarly bent and financial talent that existed in the Bloom family. Mitzi Reisen, Clarence's widow, wryly recalled how:

> The Reisens were a literary family in Vilna and Avrohom was a famous poet. Clarence's father made the money in the lumber company that supported all of the *luftmenschen* in the family. It wasn't Dow Chemical but several families did very well from it. There were other Jews in the lumber business too but his ended up as one of the biggest.[17]

Horace Bier was another Federation president who was successful in business. Bier's company manufactures electrical cable connections for Con Edison and other utilities.[18] Dan Drench, yet another past Federation president, made electronic components for navigational equipment. At its height the company's annual volume in sales was about $9,000,000 and it employed about 75–80 people.[19]

Some entrepreneurs entered more unusual lines of work, doing very well in them. One such instance is that of Philip Konvitz, son of the well-known Newark rabbi, Joseph Konvitz, and brother of the constitutional law scholar, Milton Konvitz, again demonstrating the confluence of scholarship and business, and, in this case, religion too, that characterized so many Jewish families. In an interview, Philip talked about his business and it was clear that this is a man for whom business and hard work, for that matter, is life itself:

> I've got the largest bail bond business in the country. We do a billion dollars worth of liability business a year. It's called International Fidelity Insurance Company. We're in every state in the country and in Puerto Rico. We also do bail and civil bonds. I'm chairman of the board even today, at eighty-four. I start at 7:00 A.M. I'd start at 4:00 A.M. but we don't open until seven.[20]

Looking at the larger picture, it becomes clear that men like Hollander, R.G. Salomon, and Aronson, were representative of a larger group of innovative industrialists, complemented by skilled craftsmen at every level, whose creativity energized the city. Some were Jewish and some were not, but they were united by a desire to do things, to build, and to leave their indelible stamp on this world. Newark seemed to attract such people in unusual numbers and they could be found in practically every line of work. In turn, their presence in Newark attracted leading inventors such as Seth Boyden, Thomas Edison, and Edward Weston, thus further enhancing the city's reputation as a major industrial center in the U.S.

Real estate started small in Newark as far as the Jewish community was concerned, but even so it was evidence of a desire by Jews to own property. Isaac Newman came to Newark in 1845 as part of the German-Jewish migration and opened a boarding house on River Street. Two years later, Bernard Hauser arrived and shortly after opening a grocery store at the intersection of Prince and Springfield, he bought the property there, renting out apartments to his fellow Jews. This presaged what was to happen later as Jews became prominent in this field.

Among the most important real estate firms in the city were Feist and Feist, Leslie Blau, Krasner and Stavitsky, and Louis Schlesinger. Like many other successful Jewish businessmen, Schlesinger was active in Jewish organizations, among them the Jewish Children's Home, the Hebrew Free School, Temple B'nai Jeshurun, and, nationally, as a member of the Executive Board of the Union of American Hebrew Congregations and as a supporter of the National Farm School in Doylestown, Pennsylvania.[21]

In addition to their involvement in the Jewish community, there was a belief by prominent Jews that to be an American in good standing it was necessary to display interest in non-Jewish affairs too. After all, in their business dealings, Jews and gentiles interacted with each other and, in the course of conversations, had ample opportunity to make mention of their respective civic activities, activities which produced the glue that cemented relationships based on a shared vision of what America should be. This vision was exemplified by organizations such as the Downtown Club and the Newark Athletic Club, both of which Schlesinger joined, not to mention traditional American societies such as the Elks, Masons, and Rotarians and nondenominational charities.[22]

The development of the automobile, the construction of highways, general prosperity, and the interplay between higher city taxes and the movement of business to the suburbs, reconfigured the real estate playing field as well. As a result, builders gravitated to the new Jewish areas. One early builder, Morris Rachlin, is a good example of this trajectory. At first, in the 1880s, he put up hundreds of homes in the Prince Street area. He also built upscale apartment buildings in the city, such as the Savoy and the Royal, on South Broad Street.

Rachlin then branched out into several of the more suburban areas of Newark. The endeavor that had the greatest impact on the Jewish community, in terms of size, was probably his project in Clinton Hill, where he bought and developed large tracts of land for private and two-family homes. This opened the door for shopping areas to serve the population that no longer wanted to go downtown for every purchase and in this way new centers of Jewish life sprang up.[23] This trend was repeated in the post-World War II era, with entrepreneurs like George and Maurice Levin building thousands of apartments in the Oranges, Irvington, and other areas which had become attractive for the Jews of that time. Later on, Maurice's son, Martin, played a major role, together with Alan Sagner in developing the Livingston community. Sagner was also instrumental in the expansion of Beth Israel Hospital and served as chairman of its board. He was also chairman of the New York Port Authority. An important adjunct industry that was critical for the success of these developments was that of the real estate appraisers. Among the most influential Jewish firms were those of Franklin Hannoch and George Goldstein, who was also the chairman of Blue Cross.

Real estate was a chancy business, highly sensitive to the fluctuations of the market and many more failed than succeeded. There was, for instance, the panic of 1893, about which Rachlin recalled:

> I can remember going through the streets begging people to move in without paying rent, just in order to prevent the water pipes from being frozen and bursting.[24]

The disaster best remembered by Americans is the one which most affected them—the Great Depression that began in 1929. The most dramatically affected groups were those in the volatile stock market and the real estate industry. In his 1970 autobiography, Louis Kasen, former president of the Synthetics Plastics Company and a past chairman of the United Jewish Appeal, recounted what happened to one of the largest developers, Abraham Lefcourt:

> The boom in securities was accompanied by a wild rush in the building trades when mortgage money was plentiful and rental space was at a premium; but when the market crashed the real estate industry crashed with it. Mr. Lefcourt was one of the biggest real estate operators in the New York area. He built the tallest and most modern building right in the best part of the center of Newark and he named it the Lefcourt Building which was his pride and joy. It is now [1970] about forty years old and is still considered one of the best buildings in Newark. It is now called the Raymond Commerce Bldg. Only a few weeks after the crash the banks started to tighten up on mortgage money and Mr. Lefcourt was unable to renew his loans in spite of the fact that he had the most valuable properties in all his locations. Mr. Lefcourt too could not face his tragedy and he threw himself out of a top floor of the Lefcourt Building that he cherished so much. The epidemic of suicides continued. It was contagious until people got used to their misfortunes and regained their equilibrium.[25]

Banking was never a Jewish profession anywhere in America and Newark was no exception. While today, Jews have achieved a greater degree of acceptance in American society, in the Newark of fifty years ago many gentiles were simply uncomfortable among Jews. Since the banking business was always tied in with social connections this created entry problems for them as a group. Even in Jewishly influential New York, for example, wealthy banking families like the Seligmans and Kuhns were socially discriminated against by their gentile counterparts. Moreover, knowing that there was discrimination in banking, many talented Jews shied away from the field and this created its own self-fulfilling prophecy.[26]

There were exceptions. An important bank for the Jewish community was the West Side Trust Company, founded, in 1896, by Meyer Kussy, which gave loans to the Springfield Avenue merchants and others who had difficulty obtaining assistance from the old-line establishment banks. The bank remained independent until it was merged into the Bank of Commerce in the 1960s.[27] Milton Lesnik became involved in 1950 with the Broad National Bank of Newark and was made chairman of the bank in 1960. Broad had been created as a labor bank in 1925, an institution where unions and their members could obtain loans and mortgages. Today, while the bank has non-Jewish officers, the majority, including the present Chairman/CEO, Donald Karp, are Jewish. In 1997, Broad National had assets of over 85 million dollars.[28] Significantly, the barriers in the banking industry have come down quite a bit today and there are numerous members of the Jewish faith occupying high posts in banks, both in New Jersey and throughout the nation.

Other instances exist of Jewish involvement in smaller Newark banks. Louis Lippman founded the Vailsburg Trust Company in 1923. Lippman was an active Republican and served as an alternate delegate to the Republican Convention that nominated Warren Harding for President. He was also active in Jewish life as secretary of Beth Israel Hospital, a member of Temple B'nai Jeshurun, and many other Jewish organizations.[29] Milton Wigder, owner of Wigder Chevrolet, was another Jewish banker. Among the banks with which he was involved were the Village Bank of South Orange and the Suburban Bank in Livingston.[30]

The dry goods business in Newark had a significant Jewish presence from the 1840s on when stores like Ullman and Isaacs, Klein and Thalheimer, and Hart and Dettelbach, opened. Two Jewish family names, however, became synonymous with large-scale retailing in Newark—Plaut and Bamberger. Together with the Hahne family, which was not Jewish, they made up the three largest department stores in Newark.

Department stores did not become part of Newark's business life until the 1870s and the first, established in 1870 on Broad Street by L. Simon Plaut, together with Leopold Fox, was L.S. Plaut, also known as the Bee-Hive. The Plaut family, whose roots were in Germany, had first settled in Hartford, Connecticut and Simon Plaut had cut his teeth there, working in his father's establishment for three years. Plaut founded the business at age twenty and it quickly became known for a then radical innovation, a one-price system, as opposed to the previous way of doing business by haggling over the cost of various items. In 1882, the Fox-Plaut partnership broke up and Simon's two brothers, Louis and Moses, joined him in the business. Louis had actually begun working in the store four years earlier, starting out as a $2.00 a week bundle boy and porter whose main job was to sweep the floor every day.[31]

Eventually, the store grew to the point where it occupied an entire square block, bounded by Cedar, Halsey, and Broad Streets, and the old Morris Canal bed. In addition to its one-price policy, the Bee-Hive also pioneered in the area of worker benefits, becoming one of the first to set up a mutual benefit program for store employees. It also adhered to a policy of promoting from within, thus insuring high worker morale. In 1923, the store was sold to S.S. Kresge in a $17,000,000 deal.[32] Like Plaut, Louis Bamberger was not from Newark. He came from Baltimore and it is interesting that Newark lies about midway between Hartford, Plaut's birthplace, and Baltimore.[33] Perhaps both of them saw something special in the "City on a Hill." In any event, it is clear that Bamberger, after learning the business in his uncle's dry goods store and then operating a wholesale outfit in New York, waited almost two years for what he felt was the right location in Newark. That turned out to be the corner of Halsey and Market Streets. He bought the Hill and Craig store there, in 1892, in a bankruptcy proceeding, joining forces with two partners, his brothers-in-law, Felix Fuld, and Louis M. Frank. (Caroline Bamberger Fuld married Felix Fuld after her first husband, Louis Frank, died.)

In 1912, L. Bamberger and Company, which had already undergone several expansions, took up a full square block with Halsey, Market, Washington, and Bank Streets on each of its four sides. Its success was due, in no small measure, to its ability to market itself as a premier store aimed especially at the upper middle classes. A key vehicle for promoting that view, was *Charm*, its glossy, in-house publication. Moreover, as John O'Connor and Charles Cummings have pointed out, sales people were trained to treat all customers with great respect, thus making Bamberger's a place where the middle classes "could expect the same high level of dignified personal service as the the wealthy scions of high society." By 1924, the store had grown to the point where it employed 2,800 people. And, as was the case with the Bee-Hive, Bamberger's exhibited enlightened attitudes towards its employees, providing them with benefits, pension plans, and other incentives. In 1928, the year before the store was sold to R.H. Macy, Bamberger's enjoyed annual sales of $38,000,000, ranking it fourth in the country among department stores.[34]

What was the true significance of these enterprises in terms of the Jewish community? Clearly, the financial success of those who owned them was helpful to Jewish life because it made possible their donations to Jewish causes and organizations. Among the many endeavors with which the Plaut family was associated were the Jewish Children's Home, Plaut Memorial Hebrew Free School, United Hebrew Charities, the Y, and Temple B'nai Jeshurun, where Louis Plaut was a trustee. The family also supported non-Jewish organizations, among them the Red Cross, Navy Club of the United States, National and Newark Chambers of Commerce, Newark Musical Festival Association, and the New Jersey Historical Society.

Bamberger was also involved in many causes, though his innately shy and retiring nature sometimes prevented that fact from becoming widely known. For example, in 1930, Bamberger, who had made a major capital gift to the Y, was urged to take on its presidency but declined on the grounds that he had never wanted to be in "the front line." He did, however, offer financial support to the Y if someone else would take the position. And so it was. While someone else took on the job, he gave $25,000 a year for two years.[35]

In 1928, Bamberger was also a major donor to the new building for Beth Israel Hospital. Other groups that benefited from his largesse included the Jewish Theological Seminary, the American Jewish Relief Committee, the Palestine Foundation Fund, the Emergency Committee on Jewish Refugees, and the Jewish Children's Home. In addition, he was a steady supporter of the local United Jewish Appeal. Not to be overlooked is the pressure brought to bear by Bamberger and Fuld on Newark's non-Jewish businessmen to join with their Jewish coreligionists in supporting a united drive for the Community Chest in 1923.

Bamberger was also very active in causes and projects that were not specifically Jewish. He is perhaps best known in Newark's larger community for his donation of the buildings for the Newark Museum and the New Jersey Historical Society. He also presented to the Society a full set of autographs of the signers of the Declaration of Independence. To help the museum, he gave it many art, archeological, and scientific objects from his own personal collection. Bamberger was also a patron of the Newark Public Library.

Outside of Newark, his greatest contribution was an initial $5,000,000 gift, together with his sister, Caroline Fuld, to help create the famed Institute for Advanced Study affiliated with Princeton University. Bamberger had originally wanted to build a medical school for Jewish students who faced discrimination but he was persuaded by Abraham Flexner, a respected scholar, to select Princeton because it was an excellent way to capitalize on the Jewish bent for scholarship at a very prestigious university. Flexner became the first director of the Institute, which was housed on a site adjacent to Princeton. Finally, Bamberger's ownership of WOR radio, with its music programs and talk shows, helped make cultural programming accessible to the masses. Music was a strong interest of his, and he endowed music festivals and scholarships for young people.[36]

The Fulds were equally generous with their wealth and in a variety of ways. Caroline Fuld had a lasting effect of a different sort on Newark when she donated about 2,000 cherry blossom trees, imported from Japan, that she had raised on her estate, to the Essex County Park Commission. The Commission had them transplanted to Branch Brook Park, where they have bloomed every spring since. An active member of Hadassah, Mrs. Fuld also gave generously to the Jewish Day Nursery and Neighborhood House and, on the national level, she served as president of the National Council of Jewish Women. The Fulds gave $500,000 to Beth Israel Hospital and Felix was an active participant in his congregation, B'nai Jeshurun. Both Bamberger and Fuld were members of the American Jewish Committee.

One can clearly discern, in the charitable giving patterns of Louis Bamberger, a propensity to give to both Jewish and non-Jewish causes. Did this reflect an insecurity on his part, a quest for social acceptance? Certainly Jews did not feel completely secure in early twentieth-century America and many undoubtedly wished to appear worldly in the eyes of their fellow Christians. On the other hand, there was no need for Bamberger to give to any Jewish causes and, indeed, plenty of wealthy Jews, gave nothing or almost nothing to the Jewish community. By contrast, Bamberger gave to many Jewish institutions and none of his comments or actions suggest even the slightest semblance of discomfort with his identity as a Jew.

Some might interpret the size of his gifts to the Institute for Advanced Study and the Newark Museum, compared with his gifts to Jewish groups as evidence of a bias in favor of non-Jewish giving, based on a desire to win acceptance in the larger American society.[37] In this writer's view, that would be an oversimplification. A man of Bamberger's sophistication possessed a very clear understanding of the Jew's place in American society, namely a view that expanding educational and cultural opportunities for Americans in general would ultimately benefit Jews even more than the average American because of the proclivity of Jews to aspire to succeed in these arenas. In other words, Bamberger knew that in giving to the Institute, he was probably benefiting his Jewish brethren the most because they were likely to win acceptance to such an institution more often, proportionately, than members of other groups. In fact, given the manifestations of anti-Semitism, particularly in the form of quotas, that had appeared at elite institutions such as Columbia and Harvard during this period, endowing the Institute on its own campus at an equally prestigious institution, namely Princeton, was most likely an answer to such practices, not an expression of a desire to promote assimilation. Moreover, in the larger scale of things, in terms of having an impact on society as a whole, be it Jewish or Christian, the Institute as a world-renowned center was probably more important than individual Jewish organizations, hence the justification for the larger contributions.

Given these realities, and considering his involvement with the Jewish community (not to mention that of his sister) it seems safe to conclude that Louis Bamberger identified as a proud Jew, irrespective of who received his money. Yes, philanthropic gifts to places like the Institute "synthesized his American and Jewish concerns."[38] And that is a synthesis that typifies the identifications of American Jews in general as a people who are both American and Jewish, in the fullest sense of each term.

The salutary effect of known Jewish names such as Plaut and Bamberger on the Jewish community at large cannot be overestimated. True, these were German Jews and by the 1920s more than half of Newark's Jewish population was of Eastern European extraction. Still, they were Jews and that must have given the community a distinct sense of pride in the achievements of their larger ethnic group. Even more than real estate, leather, law, or education, retail stores were highly visible in the public mind. They were, after all, household names. There was vicarious gratification in hearing people say "I'm going to Bamberger's, [or 'Bam's,'] to buy a gift." or to see advertisements extolling the virtues of Plaut's Department Store. For the immigrants it meant that the American dream was eminently attainable. In that sense, Bamberger's and Plaut's effect on the community was profound, for it was a vehicle for both pride and hope in a group that wanted to believe in their efficacy.

The list of important businesses both retail and wholesale that began in Newark or that were founded by Newark natives could easily stretch into the hundreds and space does not permit a detailed enumeration of them. In all of these cases, be it Leonard Kurland's fixture manufacturing company or Howard Levine's twelve-volt products company, the story is invariably one of sheer grit and determination, coupled with hard work, creative thinking, and sometimes a measure of plain good luck.[39] To demonstrate the process, let's take one more example of a Newark-based business because it is a textbook case in how such businesses got started:

Max Polaner came from Europe in 1885. A housepainter by trade, he soon became a fruit peddler, eventually opening up his own fruit and vegetable store. There was, of course, no refrigeration in the 1880s so, to preserve it, Grandma Polaner made the fruit into jam. Around the same time, in Ohio, a German named Smucker was doing the same thing. Polaner's jam was sold in the store and soon other shopkeepers began buying it from him, thus turning Polaner into a distributor. The business began on 15th Avenue, soon expanding to a larger facility on 16th Avenue. A small factory was built and the making of sauerkraut also became part of the enterprise. By 1910, the company was producing peanut butter, in addition to its mainstays of jam and jelly.

The business survived the Depression, though it was rough going for a while. Eventually, however, it prospered and adapted to the changing times. Grandson Leonard attended MIT where, among other things he studied food technology, a subject that was of significant practical help to him in his business. In 1986, when he sold the business, annual sales were a whopping 32 million.[40]

Then there were native Newarkers whose businesses were not limited to Newark, but who were immensely successful. Alex Aidekman, for example, grew up poor on a farm in Maplewood, where he was born in 1914. Together with two other partners, Herbert Brody and Milton Perlmutter, he founded the immensely successful Shoprite and Pathmark chains. In 1980, for example, the Pathmark stores alone rang up sales of 2.3 *billion* dollars.[41] Aidekman certainly helped Newark's Jewish community, giving generously to Jewish charities and organizations including a gift to the MetroWest Federation worth about $2,000,000, in return for which its complex was named the Aidekman Campus. Of equal importance is Allen Bildner, who owned King's Supermarkets and who is very much involved in the Jewish community. Another example of a Newarker who made good is Bernie Marcus, now resident of Atlanta, and CEO of Home Depot, a company which, in 1995, did 16 billion dollars in sales.[42] Marcus, who grew up in Clinton Hill, is from the younger generation of Newarkers, having graduated high school in 1947. A third well-known name is Lechter's. The hardware chain was built up by Albert Lechter, a 1946 graduate of South Side High School who currently resides in Livingston. The seeds for this idea were probably planted by his grandfather, who had a small store on Prince Street and, in fact, it was Lechter who reportedly persuaded Marcus to switch from his job as a pharmacist to the home improvement business. Lechter has done quite well in his own right, with some 650 stores located all over the country.[43]

The Professions and the Arts

Jews entered a variety of professions. Some, such as engineering, were inhospitable to them, while others were not. Space does not allow for a detailed discussion of each field so we will only focus on some of those that were most attractive to people in the Jewish community. One of them, law, has always been a popular profession for Jews and, over the years, thousands of Jews have practiced in Newark. Wherever Jews have been granted civil equality they have entered law and in Western countries, including the U.S., they have been overrepresented in the field. Within the context of this discussion it is only possible to mention some of the most prominent such individuals in the community.

One of the best-known early lawyers was Samuel Kalisch, who became a New Jersey Supreme Court Justice in 1911. A specialist in the field of negligence, he was, nevertheless, well grounded in all aspects of criminal and civil law and achieved a reputation as an outstanding jurist. Kalisch was an excellent litigator and had a flair for the dramatic. On one occasion, in a negligence suit against Western Union Telegraph Company, Kalisch brought tears to the jury's eyes when he compared the armless plaintiff to the statue, in the Louvre, of the Venus de Milo.[44] Kalisch, whose father, Isidor, was the rabbi of Temple B'nai Abraham, was active in Jewish affairs and worked together with Louis Marshall on behalf of the American Jewish Committee. There have, in fact, been numerous Jewish judges in Newark, at one time or another, among them, Louis R. Freund, Joseph Siegler, Joseph Weintraub, Nathan Jacobs, Morris Shapira, Leonard Kalisch, Martin Greenberg, Julius Feinberg, Kenneth Stein, Leon Milmed, Joseph Lerner, and Leo Yanoff, who is still active today. In 1997, at age eighty-six, Yanoff, also a past Federation president, was the oldest sitting judge in New Jersey.

Other attorneys who achieved prominence early in the twentieth century were Samuel Leber, who specialized in real estate and who was a president of the Essex County Council of Jewish Agencies and Louis Hood, general counsel of Fidelity Union Trust Company, the largest bank in the state. Hood was an 1878 Yale College graduate and he received his law degree from Columbia. He also served as the prosecutor for Essex County and was president of the Essex County Bar Association. Another Jewish attorney who was an Essex County prosecutor, was Jacob Newman. There was the firm of Stein, Hannoch, and McGlynn which had several well-known Jewish members. Leo Stein was president, for a time, of the Lawyer's Club of Essex County[45] and Joseph Weintraub was named chief justice of the New Jersey Supreme Court in 1957. Herbert Hannoch was president of the Jewish Children's Home and Aaron Lasser became president of the Y. Other highly respected members of the bar were Emmanuel Lowenstein of Lowy, Lowenstein, and Leber and Nathan Kussy of Kussy, Kohn, and Cohn. Mention should also be made of Samuel Kessler and Robert Grossman, each of whom served as New Jersey assistant attorney general in the 1920s, a time when only two or three individuals held that office at a time. Prior to this appointment, Kessler had also been an assistant U.S. attorney.

Milton Unger was a successful lawyer who served as president of the New Jersey Bar Association and Alan Lowenstein heads one of the largest law firms in New Jersey, Lowenstein, Sandler, Kohl, Fisher, and Boylan. Other lawyers who gained recognition in the field and/or the Jewish and general communities, include Nathan Bilder, Dave Stoffer, Israel Greene, Meyer Ruback, Emmanuel Scheck, Morris Schnitzer, and, of course, Meyer Ellenstein. In 1947, the state held a constitutional convention, changing the Constitution for the first time since 1844. As vice chairman of the Judiciary Committee, Nathan Jacobs played a key role in many of the changes made, changes which helped open up the judicial system to broader participation among all minorities, including Jews.[46]

Anti-Semitism was present in the legal profession just as it was a factor throughout America but it really became an issue in the 1920s when Jews began challenging the old guard. In earlier years it was not that great a problem. That's why a Louis Hood could become general counsel to the state's largest bank in the beginning of the century. Meanwhile, however, it had become common in major American cities with substantial Jewish populations to have both Jewish and gentile law firms. This was true in New York City and in Newark. A notable exception was Hood, Lafferty, and Campbell. Hood was, of course Jewish, and Lafferty and Campbell were Protestant. Some law firms were quite helpful to the Jewish community. For example, Alan Lowenstein's firm has given *pro bono* service to the MetroWest Federation for over fifty years.

One attorney who achieved international recognition was Milton Konvitz, the son of Rabbi Joseph Konvitz, and brother of Philip Konvitz, who owns the bail bond business mentioned earlier. Konvitz is a first-rate scholar of constitutional law who is a professor of industrial and labor relations at Cornell University. His books have been cited on numerous occasions in U.S. Supreme Court opinions. The author of hundreds of articles and many books, he has long been active in Jewish organizations and was, for several years, the staff counsel of the American Civil Liberties Union. Locally, he also did a stint as general counsel to the New Jersey State Housing Authority. Konvitz was actually born in the holy city of Safed, Palestine, and spoke no English when he arrived in America at the age of eight.[47]

Women were also active in the legal profession, though, owing to the general difficulties that often faced women entering the professions, they did have had trouble advancing. The terminology in an August 8, 1930 *Jewish Chronicle* article gives a hint as to the problem. In noting that only twenty-two of the 331 graduates of that year's New Jersey Law School class were women, it refers to them as the "girl graduates."[48] Whatever discrimination they faced in 1930 was nothing when compared to the situation two decades earlier. And the fact that even twenty-two women graduated probably had a good deal to do with one woman who pioneered in the field—Elizabeth Blume:

Born in 1892 in Newark, Blume attended Newark public schools, graduating from Barringer High School at the age of sixteen. An article in the March 1, 1922 issue of the *Newark Ledger* aptly described her determination, from early on, to make her mark on this world:

> The eighth grade in one of the Newark public schools was about to graduate and the teacher desiring to learn what her young hopefuls aspired to be when they stepped into the big wide world, circulated questionnaires. Sorting them over later, the preceptor came to one that brought a frown to her face. She quizzically read it over again and then said, with emphatic disapproval: "Well, I never thought that I would teach a girl who didn't know the difference between a man's work and a woman's."
>
> The slip of paper which had caused the good teacher's consternation read: "Elizabeth Blume, Lawyer."

Miss Blume was then perhaps twelve years old but she she realized it was no time for her to argue. So she glanced at the slip the little girl who sat across the aisle had filled in and saw that she had written "Nurse" opposite her name. So Miss Blume meekly wrote on the slip which the teacher had returned to her, "Elizabth Blume, Nurse."

But she didn't mean it. And in the high school she read "The Merchant of Venice" and of wise Portia and it only sealed her ambition to become a great barrister.[49]

Blume graduated in 1911 at the ripe old age of eighteen from the New Jersey Law School, forerunner to Rutgers Law School. Too young to take the bar exam, she had to wait two years. Then, at twenty-one, she became the first woman in New Jersey to practice law, and was granted the right to try cases in the U.S. Supreme Court in 1922. Specializing in the criminal area, she also became the first woman to try a murder case. (She won.) As an American Jewish Congress delegate, she supported the drafting of the Balfour Declaration, in 1917. The legal and Jewish organizations that she was involved in fill an entire column in a biographical encyclopedia published by the Lewis Publishing Company. Suffice it to say that she proved that a woman can do very well if given the opportunity and was an excellent role model for women of her time.[50]

Medicine was an especially popular choice for Jews. As usual, there was discrimination against them when they first sought to gain a foothold in the profession. Arthur Bernstein, a prominent Newark physician, described the difficulties he encountered in the early 1930s:

I was interviewed for Penn by the dean. I had gone to Penn as an undergraduate. The dean said to me: "I might as well tell you right now that you do not have a chance here because we took in the ten Jewish boys that we always take in and that is our quota. We also take ten Catholics and the rest are Protestants." I said, "That's not fair," and we got into an argument and he said: "Why is it that Jewish mothers always want their sons to be doctors?" I said: "Dr. Pepper, you're wrong. That's not true. My father wants me to be a cantor, my mother wants me to be a rabbi. I want to be a doctor." Finally, after about forty minutes, he said, "My God, this was supposed to be a fifteen minute interview. Get out and don't ever come back."

Then I went to the president of the alumni association with my records. He was a non-Jewish doctor with a German name. He asked to see my grades and he said: "What! With these grades they didn't take you?" He sat down and dictated a letter in which he said, among other things: "I had no grades anywhere near this good when you took me in. I can assure you that if you don't take him in, you will never get another penny from the alumnae of the Newark area." And I got in and I went.[51]

Even when Jews were admitted to medical school and did well in their classes, they faced prejudice when it came to hospital placement and it was this that provided much of the impetus for the founding of Beth Israel Hospital. Arthur Bernstein recalled how, when he first began his practice, he applied to St. Barnabas Hospital, requesting admitting privileges. The answer came quickly, stating bluntly: "We do not accept Jews on our staff."[52] Bernstein's experience typified that of many Jewish physicians who were finding it difficult to obtain positions in area hospitals. A further stimulus for the creation of Beth Israel was that the Jewish community simply wanted a facility it could call its own, one where Jews would feel comfortable.

The idea of a specifically "Jewish" hospital did not initially meet with great enthusiasm. Many in the German-Jewish establishment viewed such an effort as very parochial and opposed to the idea of Jews being as American as any other group. According to two physicians at the time, Aaron Parsonnet and Max Danzis, their limited perspective:

> precluded the foresight and realization that within a short period the steadily increasing mass of immigrants will constitute a communal problem with many ramifications—educational, religious and medical. Being brought up as they were with the long-established native population made them feel that a Jewish hospital was unnecessary.[53]

Implicit in these observations is the idea that the East European immigrants were thought of as people in need of help and that doing so would redound to the credit of the Jewish community as a whole. In that sense it resembled the efforts of German Jews to build religious institutions for the immigrants, most notably the Jewish Theological Seminary in New York City.

In 1900, the Daughters of Israel Hospital Association raised $4,000 that went toward the purchase of a small wooden-frame building at the intersection of Kinney and High Streets. Two years later, Beth Israel Hospital was formally chartered, the result of a merger with another group, whose members included physicians, the Hebrew Hospital and Dispensary. The original staff at the time consisted of about twelve doctors, of whom eight were recent graduates. The hospital's first president was Dr. Victor Parsonnet. He and Dr. Max Danzis were probably the most prominent physicians of that early period. Some other well-known practitioners at the time were Armin Fischer, Marcus

Seidman, Emanuel Schwarz, and Clarence Rostow.[54] Doctors did not, incidentally, follow the same smooth path then into medicine that Jewish children of a later, more prosperous generation would. Danzis, for example, supported himself with various odd jobs at night. He was an errand boy for a paper-wrapping company and a hatter who actively participated in the famous hatters' strike of 1894. In fact, he studied engineering first, switching to medicine after discovering that the field was not suited for him.[55]

Six years later, the hospital expanded to accomodate eighty beds and, by 1928, after $4,000,000 had been raised, it had moved to a new facility on Lyons Avenue. There, it became a 500 bed institution, servicing the community in general, as well as those too poor to pay the full cost of hospital treatment and care. In the decades that followed, Beth Israel became a world-class institution, offering first-rate care and innovative treatment in many areas of medicine. It was among the first hospitals in the U.S. to engage in kidney dialysis. Its world-renowned doctors included the surgeons Eugene Parsonnet and his son, Victor Parsonnet. Eugene trained many of the best surgeons in the state. He was twice chairman of the local United Jewish Appeal Campaign. In addition, he was the national collegiate wrestling champion while at Harvard, as well as a champion swimmer who swam together with the legendary Johnny Weissmuller. Victor developed the world's first nuclear pacemaker, was the first to do heart transplants in New Jersey, and began the state's first major cardiac bypass program in 1969. Together with David Biber, Mervyn Welkind, and several other physicians, Victor also developed the first cardiac catherization lab in New Jersey. A man of many interests, he is currently the chairman of the New Jersey Symphony Orchestra.[56]

Among its specialties, Beth Israel Hospital became known for research in blood diseases and the Rh factor was discovered there by Dr. Philip Levine. Oscar Auerbach, a noted pathologist, was one of the first, in the 1960s, to demonstrate, over and over again, the relationship between cancer and smoking. William Ehrlich was the first certified neurosurgeon in the state and Gabriel Yelin, together with Lester Goldman, developed a treatment for pernicious anemia.[57] The hospital also established an excellent school of nursing. One of its most distinguished trainees was Paula Ben-Gurion, wife of the esteemed Israeli prime minister. Finally, there was Dr. Henry Kessler, who gained fame in the field of rehabilitation medicine.

Jews also entered pharmacy and, in the early days, pharmacists had greater influence on medicine than today, prescribing, as well as selling, medications. Moe Berg's father, Bernard, was a pharmacist as early as 1906, and his work was depicted in the following terms:

> Customers would come into the store and describe their own or their child's symptoms. If things sounded serious, they were told to see a doctor. Otherwise, Bernard treated the affliction himself.[58]

Many received their training at the New Jersey College of Pharmacy in North Newark and were active in the professional associations such as the Independent Druggists' Alliance.[59] While the majority of pharmacies in the early days were small, there were some chains, one of which was the Schwarz chain of drug stores, which pioneered the concept of cut-rate prices.[60]

Dentistry was yet another field that Jews found attractive. Newark Jewry's most public dentist was its only Jewish mayor, Meyer "Doc" Ellenstein. Although he graduated at the top of his Columbia class in 1912, Ellenstein did not remain in dentistry for long, opting instead for a political career. Here again, Jews faced the usual prejudices. In dental school, Jews were limited to the Jewish fraternities, usually Alpha Omega and Sigma Epsilon Delta. The Newark Dental Club was founded because Jews experienced difficulty in gaining membership in certain associations. This was not true, however, of the Essex County Dental Society, which numbered several Jews among its early presidents—Abraham Wolfson in 1929 (He was a prominent orthodontist), Jacob Schaffer in 1933, and Matthew Rouse in 1936. Still, in those days, Jews accounted for a small proportion of the membership. Today, by contrast, the Society is predominantly Jewish and Italian.[61]

Accounting was a field with a heavy concentration of Jews and many of the firms were quite successful. Some accountants, such as Milton and Lester Lieberman, who did the work for most of Newark's funeral homes, Samuel Klein and Company, which specialized in municipal accounting, and Bederson and Company, a bankruptcy firm, carved out special niches for themselves. Others, like Puder and Puder, Besser and Company, and Granet and Granet, were in a number of areas. During the 1940s, J.H. Cohn and Company was probably the biggest independent accounting firm in the state and had a number of important banks as clients.

Why did Jews enter accounting in relatively large numbers? Besides the fact that they could obtain degrees in less time than in many other professions, a major factor was the ease with which they could enter the field. Unlike banking or insurance, an accountant could open up a one or two person firm and function independently without worrying about discrimination. In larger organizations this was not possible and Jews did face prejudice in general in the economic workplace during the first part of the century and even beyond.[62] In addition, Jews as a group were often stereotyped as being smart and sharp with figures, be it business or accounting, and this image worked in their favor when it came to attracting clients.[63]

When Harold Glucksman began his career as an architect in 1937 there were perhaps a half dozen Jews in the profession. Among them was the firm of Frank Grad and Sons, which won a competition for its design of the famous traffic signal, built, in 1925, at the intersection of Market and Broad. In 1926, a survey firm hailed it as "the busiest traffic center in the world." The signal, made of bronze and stone, was known throughout the country and featured an officer inside it who changed the signals manually. Today, incidentally, it rests in a Clifton, New Jersey cemetery. Grad was the largest Jewish architectural firm in Newark and designed many major buildings in the city, among them the National Newark and Essex Building and Beth Israel Hospital.[64] The firm was also involved in the design of the vertical assembly building used for space explorations at the NASA Space Center in Florida.

At first, there was discrimination against Jews in the profession but, as usual, they persevered and overcame. The oldest Jewish firm was Lehman and Company, which celebrated its 100th anniversary in 1996. Among their projects was the Federal Post Office and the Federal Office Building, renamed today after former Congressman Peter Rodino. Lehman remains an influential firm with licenses in forty states.[65]

Barney Gruzen, a resident of Maplewood, was another important name in the field and his firm did a good deal of work for the state, including modernistic prison buildings. They also designed buildings used by the Jewish community, among them Daughters of Israel Geriatric Center, The Y in West Orange, and Temple B'nai Abraham in Livingston. In this context, the name Burton Berger is worthy of mention. Formerly with Gruzen, he designed the MetroWest Whippany campus. Another important firm was Kruger and Fava, who designed schools for the Newark Board of Education.[66] Finally, one of the top architects in the world, a winner of many awards, is Richard Meier.

Meier was raised and educated in Newark and began his illustrious career there. Among his projects are the Barcelona and Getty Museums. Last year he received the prestigious Gold Medal from the American Institute of Architects.

While engineering was not a Jewish profession, one Newark resident who received his degree in the field from Massachusetts Institute of Technology, made a substantial impact on the outside world. David Lasser, who grew up in Newark, is credited with having written, in 1931, the first English-language book to present the idea that space travel is not something fictional, but rather, a real possibility. At the time this was a revolutionary concept and his book, *The Conquest of Space*, had an important influence on the thinking in this area. Lasser was also one of the founders of what is today The American Institute of Aeronautics and Astronautics, a 41,000 member organization based in Washington D.C.[67]

The arts have traditionally been a path leading to upward mobility for minorities in America and Jews were no exception to that rule. Among the most famous celebrities who came from Newark or who lived and/or worked there were the comedian, Jerry Lewis; the playwright, Moss Hart; the composer, Jerome Kern; the entertainer, Fanny Brice; the producer, Dore Schary; and, of course, the writer, Philip Roth, who has delineated Jewish Newark, from his unique perspective, to millions of readers.[68]

Roth was born in Newark on March 19, 1933 and is the author of twenty-two books. A graduate of Bucknell University, he has taught at many colleges and universities, including Princeton and the University of Chicago. His books have achieved widespread popularity and he has won many awards for them. More than anyone else in the world, Roth has enlightened readers everywhere about Newark, for it occupies a prominent, indeed, central place, in his work. He is intimately familiar with its people, its neighborhoods, and its social and cultural institutions. Although he is often critical of Newark in his writings, it is clear that he has a great deal of love and affection for the city of his youth.

Other personalities in the arts included Marion Parsonnet, Norman Tokar, Jed Harris, and Herman Shumlin. Many of these people first received their opportunities at the Y under the guidance of George Kahn. Burton Shevelove was an important producer of Broadway musicals, including, *A Funny Thing Happened on the Way to the Forum* and *Bye Bye Birdie*. Richard Schechner became chairman of the Drama

Department at New York University and Ina Golub established herself in weaving. Michael Lenson, brother of the humorist, Sam Levenson, made his reputation as an artist, as did Jean Schonwalter in sculpture. In some cases, the involvement with Newark was purely coincidental, an accident of birth, and in others, the city's proximity to the Big Apple made it a natural alternative to those hungry for both employment and receptive audiences.

In journalism and public relations there was Morris and Julius Scheck, Max Wiener, William Ratner, William Pages, Philip Hochstein, Harry Weingast, and Mort Pye. Pye effectively used his position to sponsor the creation of the Sports Authority buildings in the Meadowlands and, more recently, the New Jersey Center for the Performing Arts. He was also a brother-in-law of the publisher, Samuel I. Newhouse, who merged the *Newark Ledger* with the *Star Eagle*. Eventually, that paper, the *Newark Star-Ledger*, became New Jersey's leading newspaper.

Politics

Over the years, many Jews were elected to public office in Newark. In 1889, Leonard Kalisch became the first Jew elected to the New Jersey State Assembly. Later on, in 1916, Edward Schoen would become the first Jewish Speaker of the State Assembly. There were some early Jewish suburban mayors, namely, Isaac Shoenthal of Orange, in 1904, and William Hauser of Bloomfield, in 1911. In subsequent years, a number of Jews were elected to the post of city councilman.

The major Jewish figure on the political scene, was Meyer "Doc" Ellenstein, who was Newark's mayor from 1933 to 1941. He was a controversial figure. Charges of corruption, particularly with respect to the building of Newark's airport, dogged him throughout his career, but none of them ever stuck. He was indicted once and tried twice. One trial resulted in a hung jury, the other in an acquittal. He was hurt, however, in terms of his reputation, by his association with Longy Zwillman, a childhood friend, with whom he remained on good terms.[69] He was also a colorful individual, as we can see from the following story told by Philip Konvitz, a supporter of his who served in his administration and knew him quite well:

He was a great fellow, a dentist, a lawyer, and a two-fisted man. One time a man came to see him and they talked for a long time. At one point, Ellenstein said to him: "You can talk to me about city politics all you want, but if you attack me I'll take you outside and knock the living shit out of you."[70]

He probably could have. Ellenstein was once an amateur boxer who went by the moniker of "Kid Meyers." After deciding that fixing teeth was more lucrative than knocking them out, he became a dentist, graduating at the top of his Columbia University class, in 1912. In addition, he was also a lawyer before entering politics.[71]

There were certainly questionable appointments and other problems during Ellenstein's tenure and he was definitely involved with the "bootlegger's crowd," but Ellenstein was also something of a Robin Hood, helping poor people whenever possible. His closest friend, Harry Wagman, reportedly described him as "kind, considerate and caring." When he died, in 1967, he left about $200,000 to his wife and, after her death, the money from the residual estate was bequeathed to what is now the Jewish Community Center of Metropolitan New Jersey in West Orange.[72]

In 1953, Newark's voters chose the reform-minded Leo Carlin over the establishment candidate, Ralph Villani. Alan Lowenstein was instrumental in Carlin's administration, playing a major role in the creation, in 1953, of a Charter Commission, which he headed.[73] In 1956, Carlin was opposed for relection by a Jewish councilman, Jack Waldor. Waldor lost, but he was, nevertheless, a man who accomplished much in many areas. A state senator, he was also national commander of the Jewish War Veterans and author of a book, *Peddlers of Fear*, an expose of the John Birch Society.[74]

Jews also made their mark on Newark's political establishment as appointees. In 1941, for example, under the new mayor, Vincent J. Murphy, Philip Schotland was made an assistant corporation counsel, as was Thomas Parsonnet. Another case in point was Sam Convissor, who served as executive assistant to Mayor Hugh Addonizio. Jews served in various capacities in all city administrations beginning even before the turn of the century, and on up to the present, but the most important appointee was probably Harry Reichenstein, the city clerk from 1933 to 1972. He was one of the most powerful men in city government and used his knowledge of the rules and regulations governing the city to great advantage. Another influential administrator (though not under the mayor's direct control) was Louis Danzig, who headed the Newark Housing Authority from 1948 to 1969.[75]

Labor, Sales, and Small Businesses

People like Aidekman, Hollander, and Bamberger, were the Horatio Algers of the Jewish community. Their successes may have inspired others, but for most immigrants and even their children real life was a far cry from whatever dreams they may have had. Yes, there was no tsar to oppress and starve them and they could certainly try their best to climb out of the poverty in which they found themselves upon arrival on these shores, but doing so was no easy matter. Uneducated and unconnected, their struggle to make ends meet was often incredibly difficult and supremely frustrating. One Newark resident in her sixties, a retired personnel director who requested anonymity, recalled her father's efforts at making a life for himself. It was not a pretty picture:

> My father came from a very poor family, so poor he couldn't have a bar-mitzvah because he couldn't afford a suit. He never owned underwear; he never wore shoes in the summer. He worked in a factory in New York. Why he lived in Newark I don't know. He was malnourished and the soup he had was usually whatever was left from the vegetables. In the house my uncle threw my grandfather out for whatever reason and eventually he committed suicide. Those were my memories.

The immigrants worked in every conceivable industry. They were leather cutters, glass cutters, jewelry polishers, brewery workers, hatters, construction laborers, whatever they could find. Their often miserable conditions in the shops and factories were of no interest to anyone who counted, that is, with the exception of the labor organizers and the muckrakers who wrote about work and life in the slums. The following account of a woman who ended up working as a "wrapper" in the Charm Lollipop Factory was typical of the working conditions that prevailed. She had applied for a job as a Hebrew teacher but was forced to look elsewhere because of a teachers' strike at the school:

> Gail entered a factory for the first time in her life. The noise of the running machinery was deafening. She could hardly hear her sister's voice, telling her to sit near her, alongside a huge table, where many girls were sitting, grabbing lollipops from a rapidly moving chute, placing them on small papers and wrapping them quickly. . . . Ann showed her how to place the lollipops in the proper position on the small piece of paper provided, then fold the paper around the lollipop and tightly fasten it around the stick.[76]

The organized Jewish community did its best to help the newcomers and there was a plethora of organizations that tried to smoothe their passage into American life. There were various groups, called *malbish arumim* (literally, "clothing the naked") societies that serviced the immigrants. Their activities ranged from providing clothing, shelter, and food for the poor to assisting them in securing employment. There were children's homes, especially for orphans, and nursing homes for the aged, but the most important organization, on the whole, was probably the Jewish Family Service Association, because it provided the broadest range of services to the needy. The greatest contribution of these organizations was in easing the immigrants' transition from the old to the new.

The labor movement, encompassing socialism, communism, anarchism, and nonpolitical worker unions, took up the cause of the downtrodden from a different direction. They fought for jobs, better wages, working conditions, and benefits. And during the Depression, their stock rose considerably. As one chronicler of the period, a Newark native, put it:

> Charity groups helped by the cities established soup kitchens everywhere in schools and other public buildings to feed the hungry hordes and on every corner prosperous looking men and women were peddling apples at five cents apiece. The Communists had a field day. That terrible panic was their golden opportunity to prove to the masses that it was the end of the decadent rotten and imperialistic capitalistic system and it was time to throw over our oppressors and establish a real democracy for the people just as they did in Russia. . . . What saved us from a revolution was that the left wingers were not properly organized. There was no other political party of the left outside of the Socialist party which was a far cry from the Communists.[77]

From the 1920s on through the 1950s, the unions had a strong presence in Newark, especially in the needle trades and in the electrical and leather industries. The largest union was probably that of the electrical workers and it was divided into factions, which merged in 1955. One was the United Electrical Workers Union and it was communist controlled. The other, which was anticommunist, was the International Union of Electrical Workers. The size of the union was directly related to the fact that, after the Depression, factories opened up to respond to the needs created by America's entry into World War II. One of the most prominent Jewish labor leaders was Joel R. Jacobson, who headed the AFL-CIO in New Jersey, and who, as a social democrat, fought against the communist influences in his organization.[78] According to the sociologist, Stanley Aronowitz, who lived in Newark's Clinton Hill section in the 1950s, Newark's Jewish community was decidedly shaped by its strong industrial base:

While New York City more closely resembled Los Angeles and San Francisco, Newark was more similar to Chicago and Cleveland. The industrial range was more broadly distributed, from the needle trades to heavy machinery. Because of this strong working-class base, a significant portion of Newark Jewry became more culturally integrated into American society as a whole.[79]

In the end, most Jews accepted a capitalist-oriented, liberal approach that had them voting Democratic even as they struggled to become part of the propertied classes. The majority of those who worked for others longed most of all for the chance to work for themselves. Housepainters opened hardware stores and factory workers opened their own shops, while others traded in blue collars for white ones, even if it meant continuing to be in the employ of others, anything to improve their status. Listen, for example, to the journey of Esther Kesselman's father as he went from one type of job to another:

My father worked in a leather factory. I remember, as a little girl, how my father detested his hands. He used to have callouses, about one-quarter of an inch high, stained with brown from the tanning of the leather. He vowed he was going to get out of it. He even went to Buffalo because he thought he could find a better job, but there was too much anti-Semitism there. He started to work for the Prudential Insurance Company. He had one pair of pants. When I was nine years old my father was pressing his pants. Then he would polish his shoes, clean his nails, brush his hair, take a bath, and dress himself up elegantly. You would think he was a wealthy man. Then he would go to these homes and try to sell them insurance.[80]

Kesselman's father eventually achieved some measure of success as a salesman for the Griffith Piano Company. Others, such as Philip Roth's father, who worked for Metropolitan Life, made a permanent career out of selling insurance. As we can see from the following observations by Roth, it was by no means the big time, but, at the very least, it connoted respectability:

the home-office executive whom my father would trek from New Jersey to see was the superintendent of agencies, a Mr. Wright, whose good opinion my father valued inordinately all his life and whose height and imposing good looks he admired nearly as much as he did the man's easygoing diplomacy. As my father's son, I felt no less respectful toward these awesomely named gentiles than he did, but I, like him, knew that they had to be the very officials who openly and guiltlessly conspired to prevent more than a few token Jews from assuming positions of anything approaching importance within the largest financial institution in the world.[81]

There was this idea of status by association that people everywhere have, working for a very large firm, doing business with large entities, and the Jews of Newark were no different. In that vein, the owners of a dry cleaning establishment wrote in their autobiographical account: "We used to do the cleaning for Bamberger's, Kresge's, Hahne's, and also for Proctor's Theatre."[82] And if their services were valued by these companies, were they not then more worthy?

For most, however, there was not even that small satisfaction. They lived by the sweat of their brow, hoping only to make ends meet. Thousands of salesmen could only be called peddlers and they have remained anonymous, remembered only by their families, if at all. Thus, one resident described how his immigrant father sold a veritable cornucopia of items so varied that they conjured up the image of a portable department store. These included clocks, springs, rugs, wringers, albums, lace and chenille curtains, jewelry, furniture, clothing, dry goods, and all kinds of table covers. How did he know? It was written on one of his father's "business cards."

Innumerable Jews in Newark earned their living as small shopkeepers. Mamie Bogner's father, Hyman Mirsky, came to the city from Russia in 1912 and ran a small candy store in Irvington for four years. He then moved to a location on Belmont Avenue and stayed there for the rest of his life. He was never even able to join a synagogue because he was open seven days a week from 6:00 A.M. until 11:00 P.M. He allowed himself but a short nap in the afternoon, during which time his son or wife took over until his return. He attended synagogue only on the High Holy Days.[83] Similarly, Hannah Litzky compared her father's life as a candy store owner on Bridge Street to the main character in Bernard Malamud's novel, *The Assistant*: "He felt he had to be there at five o'clock in the morning so that the men who were going to work on that shift would be able to stop in and buy their cigars or their cigarettes, or their newspaper, or their bar of chocolate."[84] That was another way of investing labor with importance. Someone needed you, someone was counting on you, and so you had to be there.

Some people combined store ownership with labor because one job was not enough. Bernard Menkes' father was an egg candler, which meant that he evaluated eggs by holding them up to the light of a candle. To augment his meager income, he had a small butter and eggs store on Chancellor Avenue. Ultimately, he became a beneficiary of the trend towards larger stores, ending his career as a dairy manager for a Food Fair supermarket. Another egg candler was Sam Wolf, who sold eggs on a wholesale basis to Newark restaurants.[85] Success, on a major level, was reached by his son, Carl, who became the CEO of Alpine Lace Brands, one of the largest low-fat cheese companies in the U.S. Its corporate headquarters today are in Maplewood.

Others went into areas where the work, while not especially pleasant or edifying, offered a chance to, as they say, "make a living." Myron Katz's grandfather, Louis Brownstein, operated what was, in the 1920s and 1930s, one of the largest live poultry markets on Prince Street. It was a family business and even the young were expected to help out:

> I remember going to Brownstein's Poultry when I was six or seven years old. I used to carry the fowl by the legs and wings so they wouldn't open up, to the *shochet*, I did it after school, especially on Thursday, which was our busiest day. It was expected that we would work there after school, though not every day. That business supported my grandfather, father, and three or four of my uncles. There were cages on each side of the aisle. It was thirty to forty feet wide and 150 feet long. We had pigeons, ducks, geese, chickens, and they came from Somerset County, Mount Freedom, and Vineland.[86]

It did not matter. For most Jews, coming as they did from lands where rulers had decreed that Jews were unassimilable and unworthy of equal rights, no job that paid a decent wage for an honest day's work could be refused outright. And so, when Jacob Scarr, who responded to an ad for a charcoal salesman, was told: "This job is not for you. It is a dirty job. You get smeared up with charcoal and charcoal dust," he asked: "Does this job pay enough for a man to change his clothes while he is on the job?" The boss saw the determination on his face and said: "Come in to work tomorrow morning at seven."[87]

Matters of pride and self-respect were not only an issue when it came to physical labor. Former New York mayor, Edward Koch, moved to Newark from the Bronx at the age of seven. His father, who had been in the fur business, was broke, and, as a result, had to take a job working for Uncle Louie in a catering hall, known as Krueger's Auditorium. He was given a lease on the hatcheck concession. The money was not very good and Koch senior was often forced to work a second, and even a third job. The following account demonstrates that his son was clearly able to extract a positive lesson from the experience:

> When I think of my father and the work that defined him during those years I recall his checking coats until two-thirty in the morning on weekends, or midnight during the week; and being up at four-thirty in the morning, ready to take the train

from Newark to his day job in New York, or to get a head start on the other job seekers. He worked hard all his life, and he passed that ethic on to me. From my father I also learned how to get by on very little sleep; to this day I get up at five-thirty each morning (my father was tougher than I am).[88]

That was the good part. But Koch also remembers some other things, one of which was how his uncle charged each guest a quarter to check their coats but gave his parents nothing from that amount, leaving them totally dependent on tips. He talked about his feelings with evident bitterness:

> I was distressed for my parents. It was a terrible, unseemly way to make a living, to be dependent on the charity of other people. It was honorable work, but tiring, boring, and mindless—and it was demeaning to have to ask for tips. The humiliation of those nights has never left me, and I have never forgiven my uncle for the way he treated us . . . even though I am sure he saw things a little differently. . . . As distasteful as this arrangement was, it was the only steady job my father had . . .
>
> The lasting scar from that experience has been my reluctance as a fund-raiser. I am plainly lousy at it. . . . When I ask for a contribution, I can still hear that plaintive cry: "Please don't forget the hatcheck boys, we only work on tips!"[89]

For others, there were different drawbacks, such as danger and punishment by association. Eddie Rosenthal's father owned a restaurant in downtown Newark, near the Loew's Theater. One night, Dutch Schultz came there for a meeting and was murdered. According to one version, the rubout had been set up by Lucky Luciano. The restaurant was subsequently closed down and Rosenthal lost his liquor license.[90] While this was obviously an atypical incident, those who did business in Newark's grittier neighborhoods faced real danger and risk from gang warfare, petty crime, and robberies.

Those who operated downtown functioned as individuals but in the Jewish neighborhoods of Newark, merchants sometimes formed associations, of which the best known was probably the Springfield Avenue Merchants Association. In the days before malls, shopping strips like Bergen Street, Springfield Avenue, and Clinton Avenue, were the main attraction for shoppers. The modes of transportation were buses, trolleys, and a good pair of legs. Unlike today's often disengaged salespeople, those who waited on customers were usually owners or their family members and one felt that they cared and were knowledgeable about their merchandise.

Ed Brody, a former shoe store owner and co-chair of the Jewish Historical Society of MetroWest's Oral History Committee, has written a loving portrait of the neighborhood merchants' associations in those days:

> Jack Tabachnick did not just sell appetizers, but his outside sign proclaimed in large letters that he was the "Herring King." Charlie Schultz, who sold appliances, became "Prince Charles" of Prince Range. Harry Lehr had the store with the most cigars in all of Newark. Max Sherman had six or eight vans that his salespersons/decorators used to advise you in your home on interior decorating problems. After all, if your drapes were not made by Sherman Decorators, people would think you purchased them at S. Klein's. Other stores often advertised themselves as "N.J.'s Largest."[91]

This feature exists in all "pre-megalopolis" locales. In Jerusalem, for example, strollers along Jaffa Street will pass stores called, "The Falafel King" or "The Sandal Empire." Such seeming hyperbole was actually true at a certain level, for to those who lived in these Newark neighborhoods, local shops were often the only places they frequented. Downtown was reserved for special occasions only. More than anything, perhaps, these shopping areas contributed mightily to the sense that Newark was a real community. Unlike today's suburban malls, the stores, whose owners invariably lived nearby, were venues for catching up on the latest gossip, for socializing, and for general social interaction. In this way, the community solidarity that characterized Newark's neighborhoods was reinforced and economy and society were intertwined to the point where they became almost a seamless web.

The merchants' associations were often highly organized. The areas were densely populated; for example, at one time, the eight-block, Bergen Street shopping area in Weequahic contained no fewer than 150 stores. Formed to benefit from the strength of numbers, the associations offered police protection, better snow removal, group health insurance, and lobbying for improvements such as special parking lots for shoppers. In some cases, they even became the vehicle for formal dinner dances attended by the merchants and their friends.

Speakers at their meetings ranged from bank presidents to Rabbi Zev Segal of the Young Israel synagogue. To attract customers, promotional events were held. Typical of such efforts was an Easter Egg Hunt by the Bergen Street merchants, with prizes awarded to those who came the closest to guessing the number of eggs hidden by storeowners in their display windows.[92] The Springfield Avenue Association even enlisted the aid of Broadway producer, Dore Schary, for a promotional campaign. Schary promptly dubbed the avenue "The Great White Way."

As Jews continued their inexorable march to the suburbs, the businesses declined, though for a long time, they simply readjusted to the black clientele that replaced their own coreligionists. The end was signaled by the devastating riots, accompanied by fires and looting. Arnold Mirsky, who owned a furniture store, recalls how, around the time of the riots, "We began to notice that customers would leave the store every five minutes to see if the car was still there."[93] And Brody writes of a fine dress shop, completely emptied of its merchandise with the exception of one lone dress, on which was pinned a note, proclaiming: "You're still in business." Humorous to some, perhaps, but not to those who had invested a lifetime of sweat and tears in their enterprises.

Last, and perhaps least, though certainly not inconsequential, there were illegal activities. As has already been noted, there was a flourishing crime industry in Newark, led by Abner "Longy" Zwillman. Given its scope, it was clearly not a one-man operation and there were many who earned their keep in Zwillman's employ. Eddie Rosenthal's father was a good example of this phenomenon:

> My father became a bootlegger during Prohibition. In fact, the whole street on Lehigh Ave. was in it. There was a fellow, Niggy Rutkin, [a well-known Zwillman associate] who later became connected with Reinfeld Liquors. They bought alcohol, colored it, added stuff to it, and mixed it. There was a chubby fellow nearby who owned a bottle store on Clinton Place. I used to buy bottles there with my father. They even had fancy bottles, the kind you slip straw over.[94]

Many of these people were not really criminal types; their presence on the margins of such activities is simply evidence of how pervasive these activities were. Most, like Rosenthal's father, were not really comfortable doing these sorts of things:

> But my father wasn't that type of man; he wasn't rough, so he got a little nervous and turned it over to someone else. But we were living very well, Cadillacs and all. We had a live-in maid.[95]

Rosenthal reports that his brothers ran one of the biggest crap games in the city and that he himself made money running errands and buying cigarettes for the players.

Further evidence of involvement can be discerned from control of various industries by organized crime. In his book about Zwillman, *Gangster #2*, Mark Stuart writes about mob control of Newark's economy. For example, window-cleaning companies that did not belong to the mob's "asssociation," were visited by local goons, usually Abe Lew, Zwillman's cousin, and Ira Berkowitz, and warned to either use companies that they recommended or face an employee strike. The strike threat weapon was also used at one time against Bamberger's Department Store and those who negotiated on the employees' behalf were Zwillman's people.

Zwillman's reach extended to many unions—retail clerks, motion picture projectionists, etc., and it is safe to conclude that many small-timers made money from it and that, given the way in which neighborhood connections developed, quite a few of these individuals were Jewish.[96] Along with the unions there were slot machine operations, numbers games, plus all sorts of legitimate spinoffs, through which illegal financial gains were funneled.[97] Legitimate companies like Reinfeld Distributors were created after repeal from what had been illegal bootlegging operations during Prohibition.[98] In fact, Zwillman's career in bootlegging began when, as a teenager, he transported liquor from Boston to Newark for Joe Reinfeld, eventually becoming Reinfeld's partner.[99] As for Reinfeld, he later became Lord Renfield.

Notwithstanding the presence of Jews in these enterprises, it accounted, as is true of criminal activity elsewhere, for only a small proportion of what Jews as a group did economically. Jews, like the Italians, Irish, and other immigrant groups, had their share of criminals, but the overwhelming majority were honest and law-abiding citizens and as we have seen in this chapter, made their contributions in many spheres of economic activity.

Perhaps the most important outcome of Jewish economic success in the larger sense is that it made Jewish philanthropy possible. Had Jews not succeeded to the extent that they did, then the social and cultural institutions they built would simply not have existed. There would have been no Y, no agencies to help the community, no synagogues, and no Jewish schools. Thus, Jewish identity and Jewish continuity were directly influenced by the fact that Jews did well in Newark, just as they did elsewhere. Not to be ignored, however, is the fact that Jews valued their own culture and saw it as worth preserving. That, of course, was part of a tradition that has spanned the centuries throughout their long history.

Education

Whatever success Jews achieved in fields such as law, medicine, architecture, education, the arts, and even business, they owed, in large part, to their education. Learning was clearly an avenue to success in America, and Jews, by virtue of their age-old emphasis on this area, were well equipped to take advantage of the opportunities offered by their new homeland. This discussion, concludes, therefore, with a look at how education, an important key to economic success, developed in Newark.

That it was valued by the city's Jews can be seen from the interest in study displayed by the German Jews who arrived here in the mid-nineteenth century. When the first known evening classes for the foreign born opened at the Morton Street School in 1857, a number of Jews enrolled there. Newark's Jews were particularly fortunate in that the Protestant elite, which controlled the city, very much desired a first-rate school system and actively supported efforts to create one. To build it, they brought in the best teachers and administrators from around the country. In fact, Newark educators emphasized that immigrant groups be given schools of "especial excellence." Addison B. Poland, who became the system's Superintendent in 1901, took a strong position on this matter:

> There is no other factor in our American political or social life that equals a good public school in democratizing, socializing, and, in general, Americanizing our foreign population, old as well as young. . . . Good schools cost money. Crime, poverty, ignorance and vice also cost money, both to prevent and to punish.[100]

Jewish children attended elementary schools in their neighborhoods and the thirst for learning that so many of them evinced greatly raised the level of education in these institutions. Good students ask good questions and good teachers respond to students who stimulate them. The schools were named after the streets on which they were situated and among the most popular were, Hawthorne, Chancellor, Avon, Maple, Bragaw, Bergen, and Peshine. Outside one of these schools, on 18th Avenue, there still hangs a sign that says: "The public school is the best defense of a democratic nation." It was a vision shared by both Newark's Jews and the businessmen and industrialists who helped found them. The driving force behind their ambitiousness was often their parents and the community in general. As Philip Roth put it in

American Pastoral, "You must not come to nothing. *Make something of yourselves!*"[101]

It was in the high schools that students really developed the ability to think critically and independently. The major secondary schools in Newark were Barringer, East Side, West Side, South Side, Central, Arts, and Weequahic. A student at West Side High recalls it as the place where he studied Latin for three years, was exposed to Cicero, Virgil, and Ovid, as well as topics like evolution, the right to unionize, and whether or not the Marines should withdraw from Nicaragua, all of which were hotly debated in class and at school assemblies.

Some families, usually of German background, sent their children to private schools, which, as always, had a certain snob appeal. There was also a belief that attendance at such institutions increased the likelihood of being admitted to the best colleges. Not unexpectedly, Jews who went to places like Newark Academy experienced some anti-Semitism but it was apparently nothing serious. There were probably not enough Jews there to make anyone feel threatened by them.[102]

Each high school had its partisans—Barringer, South Side, etc. Ed Koch felt he received an excellent education at South Side even as he candidly admitted that he was "a fairly solid, unspectacular B student," there.[103] No school was more Jewish than Weequahic. During the mid-1930s, 1940s, and 1950s, it was almost entirely Jewish. One has only to look at the different school songs to get the message. At East Side High, which had Jewish students, the school chant was quite general and bland:

> Hail, all hail, dear East Side High School
> Green thy memory be
> By the bond of happy hours
> Are we bound to thee.

Weequahic's official song was equally tame:

> From our great wigwam
> on the hill
> Where stand our totems
> gleaming high
> We chant your praises
> with a will

To you all glory will
come nigh
So hail Weequahic
all hail to you
To you we bring
our honor true
Your name forever ring
To you Weequahic High we sing.[104]

On the other hand, the unofficial Weequahic song, which appears in *Portnoy's Complaint*, was unabashedly Jewish and also mockingly self-confident:

Give a yell, give a yell
A good, substantial yell
And when we yell, we yell like hell
And this is what we yell
Ikey, Mikey, Jake, and Sam
We're the boys who eat no ham
We play football, baseball, soccer
We keep matzohs in our locker.
Aye, aye, aye, Weequahic High!

And then there is the song, also recorded in *Portnoy's Complaint*:

White bread, rye bread,
Pumpernickel, challah,
All those for Weequahic,
Stand up and hollah![105]

These chants were usually on display at sporting events, which, given the talents of most of the Jewish students, certainly livened up what was usually a disappointing outcome on the field. Still, there were exceptions. Moe Berg, who went on to play major league base-ball, was selected, in 1918, as a third baseman for the *Newark Star-Eagle*'s "dream team," made up of the city's schools.[106] A number of football teams at Central High School, coached by Charles Schneider, boasted many Jewish players and were quite successful. In later years, Sam Convissor was the only Jew to play basketball for Central's bas-ketball team the year they won the state championship.[107] And, of course, Roth's fictional super athlete in *American Pastoral* was based on a real life counterpart, "Swede" Masin, who attended Weequahic High. In, *The Facts*, Roth describes what he calls, the "postgame pogrom" that broke out when Weequahic beat Barringer High for the first time in its fourteen year existence:

> The nearest bus was already almost full when I made it on board. . . . By then there were easily ten or fifteen of the enemy, aged twelve to twenty, surrounding the bus and hammering their fists against its sides. Fred Rosenberg contends that "every able-bodied man from north Newark, his brother, and their offspring got into the act." When one of them, having worked his hands through a crevice under the window beside my seat, starting forcing the window up with his fingers, I grabbed it from the top and brought it down as hard as I could. He howled and somebody took a swing at the window with a baseball bat breaking the frame but miraculously not the glass.[108]

Reada Jellinek, a librarian at Weequahic, recalled that "The Italians were so mad that night, they came and threw rocks on the field."[109]

Weequahic's primary claim to fame, and justifiably so, was its student body and its faculty. It achieved a reputation as one of the best high schools in the country, in the same class with Scarsdale or Great Neck High Schools, both in New York. Ruth Fien gives us a pretty representative description of how it felt to go there:

> I loved my experience in Weequahic High. The teachers were fabulous, the breadth of courses was spectacular. I thought it was an extraordinary educational experience. My teachers had a profound influence on me.[110]

The faculty at Weequahic High was outstanding, by all accounts. Helen Stevenson headed the History Department, Robert Lowenstein chaired the Language Department, and there was David Weingast, Alice Saltman, Sadie Rous, Isaac Ellis, Raeburn Higgins, Charles J. Schneider, Julius Bernstein, Charles Brodsky, and many, many more. Their dedication showed, not only in their teaching, but in the activities they planned. Hannah Ginsberg Litzky, who taught there for many years, took her students on trips whenever possible to see plays, museums, and the like, traveling as far as Stratford, Connecticut to see Shakespearian plays. Its reputation remained good even into the sixties. Phyllis Lauer, who graduated in 1964, when most Jews had already left Newark, praised the teaching staff too, in particular, Simon Chasen, who taught Hebrew and French. She noted that through the Hebrew class, which also included Jewish history, she and other students learned to appreciate their cultural heritage.

Litzky described her experience at Weequahic as "a love affair" between her, the students, faculty, and the school as a whole. She came from a literary family and her most famous relative was her nephew, the late Allen Ginsberg, whose own father, Louis, was also a teacher, as well as a highly regarded poet. Reminiscing about him in 1986, she observed:

> I am more an appreciator than a creative artist. Allen was born with it [the creative spirit]. Everybody knows the name of Allen Ginsberg and his sometimes bizarre behavior and his rebellious attitudes. He is a wonderful human being, a very fine poet, and what is particularly important to me is his very strong devotion to the family. And his career is pretty much an open book. You know, his homosexuality, which he doesn't want to hide, in fact, as one of the leaders of the beat generation. He's really a prophet in the biblical sense, I feel—his teachings about peace, his anti-nuclear stance, his poems for freedom of creativity.[111]

The staff had terrific raw material to work with. In its halcyon days, Weequahic's students were among the best in the land. And, as attested to by the esprit des corps that characterizes their reunions, they regarded Weequahic as the place where the seeds of their desire to excel and the wherewithal with which to do so, were planted. To speak of Newark without taking note of Weequahic is impossible, for it represents much of what Newark's Jews loved about their city. They knew their school was first rate and, thus, they reasoned, so were they.

There were schools in the suburbs that were also quite good, the best of which was probably Columbia High School in Maplewood. Some will say that, at certain points in its history, it was the equal of Weequahic and that may be so. But because it was not predominantly Jewish it was not regarded with quite the same affection. The Jewish community never thought of it as "their school." In fact, graduates remember some anti-Semitism there and, as a rule, Jews did not mix socially with those who were not Jewish. Certainly what happened to Franklin Hannoch, Jr. at Columbia could never have happened at Weequahic:

> I ran for president at Columbia High School, in 1945. And there I experienced anti-Semitism. One day I came to my locker and found that all my books had been ripped in half. And scribbled on one of them was: "Jew won't get to be president." So what do you do? I went to the assistant principal and I said, "I don't want to make a big deal about it, but I need a new set of books." And I did not get to be president of the school. And it was because I was Jewish. At that time Jews were less than 10 percent of the [school] population, but that's the way it was then. I was very popular in general because of my athletic ability, but people resented it when Jews did well.[112]

Negative encounters with the gentile world became even more common as Newark's Jews went to college, especially in the 1920s and 1930s, though not everywhere. Nat Dunetz attended New York University and did not have any difficulties, but many Jews elsewhere did. Seymour Epstein went to Princeton in 1936, where there were sixteen Jews in a class of 600. The eating clubs discriminated against Jews and he was only able to get into the one at the bottom of the social scale, largely because it needed members and was ready to accept anyone who applied.[113] The experiences of Harold Grotta and Bud Davis, both of whom attended the University of Virginia in the early 1930s, were all the more vivid because they had been led to believe differently. According to Harold Grotta:

> I went to the University of Virginia because a letter from their president appeared in the *New York Times* extolling its virtues and saying there was no prejudice there. So I went. There were maybe twenty Jews in the class.[114]

As a result, Davis was all the more surprised when:

> I was waiting for a squash court and when my turn came, the guy refused to get off. He was from the South and he said, "I'm not getting off for any Jew." So we went outside in the back and we went at it.[115]

Even closer to home, there were difficulties. In its October 17, 1930 issue, the *Jewish Chronicle* featured a page one story, titled: "State Groups Will Meet Tuesday to Sift Discrimination Charges at Rutgers; Allegations Denied." The story concerned reports of a quota system limiting the number of Jews admitted to the college.[116]

Education was, of course, a popular profession in Jewish communities everywhere. Within the Newark public school system, a number of Jews achieved prominence in the field of education. Among the best known were William Weiner, named principal at Central High School in 1912, the first Jew to hold such a post in the U.S.; Max Herzberg, Leon Mones, and Julius Bernstein, all principals at Weequahic High School; Leo Litzky, principal of East Side High School; and Charles Brodsky, holder of the same position at West Side High School. Mones was eventually promoted to assistant superintendent of schools in charge of Newark's high schools, the highest position achieved by any Jewish educator in Newark. Bernstein was later named superintendent of schools in Livingston. There was also Isaac Lowenstein, who served as school secretary to six successive school superintendents and as secretary to the Board of Examiners. He was the dean of Newark city employees, having been in the school system for fifty-nine years. Lowenstein was also president of the Y.

As a rule, Jews were able to secure teaching positions only in urban centers such as Newark, Paterson, or Passaic. Communities such as Irvington, Bloomfield, or Montclair were essentially closed to them. Isidore Hirschhorn remembers his struggle, in 1936, to find employment upon receiving his teaching degree from Montclair State College. After approaching the college's placement director several times, an interview was finally arranged with a member of the Hawthorne Board of Education. Hirschhorn recalled with bitterness how, as he was interviewed, he "walked alongside the gentleman, who continued to mow his lawn," as he talked. Needless to say, no job was offered.[117]

Over the years, the progress of Newark's Jews in education followed the same path as it did elsewhere. Initial bias, a period in which it is overcome, followed by the advance of African Americans in the field, as the inner cities turned predominantly Black and Jews moved out. Brooklyn's Ocean Hill-Brownsville school district was perhaps the best known setting for the conflicts over turf and control that inevitably ensued, but the picture was pretty much the same everywhere else too. Jews did not take kindly to being pushed out and African Americans did not appreciate the white presence in ghetto schools, even if the instructors were highly qualified. Litzky's description of the situation is representative of the attitudes of most Jews at the time:

> My husband was then [in the 1960s] principal of South Side High School. He felt a very strong commitment, as I did always, to Newark. We wanted integration to work. But when we began to be threatened by the violence and the crime, we just couldn't stay any longer. There was a big turnover in the faculty and my English teacher colleague was replaced by a black militant in college guidance [who wrote articles] claiming that the Guidance Department was a fraud. . . . It was just not a good situation for me.[118]

Many Jews who were educated in Newark's schools, whether at Weequahic or elsewhere, later made their mark in the field of higher education. Some examples are Yehuda Reinharz, currently president of Brandeis University; Melvin Tumin, former professor of sociology at Princeton University; Nathan Winter, former Jewish studies professor at New York University; Norman Samuels, provost at Rutgers University at Newark; Janet Lipman, professor of sociology at the New School for Social Research; Robert Rotberg, who taught political science at MIT for many years; Leslie Fiedler, professor of English at SUNY Buffalo; and Robert Eisenman, noted Dead Sea Scrolls scholar and chairman of the Department of Religion at California State University at Long Beach. Rotberg, who grew up in South Orange, was an athletic star as well as a brilliant student at Princeton, whose all-around abilities were recognized when he was named a Rhodes Scholar in 1957. And in Newark today, other Jews such as Saul Fenster, president of New Jersey Institute of Technology, occupy important positions in higher education.

American Jews in general understood that in making their way through the world of work they started out with the disadvantage of their background. They believed that they had to do much better than average to succeed. Ultimately, this had a great deal to do with their ability to prevail and do well in life. The combination of home and community gave them the self-confidence and work ethic to deal with discrimination and Newark's Jews were no different from Jews anywhere else in this regard.

Notes

1. Sarah Kussy, *The Story of Gustav & Bella Kussy of Newark, N.J.: A Family Chronicle*, booklet, n.d., 12,13.
2. Evelyn Goodstein, interview, August 8, 1996.
3. *Robert Nathan Report*, United Jewish Appeal Survey, 1947.
4. Abner R. Gold, "JVS' 'Mr. 5,000' is Typical in Desire to Earn Own Living." *Jewish News*, February 12, 1954, 20.
5. *Jewish News*, July 28, 1950, 5.
6. Benjamin Kluger, "Growing Up in Newark," *Jewish News*, September 8, 1977, B6.
7. Mark Stuart, *Gangster #2: Longy Zwillman, The Man Who Invented Organized Crime* (Secaucus, N.J.: Lyle Stuart, 1985), 20.
8. Frieda Mayers, interview, December 15, 1995, Jewish Historical Society of MetroWest.
9. Evelyn Goodstein, interview, August 8, 1996.
10. John T. Cunningham, *Newark* (Newark: The New Jersey Historical Society, 1988, rev. ed.), 182.
11. Philip Roth, *American Pastoral* (New York: Houghton Mifflin Company, 1997), 11-12.
12. "A. Hollander & Son—Industrial Leader," *Jewish Chronicle*, Fifteenth Anniversary Issue, April 24, 1936, 25, "A Hollander & Son's Splendid Record Marks Triumph of Great Perseverance," *Jewish Chronicle*, Twentieth Anniversary Issue, June 20, 1941, 83.
13. Dan Shiman, interview, November 30, 1994; Sol Goodman, interview, October 30, 1994, Jewish Historical Society of MetroWest.
14. Roth, *American Pastoral*, 25.

15. "L.V. Aronson—Newark's Civic Leader," *Jewish Chronicle*, Fifteenth Anniversary Issue, April 24, 1936, 54; "L.V. Aronson Entertains Civic Leaders Aboard his Yacht," *Jewish Chronicle*, July 30, 1931, 2; "William Schiffenhaus' Passing is Mourned by Whole Community," *Jewish Chronicle*, April 25, 1941, 1.
16. Bernard Bloom, interview, August 5, 1996.
17. Mitzi Reisen, interview, September 20, 1996.
18. Horace Bier, interview, December 2, 1996.
19. Dan Drench, interview, August 12, 1996.
20. Philip Konvitz, interview, April 8, 1997.
21. "Louis Schlesinger has Cure for City's Problems," *Jewish Chronicle*, Twentieth Anniversary Issue, June 20, 1941, 61.
22. Frank Schlesinger, interview, July 21, 1997.
23. "Newark of Yesterday, Today, and Tomorrow, With the Stamp of Morris Rachlin, Master Builder, Indelibly Printed on Each Phase," *Jewish Chronicle*, September 23, 1927, 1.
24. Ibid.
25. Louis Kasen, *Love is Not a Potato* (n.p.,n.d.), 220.
26. William B. Helmreich, *The Things they Say Behind your Back: Stereotypes and the Myths Behind Them* (New York: Doubleday, 1982), 26-27; Franklin Hannoch, Jr., interview, August 20, 1996.
27. Bella Milmed, interview, August 14, 1996; Ray E. Mayham, "President of West Side Trust Company Recalls Great Ability of Meyer Kussy," *Jewish Chronicle*, Fifteenth Anniversary Issue, April 24, 1936, 40.
28. Donald Karp, interview, July 21, 1997. For more detailed information about the bank's history, see *Broad National Bancorporation, 1985 Annual Report* (available through the bank.
29. "Vailsburg Bank Opening Creates Wide Interest," *Jewish Chronicle*, April 6, 1923, 1.
30. Franklin Hannoch, Jr., interview, August 20, 1996.
31. *Jewish Community Blue Book, Newark, New Jersey* (Newark: Jewish Community Blue Book Publishing Company, 1924), 670-71.
32. "Louis Plaut Passes Away in Los Angeles at Age of 82," *Jewish Chronicle*, January 8, 1943, 7; "Plaut Observes Anniversary in Newark Concern," *Jewish Chronicle*, April 6, 1923, 1; Barbara Lipton, "Newark Long Ago: 19th Century Photographs from the Museum's Collections," *The Newark Museum Quarterly*, 26 No. 4, Fall 1975, 12.
33. The distance between Baltimore and Newark is 185 miles while 140 miles separates Hartford from Newark. Whatever, the case, it is interesting that for both of these individuals, Newark, a city not in their immediate area, seemed so attractive as a business opportunity.
34. *Jewish Community Blue Book, Newark, New Jersey* (Newark, N.J.: Jewish Community Blue Book Publishing Company, 1924), 644-45. See also, John E. O'Connor and Charles F. Cummings, "Bamberger's Department Store, *Charm* Magazine, and the Culture of Consumption in New Jersey, 1924-1932," *New Jersey History* 102, nos. 3-4 (Fall/Winter, 1984), 1,4,22.
35 This was only one of numerous instances where others received credit for activities that he backed.
36. Laura Smith Porter, *From Intellectual Sanctuary to Social Responsibility: The Founding of the Institute for Advanced Study, 1930-1933*. Ph.D. dissertation, Princeton University, 1988, 110-11. Based also on a talk given by Elliott Shore at a meeting of the Jewish Historical Society of MetroWest on November 10,

1997. Felix Bamberger and Caroline Fuld had, at first, wanted the Institute built on their East Orange estate, but were convinced by Flexner to opt, instead, for the more academic environment of Princeton.

37. Ibid., 75.

38. Ibid., 79.

39. Leonard Kurland, interview, December 26, 1994, Jewish Historical Society of MetroWest; Howard Levine, interview, August 29, 1996.

40. Leonard Polaner, interview, August 14, 1996.

41. Lynne S. Dumas, *Elephants in my Backyard: Alex Aidekman's Own Story of Founding the Pathmark Supermarket Powerhouse* (New York: Vantage Press, 1988).

42. Bernie Marcus interview with Paul Silberberg, "Entrepreneurship in America," Rittenhouse Hotel, September 13, 1995.

43. Thomas Weinstock, interview, July 24, 1997.

44. Robert H. McCarter, *Memoirs of a Half Century* (autobiography, n.d., n.p.), 95-99.

45. "Lawyer's Club to Close Season by Annual Dinner," *Jewish Chronicle*, April 6, 1923, 1.

46. Virginia Grumbach, interview, August 12, 1996; Leo Yanoff, interview, November 24, 1996.

47. Milton Konvitz, interview, April 8, 1997.

48. "Some of Newark's New Female Barristers," *Jewish Chronicle*, August 8, 1930, 6.

49. Joseph F. Folsom (ed.), *The Municipalities of Essex County, New Jersey, 1666-1924* (New York & Chicago: Lewis Historical Publishing Company, 1925), 106-07.

50. Ibid.; "Miss Blume First Jersey Girl to Act as Murder Counsel," *Newark Morning Ledger*, April 29, 1918, 1.

51. Arthur Bernstein, interview, January 21, 1994 and July 28, 1994, MetroWest Jewish Historical Society. For another account of anti-Semitism in the medical profession, see Nicholas Dawidoff, *The Catcher was a Spy: The Mysterious Life of Moe Berg* (New York: Pantheon, 1994), 304.

52. Arthur Bernstein, interview, October 27, 1994.

53. Max Danzis and Aaron E. Parsonnet, "Development of Medical Profession," *Jewish Chronicle*, Fifteenth Anniversary Issue, April 24, 1936, 49. Arthur Bernstein concurred with this generalization, asserting: "Even after they [the German Jews] built Beth Israel they continued going to Presbyterian Hospital and St. Barnabas." interview, October 27, 1994. Aaron Parsonnet was one of the founders of the American College of Cardiology.

54. "Development of Medical Profession", 49. Victor's wife, Augusta was one of the first Jewish female medical students in the U.S. She dropped out, however, for financial reasons, to enable her husband to complete his medical studies. Augusta was also a leader of the Women's Suffragette Movement in New Jersey. Some other prominent physicians in this early period were Bernard Greenfield, Max Feldman, and Maurice Asher.

55. *Jewish Community Blue Book*, 647.

56. Victor Parsonnet, interview, August 6, 1997. Others who worked with Parsonnet on the Catherization Lab were Harold Goldberg, Sanford Lewis, I. Richard Zucker, and Lawrence Gilbert.

57. Ibid. The dental clinic at Beth Israel was considered the finest in the state. Lawrence Churgin, interview, August 11, 1997.

58. *The Catcher was a Spy*, 22.

59. Muriel Bloom, interview, August 5, 1996. Bloom's father was President of the Alliance.

60. "Schwarz Drug Stores Have Been in Business Almost Half of Century," *Jewish Chronicle*, Twentieth Anniversary Issue, June 20, 1941, 96.

61. Jay Weiss, interview, August 7, 1997. According to Lawrence Churgin, Jews could belong to the Essex County Dental Society, but, with few exceptions, they "couldn't get anywhere." Some societies, such as the West Essex Dental Society, barred Jews from membership altogether. Churgin attended New York University Dental School, where Jews were well represented, both as students and as faculty. His father, Leopold, founded Churgin Dental Labs in 1918, which eventually became the largest in the state. Lawrence Churgin, interview, August 11, 1997.

62. Ruth and Jerome Fien, interview, August 5, 1997.

63. *The Things they Say Behind your Back*, 13-16, 20-24.

64. Harold Glucksman, interview, August 6, 1997.

65. Gerard Schaefer, interview, August 6, 1997.

66. Jerome Fien, interview, August 7, 1997. Fava was not Jewish. As Fien noted, there was also Herman Litwack, for many years Secretary of the New Jersey State Board of Architecture.

67. Lawrence Van Gelder, "David Lasser, 94, a Space and a Social Visionary, *New York Times*, May 7, 1996, B8.

68. Kern was born in New York City, but lived in Newark for ten years and graduated from Barringer High School.

69. Mark Stuart, *Gangster #2: Longy Zwillman, the Man Who Invented Organized Crime* (Secaucus, N.J.: Lyle Stuart, 1985), 132.

70. Philip Konvitz, interview, April 8, 1997.

71. Based, in part, on Paul Stellhorn's paper about Ellenstein. "Champion of the City: The Political Career of Meyer C. Ellenstein," *Annual Meeting of Jewish Historical Society of MetroWest*, June 9, 1997.

72. Milton Keshen, "Letter to the Editor," *Jewish News*, July 10, 1997, 7.

73. Angelo Baglivo, "Pledge Given to 'Clean House,'" *Newark Evening News*, July 1, 1954,1.

74. Jerome Waldor, interview, December 2, 1996.

75. Dorothy M. Guyot, "Newark: Crime and Politics in a Declining City," in Anne Heinz, Herbert Jacob, and Robert L. Lineberry (eds.), *Crime in City Politics* (New York: Longman, 1983, 144-45.

76. Gail Schaffer, *Memoirs of an American Sabra Hebrew Teacher* (North Miami, Fla: Renaissance Booksetters, 1977), 40.

77. *Love is Not a Potato*, 221.

78. Most of this discussion is based on an interview with Stanley Aronowitz on January 9, 1998.

79. Ibid.

80. Esther Kesselman, interview, September 20, 1995, Jewish Historical Society of MetroWest.

81. Philip Roth, *The Facts: A Novelist's Autobiography* (New York: Farrar, Straus & Giroux, 1988), 22.

82. Rose D. Katz, *Golden Memories* (no publisher, no date). Available at Newark Public Library.

83. Mamie Bogner, interview, October 7, 1993, Jewish Historical Society of MetroWest.

84. Hannah Litzky, interview, November 19, 1986, Jewish Historical Society of MetroWest.
85. Bernard Menkes, interview, August 5, 1996; Sam Wolf, interview, August 10, 1997.
86. Myron Katz, interview, August 5, 1996.
87. Jacob Scarr, *Listen, My Children: A Grandfather's Legacy* (Philadelphia, Pa: Dorrance, 1972), 216-17.
88. Edward I. Koch, with Daniel Paisner, *Citizen Koch: An Autobiography* (New York: St. Martin's Press, 1992), 12-13.
89. Ibid., 12-13.
90. Eddie Rosenthal, interview, April 2, 1994, Jewish Historical Society of MetroWest. See also, Guy Sterling, "Hail of Bullets Polished Legend of Dutch Schultz," *Newark Star-Ledger*, October 22, 1995, 31.
91. Ed Brody, *The Neighborhood Merchants Associations in Newark, N.J.: A Personal Recollection*, August 1995, unpublished paper, 8.
92. Ibid., 15-20.
93. Arnold Mirsky, interview, October 10, 1993, Jewish Historical Society of MetroWest.
94. Eddie Rosenthal, interview, April 2, 1994, Jewish Historical Society of MetroWest.
95. Ibid. Even the rabbis got into the act, selling their wine permits for sacramental wine to bootleggers. See Jenna Weissman Joselit, *Our Gang: Jewish Crime and the New York Jewish Community, 1900-1940* (Bloomington: Indiana University Press, 1983), 97.
96. *Gangster #2*, 130-31.
97. Ibid., 76.
98. Alan Block, *East Side-West Side: Organizing Crime in New York, 1930-1950* (New Brunswick, N.J.: Transaction Books, 1995), 139- 40.
99. Albert Fried, *The Rise and Fall of the Jewish Gangster in America* (New York: Holt, Rinehart & Winston, 1980), 119.
100. John Cunningham, *Newark*, 214.
101. Philip Roth, *American Pastoral*, 41.
102. Don Rubenoff, interview, August 20, 1996. Some of those who attended the school included Rubenoff, in the mid-1940s; Eugene Thomas, and Marion Parsonnet, around 1915-20; and the Thom boys, Victor J. and Albert, in the late 1930s.
103. Edward Koch, *Citizen Koch*, 16,21.
104. As supplied by Fred Rosenberg, a Weequahic alumnus.
105. Philip Roth, *Portnoy's Complaint* (New York: Random House, 1969), 55. Fred Rosenberg has provided the following additions to the song: *Give* a good substantial yell; After "this is what we yell," insert: Alamen, alamen, alamen cocktail, yiscot a- boom-boom.; We play football, *we play* baseball, *we play* soccer. *Portnoy's Complaint*, it should be remembered, is a work of fiction, not bound by the rules of historical accuracy.
106. Nicholas Dawidoff, *The Catcher was a Spy*, 26.
107. Sam Convissor, interview, January 10, 1997, Jewish Historical Society of MetroWest.
108. Philip Roth, *The Facts*, 27.
109. Reada Jellinek, interview, March 28, 1995.
110. Ruth Fien, interview, November 24, 1996.
111. Hannah Litzky, interview, November 9, 1986, Jewish Historical Society of MetroWest.

112. Franklin Hannoch, Jr., interview, August 20, 1996.

113. Seymour Epstein, interview, August 12, 1996.

114. Harold Grotta, interview, August 29, 1996.

115. Bud Davis, interview, August 29, 1996.

116. For more on this, see Ruth Patt, *The Jewish Experience at Rutgers University* (Somerset: Jewish Historical Society of Central New Jersey, 1987).

117. Isidor Hirschhorn, *Recollections*, unpublished, undated paper.

118. Ibid. At the time of the riots, many of Newark's public school teachers were Jewish. From that time on, Jews were slowly but surely forced out of the field. Moreover, they were no longer able to obtain positions at the higher administrative levels, regardless of their qualifications. There was a lawsuit (Porcelli vs. Titus), protesting the situation, but to no avail. At one point, striking teachers, including a number of Jews and blacks, were beaten by others who were on the side of those who had taken over the educational administration of Newark's schools. This information is based on correspondence from Stephen B. Levitt to the author, dated, October 14, 1997, and on the following articles: Richard J.H. Johnston, "Teachers Beaten in Newark Strike," *New York Times*, February 3, 1971, 1; Robert Braun, "School Peace Talks May Resume Today," *Newark Star- Ledger*, February 3, 1971, 1.

4

Social Life and Culture

When one listens to Newark's Jews wax nostalgic as they reminisce about the Newark that was, the word that comes to mind most often is "community." It is a word that encompasses all of the many-layered aspects of a cohesive society—family, friends, synagogue, school, neighborhood—the stuff that social and cultural life is made of. Take these words and you have the basis for a community of like-minded individuals who genuinely enjoyed being with one another and who now look back with pride on what they built. Moreover, as is so often the case, the fact that what they had is no more, seems to magnify the sense of loss even more than might actually be the case.

Often, when former residents think about the life they had in Newark, it is as though every disappointment they experienced since leaving there, could have been avoided had things stayed the same. Ask Myron Katz, now a resident of Lake Hopatcong, how he feels about the good old days in Newark and his face takes on a wistful glow as he looks out over the lake in front of his house:

> The kids today, they couldn't appreciate that way of life. With kids spread out all over, with divorces, and everything else. When I made a decision, I thought about my mother and father. I never rebelled as a teenager. We used to have a picnic every year. And the Brownstein family truck used to pull up with turkeys and chickens and eggs. There were eight children in the family. And they'd invite cousins and friends. We'd have maybe 100–200 people—We'd look forward to it. We had so much fun and it was a ball. You felt so good about things. You gotta go back to family ties.[1]

We see here how family and community are intertwined. When Katz talks about the "kids spread out" he is lamenting the loss of compactness that gave Newark residents a feeling of closeness. It is a fact that Newark was small in size and hemmed in by suburban communities fiercely opposed to being incorporated by it. When he complains about divorces, Katz is expressing his dismay over the loss of close family ties, which were an integral part of life in those days. And his description of family get-togethers reminds us, and him, that it was in Newark that these get-togethers took place.

For Philip Roth, there is the sense of intimacy and familiarity among friends as well as the idea that one's whole life revolved around the neighborhood:

> . . .fifty years later, I ask you: has the immersion ever again been so complete as it was in those streets, where every block, every backyard, every house, every *floor* of every house—the walls, ceilings, doors, and windows of every last friend's family apartment—came to be absolutely individualized? Were we ever again to be such keen recording instruments of the microscopic surface of things close at hand, of the minutest gradations of social position conveyed by linoleum and oilcloth, by yahrzeit candles and cooking smells, by Ronson table lighters and venetian blinds? About one another, we knew who had what kind of lunch in the bag in his locker and who ordered what on his hot dog at Syd's; we knew one another's every physical attribute—who walked pigeon-toed and who had breasts, who smelled of hair oil and who oversalivated when he spoke; we knew who among us was belligerent and who was friendly, who was smart and who was dumb; we knew whose mother had the accent and whose father had the mustache, whose mother worked and whose father was dead.[2]

Newark's Jewish community, and Weequahic in particular, was one extended family. Everyone knew one another. Thus, when its residents moved to the suburbs, they lost something irretrievable. The homes were private, the synagogues further away, the stores not within walking distance. True, some communities forged new identities, but they were smaller in size and did not have nearly as many synagogues, Hebrew schools, and shops. As a result, the rhythm of life changed forever and the connections were lost.

Many former Newarkers kept their attachments alive, nevertheless, via visits to the city and involvement in its activities. For example, Cantor Eliezer Schulman sang for the Hebrew Academy of Essex County for eighteen years after he left Newark, at no compensation. One year he was given a kiddush cup as a token of gratitude, another year a bathrobe. Why did he do it? Because he loved the Newark of his childhood.[3]

Paradoxically, the fact that Newark was so close to New York City caused its inhabitants to feel a need to separate, to find a way in which they could be distinct and define themselves as such. David Mallach provided some insight into what constituted the Newarker's self-image:

> There was always a "New Jersey nationalism." It's that: "We are not New York; we don't do things the way they do in New York. And we are not obnoxious pushy Jews like they are." There's a view here that we're civil. Even if it's a myth, if you develop it long enough, it becomes reality. Bergen County is much more like New York than we are. They define their community by the George Washington Bridge.[4]

Such stereotypes and generalizations are a powerful weapon when people need to deal with the insecurities engendered by proximity to a world capital. Still, stereotypes do have "a kernel of truth." The small-town environment and the resultant lack of anonymity encouraged civility and even friendliness. You could not disappear into Weequahic, though, if you found it stifling, you could escape, an option chosen by more than a few. And the juxtaposition with Bergen County reaffirms the presumed specialness of Newark, namely that it is not simply another bedroom community appended to New York City.

Were the Jewish neighborhoods of Newark really different from say, the West Bronx and Flatbush in New York, or from Northeast Atlanta? It is a difficult question to answer, for the qualities attributed to Newark's neighborhoods—closeness of buildings, compactness, heavily Jewish public schools, special eateries, bathhouses, and the like—existed elsewhere too. Even the fact that so many of Newark's residents never moved that far away from the core city is not unique.

The answer lies in W.I. Thomas' sociological dictum: "If people define situations as real, they are real in their consequences." For what mattered most was that Newark's Jews saw themselves as possessing a bond that stemmed directly from the experiences which accompanied growing up in Newark and they related to each other as such, so much so that others took note of it when they observed Newarkers interacting at a bar mitzvah or even waiting at a bus stop to pick up their children from summer camp. This feeling of esprit des corps was probably most due to a certain mix of individual personalities, family socialization, and a group dynamic that was set in motion whenever residents came together in school, temple, various organizations, and at social events. Whether or not the feelings of solidarity were stronger in Newark than elsewhere is debatable, but these are the factors that generally account for such perceptions.

If people have a need to be accepted, to feel rooted, then pre-World War II Newark filled that role admirably, especially for Jews. Roth summed it up best in *The Facts*:

> Not only did growing up Jewish in Newark in the thirties and forties, Hebrew school and all, feel like a perfectly legitimate way of growing up American but, what's more, growing up Jewish as I did and growing up American seemed to be indistinguishable. Remember that in those days there was not a new Jewish country, "a homeland," to foster the range of attachments—the pride the love, the anxiety, the chauvinism, the philanthropy, the chagrin, the shame—that have, for so many Jews over forty, complicated anew the issue of Jewish self-definition.[5]

The range of social activities engaged in by Newarkers was incredibly broad and varied. These included theaters, movies, concerts, and operas; bicycle and motorcycle races, boxing matches, and professional baseball games; circuses, parades, visits to the bathhouses, medicine men shows, poetry readings, and dances.

They also belonged to a plethora of organizations. Their avid enthusiasm for such groups becomes clear from even a cursory examination of the "Community Calendar" which appeared weekly in the *Jewish News*. There were, on an average, more than fifty meetings a week, sponsored by organizations such as the American Jewish Congress, B'nai Brith, the Miriam Auxiliary of Oheb Shalom, the Six O'Clock Club of B'nai Jeshurun, Mizrachi Women, the Jewish War Veterans, the Tarnopoler True Friends, and a whole host of synagogue sisterhoods, men's clubs, and youth organizations.[6]

The degree of interest in these activities can also be gleaned from a 1948 study by the Federation. Fraternal organizations reported a membership totaling 14,523 people; another 10,940 individuals belonged to civic and service organizations. The most popular leisure-time activities in order of frequency were, movies and theaters, card games, concerts and lectures, sports, radio shows, and reading.[7]

Equally important were the informal ways in which Newarkers relaxed. To escape the blazing summer heat, they sat on the fire escapes outside their cramped apartments, hoping to catch a cool breeze as they took in the street scene below. Sometimes the children would stage skits for their neighborhood friends. Refreshments were apt to be served, usually cookies and lemonade. The more sophisticated of these shows included an admission charge, with purchasers given tickets made of colored construction paper and with children pulling sheets along clotheslines to delineate each act in the shows.

Up and down the streets, women sat on the concrete stoops in front of the apartment buildings and on an occasional bench, gossiping and exchanging information about shopping, schools, the best doctors, available apartments, and so on. As they talked, they cast approving or disapproving glances at passersby, eyeing with suspicion any strangers who chanced by. Every once in a while peddlers would come along, shouting out their wares—"knives for sale," "cheap umbrellas," "fresh vegetables." And in every neighborhood, there was the ubiquitous candy store, hangout for generations of local youths. Inside, youngsters drank egg creams and ate banana splits, occasionally whirling themselves around the red, plastic covered, and silver-bordered stools that lined the soda fountain area. And they listened, often with keen interest, to their favorite singers, warbling tales of love, heartbreak, and adventure. The music often served as a backdrop to the conversations with girlfriends and boyfriends that transpired in the wooden telephone booths whose folding doors gave them the privacy that was so often lacking in the crowded and noisy railroad flats typical of those days.

A favorite activity was swimming. In the nineteenth century, the Morris Canal was used primarily to carry coal from the Pennsylvania mines to New York Harbor, but, in the twentieth century, for Jacob Goodstein and his friends, the canal achieved popularity as a swimming hole. The Raritan River served a similar purpose for Ben Arons.[8] Others found more esoteric, but equally enjoyable, outlets for recreation. Bernard Menkes and his buddies were fond of disabling the guy wire of the trolley car's electric line and putting it out of commission, thus forcing the driver to reset the line.[9]

The following description of a childhood spent in Newark's Down Neck area, gives us a sense of the flavor, vitality and energy that characterized life in these neighborhoods:

> Ferry Street was surrounded by powerful attractions for a little boy: the forbidden tracks of the New Jersey Central Railroad, the fire engines charging out of Engine #5 and Hook and Ladder #4, East Side Park, Keisch's yard, the river and the docks, the boys diving off near the Jackson Street Bridge, bellywhopping on Flexible Flyers down the snowy incline of Congress Street, baseball in the summer, playing on and on tirelessly until there was hardly a flicker of light, and coming home to be scolded (mildly) and washed and fed. Out front, the organ grinder came along to play his wistful melodies.[10]

And then, our chronicler gives us a bird's-eye view of all of the different ways in which one could pass the time in those days, both within and outside Newark:

> What were our other diversions? Simple things, snatched from the grudging, work-filled hours of the week. There were theater parties at Elving's Metropolitan, Newark's version of the Yiddish stage located near Prince Street, and Prince Street itself, a local version of the Lower East Side, with its crowds, its pushcarts, its peddlers and its bargain stores, and the most aromatic bakeries and mouth-watering delicatessens this side of Delancey Street. We went on trips to Coney Island where my father loved to bathe in the *yom* [ocean], Luna Park, the Hippodrome, the Bronx Zoo. Newark offered us boating on Weequahic Park Lake or we sat in the stands to watch the harness racing. Or we headed to the other end of the city, to the bosky dells of Branch Brook Park.[10]

The Jews were not the only ones who loved Newark. The Germans had their parks, the Hungarians their dance halls, most notably Doelger's. And for the Poles, there were St. Stanislaus and St. Casimir, the equivalents to Oheb Shalom and B'nai Abraham. North Newark was as meaningful to the Italians as Weequahic was to the Jews. And while the Jews watched their favorites box, the Irish did the same, as well as rooting for their heroes in the Gaelic football games.

Of perhaps greatest significance to the Jews, given their cultural antecedents, was family. Philip Roth phrased it as a prayer, *"Hear, O Israel, the family is God, the family is one."*[11] The activities in which they engaged were all the more resonant historically in the reverberations of their collective memories, because they evoked loving images of families enjoying life with those whose company they most cherished. And so, Newark became a tableau against which was framed that which they held most dear—life within the accepting and unquestioning world of their loved ones.

Saturday and Sunday excursions often consisted of visits to relatives. The communities in which they lived—Paterson, Jersey City, and the Bronx, became special because in the homes of those whom they loved, they became places that were friendly and inviting. If you went to Aunt Goldie and Uncle Ben, they took you for a walk in a new park, or to a local restaurant, or a nearby amusement park, not to mention a delicious dinner in their home.

Most of all, although parents worked hard, they seemed to spend more time with their children. To be sure there were divorces, deadbeat fathers, and unhappy families, and there were orphanages and homes for unwed mothers. Yet, all in all, there seemed to be a greater feeling of closeness and warmth and family interactions that stemmed primarily from the fact that life was more interdependent in general. People lived in close proximity and were therefore compelled to deal with each other on every level. Families with more than one car were unusual. As a result, activities requiring travel tended to be those that everyone could do together. Teenagers were much less likely to attend college away from home and few parents had the money for sleepaway camps. If they could it was for two or four weeks, not an entire summer. Those who grew up in those days remember their parents reading them bedtime stories—perhaps from the Uncle Wiggily series or a portion of Booker T. Washington's autobiography. They recollect how weekends were reserved "for the children." No one would say: "Take my kids for two weeks while we go to France." In fact, few parents could have afforded such luxuries.

One of the more striking aspects of Newark's social and cultural life was the quality of its offerings. Museums, parks, theaters, and libraries operated at a high level and reflected a clear desire for excellence. That, in itself, made it much more likely that those who benefited from what was available would be deeply impressed by their experiences. To understand the degree to which these realities impacted upon the lives of Newark's inhabitants we need to examine daily life there somewhat more closely.

Small Pleasures

Walking has always been a popular avocation for both urban and rural dwellers and Newark was certainly an interesting place for it. There were neighborhoods, both familiar and unfamiliar, and there was downtown, with its tall buildings, city landmarks, and department stores. People walked everywhere, with friends, relatives, or simply by themselves and in so doing they deepened their ties to the city.

In the days before automobile travel, there were hay rides for those city dwellers interested in an excursion to the country. A popular trip for Jewish youth was the annual May ride, which took them over country roads by horse-drawn wagons, usually to Union Hill or Carlstadt.[12] Individuals fortunate enough to own buggies also took short trips to see the farms and villages that surrounded Newark. Another popular mode of transportation was the trolley car. As they rode to Olympic Park or other recreational destinations, passengers would look out from the open-sided cars and gaze at the billboards. "Drink Moxie!" exclaimed one, featuring a man in a white soda fountain jacket thrusting an outsize finger at the viewer. Tobacco ads, such as "White Owl Cigars," or "Fatima Cigarettes," were especially common.[13]

With the advent of the automobile age, new opportunities arose to venture further and in greater comfort. Those wealthy enough to own cars remember them with great fondness. Vera Verosub reminisced about her family's Studebaker Touring Car:

> If it would be raining, we had to snap the isinglass windows into place to keep the car and us dry. On the running board, there was a large storage box for tools and a jack in case we had a flat tire. . . . There were small cone-shaped vases attached to the inside windows which contained fresh flowers and water. Our car was light tan, with a canvas roof stretched from front to back. It had silver spoked wheels and white wall tires. Everyone felt very important whenever we took a trip in our wonderful car. Not many of our friends had such a luxurious car; many did not even own a car of any kind.[14]

Spending time in the local parks were among the favorite activities. As a boy scout, Saul Schwarz hiked and camped in the Surprise Lake and South Mountain Reservations. Ed Koch went to nearby state parks with his family for picnic outings. In reality, parks were an established part of Newark's cultural and social life by the mid-nineteenth century. Sarah Kussy's description demonstrates how the park and the beer gardens were intertwined with the life of German Jewry and how they provided them with the chance to meet German Christians in a setting that allowed them to become friendly:

> People would also gather for a social afternoon or evening, on a hot summer day and order drinks and pretzels. Voight's, Gegen's, and Caledonian Parks were all near our home. Doelger's Garden on Spruce Street beckoned invitingly to those who cared to bowl, or just sit with their families or friends, to enjoy a cup of coffee or a glass of beer and *Handkase* or *Schmierkase* (hand cheese, or pot cheese).[15]

Every park, well-known or unknown, had its own identity as well as its loyal following. And they were used not only for simple recreation but for meetings of all kinds, as places where you went to sort out your thoughts when there was a crisis, or as areas where gangs claimed turf rights. In an era when a house with a lawn was but a distant dream for most, parks were their only lawns and therefore far more important than today. West Side Park, which ran from 13th to

17th Streets and from 16th to 18th Avenues, was a good example of a multipurpose center. People took walks there along the beautiful trails, but during the summer months there were concerts and in the winter its slopes attracted many sledders. In addition, there were tennis, baseball, and a very picturesque, if small, lake to enjoy.

To the southeast, there was the much larger Weequahic Park, known for its sleigh riding and ice skating, among other activities. And north of West Side Park, there was equally large Branch Brook Park. Visitors came from everywhere to lie on blankets and listen to the concerts that were frequently held there.

Then there was Olympic Park, with its oversized "Smile" sign that beckoned to those outside, inviting them to enjoy its many amusements—rides, elephant shows, and games of various kinds. One of the more interesting events was the dance marathon, a featured entertainment at Dreamland Amusement Park. An innovation of the Depression era, its purpose was to provide subsistence income for the winners, who desperately needed the money during those difficult times. Bleachers were set up for the spectators, who watched as the dancers tried to remain on their feet for hours on end. Sometimes, a dancer fell asleep from exhaustion and the partner would have to drag him or her around the dance floor until they collapsed together. Contestants were allowed to rest for fifteen minutes out of every hour and in the evening as well. The competition was very keen, with contests lasting for many hours.

The best way to a man's memory, as well his heart, may be through his stomach and it would appear that the same applies to women. When Newarkers talk about their lives in that city, they often associate the good times with the food they ate and the restaurants they patronized. Prince Street, the main shopping thoroughfare for first-generation Jews, was a popular spot for those looking for Jewish food. The pushcarts and stores were well-stocked with Jewish favorites such as pastrami, corned beef, pickles, farmer cheese, herring, rugalach, and so on. Perhaps the first kosher restaurant in Newark, owned by one Samuel Arm, was located a block away, on Broome Street.[16]

Another establishment from the early days, a kosher Romanian eatery, was Rice's, located on Belmont Avenue, where Ben Arons savors the memory of the *knotzlach* (small kebabs) he ate, as well as delicious steak served on a wooden platter with grooves in it to catch the juices. The Rices were a friendly couple who used to call their regulars "their children." It was an informal sort of place. No one wrote down orders and no bills were given at the end of the meal. Everything was based on memory and somehow the system worked, for Rice's was always crowded. Restaurants were, in some instances at least, a form of entertainment, as the following Yiddish ad in the November 27, 1925 issue of *The Jewish Voice*, suggests:

Meet your friends in
Gutmann's Romanian Kosher Restaurant
79 Mercer Street
Music is played every evening while you dine.

There were delis, in those pre-cholesterol awareness days, wherever Newark Jews lived, be it Clinton Hill or Weequahic. Among the best known were Reinfeld's, Kartzman's, Peterman's, Kozake's, Tabatchnick's, and, on the West Side, Fructbaum's. Each one had their loyalists who swore by the offerings, telling anyone who would listen: "The pastrami sandwiches there, you can't beat 'em. They're the greatest!"—and treating the information imparted as though the discovery was theirs alone and you were being let in on a big secret. For the more health conscious, or simply for a change, there were dairy restaurants. Newark's riposte to New York City's Ratner's or Rappaport's, was the Ideal Dairy, Tobin's Dairy, and many others along Prince, Springfield, Clinton, and Halsey, whose names have long since been forgotten through the passage of time, places where one could order anything from borscht to red snapper and where waiters with starched napkins on their arms made wisecracks about flies doing the backstroke in your potato soup.

And who could forget the bakeries? Again, each had their supporters. In a memoir, Helen Judd wrote of the distractions of Silver's Bakery, located across the street from the Hawthorne Avenue School:

The third bell sounds and we sit quietly in homeroom, listening to Mrs. Black make the day's announcements. I try hard to pay attention, but the smells of freshly baked bread and cakes from Silver's Bakery across the street drift through the open windows. I think about the taste of warm rye bread, puffy rolls, chocolate seven-layer cake, Charlotte Russes with heaps of whipped cream.[17]

Another favorite was Keil's Bakery, equally famous within its little world, specializing in delicious rye, corn, and pumpernickel breads. The Bergen Street Bake Shop had a reputation for excellent challah.

Others were partial to Schachtel's Bakery, on Broome Street, renowned for its salt sticks and hot rye bread, or to nearby Wigler's Bakery on Mercer Street, as well as Watson's Bagels on Clinton Street. Naturally, since most bread is not eaten fresh out of the oven, those experiences, preceded by anticipation as one went to the bake shop, are likely to stay in peoples' minds long after they happen. For small children, there were other associations. Their idea of culinary excellence was to be found in the candy stores, where they consumed as many jaw breakers, Chiclets, gumdrops, pretzel sticks, malt balls, and licorice whips, as their funds would permit. These were, of course, the days, when ten cents went a long way.

As with the bakeries, several hot dog places vied for the affections of Newark's Jewish inhabitants. For many youngsters, a day in Weequahic Park followed by hot dogs at either Sabin's or Millman's, on Meeker Avenue, was a perfect combination. They were household names in the Jewish community as can be seen from an ad that ran repeatedly in *The Young Israel Review*: "Sabins—For delicious kosher Hebrew National franks." It seems you were either a fan of one or the other, but, in any case, there was wide agreement on the quality of the hot dogs served at Syd's Luncheonette on Chancellor Avenue. Incidentally, Syd's is still in business today, in nearby Vauxhall. Also, in those days, Pal's Cabin, now a West Orange restaurant was a small hot dog and ice cream place. And for those who did not like hot dogs, there were potato knishes and hot buttered sweet potatoes, sold from yellow pushcarts. For those interested in a sandwich, Stash's, on Nye Avenue was a popular stop.

When the weather turned warm, it was time for cold refreshments, ices and ice cream. Italian ices cost two cents in the 1930s and a typical street scene was a bunch of kids crowded around a vendor as he poured cherry, lemon, or orange syrup from a bottle, over a cup filled with shaved ice. Today, these treats still flourish in the poor neighborhoods of American cities.

Most memorable, however, for generations of children, were the Good Humor trucks (later challenged by the more musically endowed Mr. Softee). At first, Good Humor was sold only from three wheeled bikes and then, later on, from white, little square trucks with bells that rang to herald their arrival and which cruised Newark's residential areas. Esther Blaustein, author of an intriguing family memoir called, *When Momma was the Landlord*, loved Good Humor as much as any child, but was especially resentful at what she perceived to be its discriminatory policy towards traditional Jews. Reflecting on the Passover holiday and its seemingly inconvenient appearance, she wrote:

> The whole thing seemed like a plot, with the main villain the Good Humor Ice Cream Company, may their freezers conk out. With fifty-two weeks in the year, did they *have* to start each selling season during the week of Pesach? We kosher kids . . .had to have our childish hearts torn out by the tintinnabulation of the bells, bells, bells on those rotten ice cream wagons. What did Edgar Allan Poe know about how a bell can sound? Did his friends stand in front of *him* and eat a chocolate malt on a stick, or a toasted almond that crunched in the mouth like Mt. Vesuvius erupting, or, worst of all, a dark chocolate sundae?[18]

Rounding out the ice cream department, in addition to Henry's Sweet Shoppe, were the two Grunings stores, one in Newark proper and the other, more popular hangout, in South Orange, both known for hot fudge and for peach ice cream in season.

When it came to non-kosher restaurants, the choices were much wider and many, if not most, of Newark's Jews took advantage of them, albeit accompanied by some guilt, at least initially. In fact, the progress of Newark's Jews from, say, salads, to dairy foods, to meat, in non-kosher eateries would probably serve as a good time-line by which Jewish assimilation into the American mainstream could be accurately followed. Sometimes it was gradual, as with one woman who, over the years, went from tuna fish sandwiches, to hot fish or meatless pasta, and finally, to chicken. In other instances, the decision was both sudden and spontaneous, as was the case with one youth, who reminisced about his summer school days at Central High and how the smell of Italian sausage cooking in a nearby restaurant "got the best of me and I capitulated."

The significance of this is that Jews were responsible for Newark's general culinary map almost as much as other ethnic groups. Naturally, everyone had his or her favorites. Nevertheless, several places stood out, one of which was the Weequahic Diner, owned by Leo and Morris Bauman. Actually, the diner's origins went back to North Newark, at the intersection of Broadway and Herbert Place, where it was called the Broadway Diner, a typical trailer operation with stools and a counter. It became a landmark, however, when it moved to Weequahic. Though the decor, with green plastic covering the chairs and booths, was quite ordinary, the food was special, featuring both Jewish dishes, such as kishka and chopped liver, as well as great steaks and pies. In response to the long lines outside his establishment, Bauman developed some lines of his own, such as: "Waiting for all seats!" (said in a loud voice), or, "Sorry folks, you'll have to leave because there is no floor show tonight." Amazingly, he got away with it, partly because of his bright smile, but more likely, because the food was first rate. The successor to the Weequahic Diner, in Verona, on Bloomfield Avenue, was the Claremont Diner.

Jewish businessmen tended to favor two eating clubs in downtown Newark, the Downtown and 744 Clubs, as well as a deli called Hobby's, which is still around today. For fine dining in and around Newark, there were numerous establishments, such as Don's, Zig's, the Steuben, and the Westwood, but the most famous was the Tavern, a restaurant that dated back to Prohibition days. In terms of quality, the Tavern, on the corner of Elizabeth and Meeker Avenues, was the equivalent of New York's Le Cirque or "21," though not quite as formal. Voted by two national surveys as one of America's fifty most popular restaurants, the Tavern, founded by Sam Teiger, was truly a Newark landmark. Everyone went there to eat, but also to "see and be seen." It was the place you went to for a special occasion, an important meeting, or a date that you wanted to consider as "a night on the town."

Apparently, Teiger was a good businessman, mixing hard work, dedication to his profession, common sense, and diplomacy. It was a rare combination of an unpretentious restaurant that, nevertheless, attracted everyone, from the elite to the not so elite, all the while making everyone who entered it feel welcome. On one occasion, when a prominent corporate head absentmindedly scribbled some notes on a white tablecloth, and then was embarrassed upon realizing what he'd done, Teiger put him at ease immediately when he quipped: "It's all right. When you leave, I'm planning to sell it to the highest bidder." Teiger's ability was reflected in profits, which totaled $1,500,000 annually by 1959.[19]

The fare at the Tavern was universally recognized as being of the highest quality, from the prime cuts of meat to the desserts. The one item that sparked the greatest enthusiasm, however, was the coconut cream pie. Ed Koch, in his autobiography, remarked how "even after fifty years, I still remember it as the best I have ever eaten."[20] Considering the options available to New York City's former mayor, that is quite a statement.

There are many stories associated with the Tavern that serve to validate its reputation, but the following one not only achieves that goal, but does it in a humorous and endearing way: Dore Raynes, who lived in nearby Bayonne, decided to bring home a coconut cream pie to his wife, Dinah, an outstanding baker in her own right. The cost was relatively high, $2.50, but Dore felt it was eminently worth it. Upon tasting it she readily conceded that the pie was out of this world and that she could not bake one as good:

> "How much did it cost," she asked.
> "$1.50," lied Dore.
> "For only $1.50 it doesn't pay me to bake."
> "Okay," Dore thought to himself, "so I lied for a dollar. It's worth it."
> However, his little white lie backfired. He did not object to paying two and a half dollars for the pie for his family and guests, but Dinah began taking orders from friends and relatives for $1.50 a pie. Dore found himself bringing home two and three pies every Friday, losing a dollar on each one. He finally confessed and the deliveries stopped.
> Not long after that, the owner of the Tavern, Sammy Teiger, realized a need for a store because of the demand for the pastries. The Tavern Pantry Shop was opened on Meeker Avenue next to the restaurant and the famous pies, cakes, and desserts were available to everyone.[21]

For weddings, bar mitzvahs, and other affairs, Newark's Jews usually opted for Schary Manor, Krueger Hall, Clinton Manor, Ann Gordon's, Avon Mansion, The Essex House, and The Chanticler. Of these, Schary's, with its Green, Blue, Gold, and Oak Rooms, was probably the most popular. It was a lavishly designed hall, with collages, statues on pedestals, and gilded cherubs that hung over the wedding canopy. Innumerable parties were held there and the sign outside, "Schary Manor, Catering for Special Occasions," became its trademark.[22]

Cultural Life

As it has always done, the organized Jewish community did its utmost to keep its members within the fold by sponsoring Jewishly oriented programs as well as general activities within a Jewish environment. This was true of Newark from earliest times when unmarried tradesmen ate their Sabbath meals in the boarding houses where they had taken up residence. There they caught up on the latest communal gossip, sang, and talked about business and marriage.[23]

In the days before Jewish community centers, the synagogue filled that role. Men would gather around the pot-bellied stove inside and discuss the day's events, catch up on who was doing what, joke, relax, and just generally enjoy the feeling of companionship that came from being with their coreligionists. There were also Purim balls, picnics, and fairs, and the support which these events attracted gave rise to the general belief that a permanent center where Jews could engage in a wide range of leisure pursuits, was needed.

The most important Jewish organization in Newark for the masses of Jews who lived there was the Young Men's Hebrew Association, first organized in 1877. Four years later, it leased a building on Plane Street from the brewer, Gottfried Krueger, one which contained both sports facilities and space for cultural events. In 1898, it closed temporarily due to waning interest and competition from the No Name Club (which later evolved into the Progress Club), but was eventually reopened.

Under the leadership of Abe Dimond, and with the financial backing of philanthropic individuals such as Louis Bamberger and Felix Fuld, a large center was built at the intersection of Kinney and High Streets and it opened in 1924. It is worth mentioning that from 1905 on, a Young Women's Hebrew Association, founded by Sigmund Kanengiser, had also been functioning and quite well at that. Later on, it merged with the YMHA. There was also a Hebrew Club and several other smaller groups. It soon became clear that all of them would be best off by joining together as a single Y and those most responsible for effecting that were a young social worker named Michael A. Stavitsky, who was to become a major communal force, and Morris Schutzman, another important leader.

The Y was significant because it was the place where so many things happened—social, intellectual, religious, cultural, and recreational. People, especially the young, needed a central address where they could meet each other. After all, they and their parents had come from different countries, belonged to different synagogues, and had different family histories. By doing things together they got to know each other and relationships, many of them enduring, were formed. As Jerry Lehman recalled: "Many of the Y people married each other. And let me tell you something—those marriages stuck. A Y marriage was a *good* marriage."[24] Saul Schwarz elaborated further on what the Y meant to him:

> The Y was almost everything to me and my friends, all children of immigrants. You met friends there, you made friends there, learned about music and books,

free High Holy Day services, and found out about the larger Jewish community. Unlike B'nai Jeshurun, we were always welcome, no matter how poor our clothing and even if we sometimes spoke in Yiddish. Nurin's luncheonette, I called it Nurin's Nauseous Nook, was a favorite gathering place. Even when we moved out of the Third Ward, we kept returning to the Y.[25]

The Y was more than simply a vehicle for discovering and expressing culture, important as these goals were. It was designed to do so within a Jewish framework. To provide the vision and organization necessary for achieving that goal, Dr. Rabbi Aaron G. Robison, executive director at the famed 92 Street Y in Manhattan, was lured to Newark. Upon his arrival, Robison predicted that the Y would become "the town hall of the Jewish community, the one place in the city where Jews of every age, both sexes, and of every condition of life and belief, shall meet for common purposes." Robison also brought with him Harry Friedgut, who served with distinction for many years, as the organization's educational director.[26]

There were glee clubs, drama and dance clubs, the Hazomir Choir, lectures by well-known personalities, literary and debating clubs, and arts and crafts. George Kahn put on innumerable plays through the years with local talent that became nationally known, such as Moss Hart and Dore Schary, and he developed the very popular "Bits of Hits" programs, consisting of selections from well-known plays and dramas. Friedgut directed the educational programs and they were uniformly of high caliber. Through the years an incredible array of outstanding artists and lecturers appeared there, including Sergei Rachmaninoff, Fritz Kreisler, Arthur Rubinstein, Hendrik Van Loon, Philip Roth, I.B. Singer, Vincent Price, Ida Kaminska, and Jessica Tandy, to name just a few. And the programs were geared to a broad age range, encompassing everyone from nursery school age to senior citizens, and all those who fell in between. Friedgut also organized a chamber music series which is still in existence today.

The Y blended Jewish culture together with its activities in such a way that they came to be seen as part of everything it did. It was not simply the fact that there were holiday services there, a Yiddish lecture series, Purim carnivals, and the Hazomir Choir. Rather it was the values that were transmitted:

All the time we were growing up, the Y helped to shape the ideas we lived by and nurtured the faith we believe in. Through its group work methods, the Y brought the age-old ethics of our people home to us. We sang Jewish songs and observed and celebrated our Jewish holidays. We also learned the meaning of *tsedaka* [charity] through participating in the UJA. In this way we learned to live Jewishly.[27]

The Y ran summer day camps, and the values extended there too. In the words of a former camper:

> To us, the Y was never just a building. It accompanied us everywhere—its spirit pervading our actions, its philosophy guiding our lives. In the summer we took it with us to the Y day camp and the New Jersey Y Camp. It was part of the atmosphere like the air we breathed, the clothes we wore, the green grass, the surrounding woods.[28]

The Y also provided a home for that most American of institutions, the Boy Scouts. Saul Schwarz joined Troop 52 at the age of twelve and views the four years during which he was a scout as a defining period in his life. Naturally, he learned things like knot-tying and map-making and competed in sports events, winning a wading championship, but on a deeper level, he made friends and learned about the idea of patriotism, general values of loyalty, honesty, and hard work, and established lasting friendships. These have stayed with him his entire life and he associates them closely with the Y.

Last, but certainly not least to those who participated, were the sports and recreational facilities. The Y had a full range of activities— swimming, basketball, fencing, wrestling, boxing, gymnastics, hiking, parties, games of all sorts. To be sure, people who worked all day needed a place in which to relax in the evening and on the weekend, but of what *Jewish* significance was volleyball or swimming? The answer lay in the opportunities for camaraderie. There were Jews who were not interested in its Jewish cultural offerings; they saw the Y simply as a place with a nice basketball court or a first-class pool. But the locker-room conversations with people of similar backgrounds inevitably led to other activities when people discovered common ground. A business relationship would form and once these individuals had worked together one would perhaps persuade the other to become involved in a Jewish cause. One friend would invite the other to his or her home for a Friday night dinner, introducing his or her more assimilated counterpart to a *Shabbat* meal. Out of that would come genuine interest in one's heritage, to be nurtured and one day taught to one's children. In these small ways the Y awakened Jewish consciousness without making otherwise wary members feel they were being pushed or brainwashed.

The Depression hit the Y quite hard; many of its programs were cut or curtailed. The large donations became smaller and good people felt compelled to leave. Friedgut took his music program to the Mosque Theater and Stavitsky began spending more time at Temple B'nai Abraham. Nonetheless, the Y made it through the 1930s and once the war began, it came alive again. Soon, however, it faced another challenge—with so many Jews having moved to the suburbs there was a need for additional facilities near their homes. In short, the Kinney and High Streets location was becoming obsolete. Recognizing the challenge, the organized Jewish community established new branches and a variety of clubs in Irvington, the "Reservation" area, South Orange, Millburn, Verona, Hillside, Nutley, and numerous other communities. Most important, in 1954, the Y at Kinney and High was sold. It was bought by a black Masonic society which promised to pay $200,000 but could come up with only half that amount. Today, the building through which uncounted members of the Jewish community had passed, is home to a black, church-affiliated school.

For the next five years, the Y operated wherever it could, in synagogues, schools, and other locations, and, in 1959, a new Y came into existence on Chancellor Avenue, in Newark's Weequahic section. The programs continued to be excellent, with one of the most memorable having been the Israel Exhibition and Trade Fair, held in 1963. The idea for the fair, which displayed Israeli products of every type, belonged to Frances Nusbaum, and it was so successful that it was repeated in 1965. But the building was long and narrow and it soon became clear that it was inadequate to meet the demands of a burgeoning Jewish population that continued its westward movement away from Newark, one with increased leisure time and, with newfound affluence, greater demands for a more spacious facility.

The Jewish community again rose to the occasion and, in 1969, the Y opened its doors in a new location, on Northfield Avenue, in West Orange. The building, designed by the firm of Gruzen and Partners, won an award from the American Institute of Architects. Eventually, the growth of the community necessitated the construction of a second cultural and recreational facility in addition to the Northfield Y, namely the one at the Aidekman Campus of MetroWest, in Whippany, one which serves at least three counties—Essex, Morris, and Sussex.[29]

Besides the Y, there were many other Jewish groups that met regularly and which tremendously enriched Jewish communal life in Newark. First, there were the *landsmanshaftn*, Jewish societies whose meetings were both social and cultural affairs. Sometimes there were dinner dances and, on other occasions, lectures on topics as diverse as "The American War Effort" and "Jewish Education." There were many European communities, both from large cities and from *shtetls* (small towns) represented in Newark. Among those listed in the Jewish newspapers were: Warschauer, Chudnover, Boryslawer, Tarnopole, Bialystoker, Berdichever, Minsker, Bolechower, Gombiner, and Rzeszower. Another social constellation revolved around family circles and each week, meetings were announced for different families. The Hyman and Becky Lesnik Family Circle or the Reich-Greenberg Family Circle would announce a gathering at a member's home, with the lack of specifics suggesting that its purpose was purely social.

There were also different fraternal lodges and veterans groups that met, sponsored social events, had cultural programs, and which often held fund-raisers for various good causes. The largest group nationwide was probably the Independent Order Brith Abraham. The influence of these orders can be seen from their fund-raising efforts. In the first fifty years of its existence, from 1886 to 1936, the Order disbursed upwards of $35,000,000 in death benefits to widows and orphans. It had also allocated more than $10,000,000 to be paid to members who were sick, in need, and in distress. Many of Newark's most prominent citizens, including Elizabeth Blume, New Jersey's foremost female attorney, her husband, Max Silverstein, and Mayor Meyer Ellenstein belonged to Brith Abraham. Another large and important order was the International Order of Brith Sholom. Like Brith Abraham, it counted numerous influential Newarkers in its ranks, such as Sigmund Kanengiser and Martin Levy, quite a few of whom achieved national prominence in the organization.[30]

The various Jewish organizations, like the B'nai Brith, Agudath Israel, Mizrachi, the Workmen's Circle, the National Council of Jewish Women, American Jewish Congress, and the American Jewish Committee, also met regularly. In addition, there were special organizations. Tuberculosis had always been a problem for immigrants and long after the major immigrant period ended in the mid-1920s, organizations such as the Deborah Consumptive Relief League, continued to sponsor events. It was not only the goals of the League that mattered to those who belonged, but the reinforcement of the bonds of fellowship that such meetings strengthened and maintained. And, of course, there were the Bikur Cholim societies, set up to visit the sick in local hospitals and in their homes.

The proliferation and growth of at least certain organizations was often tied into immigration. When it slowed, the organizations either died out or became inactive. Thus, it was not surprising to see renewed activity in this area when Holocaust survivors began arriving in the U.S. and in Newark after the war. In 1950, with the assistance of Dr. Curt Silberman (who had earlier helped German-Jewish refugees in the 1930s adjust to life in America) and Theodore Isenstadt, then executive director of the Jewish Family Service Association, the Newcomer's Club was formed. Its avowed purpose was to give the survivors both a place and a forum within which to discuss their problems. It was also an opportunity for social gatherings, with dancing and music, and the response was enthusiastic, with up to 200 members participating in events. Such assistance from the community came at a critical period in the newcomers' lives since many of them were literally starting over again, both occupationally and in terms of rebuilding their lost or broken families.[31]

As elsewhere, there were Jews in Newark who wanted to link up with Zionism. The idea of playing a role in the establishment of a Jewish homeland appealed to them and, as a result, they were attracted to organizations that emphasized it. Sarah Kussy and Leon Kohn put Newark Jewry on the Zionist map, so to speak, in 1905, when they traveled as delegates to the Federation of American Zionists' convention, then being held in Tannersville, New York. A few years later several Zionist clubs, most notably Ohavei Tzion and Tikvat Tzion, joined up with the newly formed national Zionist organization, Young Judea.[32]

Then, in 1914, Sarah Kussy led others in starting a Hadassah branch in Newark. Eventually, Hadassah's local members numbered in the thousands and they participated in every aspect of Jewish life. Led by people like Israel Cohn and Michael Hollander, Newark's Jews lent strong support to renewal projects in Israel, including the planting of millions of trees under the direction of the Jewish National Fund.[33]

As with the Y, many of the Zionist groups served a dual function— Zionism and friendship with like-minded souls. Typical of such efforts was the Chug Ivri, a cultural club. It was chaired by Charles Ehrenkrantz, principal of the Newark Talmud Torah and it regularly invited Zionist-oriented speakers and entertainers. Another club was

Tzeirei Tzion. For them, participatory activities, singing Zionist songs and dancing the hora, were what they enjoyed most, as well as discussions and trips. At one point, Tzeirei Tzion performed a play called *The Chalutzim* at the Y, and donated the proceeds from ticket sales to Israel.[34] The connection of these groups to Zionism was strengthened even more when they got together with members of like-minded organizations from Passaic, Elizabeth, Paterson, and other nearby communities. It gave them a feeling that they were part of something really important, something that was making history.

Politics, with its intellectual and idealistic traditions, has always held a certain attraction for Jews. In the general sense, Newark's Jews were as patriotic as anyone else and they were so from early on. Sarah Kussy writes of her father's feelings vis-a-vis politics in the post-Civil War period:

> On election day father walked to the polls with shoulders erect and cast his vote. It put him on terms of political equality with the President of the United States. That is what it meant to be an American! . . .Father loved to discuss politics with his farmer friends—Meeker, Johnson, Farrow, Jenkins. . . . With them he could discuss political differences without rancor; they would pummel each other with witticisms—and here father was master of them all.[35]

Judging from other accounts of the times, interest in such matters was shared by many in the German-Jewish community.

Jewish political involvement reached its height during the Depression, when economic conditions caused widespread disillusionment with the system. The Young People's Socialist League, the Jack London Club, the Workmen's Circle and other, similarly oriented organizations became very popular among the young, who were searching for something to believe in. There were rallies in parks as well as in halls normally used for weddings and bar mitzvahs, often accompanied by the singing of the Internationale. Others joined up with radical elements in the labor movement, participating in sit-down strikes and demonstrations. Molly Rosenberg tells what it was like:

> I belonged to a gang of kids. We were all from Weequahic High School and some from South Side High School. The gang of kids I went with were all very politically motivated to protest a lot of things we thought were unjust. This was the heyday of the Communist Party in Newark. There were meetings held with lectures. I remember hearing Paul Robeson one time. I remember hearing Sinclair Lewis speaking to an auditorium of people interested in political situations.[36]

Only a segment of the young were political activists, but it was quite clear that they were among the brightest in the community. Later on, their commitment became mixed in with pragmatic considerations as World War II drew closer and the draft became a problem for many. By 1942, however, it had become clear that Hitler was not only America's enemy but an implacable foe of the Jewish people, leaving only the most assimilated members of the community in the isolationist camp. The end of the war in 1945 marked a time when people tried to put their lives together to create some semblance of normalcy to counter the dislocations brought about by the protracted conflict.

Then came the 1950s, the McCarthy Era, and a climate of fear spread throughout the Jewish community. Many who were sympathetic to communism were persecuted and lost their jobs, especially in the school system. Liberals, too, became afraid, lest their enlightened views be mistaken for allegiance to the principles of communism. As a result, many became inactive politically and turned their attention inward, to careers, family, and nonpolitical pursuits.[37] Only when the Kennedy Era ushered in a period of social activism, did things begin to change.

If the true benchmark of a city's culture is to be measured by its main library and major museum, Newark would be in the first rank. From the onset, when it was founded in 1887, the library was regarded as an institution open to all. In a May 1888 article, the *Sunday Call* asserted: "Let it be known from the start that this is to be a people's library and that the struggling artisan is to be as welcome to its precincts and its privileges as the scholar and the millionaire."[38]

John Cotton Dana, librarian par excellence from 1902 until his death, in 1929, built up the reputation of the library to the point where it became one of the best known in the country. Not only did he create great collections, books as well as periodicals, but he generated tremendous public enthusiasm for the library by making Newarkers feel that a world-class library was crucial for its residents' intellectual progress. In addition to its obvious benefits, a first-rate library served a latent function—it allowed Newarkers to take pride in themselves and in their city. They could tell potential detractors that their city was one where learning and culture were esteemed. They could also have told them that Washington Irving had been a frequent visitor to Newark and in the *Salmagundi Papers* had claimed inspiration for some of his work from the city. Moreover, Stephen Crane was born on Mulberry Place and Mary Mapes Dodge grew up in a house at the corner of Elizabeth and Renner Avenues.

For "the people of the book," such an institution was a godsend and they used it constantly, both to help them reach their academic and professional goals and simply for the pleasure of reading, a habit instilled in them by their immigrant parents. To them the massive stone structure with the green slanted roof was a home away from home. Newark actually had many fine branch libraries, but its crown jewel was the main library. What made it so unusual was that its high level of quality was not in any way intimidating. It had a truly comfortable fit, like a well-worn glove, that made everyone feel at home in it. Most important, all of its stacks were open, a concept pioneered by Dana. Although *Goodbye Columbus* has been immortalized for its account of a lavish Jewish wedding and its tale of budding romance, it contains an excellent description of the Newark Library that beautifully captures its essence:

> I walked up the three flights to Stack Three . . .past the reading room, where bums off Mulberry Street slept over *Popular Mechanics*; past the smoking corridor where damp-browed summer students from the law school relaxed, some smoking, others trying to rub the colored dye from their tort texts off their fingertips; and finally, past the periodical room, where a few ancient ladies who'd been motored down from Upper Montclair now huddled in their chairs, pince-nezing over yellowed, fraying society pages in old old copies of the Newark *News*.[39]

Remarkably, this description quite accurately sums up the library today. The same types of people described by Roth thirty-five years ago still populate it every day.[40]

Throughout the years, Newark was fortunate to have several excellent newspapers, namely the *Sunday Call*, the *Evening News*, and the *Star-Ledger*. This was crucial, for people are often literary captives of their local news organs. As a result, Newark residents knew what was happening in the world and benefited from intelligent commentary on national and world events. The *Jewish Chronicle* served a similar function for the Jewish community. While it had its critics, the fact is that the newspaper provided adequate coverage of Jewish life, both locally and elsewhere and its regular appearance as well as that of its worthy successors to the present day, provided local residents with a forum for expression and linked up the community with Jewry elsewhere. To be sure, people read many other things as well. Depending on the time period, their reading habits tended to reflect what was popular in the larger society, be it *Life* and *Look* magazines, *Reader's Digest, Saturday Review,* and *Parents' Magazine.* For children, there were authors like Louisa May Alcott, Booth Tarkington, and, no doubt, Mark Twain.

The Newark Museum actually began operations on the fourth floor of the Newark Library. Eventually, the Museum acquired its own beautiful building, a gift from the philanthropist Louis Bamberger, but the impetus again came from Dana, who had initially pushed the city fathers into recognizing the need for a quality museum. Over the years, the Museum, in addition to serving as a valuable repository of Newark's history, brought many important exhibits to the city and was thought of by many professionals as the best small city museum in the country. Certainly generations of Newarkers appreciated its offerings, from personal and family visits, to classroom trips. Newark's commitment to the Museum has continued even through its darkest financial periods. During the 1980s, the city spent about $7,000,000 updating and refurbishing it.[41]

Literary interests were part of the Jewish community's life from the beginning. Congregation B'nai Jeshurun was home to the Daniel Webster Debating Society which sponsored discussions on slavery and other relevant issues of the times. Oheb Shalom followed a parallel course, establishing the Lasker and Montefiore Literary Societies. One of the earliest literary figures, albeit part time, was Nathan Kussy, who, despite a busy legal practice, managed to write several novels and playlets. One work of fiction, *The Abyss,* received favorable reviews in several leading newspapers, including the *Los Angeles Times* and the *San Francisco Bulletin.*

Louis Ginsberg, on the other hand, was a full-time writer and teacher of literature. His poetry appeared in the *New York Times,* the *New Republic* and was also published in book form. One of his poems was called "In the Newark Library":

> Prophet and poet, priest and sage
>   Are living here anew;
> From alcove and from crowded stack
>   They look again at you.
> Here Keats is watching eagerly
>   Wherever Beauty gleams;
> Shakespeare is gazing in your heart;
>   And Shelley, in your dreams.[42]

Louis was the father of the more famous Allen Ginsberg, but, if one is to judge from a comment that appeared in a 1959 *Jewish News* article about the two, it was Louis who was seen as more acceptable, at least by conventional standards:

> Louis Ginsberg is a poet who finds beauty in concrete pavements, tall buildings and electronic brains. Allen Ginsberg is a poet who finds beauty in very little. This, essentially, is the difference between father and son, the elder, a Newark-Rutgers evening college lecturer, and the younger, a leading poet of the "beat" generation, and author of Howl![43]

In the article, Ginsberg senior was critical of the quality of work produced by the beats, but said that the writings of some, like his son, would survive "after their eccentricities and lack of balance have been washed away by time and maturity."[44] Louis Ginsberg, incidentally, spent the first thirty years of his life in Newark and moved to Paterson in 1925, while Allen, although born in Newark, was raised in Paterson.

For Jews, a city library and museum alone was insufficient to meet their cultural needs and here the Y again met the demand through book fairs and classes taught by painters, sculptors, musicians, and dancers. Jewish Music Month was commemorated and there were film festivals and Jewish thematic art exhibits as well. The Y also brought noted personalities to Newark. One lecture, held in 1930 at the Newark Armory under Y auspices and featuring Rear Admiral Richard Byrd, attracted 10,000 listeners.[45] Six years later, the Y invited Amelia Earhart to Newark as a speaker.[46]

The Y, while a leader in such programs, was by no means the only organization to hold them. Temple B'nai Abraham also became a center of cultural activities, especially in the musical arena. And there were literally hundreds of lectures given elsewhere by people of note. For example, in December of 1947, the renowned anthropologist, Margaret Mead, spoke at the invitation of the Jewish Family Service Association. In May of 1961, the Reverend Martin Luther King was a guest speaker at Temple Sharey Tefilo. In 1966, the black psychologist, Kenneth Clark, lectured at B'nai Abraham. Needless to say, suburban synagogues also had speakers, such as an April 11, 1965 speech at a Livingston temple by the literary critic and historian, Irving Howe.[47] There were also speakers sponsored by non-Jews whose topics were sometimes of Jewish interest and which were reported as such by the Jewish media. For instance, the October 25, 1940, issue of the *Jewish*

Chronicle, carried an article about a forthcoming talk by Count Jerzy Potocki on the future of world democracy. It was underwritten by Mrs. Parker O. Griffith. With the rise of Hitler and World War II, Jews were keenly interested in the topic of democracy.[48]

A look at what lectures were given and when, is an excellent way to assess what was troubling the Jewish community at various points in its history, or simply capturing its attention. Thus, lectures in the 1960s spoke of culture clashes between the generations, civil rights, and the Vietnam War, while the 1970s featured the Middle East and a rising awareness of issues related to Holocaust survivors. All in all, the richness and variety of offerings available to Newarkers made for a life that greatly expanded the cultural horizons and knowledge of its residents.

As noted earlier, the man most responsible for the outstanding quality of the Y's cultural programs was George Kahn. But not everyone had a positive experience with him. Jerry Lewis, for example, who grew up in Irvington, was quickly shown the door by Kahn, who saw him as a little too brash. And Kahn was known as a demanding individual who insisted that everything he became involved with be done as well as possible. But the overriding characteristic of the man, in addition to his talent, was that he cared and gave it his all. Little wonder, then, that the Jewish Welfare Board, turned to him during World War II to help organize programs for the soldiers. Kahn developed innovative programs for the GI's, incorporated in what was known as the "Social Lyceum" and which were performed in hospitals and camps at war bond rallies.[49] On March 31, 1964, the Jewish community paid tribute to George Kahn for his forty years of service to the Y. Also honored were Fritzi Satz, director of Physical Education, and Dore Schary, local boy made good who was first appreciated for his talents at the very same Y. Fittingly, the evening featured a performance at the Hollywood Theatre in East Orange, of the play, *Act One*, written, produced, and directed by Schary. The all-star cast included Jason Robards, Jr., Jack Klugman, Eli Wallach, Sam Levene, George Segal, and Bert Convy.

Newark's leaders in the arts knew that appreciation of culture had to start when one was young. With that in mind, the Y created a youth orchestra and symphonic band under the directorship of William Weiss, head of Barringer High School's Music Department.[50] With the help of Lena Griffith, Rose Parsonnet and Leonard Shiman organized a classical music concert series at the Y that continues to this day. Founder of the Griffith Music Foundation (Her husband was president of the Griffith Piano Company.), Lena Griffith was a key supporter of programs for young people. She helped them, not only through concerts that appealed to the young, but by giving scholarships to promising students. Although not Jewish, she backed many Jewish causes and, in 1950, brought the Israel Philharmonic Orchestra to Newark. In her view, music was an excellent common denominator for different cultural and religious groups and she actively promoted that philosophy through her leadership as treasurer of the National Conference of Christians and Jews.[51] When the Music Foundation dissolved, Moe Septee undertook to promote classical music events at the Mosque Theater, including soloists such as Arthur Rubinstein, Nathan Milstein, and others.

The fruits of these peoples' labor were most clearly realized when young people were accepted into top music schools such as Juilliard in New York and Curtis in Philadelphia. There was Eric Friedman, a violinist who was a soloist with the New York Philharmonic Orchestra at age thirteen; Michael Tree, a violist who was a student of Efrem Zimbalist at Curtis for ten years, a member of the Guarnieri String Quartet, and who has recorded for RCA and Columbia Records; Jill Bengelsdorf, a Juilliard graduate and Fulbright winner, who did outstanding work with the Canadian Broadcasting System; and Kenneth Amada, a finalist in 1956, for the Leventritt International Piano Competition.[52] Mention should also be made of Marion Parsonnet, who became a respected director and writer of films, including *Cover Girl* and *Gilda*. He also produced one of the first television medical shows, *The Doctor*.

But most of all, the legacy of Newark's promoters of the arts can be seen in the thousands of people who simply developed an appreciation and understanding of how music and art can enrich one's life. With respect to the latter, there were many classes given by a variety of organizations in painting and sculpture and there were also important art galleries in Newark. The most highly regarded of these was Rabin and Krueger, on Halsey Street. This gallery, in particular, encouraged many Jewish artists, including Chaim Gross and the Soyer brothers, to exhibit their works there. Bernard Rabin himself enjoyed an international reputation in the art world and was named the head restorer in Florence, Italy, when floods hit that city and damaged so many of its works of art. Still alive and well, he remains active, working at the Norton Museum in West Palm Beach and as a restorer for the Huntington Museum in California. First-rate art exhibits were also presented in later years, when the Y moved to its Northfield Avenue location. Among the exhibitions were, "A Century of East European Immigration," "Art in a Concentration Camp: Drawings from Terezin," and "Judaica Now."[53]

Newark also developed a reputation as an excellent forum for the theater. It had the advantage of being near New York City and new productions often tried out there first. In addition, people preferred to perform there because of Newark's proximity to Gotham. Actually, Newark's Jews had theater as a form of entertainment as early as the nineteenth century. *The Newark Morning-Register* wrote in its September 29, 1881 issue, of a play put on by the Elks, a German-Jewish organization and there were other productions within the community too.

The "Bits of Hits" performances at the Y can hardly be characterized as an amateur-level production, even though they were not what would be called "the legitimate stage." Performed at Krueger Auditorium, they played, invariably, to packed houses, meaning upwards of 2,000 people. The cast was large, usually between sixty to eighty members, many of whom acted at a high level. For the Y, professionalism in this area has been a constant through the years. In more recent times, important groups like the National Shakespeare Company and the Cafe La Mama Troupe, have appeared at the Northfield Y. Although Kahn is no longer there, his spirit is apparently very much alive judging from all of the different ensembles that are housed there, such as the Northfield Players, the Y Orchestra, and the Teen Drama Group.[54]

For the immigrants, however, in terms of making the transition and simply as a chance to relax, the Yiddish theater was of critical importance. New York's theaters were better known and of higher caliber, but Newark had nothing to be ashamed of. Between 1922 and 1944, Elving's Metropolitan Theater was the place to go for Yiddish plays and operettas. The plays were mostly written by Bernard and Rose Elving and reflected the problems faced by their audiences—adapting to life in America, broken romances, ungrateful and rebellious children, intermarriage, and bringing the whole family over from the *shtetl*. Whatever the quality of the performances, Elving's, which featured stars like Menashe Skulnik, Moishe Oysher, and an assortment of lesser lights, filled a real gap in the community.

The regular theater also catered to the immigrants, or at least the Jewishly identified. The following ad appeared in the *Jewish Chronicle*:

Orpheum Theatre
MATINEES DAILY - ALL SEATS 30 CENTS
Regal Fischer Corp.
PRESENTS
"PERSECUTION"
adapted from the great biblical story
The Book of Ester [sic]
SEE
The reason for the great feast of Purim
Ester's sacrifice to save her race
Mordecai's triumph and the deliverance of the Jews

Some of the more popular theaters in the 1920s and 1930s were, the Branford, Loew's, the Terminal, the Adams, Proctor's, the Ritz, the Shubert, the Broad, and the more "intellectually oriented" Little Theatre, which served coffee in cappuchino-style cups. Generally, they featured dramas, musicals, and comedies aimed at the general public, not ones with Jewish themes, though the producers and directors were often Jews. Some examples of the fare follow:

ARTHUR HAMMERSTEIN's
LUANA
A musical romance of the South Seas
Music by Rudold Friml
Broadway's Best Cast Including
RUTH ALTMAN - ROBERT CHISHOLM - JANS & WHALEN
JOSEPH MACAULAY - ETHEL NORRIS - LILIAN BOND
Singing and Dancing Chorus of 80
Prior to Engagement at Hammerstein's Theatre, New York
***
SHUBERT THEATRE
PAT ROONEY and MARION BENT
THE DAUGHTER OF ROSIE O'GRADY
"Delightful Show" *Inquirer* "Full of Pep" *Ledger*
Pulse stirring music by Pat Rooney's
SYNCOPATING SYMPHONISTS

These shows acculturated the immigrants to life in America, but some-times they also reflected both the strains and the possibilities of multicultural life in the New Land. The same issue of the *Jewish Chronicle*, dated January 22, 1926, contained reviews of a film, called, *Under Western Skies* and a Broadway "musicomedy" entitled *Kosher Kitty Kelly*. About the film, the reviewer wrote:

> The Oregon wheat belt and the old clash between Eastern capitalists and Western farmers form the theme for "Under Western Skies." . . .The greater part of the picture was filmed in Eastern Oregon during the harvesting of the wheat. The harvesting machines are shown at work reaping and binding the golden products of the soil that go to help feed the world. The toil and labor of it all are vividly illustrated. In contrast there is the smug complacency of a group of capitalists who in their Wall Street offices are scheming to ruin the farmers.[55]

It does not require much imagination to see where Jews fit in with this approach. The average American associated Wall Street and capital-ism with Jews and the message was clear. "Good Americans," must fight the greedy bloodsucking Jews who are trying to exploit the hon-est and hard-working farmers. Viewing such films, even in relatively safe Newark, could scarcely have made the typical Jew feel comfort-able about how accepted Jews as a group were in this country.

Kosher Kitty Kelly, on the other hand, playing at the Broad Street Theatre, represented a different danger, that of assimilation and inter-marriage. Described by the reviewer as the "'Abie's Irish Rose' of musical comedy," it was a story of Irish-Jewish life. While it did not claim to deliver a real "message," the tone was upbeat—different groups could get along if they tried. Issues regarding the importance of cul-tural survival were not really dealt with, but for Jewish viewers, the theme certainly caused them to reflect on their role within the larger gentile community.[56]

Perhaps the best-remembered showcase for the arts was the Mosque Theater, which was the scene for many important events and produc-tions. The Mosque was originally a movie house and the first film shown there, *Beverly of Graustark*, starred Marion Davies. In addition to dramatic plays, stars of the opera appeared there, as well as impor-tant political figures like Interior Secretary Harold Ickes. Judy Gar-land, Marian Anderson, Paul Robeson, and Isaac Stern performed at the Mosque. In short, it was a place to see and to be seen.

The theater was first and foremost a place of entertainment. Impor-tant theatrical productions played in Newark and those unable or unwilling to go to New York City found that its fare more than served their needs. But it was also a place for young aspirants attracted to the arts. Take, for instance, Selma Weiss, who grew up during the Depression and who attended rehearsals for fifteen years at the Helen McHugh Studios on Washington Street. As a result, she was invited to join the chorus at the Mosque, where she sang for years, until World War II broke out and the chorus was disbanded. Looking back on that period, Weiss mused about an experience that gave meaning to her life through fellowship and work that she loved:

> I sang with the stars of the Met . . .Martinelli, Kiepura, Castagna, whenever they appeared at the Mosque. I was privileged to be on stage with them. Even as a chorister, it was a tremendous thrill. My fellow choristers were the most delightful people; our mutual love and interest in music and our genuine respect for each other kept us together in complete harmony.[57]

There was also the Frieda Lippel Dance Studio above the Loew's Theater, which trained Peggy Ann Gardner, a 1930s child movie star.

Fanny Brice, who achieved fame in drama, comedy, music, theater, and burlesque, also benefited, in an earlier era, from the Newark experience. Brice was born in New York City in 1891, but her parents, eager to climb out of the poverty-stricken Lower East Side, moved west to Newark when she was a small child. There they were saloonkeepers, a natural choice in a city with a large working class. Not much is known of her life in terms of schooling, friends, where she lived, in part, because she made a seemingly conscious effort to play down the ten years in Newark. Instead, she preferred to romanticize her life by concentrating on her New York roots and her "rags to riches" story which began in "the ghetto."[58]

Nonetheless, in what was probably an unguarded moment, Brice touched on one aspect of her life that revealed the important formative impact that Newark had on her long and successful professional career:

> In talking about her life, Brice virtually erased her Newark experience. She did tell one reporter in 1925 that she had lived in that city "from the time she was a little tot until she was twelve years old" and claimed that "Her first impressions of the stage were formed and her ambition to be an actress was fired [there]." She reminisced about "trotting down to Washington Street" to Blaney's Theatre where "the old blood-and-thunder melodramas" used to play and admitted that she could always find a way into the theatre without buying a ticket. "My favorite dodge," she confessed, "was to sneak into Blaney's Gallery while they were airing and cleaning the house in the morning at nine o'clock and hide until matinee time."[59]

Irrespective of her efforts to rewrite her own history, these reminiscences, focusing on an area that she chose as her life work, speak for themselves. Ten years of one's childhood spent in a city had to have had a significant effect, and, judging from these comments, they clearly did. It is interesting, though obviously coincidental, that during this period in her life, the great song writer, Jerome Kern, also lived in Newark, graduating, in 1902, from Barringer High School. Kern was a few years older than Brice and they probably never even met in Newark. However, Brice did perform in productions for which he had written the music, namely the musical comedy, *Nobody Home* and the *Ziegfield Follies*, for which Kern wrote some of the tunes.

Sometimes there were "cultural happenings" at social events, featuring appearances by film stars or singers and dancers. One of the more unusual events was reported in the February 24, 1922 issue of the *Jewish Chronicle* :

> As a social event, strikingly original to its minutest detail, the fifth dance of the Century Cotillion of Newark, held Tuesday night at Proctor's Roof, was outstanding by far of all similar affairs ever held in this city.
>
> The first event on the program was a Rube Goldberg studio party, with Rube Goldberg, the cartoonist there in person as the guest of honor. All of Rube's characters were there in costume, looking as if they had stepped out of one of his comic strips. Goldberg was stunned when he entered the hall and saw hundreds of dancers attired in costumes representing the children of his brain.
>
> In the early hours of the morning the dancing stopped and a vaudeville show was put on by the Century Players.
>
> Following the show, all adjourned to the grill in the basement of Proctor's building for a beefsteak dinner, after which there was more dancing until dawn Wednesday morning.
>
> The committee in charge of the affair consisted of Sidney S. Sonheim, president; Milton Simpson, vice-president; Al Schlesinger, treasurer; Victor Lindeman, secretary; Herbert Hannoch, Leo Steiner, and Harry Stern.[60]

This description, though lengthy, is important for an understanding of the life and culture of Newark's Jewish community during the first quarter of the twentieth century. It is easy to stereotype the community and think only of the impoverished masses struggling to earn their daily bread. That was certainly true of the community as a whole, mostly the Eastern European immigrants.

Yet it is equally important to understand that those who made the decisions for the Jewish community were people, primarily of German-Jewish descent, who had lived here for fifty years and had achieved a certain level of success. The party described above, the food, the entertainment, and the location all bespeak a life of luxury and ease that characterized the city's Jewish elite and it is important to understand that it existed and operated within the larger social framework of Newark, country clubs and all, for better or for worse. To the Eastern European masses, these Jews represented something attainable, though barely so, it seemed at the time. If nothing else, however, they were a sign that at least some of Newark's Jews could rise higher as time went on.

Throughout the years that Newark was a major Jewish population center, the black and Jewish communities maintained contact in varying degrees. There were friendships and business relationships, some of which are recalled with fondness by both sides. Many Jews were also quite interested in black culture, going to nightclubs that featured black bands and to jazz bars, like the Blue Mirror, where they would listen to the hip language of blacks, then known as "jive talk."[61] In *American Pastoral*, Roth mentions jitterbugging as a high school activity and talks about evenings spent listening to jazz and bebop.[62] Although a work of fiction, the following description in his book is clearly based on real-life happenings in Newark, at least in the general sense:

> It was Mendy Gurlik (now Garr) who'd taken me with him to the Adams Theater to hear Illinois Jacquet, Buddy Johnson, and "Newark's own" Sarah Vaughan; who'd got the tickets and taken me with him to hear Mr. B. Eckstine, in concert at the Mosque; who, in '49, had got tickets for us to the Miss Sepia America Beauty Contest at Laurel Garden. It was Mendy who, some three or four times, took me to watch, broadcasting in the flesh, Bill Cook, the smooth, late-night Negro disc jockey of the Jersey station WAAT. *Musical Caravan*, Bill Cook's show, I ordinarily listened to in my darkened bedroom on Saturday nights. The opening theme was Ellington's "Caravan," very exotic, very sophisticated, Afro-Oriental rhythms, a belly-dancing beat—just by itself it was worth tuning in for.[63]

What Roth is enunciating here is a certain fascination that black culture had for the Jewish youth of his generation.

What black music on the radio did for Roth and his friends, the "Lux Radio Theater" did for Esther Blaustein. She remembers sleeping on a cot in the living room, listening, as her mother ironed, to Cecil B. de Mille's introduction, followed by a movie adapted for radio. She probably never found out the ending to half the movies she heard, because, more often than not, the muffled radio voices lulled her to sleep.[64] For others it was the soap operas—Yiddish, *a la* WEVD (ever "the station that speaks your language") for the immigrant generation, and "My True Story" and "Whispering Streets" for those who were more Americanized.

Burlesque, especially at the Empire Theatre on Washington Street, was another favorite pastime. While this may conjure up thoughts of strippers and peep shows in the minds of contemporary readers, the offerings were quite tame by today's standards. Patrons saw a woman cavorting in a g-string, but it was more slapstick or vaudeville and the audience was a mixed one. In fact, according to Arthur Bernstein, who was, for a time, the "official" physician for Minsky's Burlesque House, a good number of the performers were college students who viewed the job as a necessary evil to help pay their tuition expenses.[65]

Best of all, perhaps, were the movies, double features, of course. The Rivoli, the Ironbound, Olympia, Cameo, Park, Hawthorne, Roosevelt, Elwood, and so on. Each neighborhood had its favorites. The names fairly sing in the hearts of those who went there as they bask in the remembered glow of their innocence and their carefree lives. A nickel or a dime would buy entrance to a double feature, perhaps a Tom Mix western, a Charlie Chaplin comedy, a Ginger Rogers-Fred Astaire musical, or a feature film staring Mickey Rooney. Often the children saw a serial, in addition to the feature films. As Vera Verosub observed:

> Each week we saw one chapter and this would stir up our curiosity and encourage us to come back the following week. The serials seemed to run forever. I can't remember when they finally ended. Some of our favorites were: "The Perils of Pauline," "Buck Rogers in the 25th Century," and "The Adventures of Flash Gordon."[66]

There was a certain excitement created by the need to wait a week for the next installment. As Elsie Feldman described it: "If you went one week and saw the woman tied up on the tracks, you'd have to wait until next week to find out *how* they got her off the tracks."[67] This was, of course, the pre-TV days. Later on, these serials became standard TV fare and when that happened, the ability to watch in the comfort of one's home, was simply another factor in the shift from a communal to a more privatized culture.

Social Life

Dating was an important part of social life in Newark. In the 1920s and 1930s, couples often met under the clock by Bamberger's. From there it was off to a dance at a nearby temple, or to the Meadowbrook in Cedar Grove, or a ride to Asbury Park where they could listen to music. The entertainment ranged from ballroom dancing and Benny Goodman to forays into black nightclubs. Afterwards, there would be dinner at a nice restaurant or a trip to the Sweet Shoppe or Grunings. Life was simpler then—there were no condom distribution programs and teenage pregnancies were far less common, though by no means unheard of. Emblematic of the times was the Clean Teen club, known as such because only milk shakes were served there.

Esther Blaustein writes about her dating adventures, giving the reader a clear sense of a time long since forgotten and rather unfamiliar to today's youth. Imagine a young man of, say, sixteen, saying to his girlfriend, after a few dates: "Do you think we know each other well enough for you to let me kiss you good-night?" Her response:

> I nodded and closed my eyes.
> He put his lips on mine. And then took them off . . .This was it? This is what made bells ring and cameras fade out in movies? This was what was described in books as "moving" and "arousing?" From doing this too much a girl could get into trouble?[68]

But this was what life was about in those days—dances, music and being beautiful and popular. There were, however, apprehensions and fears, not necessarily misplaced, that lent a certain adventure to all dating experiences, and to deal with them there were advice columns:

> As I had learned, from the advice column on the features page of the *Newark Star-Ledger*, necking was from the neck up and O.K., as long as it wasn't your first date and you liked the guy. "Petting" was from the neck down and could lead you into all sorts of trouble. It could make a girl lose control and "go all the way," possibly resulting in pregnancy.[69]

Naturally, such practices and attitudes varied greatly within the community, depending on which social circle one belonged to. There were "fast" crowds and not so fast crowds, losers, cool kids, prudes, and sluts. One group that had its own difficulties in the Newark social scene was the Orthodox. The community was small and young people were often forced to travel to New York, where the selection was wider.

Intermarriage was certainly not a problem from the 1920s through the 1950s by comparison with today's times. The number of interfaith marriages was very low. In fact, it was so unusual that one more

ecumenically minded resident of South Orange felt obliged to write a
note for the benefit of her daughter's girlfriends, saying she was:
"permitted to date anybody she wants to who is of fine character."
Nevertheless, Jewish leaders were concerned and the Jewish newspapers occasionally carried editorials on the subject.[70] A sociological
study of Jewish social life in the late 1940s and early 1950s, reported
that the incidence of intermarriage was limited to a small segment of
the population. Efforts to combat it consisted, in the main, of sponsoring a variety of programs under Jewish auspices so that the young
could meet and socialize. The problem was that Jews living in the
suburbs wanted to be accepted by their gentile neighbors. And so, to
counteract this, the same rabbis who counseled against interfaith marriage, participated in interreligious programs at the clergy level and
also at the lay level, where people visited churches and synagogues.
Deciding when to meet, when not to, and under what conditions, was
not an easy challenge for the Jewish leadership of those days.

Weddings in the first half of the twentieth century ran the gamut—
from fancy affairs at Newark's leading clubs and hotels to "home
weddings" where the party was held in the apartment of a relative who
had enough room for the entire family. Arnold Mirsky remembers his
wedding as if it were yesterday and it's not hard to see why:

> We were married in December of 1947. The record snowstorm was on December
> 26 and we were married the next day. It was at Steiner's on Clinton Avenue and
> 13th Street and we still have the pictures of the snow piled up all around. There was
> only one person who did not make it to the wedding. He had to come from way out
> in Smithtown, Long Island. We were supposed to go to Grossinger's for our
> honeymoon. But they would not take you there [due to the inclement weather]. . . . So
> we had a reservation at the Hotel Taft in New York City from our wedding until
> January 2.[71]

Benefits, balls, and parties were yet another outlet for Newarkers.
These could range from a *landsmanshaft* dinner in a synagogue social
hall, to the annual Krueger Ball in Krueger Auditorium, to a seven
course banquet at the Robert Treat Hotel on Park Place, the "in" hotel
in Newark's heyday. Dressing up in the 1920s and 1930s often meant
a black tuxedo with satin lapels and pearl cufflinks for men, while
women might wear a multilayered chiffon dress, with blue velvet, and
a matching ostrich feather protruding at a jaunty angle from a velvet
headband.[72] The following description of the setting at a 1921 B'nai
Brith ball, is fairly representative:

The Ezekiel Lodge dance at the Robert Treat on election night was a gala affair of dazzling beauty. Everything from the stimulating music of Yerke's orchestra, which chairman Milton Greenbaum had hired for the occasion, to the volumes of carefree noise produced by the noisemaking souvenirs which were distributed—everything was one huge, brilliant success . . ..The ballroom of the Robert Treat was lighted resplendently and decorated with draped American flags. The mirrors which flanked the walls reflected the images of the 300 dancing couples who came to participate in this first one of the season's affairs . . ..By 9 o'clock the ballroom was already crowded and until midnight new arrivals kept coming. The spirit was one of a huge family affair.[73]

The mood captured in this vignette is buoyant. The account is one of a clearly well-heeled stratum of Newark Jewry which busies itself in making the rounds of Newark parties and where members of the group know one another well.

But the center of social life for such people was not occasional social events, important as they were. It was the country club, where one could golf, play tennis, swim, eat in a well-appointed dining room, have weddings and other parties, that became an important part of the overall community. Here Jews, excluded from Christian clubs, created their own pecking order of who was acceptable and who was not. Exclusion of Jews existed from early on and continued for many decades. Some may remember the flap that ensued when it was publicly disclosed that former President Richard Nixon belonged to the Baltusrol Country Club in New Jersey, a club that barred Jews. In the early part of the century, however, no fuss was made regarding even blatant discrimination. It was simply a fact of life.

One of the premier Jewish country clubs came into existence because of an act of prejudice. It seems that Abe Dimond and Louis Bamberger paid a call on the president of the Essex Fells Country Club. They wanted to play golf but were told, politely, "We don't take Jews." Angered, they decided to found their own club, Mountain Ridge, persuading many of the old Progress Club members, men like Felix Fuld, to switch their allegiance to Mountain Ridge.

Paradoxically, the new institution's members, all German Jews, also displayed bias—against Eastern European Jews, a practice which lasted at least through the 1950s, with a few exceptions here and there. The response of the East Europeans was to establish their own place, the Green Brook Country Club. Eventually, a third club followed, Crestmont, and then a fourth, in Livingston, known as Cedar Hill. At one time, a popular joke about these clubs, with a bit of truth, went like this: "Mountain Ridge is old money, Green Brook, new money, Crestmont, hot money, and Cedar Hill, no money."

At one time, Mountain Ridge had a 200–person waiting list, despite a nonrefundable initiation fee. Prejudice cannot be justified on any grounds. Nevertheless, people often feel most comfortable with others of similar background because they have more in common with them. The following comments by a long-time member of Mountain Ridge pretty well sums up the attitudes that prevailed:

> There are no non-Jewish members that I know of but there have been in the past. Basically, you're proposed by other people and it's really a problem if you're accepted and you don't know the people. You sit here, you don't get a golf game; you don't get a tennis game. You're not really absorbed into the community, so to speak. Therefore, we require that if you want to sponsor someone who's new to the community, that you invite them to your home, that you have them meet members informally before they apply for membership. It's a good policy because we've had some members who just didn't fit in. It's not the warmest place in the world.[74]

Fair enough, but there are clearly segments of the population who would never be considered for membership in Mountain Ridge. Despite such snobbishness, the Club is certainly given its due by non-members who respect its power and influence. As one former Federation president put it: "They're elitist, more than they have a right to be. On the other hand, they give $4,000,000 a year to the Campaign; that's not chopped liver."

The average Jewish resident of Newark could clearly not afford a country club membership and had to look elsewhere for leisure-time pursuits, one of which was sports. The Y, with its pool, gymnastics facilities, and basketball court provided ample opportunities for such activities, but sports occupied a central place in the daily lives of most Newarkers where they lived. Different games were popular in different eras and even in different neighborhoods. Perennial favorites, many of them well-known in American cities everywhere, included jump rope, hopscotch, punch ball (usually with a Spaldeen), immies, or marbles, "off the wall," stoop-ball, boxball, and handball, both Chinese and American. In fact, Newark native, Sam Wolf, whose son, Carl, owns Alpine Lace Brands, was a champion handball player. He won about twenty-five state championships between 1940 and 1960 and was voted the greatest handball player in New Jersey of all time, by his peers.

Growing up poor, children learned how to improvise, fashioning bats from broomsticks and cubes of sugar with penciled-in dots on each side for dice. In the winter it was snowball fights and sledding, perhaps on a Flexible Flyer. The flavor of street games in those days is well-captured by Esther Blaustein:

> Against the brick walls of the houses you could play lots of games—pitching pennies, flipping trading cards (if they had not been taken away by some teacher who said they spread disease), or ball games like Russia and Asses Up. In Russia you threw the ball against the building. While it was up there you clapped, turned around, or performed another of the prescribed tasks for one-sy, two-sy, and all the way up eight-sy. Asses Up was the way you had to lean against the building if you hadn't caught the ball without a bounce. Then the winner had a chance to catch the ball off you.[75]

As for spectator sports, these ran the gamut, from motorcycle and bicycle races at Laurel Garden, to wrestling and boxing, also at Laurel Gardens and at the Velodrome, with baseball and football in between. Thousands of Newarkers remember with great fondness watching the International League Newark Bears play baseball at Bears Stadium. As a top Yankee farm team, the Bears often featured name players who were either on the way up or on the way down. Some of the famous ones were Ty Cobb, Tris Speaker, Eddie Collins, and Walter Johnson.

When it came to players, Moe Berg, who was Jewish, was Newark's answer to Yogi Berra, from nearby Montclair. Berg played in the majors for fourteen years and was also known as a brilliant, if somewhat eccentric, intellectual. He was one of only a very few Jews to play professional baseball and, as such, he experienced a good deal of anti-Semitism:

> "The people on the ball club didn't like him," says Billy Werber. "He wasn't of their stripe. He was Jewish and people were less tolerant of that then." Pitcher Herb Hash says he had little to do with Berg, explaining, "The Jewboys didn't associate with us as much as with their own kind." At six foot one and 200 pounds, Berg was a large man and not one to trifle with. If Red Sox members were casting anti-Semitic aspersions his way, they were probably doing so out of his hearing.[76]

Besides baseball, the Newark area also had track meets, horse racing, golf, ice skating, and tennis. One of the top tennis players from Newark, Dick Savitt, was Jewish. But it was probably boxing that most captured the Jewish imagination. As an oppressed minority, one often scorned as cowardly, especially in the pre-State of Israel days,

Jews loved their boxing champions, for they could derive vicarious pleasure whenever one of their own emerged victorious over a gentile opponent. Thus, Jews thronged to the local arenas to watch coreligionists like Barney Ross, Benny Leonard, Slapsie Maxie Rosenbloom, or Allie Stoltz, a native Newarker, fight. It was strange to conceive of Jews as fighters, but wonderful at the same time: As Philip Roth put it,

> boxing was, a strange deviation from the norm and interesting largely for that reason: in the world whose values first formed me, unrestrained physical aggression was considered contemptible everywhere else. I could no more smash a nose with a fist than fire a pistol into someone's heart. And what imposed this restraint, if not on Slapsie Maxie Rosenbloom, then on me, was my being Jewish. In my scheme of things, Slapsie Maxie was a more miraculous Jewish phenomenon by far than Dr. Albert Einstein.[77]

Another popular recreational pastime was to visit New York City. There they could see a show or film at the Roxy, Mayfair, Paramount, and Radio City Music Hall, which could be followed by ice-skating, the circus, or a ride atop a double-decker bus. For adults and even youngsters, there was the Yiddish theater, where they could see Jacob Adler star in *Elischa*, combined, perhaps, with a meal at Rappaport's Dairy. And there was always Coney Island. Parents would rent canvas sling chairs and carry them to the beach. Some rented rooms for the summers; others, who were better off, stayed in beach houses built on stilts in the sand.

For those desirous of being closer to home, there were trips to nearby farms where the family could swim in a pond, enjoy a picnic, and ride a horse. Everything is relative and for New Yorkers, West Orange was the sticks. Vacationers would stay at the Green and Goldman Hotels and stroll down Pleasant Valley Way. Eventually, as the area was built up, Green's became a senior citizens' residence, while Goldman's was converted into a catering hall.

For most Newarkers the major resort area was the Jersey shore and its beach communities, and the ads in the Jewish newspapers reflected that choice. The groups that opted for each community were representative of New Jersey's ethnic mosaic. Bradley Beach was perhaps the most popular among Jewish Newarkers of modest means, especially in the 1930s and 1940s. The homes were smaller and designed primarily for summer use. For the upwardly mobile, communities were forever becoming *declasse* and replaced by new "in" places. Thus, Long Branch, especially the West End, would be the place to go to, only to be replaced after a few seasons, by Deal. Asbury Park was another popular destination and, in the Northern section, year-round residents often rented out their spacious homes for the summer. Some places, like Elberon, were favored by New Yorkers, just as New Jerseyans preferred Bradley Beach. In the beginning, the nicer areas were more likely to have German Jews, but eventually, economics became the determining factor, not social background.

Other groups operated under the same stratification system. The working-class Irish gravitated to Avon, referred to as the "Irish Riviera," while their wealthier "Our Crowd type" counterparts summered in nearby Spring Lake. Long Branch was generally Italian, and Belmar was a mix, mostly Italians and Jews. Of course, there were exceptions to these patterns. One gated town, Ocean Grove, was completely owned by the local Methodist church, which offered ninety-nine-year leases, but sold nothing, thus maintaining control over those who lived there. And there was discrimination in many places. Communities like Asbury Park had separate swimming areas for blacks and residents thought nothing of it as they walked along the boardwalk dressed in straw hats, or lay on the beach.

What was it like though, in terms of daily life, for those who vacationed there? In, *The Facts*, Philip Roth gives us a glimpse, depicting Bradley Beach as:

> the very modest little vacation resort where we and hundreds of other lower-middle-class Jews from humid, mosquito-ridden north Jersey cities rented rooms or shared small bungalows for several weeks during the summer. It was paradise for me, even though we lived three in a room, and four when my father drove down the old Cheesequake highway to see us on weekends or to stay for his two-week vacation. In all of my intensely secure and protected childhood, I don't think I ever felt more exuberantly snug than I did in those mildly anarchic rooming houses, where—inevitably with more strain than valor—some ten or twelve women tried to share the shelves of a single large icebox, and to cook side by side, in a crowded communal kitchen, for children, visiting husbands, and elderly parents.[78]

Roth also writes of anti-Semitic incidents involving attacks by boys from neighboring Neptune, but these seemed to be far more the exception than the rule. More typical in the memories of those who went there was the view, at least among the youth, of these communities as the locale for a variety of "coming-of-age" experiences. As Benjamin Kluger recalled with perhaps some degree of hyperbole:

Bradley Beach was the St. Tropez of Newark's Jewish flaming youth. It was a weekly event in the summer, racing down the Cheesequake to begin the weekend in a car packed with friends . . ..After hurriedly renting a room, we baked on the beach all day. Then began the frantic quest for a date for the evening (not to have a date when night fell in Bradley Beach was akin to walking about with a form of leprosy.) The lucky ones, dressed to the nines, their faces flaming with sunlight, were off to the Hotel Scarborough in Long Branch or the Berkeley-Carteret in Asbury Park to dance cheek to cheek to "Stardust," "Dancing in the Dark" and "I'll See You in my Dreams." Late in the evening everyone "walked the boards" in Bradley or danced in the little casino that stood over the pounding surf.[79]

Not far from the shore was the Jewish community of Lakewood, with its year-round hotels—the Belmont, Majestic, and the Rose Villa. Rooms with southern exposure, dietary laws observed, sun parlors, and, to be sure, hot and cold running water in every room. Again, Roth, in *Portnoy's Complaint*, explains why one went there: "Take in the piney air all the way. This is the best air in the world, good winter piney air."[80] Over in the Morristown area, one could spend a vacation in Mount Freedom, affectionately known as Mount Friedman, by those who went there. It was close by, not too expensive, and definitely Jewish.

While New Jersey had Lakewood, Mount Freedom, and the shore, the Catskills region had its supporters too. Besides Grossinger's and the Concord, there were legions of smaller establishments, all vying for the affection of Newark's residents. In a 1935 advertisement, the Ambassador claimed to have the only sulphur swimming pool in the United States. The Commodore billed itself as "The Smart Country Club," while the Breeze Lawn in Ellenville offered "Prosperity Service at Depression Prices." Edward Koch's family so valued these vacations that it was willing to put up with a *kochalein* (bungalow) so small that it was necessary for people to eat their meals in shifts.[81]

Trends and patterns ought not to obscure the fact that people traveled to many different places for vacations. It might only be a handful of families, but for that handful, these locales represented the storehouse of memories that they were left with. One such instance, which took place in 1940, provides an interesting window on the cultural norms that predominated in those days in certain circles. In it we see the prejudices of the times as well as the steps taken to determine who "belonged":

We went away on vacations sometimes to an adult place in Maine called Bald Mountain Camp. It was in the Rangely Mountains and if you were not a German

Jew, or maybe a Hungarian Jew, or a Portuguese, you were ostracized . . ..We were "checked out." But once they found out we were German, we were invited with the Teppers, Haas, and the other German Jews. And I remember it like it was yesterday. Even as a thirteen year old, we were invited to entertain the young ladies. I can picture the maids and butlers up there.[82]

To be a part of this environment meant that one had to accept its attitudes. Yet, as the following comments bear out, such views changed over time, particularly among those born after the early 1920s, when the surge in East European immigration came to a halt as a result of the anti-immigration Johnson Acts:

"I guess, as part of my upbringing, I felt proud to be included. I don't feel that way anymore. My wife is not of German background and there's no one I have more regard for. I might tease her about her background sometimes, but it's meant as a joke.[83]

As they reflect on their childhood, the thoughts of many Newarkers turn, inevitably, to that most formative of experiences, summer camp. It is there that they have some of their fondest memories and it is there that they formed lasting friendships, both with children from their communities and those from far away places. Because camp is a total environment, the two months, or even four weeks spent there, is often more significant than the ten months spent in school.

Many children attended day camps and the most popular were those run by the Y. Both the Y facilities and nearby parks were used for activities. At the other end of the age spectrum, there was also the New Jersey Y camp for senior citizens. The crown jewels, however, of the New Jersey Y camp system, the ones which thousands of youngsters attended through the years, were the overnight camps—Cedar Lake and Nah-Jee-Wah. The camps were truly egalitarian, attracting campers from both wealthy and poor homes. They had a Jewish emphasis and many of those attending came from the Newark area. Moreover, several presidents of the camps, Clarence Reisen, Morris Reisen, and "Mike" Stavitsky, were from Newark.[84] The camps, now located in Milford, Pennsylvania, are still thriving today—Cedar Lake hosted 642 campers in 1997, and Nah-Jee-Wah, 559.[85]

Through the years, the Jewish community supported camps for children with special problems. For example, in the 1930s, the Conference of Jewish Charities sponsored the Personal Service Association Camp in Westwood, New Jersey for anemic girls. Today, there are other camps such as Round Lake Camp in Lake Como, Pennsylvania, for youngsters with learning disabilities. In 1996, Camp Nesher, for Orthodox children, opened, and, in its second year of operation, enrolled 321 youngsters.

Besides the New Jersey Y camps, there were numerous private camps, a good number of which emphasized the Newark connection. An ad in the February 12, 1926 issue of the *Jewish Chronicle*, for Camp Monterey, for boys, and Camp Owaissa, for girls, exhorted readers to, "Entrust your Children with a Newark Educator." Another Newark based outfit was Camp Weequahic, whose ads informed parents that sports activities were under the supervision of Art Lustig, a Newark school teacher, who by 1954 had logged twenty-nine years in the system. Clearly, the Newark connection was seen as a plus that inspired confidence in the camp's ability to deliver.

Not all camps that sought to attract Newarkers had such a connection or relied on one. Camp Arcady's main claim to fame in the 1950s was its baseball program, under the direction of baseball manager, Leo "The Lip" Durocher. There were small camps that emphasized personal attention. One such place was Weingart's Summer School for Boys, which operated in the early part of the twentieth century in Highmount, New York and which averaged about fifty kids a season. Among those who went were Philip Schotland and Gabriel Rich, both prominent leaders of Newark's Jewish community. Other popular camps, mostly in Maine and New Hampshire, were Winnebago, Androscoggin, Tripp Lake, Cobbosee, Kennebec, Fernwood, Wildwood, Wigwam, and Tapawingo.

The private camps had a certain snob appeal and catered to the well-to-do among Newark's Jewry. An exception to that rule was Camp Mahkeenac, located in Stockbridge, Massachusetts, and operated by Joseph Kruger, a Newark resident. His account gives us the flavor of what was involved in managing a camp and the issues that camp owners were typically concerned with. It is evident that Kruger had his own way of looking at things and was eager to put his stamp on the place that he ran:

I started in 1929 with fifteen boys. My fee was $300.00 a season, but when the Depression came, I dropped it to $200.00. The clientele was all Jewish and I had a service every Friday night until the 1960s when the war [in Vietnam] was going on and people were rebelling. By then I had about 300 kids. We drew from Manhattan, New Jersey, Long Island, and Westchester. It went by word of mouth. The main thing is to have a terrific staff and I knew every boy in the camp. I ran a highly personalized operation. If a kid was homesick, or there was a conflict, they came to see me. I had no colorwar because I didn't want competitiveness and awards. I took pride in that we took in kids who weren't necessarily rich. A lot of them came from Clinton Hill. I had Hannoch's kids and others with me and I never recognized them as part of the German-Jewish community.[86]

Finally, there were camps that were private but Jewishly oriented. A good example was Camp Modin in Maine, which numerous Newarkers attended over the years. The camp was both kosher and Zionistic, and featured religious services as well as Jewish intellectual programs. The great Jewish rabbi and philosopher, Milton Steinberg, was a counselor there and the following account by a Newark camper who requested anonymity, demonstrates just how intense the camp experience could be, especially if Steinberg was your leader:

> My counselor, Milton Steinberg, used to take walks with me and another counselor, who later became head of the Canadian Banking System, on Saturday afternoons, dressed in our white shirts and trousers, following Sabbath services. My experience led me to lay *tefilin* after I returned from Maine, something my father never did, but this was a time of questioning for me. Away from the camp influence, I soon ceased the practice. By my second summer, I was challenging Steinberg and others for answers. It wasn't too long before I reluctantly found that I could no longer accept the religious teachings that had meant so much to my family and to my friends and counselors at Camp Modin.

Needless to say, for others the influence of camp might well have been more lasting.

Notwithstanding these sometimes glowing accounts of camp life, it must be recognized that for many of Newark's urban Jewish poor, camp was simply out of reach. They could not afford it and their children spent the summers playing in the streets, sometimes getting into mischief but otherwise enjoying themselves in the way youngsters do when in the company of one another. Moreover, even for those whose parents had the money, camp was not always a positive experience simply because camp isn't for everyone. The following recollection probably resonates with at least several readers:

> I went to Echo Lake, which I hated and then to Rose Lake, around Honesdale, Pennsylvania. I just was not meant for camp. I wasn't good at sports, I started late, when I was twelve. I went for two years because I was afraid to tell my parents I hated it. Because it was expensive and I knew my parents had sacrificed to send me there.[87]

The Larger Context

As we have seen, Jews had a highly variegated social life. There were movies, games, clubs, organizations, beaches, resorts, parks, and many other forms of recreation. Of necessity, these activities often involved interacting with Jews of different backgrounds and with non-Jews. In some cases, this happened quite easily and frequently, and in others, relations were strained or guarded.

Contacts between Eastern European and German Jews were difficult in the beginning. The German Jews looked upon their Polish and Russian coreligionists with thinly disguised contempt, seeing them as uncouth and uneducated. Their language, Yiddish, was viewed as nothing more than "jargon," a bastardized form of German, and their impoverished circumstances made the German Jews want to distance themselves lest they be lumped together with them by the larger society. Newark's German Jews were no different in their attitudes than their brethren elsewhere. The same scenario of distaste and initial rejection played itself out in cities across the continent.

In the end, however, German Jews arrived at an accommodation and this was so for several reasons. First, they recognized, however belatedly, that they had a responsibility to their fellow Jews. Moreover, they came to understand that, in the Christian world, both groups tended to be seen as one and that helping them improve their lives would ultimately benefit all Jews. Finally, interdependent relationships based on mutual interests had developed that brought the groups closer together. East European Jews shopped in German-Jewish owned stores, they saw German-Jewish doctors and attorneys, they worked in factories owned by German Jews, and so on and so forth. Conversely, Eastern European Jewry exerted its own influence by familiarizing and making more acceptable to German Jewry Jewish customs and traditions, as well as Zionism. In the end, German Jewish identity was considerably enhanced by the newer immigrants, who effected a permanent change in the character of American Jewish life.[88]

In Newark, the relationships between these two communities were even more tense than elsewhere because Newark was small enough for people to know each other. For example, the German-Jewish and East European synagogues were located within walking distance of each other. Newark was small enough for youngsters to know which summer camps were for German Jews and which were not, just as their parents knew which country clubs accepted Eastern Europeans and which did not. As a result, when things worked out, people noticed, just as they did when issues could not be resolved. In short, the sting of discrimination hurt all the more when those who discriminated were known by name. Interviews with Newarkers leave no doubt that it was widespread. As Bud Davis recalled:

> My grandmother would ask me the last names of the people I went out with. They wouldn't say anything but it was clear they disapproved. The German Jews sometimes referred to the East Europeans as kikes.[89]

Nevertheless, since Newark was typical in this respect, prejudice against the East Europeans began to diminish in the 1920s and by the 1940s, with the rise of Hitler, it had become a minor factor in Newark's Jewish life, though vestiges of it remained.

One of the rules of assimilation is that the more similar groups are in terms of their culture the less prejudice there is between them. Similarly, the greater the incoming group's willingness to adapt to the dominant culture, the less discrimination it is apt to face. Finally, the smaller the incoming group is in terms of size, the more likely it is to be accepted by those who preceded them.

All of these characteristics were true of German Jewry in the mid-nineteenth century. Culturally, in terms of language, occupation, and general outlook, its members closely resembled German Christians. In fact, German Christians were generally known to look askance at the Irish, not the Jews. The Jews, incidentally, called the Irish *Beytzimers*, (from the Hebrew word *Beytzim*, for eggs, which, in German are called *Eier*, read: Irish). The Jews were certainly eager to adapt and be accepted. They ate together with gentiles, sat in parks and talked, and generally socialized with each other. And the German Christians did not see them as a threat because the number of Jews who came was not particularly large, relatively speaking.

When Newark began to grow by leaps and bounds, near the end of the nineteenth century, this changed. Poles, Russians, Greeks, Italians, and other Europeans began arriving in such large numbers that the small town feeling of Newark was lost and could, perforce, be limited only to members of one group, if that much. In addition, the pressures of urban living and the need to work long hours, often in impersonal environments, made socializing less likely. Though one might meet gentiles at work, this was less true of the neighborhoods in which most

Jews lived, like Weequahic, which were overwhelmingly Jewish. Naturally, such isolation was not the case in neighborhoods that were ethnically mixed. For example, the area around Bergen Street was mostly Italian in the late 1930s, and so the few Jews who lived there were socially integrated with them. Jerry Lehman even attended catechism classes for a short time with his Catholic playmates, just to be sociable.[90] In the same vein, Italians and Jews were socially friendly in the Clifton Avenue area, near Branch Brook Park, on Newark's North Side.[91] The same held true for Jews in the Down Neck section.

When it came to relationships with blacks, common cause was often made in terms of fighting the larger enemy of bigotry. Socially, however, friendships between blacks and Jews were unusual. Though Jews might voyeuristically enjoy black entertainment, becoming close personally was a different story. As Edward Koch, who attended integrated schools, noted in his autobiography: "I shared a desk one year with a black student . . .and the two of us were friends in school, but not out of school, which was more or less the order of the day."[92] Jerry Blum's reminiscences of Newark life in the thirties and forties, provide a fairly accurate picture of where blacks stood in the eyes of most whites:

> Black people in my day were sort of invisible. You didn't see them where we lived [Maplewood]. They were mostly in the Central Ward. They came out in the daytime and went to their jobs—housecleaning. Their opportunities were close to zero. Even when they got a good education, it didn't do much good. There were two black students in my high school class. Blacks never went to the major movie theaters.[93]

Small wonder, then, that there was no reservoir of good will to draw upon when the symbolic day of reckoning, the riots, came. The only rationale blacks could have for not looting and burning Jewish-owned stores was the way in which Jewish storeowners treated them, but certainly not (with rare exceptions) whether or not they were friends with them.

It was when Jews began the move to the suburbs that the encounters with gentiles became more common. Jews sent their children to public schools, joined the PTA and other crossover organizations. In general, they were accepted, but only after they had been living in these communities for some time. In the beginning they faced the usual resentment directed at perceived "outsiders," or as people who "want to run the town." In some cases pragmatic considerations were involved. After all, was it surprising that a local minister wanted more of his co-religionists to move into the community rather than Jews? Despite such apprehensions, Jews and Christians used the playing field of the suburbs, so to speak, to become familiar with each other's cultures, customs, and values. This was as true of, say Caldwell, Verona, and Millburn, as it was in the sociologist Marshall Sklare's famous study of a Chicago suburb.[94] One study of gentile-Jewish relations in Newark's suburbs found that 62.3 percent of the Jewish respondents had a "just neighborly" relationship with non-Jews and 12.7 percent had a very close friendship with them.[95]

In the beginning, Jews were viewed as newcomers who would both have to adjust and learn the limits of tolerance, as can be seen from the following encounter:

> We were the second Jewish family in Short Hills. . . . We had one very interesting visit shortly after we moved in and the kids started to go to the grammar schools. The minister of the Anglican church in Millburn came to visit us. It was very cordial and polite and he welcomed us to Short Hills. He said to us: "I think you ought to know one thing. Your children will have no trouble with our children at this point because they are all young. They will be invited to the parties and mingle with our children and there will be no differential. However, when they get to be sixteen, they will find they are suddenly no longer welcome at the parties of those who are not Jewish. Therefore, you have to be prepared for that." That did not really happen because, by the time they were fourteen, there were enough Jews up there so that it did not matter. When we had a party, the non-Jews came just as well as the Jews. They were welcomed at our house and our kids were welcomed at their houses. By that time the barriers had been broken [though] there were still some groups that were hard and fast in their own little groups.[96]

Relations between Jews and gentiles improved over time for two reasons. First, both groups became accustomed to living with each other and developed a sense of what principles and values were important to each community. Second, as more Jews entered the suburbs it became necessary for Christians to take into account both their presence and their priorities even if they did not like them. This held true for local politicians, school principals and teachers, as well as local merchants. The politicians wanted votes, school administrators wanted support for their policies, teachers did not want to be attacked by parents, and merchants wanted business. It was as simple as that.

In the days before Jews made the trek to the suburbs, anti-Semitism was a part of life in Newark but it was by no means a constant. Very few Jews grew up in Newark without encountering it, but for most, it usually took the form of an occasional insult hurled at them by other children as they walked to school or temple. Ruth Fien remembers being called a "Christ killer" as a rock hit her in the head, splitting it open, but she had no idea, as a seven year old, what the epithet meant. That was her only exposure ever to anti-Semitism. Others, like Hannah Litzky, were even more oblivious:

> In 1936, I and my playmates used to sing:
> "Hi Ho, Hi Ho
> We joined the CIO
> We pay our dues
> To feed the Jews,
> Hi Ho, Hi Ho."
> I didn't realize it was directed at me. But nobody ever beat me up because I was Jewish. And my school was not Jewish.[97]

Myron Katz knew very well the meaning of slurs directed at Jews and he had it out, physically, with his Irish tormentor, one Dickie Tate.[98] Dore Schary had similar run-ins with local toughs, growing up in the Third Ward. While there was friction between the Jews and their Irish and Italian counterparts, it seems that the Poles, who lived in the area around Wickliffe Street, were the worst offenders. To protect themselves, the Jews formed a self-defense group called, the Happy Ramblers. Their headquarters was the Amsterdam Moving Company, where many of them worked. Their ranks included cab drivers, "prelim" prizefighters, and young college students. Their favorite technique, when called upon for help, was to approach an unsuspecting bully and ask him pleasantly: "Russki Polski?" If the answer was yes, a fist landed in the offender's face.[99]

One area that was notorious for anti-Jewish sentiment was Irvington, where there was an active Bund organization. Jews were vociferous in their opposition to it and there are many stories of bat-wielding Jews, from Longy Zwillman and his gang, to the Edis brothers, Herbie and Joe, breaking up Bund meetings and rallies. The Bund's power declined considerably once their leader, Fritz Kuhn, was arrested by the FBI and the patriotism engendered by the outbreak of World War II made support for Nazi organizations highly unpopular everywhere.

At the same time, most Germans, who had arrived in Newark in the 1830s, did not share such sentiments. As Americans, they opposed the Nazis, though there were surely exceptions. The *Jewish Chronicle*, in a 1935 editorial, asserted that most German Americans in Newark were people "of integrity."[100] And while the Jewish community was certainly concerned about anti-Semitism in Germany, the prevailing view in the mid-1930s was that conditions were even worse for Poland's Jews.[101] Nonetheless, the local American Jewish Congress lodged a formal protest when the city of Newark appropriated $200.00 to send a Newark contestant to the 1936 Olympic Games in Germany.[102]

Newark did have periodic outbreaks of anti-Semitism, just like other American cities, but these were of limited duration and infrequent. Generally, these manifested themselves in vandalism directed against synagogues and other Jewish institutions. Sometimes Jews retaliated on their own, confronting the attackers and, at other times, they sought police protection.[103] Generally, however, these attacks were the exception, not the rule.

Looking at how Newark's Jews related to the world around them, mention must be made of organized crime. Given the fact that so many of Newark's Jews grew up in the rough and tumble neighborhoods of the inner city, it is not surprising that gangs, rackets, and gangsters were familiar to them. Not unexpectedly, there was a tendency on the part of many, especially the young, to romanticize the world of crime and to conveniently ignore its more sordid aspects. Support for such views was easy to find since Newarkers had gone through the era of Prohibition, when flouting the law had wide support among the general population. Gambling might have been illegal but many socially prominent people were regulars at the gaming tables and at the speakeasies that flourished during Prohibition. On the local level, crap games, numbers running, and bootlegging, were part of the fabric of daily social life. Philip Roth, for example, participated at the age of thirteen in a football pool run by Longy Zwillman's mob.[104]

The Depression years, with times so hard for people, gave ample reasons for those who wanted to rationalize their illegal acts. After all, they had families to feed. More important, in terms of attitudes toward crime, Longy and his men stepped into an economic vacuum, providing food, work, and small amounts of money to the needy. The vacuum existed, in part, because the Jewish community did not, in those days, have as extensive a resource system for the needy as it does today. This Robin Hood-like penchant for charity was real—Longy gave generously to synagogues, especially the Brisker Shul, where he was a member, and to local Catholic soup kitchens. People also went to him on their own when they needed coal or food.[105] Consequently, it became part of his persona.

Another part of that persona was Longy's interest in the sorts of things not commonly associated with mob figures, namely, literature and the arts. Some attributed it to the fact that he was Jewish. Arthur Bernstein was Zwillman's personal physician and knew him very well. Bernstein remembered how:

> When I made these house calls, we'd sit and talk and he was a very interesting guy. He'd read a lot and had had tutors after he went into business who taught him history, geography, and English. He had these tutors because he was Jewish. He didn't want to sound like an ignorant person. He was meeting candidates for office who came to him for money. So he decided that he needed to be polished. He was very knowledgeable and brilliant. I used to feel that when I listened to him I could really learn something.[106]

Mark Stuart, author of a biography of Zwillman, expressed it in similar terms that not only support this assessment but also present him as a charismatic figure:

> He was proud, brave, handsome, dignified, cool, polished—and ruthless, tough, unforgiving, mesmerized by money. Although he quit school in the eighth grade, he was well-read, interested in the arts, an opera buff.[107]

Opinions differ as to just how Zwillman died. Some believe that he was killed by fellow mobsters who were afraid that he would tell all he knew in order to escape a likely jail term for tax evasion. But most, including Bernstein, believe that his suicide was real, not faked. Some think it was because he had learned that he was seriously ill. Bernstein acknowledged that Longy was, on account of his chronic heart condition, never in good health, but his explanation for Longy's death has nothing to do with that. Given his knowledge of the man, it is perhaps fitting that Dr. Bernstein should have the last word on this colorful bit of Newark lore:

> In his tax evasion trial, Longy had ended up with a hung jury. But he was guilty of jury tampering, which is fifteen years in jail. So one day he said to me: "I have two options. The Italian mob does not trust me to be in jail 10–15 years. They're afraid I might talk, so therefore, they want to kill me. I don't want them to kill me because I don't want to have a headline: 'Lived by the Gun, Died by the Gun.' So, therefore, I have to find a way of committing suicide." He said this rationally, just like you and I are talking. I mean this man had nerves of steel. Absolutely. He did not want to be killed. He said: "I'm gonna get heavy aerial wire, which is very strong, and I'm gonna hang myself." I told him, "Longy, that's a miserable way to

die." And he said, "Well, I'm not gonna get anyone else involved. The only other way is to shoot myself and then it's also: 'Lived by the Gun, Died by the Gun.'" As far as I know, he committed suicide. I didn't see him the day he did it. The day after, I was in New York and I suddenly heard a siren and saw red lights flashing behind me. Two cops pulled alongside of me and one of them asked: "Are you Dr. Bernstein?" "Yes," I said. "They need you in West Orange. You better get there fast. Follow us." As his doctor I had to pronounce him dead. There were two detectives watching him as he hung there. I did so and it was a very unpleasant sight. I don't like to think about it.[108]

How important were Longy Zwillman and his confederates in the larger scheme of things? Not very. Of far greater historical significance for our story are the cultural, religious, educational, and social institutions built by Newark's Jewish community, their dreams, hopes, and aspirations, and their participation in the larger society. And yet, the Zwillman part of the story bears mentioning too. For one thing, it graphically demonstrates that things were not perfect in Newark, just as they are not perfect anywhere. The image of a thriving, dynamic Jewish community would simply not be complete without this part of the story. It would be too idealized and therefore, inaccurate. Moreover, it should be remembered, that, for Jewish Newarkers, having their own home-grown coterie of gangsters added life and color to their own lives. It gave them something to talk about, reminisce about. Without stories like the ones that grew up about Zwillman, life loses its flavor, its uniqueness, and its sense of adventure, in short, the part that makes life interesting.

Notes

1. Myron Katz, interview, August 5, 1996.
2. Philip Roth, *American Pastoral* (New York: Houghton Mifflin Company, 1997), 43.
3. Eliezer Schulman, interview, December 25, 1996.
4. David Mallach, interview, January 21, 1997.
5. Philip Roth, *The Facts: A Novelist's Autobiography* (New York: Farrar, Straus & Giroux, 1988), 122.
6. "Community Calendar," *Jewish News*, December 19, 1952, 7.
7. *Our Life in Our Time*, Essex County Council of Jewish Agencies, 1948. Pamphlet.
8. Jacob Goodstein, interview, March 18, 1980, Courtesy of Evelyn Goodstein; Ben Arons, interview, June 29, 1996.
9. Benjamin Kluger, "Growing Up in Newark," *Jewish News*, September 8, 1977, B1.
10. Ibid., B2.
11. Roth, "The Facts," 14.

12. Amy Lowenstein, *One Hundred Years of the "Y," 1877–1977: History and Guide for the "Y" Centennial Exhibition*, September 18 to November 28, 1977 (West Orange, New Jersey: YM-YWHA of Metropolitan New Jersey, 1977, unpaged).
13. Vera Verosub, *The Way it Was* (no publisher, 1992), 35.
14. Ibid., 37.
15. Sarah S. Kussy, *The Story of Gustav and Bella Kussy of Newark, N.J.: A Family Chronicle*, booklet (undated), 12.
16. Jerry Lehman, interview, June 27, 1996.
17. Helen Judd, in "Memoirs." Available at Jewish Historical Society of MetroWest.
18. Esther Blaustein, *When Momma was the Landlord* (New York: Harper & Row, 1972), 121.
19. "Let's Go to the Tavern," *New Jersey Business*, April 1959, 30–1.
20. Edward I. Koch, with Daniel Paisner, *Citizen Koch: An Autobiography* (New York: St. Martin's Press, 1992), 17.
21. Adele Finkel, in "Memoirs." Available at Jewish Historical Society of MetroWest.
22. Dore Schary, *For Special Occasions* (New York: Random House, 1961), 13.
23. Sarah Kussy, "The Story of Gustav & Bella Kussy," 12.
24. Jerry Lehman, interview, June 27, 1996.
25. Saul Schwarz, personal notes.
26. Amy Lowenstein, *One Hundred Years of the "Y."*
27. Manuel G. Batshaw, "'The Y Drew us Like a Magnet,'" *Jewish News*, June 14, 1957, 55.
28. Ibid.
29. Much of this discussion regarding the Y is based on Amy Lowenstein's fine piece on the subject.
30. "History of the Brith Abraham," *Jewish Chronicle*, Fifteenth Anniversary Issue, April 24, 1936, 82; "History of the Brith Sholom," *Jewish Chronicle*, Fifteenth Anniversary Issue, April 24, 1936, 88.
31. Helen P. Silver, "Newcomers Aid Each Other in Problems of Adjustment," *Jewish News*, July 21, 1950, 12.
32. Gershon Gelbart, Sylvan H. Kohn, and David Rudavsky, *The Essex Story: A History of the Jewish Community in Essex County, Newark, New Jersey*, booklet(East Orange, N.J.: Jewish Education Association, 1955), 54.
33. Ibid., 54–5.
34. Gail Schaffer, *Memoirs of an American Sabra Hebrew Teacher* (North Miami, Fla: Renaissance Booksetters, 1977), 62.
35. Sarah S. Kussy, *The Story of Gustav and Bella Kussy of Newark, N.J.: A Family Chronicle*, 15.
36. Molly Rosenberg, interview, September 26, 1996, Jewish Historical Society of MetroWest.
37. Arthur Bernstein, interview, October 27, 1994.
38. As quoted in John T. Cunningham, *Newark* (Newark, N.J.: The New Jersey Historical Society, 1988, revised ed.), 217.
39. Philip Roth, *Goodbye Columbus* (New York: Bantam Books, 1963), 25.
40. Based on personal observation.
41. John T. Cunningham and Charles F. Cummings, *Remembering Essex: A Pictorial History of Essex County, New Jersey* (Virginia Beach, Va.: The Donning Company, 1995), 160,175.
42. *Jewish Community Blue Book, Newark, New Jersey* (Newark, N.J.: Jewish Community Blue Book Publishing Company, 1924), 684–85.

43. "Bards of 'Beat' Generation 'Immature' to Rutgers Poet," *Jewish News*, October 2, 1959, 57.

44. Ibid.

45. "Ten Thousand Hear Byrd Lecture on Flight," *Jewish Chronicle*, October 31, 1930, 1.

46. "Amelia Earhart Will Lecture Y.M.H.A. Monday," *Jewish Chronicle*, January 3, 1936, 1.

47. "Anthropologist in Address to JFSA," *Jewish News*, November 28, 1947, 2; "Noted Leader to Lecture at Sharey Tefilo," *Jewish News*, May 5, 1961, 24; "Clark Will Speak Here," *Jewish News*, January 7, 1966, 2; "Howe Will Lecture in Livingston," *Jewish News*, April 2, 1965, 24.

48. "Future of World Democracy Topic of Town Hall Meeting in Mosque Wednesday Nite," *Jewish Chronicle*, October 25, 1940, 1.

49. Amy Lowenstein, *One Hundred Years of the "Y."*

50. Ibid.

51. "Mrs. Griffith, Civic Leader, Directed Music Foundation," *Jewish News*, December 16, 1960, 8.

52. "Our Young Artists are a Gifted Lot," *Jewish News*, June 14, 1957: 58.

53. Molly Rosenberg, interview, September 26, 1996, Jewish Historical Society of MetroWest. See Amy Lowenstein, *One Hundred Years of the "Y."*

54. Amy Lowenstein, *One Hundred Years of the "Y."*

55. "Eastern Capitalists and Western Farmers Clash in Newark Film," *Jewish Chronicle*, January 22, 1926, 7.

56. "'Kosher Kitty Kelly' Comes to Broad," *Jewish Chronicle*, January 22, 1926, 7.

57. Selma Weiss, in "Memoirs." Available at Jewish Historical Society of MetroWest. One Newark native, whose songs did well commercially, was Ralph Reichenthal (professional name: Ralph Rainger). Among other tunes, he was the author of "Thanks for the Memory," Bob Hope's theme song, and of "Love in Bloom," Jack Benny's theme song.

58. Barbara W. Grossman, *The Life and Times of Fanny Brice* (Bloomington: University of Indiana Press, 1991), 5, 7–8. There is some fragmentary evidence that the city of Newark also played down Brice's Newark connection. In an article on a forthcoming gala benefit performance by show business personalities for the Hebrew Orphanage and Sheltering Home, Fanny Brice appears with names like Milton Berle, Burns and Allen, Jack Benny, Jimmie Durante, Eddie Garr, Ethel Merman, and Rudy Vallee. Since the names are listed alphabetically, her name is first. Moreover, a cartoon drawing of her face accompanies the piece. Yet, no mention is made of the fact that she is the only one among the performers who lived in Newark. Did no one know? Did no one care? Did she ask the writer not to mention it? The issue is hardly earthshaking but the omission is curious. See "Prominent Headliners of Stage, Screen, Radio to Appear Here April 19," *Jewish Chronicle*, March 20, 1936, 1.

59. Ibid., 7. Brice also recalled singing and dancing for her father in his saloon on Sunday mornings when it was closed to the public. "My father would applaud and throw me a nickel or a dime." Ibid., 6. She also remembers sneaking into her mother's attic to play with toys stored there by a neighboring furniture storeowner. See Norman Katkov, *The Fabulous Fanny: The Story of Fannie Brice* (New York: Alfred A. Knopf, 1952) , 334.

60. "Rube Goldberg Sees His Own Characters Prance at Cotillion," *Jewish Chronicle*, February 24, 1922, 1.

61. Eddie Rosenthal, interview, April 2, 1994, Jewish Historical Society of

MetroWest. In those days "jive talk" had two meanings—discussions used to fool whites into thinking they agreed with them or accepted their authority, or a form of black slang used among blacks, generally teenagers, and usually made up of exaggerations or statements patently understood as false by all parties. See Thomas Kochman, "Toward an Ethnography of Black American Speech Behavior," in Norman E. Whitten, Jr. and John F. Szwed (eds.), *Afro-American Anthropology: Contemporary Perspectives* (New York: The Free Press, 1970), 145–62.

62. Philip Roth, *American Pastoral* (New York: Houghton Mifflin, 1997), 47,49.
63. Ibid., 48.
64. Esther Blaustein, *When Momma was the Landlord*, 59.
65. Arthur Bernstein, interview, January 21, 1994, Jewish Historical Society of MetroWest.
66. Vera Verosub, *The Way it Was*, 49–50.
67. Elsie Feldman, interview, October 3, 1993, Jewish Historical Society of MetroWest.
68. Blaustein, *When Momma was the Landlord*, 128.
69. Ibid., 160.
70. See, for example, Alter Kriegel, "Combatting Intermarriage," *Jewish News*, March 28, 1947, 4.
71. Arnold Mirsky, interview, October 16, 1995, Jewish Historical Society of MetroWest.
72. Verosub, *The Way it Was*, 27.
73. "B'nai Brith Ball was Gala Affair," *Jewish Chronicle*, November 11, 1921, 1.
74. Franklin Hannoch, Jr., interview, August 20, 1996.
75. Blaustein, *When Momma Was the Landlord*, 13.
76. Nicholas Dawidoff, *The Catcher was a Spy: The Mysterious Life of Moe Berg* (New York: Pantheon, 1994), 119.
77. Roth, *The Facts*, 28. Those interested in a comprehensive history of Jewish boxers, should look at Allen Bodner's, *When Boxing was a Jewish Sport* (New York: Praeger Publishers, 1997). There is quite a bit on Newark's Allie Stolz, especially on pp. 32, 42–3, 49–50, 87, and 91.
78. Roth, *The Facts*, 23–24.
79. Kluger, "Growing Up in Newark," B7.
80. Roth, *Portnoy's Complaint* (New York: Random House, 1969), 27.
81. Edward Koch, *Citizen Koch*, 18.
82. Franklin Hannoch, Jr., interview, August 20, 1996.
83. Ibid.
84. Matthew Elson, interview, September 25, 1996.
85. "JCC N.J. Y Camps Attendance Up," *MetroWest Jewish News*, August 21, 1997, 8.
86. Joseph Kruger, interview, September 20, 1996.
87. Paula Blum, interview, August 8, 1996.
88. Irving Howe, *World of Our Fathers: The Journey of the East European Jews to America and the Life they Found and Made* (New York: Harcourt, Brace & Jovanovich, 1976), 139, 155, 230; Moses Rischin, *The Promised City: New York's Jews 1870–1914* (New York: Harper Torchbooks edition, 1970), 95–111.
89. Bud Davis, interview, August 29, 1996.
90. Jerry Lehman, interview, June 27, 1996.
91. Isidor Hirschhorn, *Recollections*, unpublished, undated paper.
92. Edward Koch, *Citizen Koch*, 16.

93. Jerry Blum, interview, August 8, 1996.
94. Marshall Sklare and Joseph Greenblum, *Jewish Identity on the Suburban Frontier: A Study of Group Survival in the Open Society* (New York: Basic Books, 1967).
95. Morris R. Werb, *Jewish Suburbia: An Historical and Comparative Study of Jewish Communities in Three New Jersey Suburbs*, Ph.D. dissertation, New York University, 1959, 148.
96. Arthur Bernstein, interview, January 21, 1994, Jewish Historical Society of MetroWest.
97. Hannah Litzky, interview, March 28, 1995.
98. Myron Katz, interview, August 5, 1996.
99. Dore Schary, *For Special Occasions*, 83–89.
100. Anton Kaufman, "When Wise Counsel and Cool Heads Prevail," *Jewish Chronicle*, editorial, June 7, 1935, 1.
101. "Forgotten Jews," *Jewish Chronicle*, editorial, May 1, 1936, 4.
102. "Jews in Protest of Olympic Grant," *Newark Evening News*, July 7, 1936, 1.
103. See "Synagogue Hecklers Severely Beaten," *Jewish Chronicle*, October 11, 1940, 3; "Probe Sought in Shule Vandalism," *Newark Jewish Times*, May 7, 1943, 1; "Vandals Hit Local Cemeteries," *Jewish News*, May 23, 1958, 3; "Vandals Invade Local Cemeteries," *Jewish News*, September 5, 1958, 3.
104. Philip Roth, *The Facts*, 41.
105. Mark Stuart, *Gangster #2: Longy Zwillman, the Man Who Invented Organized Crime* (Secaucus, N.J.: Lyle Stuart, 1985), 107–09.
106. Arthur Bernstein, interview, October 27, 1994.
107. Stuart, *Gangster #2*, 15.
108. Arthur Bernstein, interview, October 27, 1994. The first physician on the scene was actually Franklin Simon, but Longy's wife insisted on having Bernstein come as well. Victor Parsonnet made a house call for his father at Longy's home, long after Longy's death, to see his wife. Even then, she lay in bed with a 45 revolver on the bedside table. Personal correspondence from Victor Parsonnet, December 29, 1997.

L. Bamberger & Co., Newark, c.1911

Essex House Hotel, Newark, c.1960

Bee Hive, Broad St., Newark, c.1910

Epstein's, Morristown, c.1928

Progress Club, Newark, c.1920

Jerome David Kern

Mayor Meyer "Doc" Ellenstein

Jerry Lewis

Dore Schary

Philip Roth

Abraham J. Dimond

Caroline (Carrie) Bamberger Fuld

Edward Koch

Felix Fuld

Louis Bamberger

Alan V. Lowenstein

Michael A. Stavitsky

Herman M. Pekarsky

Ralph Wechsler

Samuel Kessler

Sen. Frank Lautenberg

Miss Sarah Kussy

Trier Monument

INSTITUTIONS

United Jewish Federation Aidekman Campus, Whippany, 1992

Newark Beth Israel Hospital, Lyons Ave., Newark, 1928

Daughters of Israel Geriatric Center, Sterling Street Home, 1907

YM-YWHA, High St., Newark, c.1924

JCC of MetroWest, NJ, Salzman Bldg., West Orange, 1967

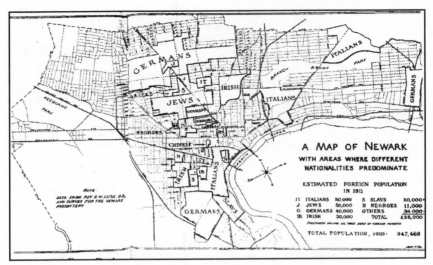

1911/Map

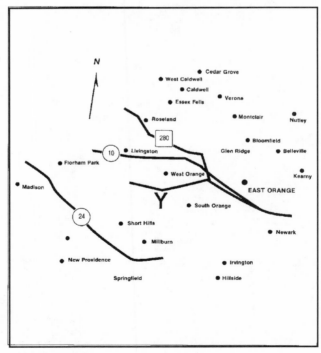

1983/Essex Map

High Street, Newark, c.1900

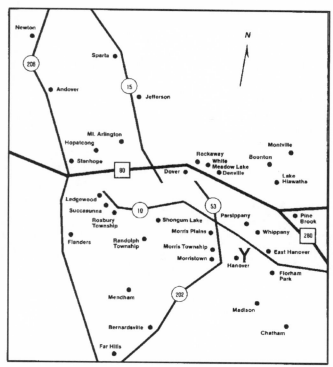

1983/Morris Map

Prince Street, Newark, c.1905

76-82 Prince Street, Newark looking N.E., c.1950

South Orange & Springfield Avenues, Newark, c.1905

RABBIS

Hyman Brodsky,
Congregation Anshe Russia, Newark

Solomon Foster,
Temple B'nai Jeshurun, Newark

Dr. Max Gruenewald, Congregation
B'nai Israel, Millburn

Dr. Louis M. Levitsky, Oheb Shalom
Congregation, Newark

Dr. Ely Pilchik, Congregation B'nai
Jeshurun, Short Hills

Dr. Joachim Prinz, Temple B'nai
Abraham, Newark

Dr. Marius Ranson, Temple Sharoy Tefilo, East Orange

Charles Isaiah Hoffman, Oheb Shalom Congregation, Newark

Isaac Schwarz, Oheb Shalom Congregation, Newark

Julius Silberfeld, Temple B'nai Abraham, Newark

Joseph Konvitz, Congregation Anshe Russia, Newark

Bradley Beach, 1905

Brach Brook Park, Newark

Camp Nah-Jee-Wah, Milford, PA

Cedar Lake Camp logo, Milford, PA

Weequahic Park

Weequahic Park Racetrack, c.1915

Krueger's Auditorium, Belmont Ave., Newark

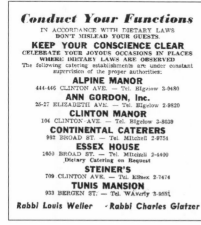

Kashrut Advertisement, 1948   Tavern Restaurant catering menu, 1941

Weequahic High School, Newark, c.1945

Nathan Bohrer/Abraham Kaufman Hebrew Academy of Morris County, c.1990

Joseph Kushner Hebrew Academy, Livingston, 1996

Solomon Schechter Upper Campus, West Orange, 1991

TABATCHNICKS   MILLMAN'S

CHEZ MODE

LEHR'S   SYD'S

WEEQUAHIC DINER

BELOV

SILVER'S   HALEM'S

TAVERN   HENRY'S

Weequahic Area, Newark

Temple B'nai Jeshurun, High & Waverly Ave., Newark

Temple B'nai Abraham, Clinton Ave., Newark, 1924-1973

Morristown Jewish Center, Speedwell Ave., Morristown, 1929

Prince Street Shul, Oheb Shalom, 1884-1911,
Adas Israel, 1911-1939, Newark

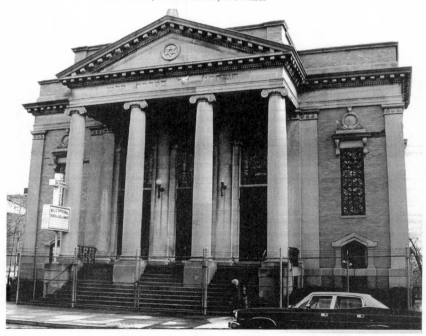

Oheb Shalom Congregation, High Street, Newark, 1911-1958

Congregation Sharey Tefilo, Orange, NJ, 1895-1922

Temple Sharey Tefilo, Prospect Street, East Orange, 1925-1981

5

Serving the Community

Long ago, in an era when the words "Federation," or "MetroWest" meant nothing to New Jersey's Jewish inhabitants, the idea of responsibility for others was already an integral part of the Jewish community. Its origins and guiding principles had been embodied for thousands of years in what the historian, Max Dimont, had dubbed, "The Portable Homeland"—the Torah. In it, one could find definitive statements regarding charity, kindness, helping the old and the sick, morality, ethics, and the obligations Jews had to each other, as well as to human beings in general.

Those who settled in Newark had come from European communities where mutual assistance was a staple of daily Jewish life, so it was not surprising that they engaged in the same activities shortly after coming here. The first such organization, founded in 1852, was the *Frauenverein Nachstenliebe* (Friendly Sisters). Its members included some of the most prominent names in the German Jewish community—Trier, Hauser, Stern, Bergstrasser, and numerous others. The annual dues were $5.00 and its purpose was to provide assistance, financial or otherwise, for its members. As time passed, however, those who belonged to it became successful to the point where they no longer needed such help. In 1927, the organization became a mutual aid society for the larger community, which had become, by then, one of predominantly Eastern European origin.

The Hebrew Benevolent and Orphan Asylum Society, later known as the Jewish Children's Home and established in 1861, underwent a similar transformation. At first, it cared for orphans in its own community and, in keeping with the noblest form of Jewish giving, its offic-

181

ers agreed never to divulge to the outside world the names of those receiving assistance.[1] By 1948, the Society had joined together with other similar groups under the name of the Jewish Child Care Association. A parallel organization, the Hebrew Orphanage and Sheltering Home, had begun operating in 1923 to serve the specific needs of Newark's Orthodox Jews. As a matter of standard procedure, the various agencies in the community routinely evaluated applicants for assistance to determine if they were deserving. This was, however, a non-Jewish innovation, for the Jews had, throughout their history, not distinguished between the worthy and unworthy poor in their midst.[2]

Other aid groups were affiliated with synagogues, of which the most important was probably the Miriam Auxiliary, whose members belonged to Congregation Oheb Shalom. Over the years, the Auxiliary contributed to many organizations, including the Daughters of Israel, American Jewish Congress, Hebrew Immigrant Aid Society, Jewish Theological Seminary, Keren Hayesod, and so on. Also important were the Hebrew Ladies Immediate Aid Society and the Hebrew Ladies Sewing and Personal Service Club, both founded in the late nineteenth century.

The most common types of organizations were the orders based on a common communal heritage. In the German Jewish community they were known as the *Kranken Unterstitzung Verein*, or, by their initials, KUV, and, among the Eastern Europeans, *landsmanshaftn*. These organizations provided loans, insurance, burial plots, but most of all, a place where the immigrants could socialize and feel at home. Yet another important type of society was the fraternal order. These were organized into lodges and, in Newark, the most significant were the Ezekiel Lodge, Tabor Lodge, Brith Abraham, Brith Sholom, B'nai Zion, and the Workmen's Circle (Arbeiter Ring).

Several important organizations were founded in the late nineteenth and early twentieth centuries, among them, the Y, the Jewish Children's Home, Beth Israel Hospital, and the Theresa Grotta Aid for Convalescents. The most important organization, however, in terms of the entire Jewish community, was what is today called the United Jewish Federation of MetroWest, or "the Federation." Through the years, it underwent various name changes and when it was first established in 1923, it was called the Conference of Jewish Charities.[3] It also existed in several locations, the first one being at 682 High Street in what was once the home of a physician. One of its locations, on Central Avenue, had originally been an automobile showroom and, subsequent to that, the headquarters of a World War I German spy ring. As the population shifted, the Federation followed suit, moving to East Orange and then, finally, to its present complex in Whippany. Today, as MetroWest, the Federation encompasses not only Essex County, but the counties of Morris, Sussex, Warren and parts of Somerset, Hudson, and Union Counties. To truly understand the importance of the Federation for our story we need to start at the beginning.

The Early Period

The meetings to establish the Conference began in 1922. Shortly theratfer, thirteen organizations came under its umbrella, some of which were Newark Beth Israel Hospital and Theresa Grotta Aid for Convalescents, the Young Men's and Young Women's Hebrew Association, and the Hebrew Benevolent and Orphan Asylum Society.[4] Jews also served on the Board of the Community Chest, which gave money to both Jewish and non-Jewish groups.

The rationale for the creation of the Conference was expressed by the noted philanthropist, Felix Fuld, at its executive committee meeting of October 14, 1922. According to Fuld, by having all local Jewish organizations join the Community Chest through one central Jewish organization, the community would have "better representation on the Community Chest Board."[5] The most important outcome, however, from a practical standpoint, was that this system was a clearinghouse. It gave the Conference the power to determine which Jewish groups would be admitted into the Community Chest and thereby receive funding from it. Thus, organizations of questionable reputation could, by community consensus, be barred from applying for financial support.[6]

The Conference's first president was Abraham J. Dimond, a dynamic individual who was a leader of several major Jewish institutions. Originally from Louisville, Kentucky, Dimond lived in Newark for several years and in East Orange from 1912 to 1937. As chairman of the Beth Israel fund-raising drive he obtained commitments of $4,000,000, a truly impressive sum for those days. He was president of the Y from 1924 to 1930, president of the Conference from 1923 to 1929, and a vice president of the Community Chest from 1927 to 1929. In addition, he was president of the aristocratic Mountain Ridge Club from 1925 to 1935. In a 1996 interview, his grandson, Don Rubenoff, presented a more personal view of Dimond:

He wanted things done his way and he was tough, but to me he was very warm. He always talked about how you have to give to people less fortunate than you. When he moved to Florida he became very involved in the community, both Jewish and non-Jewish. I remember him meeting with a group of black Baptist ministers to discuss rebuilding the church in Hollywood. He had a house in Essex Fells where he was the only Jew living there at the time, but he had no problem with his neighbors. He started off right by inviting the police chief over to his house and telling him he wanted no problems, and that was it.[7]

Because of his involvement in so many key organizations, and because the community was much smaller then, Dimond was able to exercise a great degree of control over the Conference and its board. While there is no evidence that he abused this authority, the net result of such centralization was that it led, inevitably, to a board whose members came from similar backgrounds and thought the same way on the important issues that came before it. This is reflected in the minutes of the Board during those years. By contrast, today's leaders, given the diffusion of power in the community, do not have this kind of authority.

Working as a unit was a challenge at first because the needs, priorities, and resources of the different groups were not the same. Yet, in what was to become a hallmark of the Newark Jewish community, the concept of communal cooperation generally prevailed. This position was articulated at a meeting by one of the early Board members, Frank Liveright, who argued that if any member society had money in the bank it was correct to withhold the Community Chest monies from that society to help the group that was more financially strapped at that time. Further evidence of Board control over its constituent societies, can be seen from the fact that in those early years, organizations needed to obtain permission from the Conference in order to conduct charity drives. An exception to the rule was local Jewish educational institutions, which were not part of the Conference then.[8]

As part of the general desire to consolidate and avoid duplication of effort, a decision was made, in 1926, to merge the annual fundraising campaigns of the three major Jewish communal groups into one campaign. For example, in that same year, the United Palestine Appeal raised $100,000, the United Jewish Campaign, $300,000, and the Conference of Jewish Charities, $125,000. The new organization was called the United Jewish Appeal, a source of confusion in later years because that was the name taken by the national organization when it was founded in 1939. The national UJA was actually the result of a merger between the American Joint Distribution Committee and the United Palestine Appeal, with the National Refugee Service as a beneficiary. Its major function was to serve as a vehicle by which Jews in overseas countries could be supported.

The onset of the Depression played a major role in terms of how Jewish organizational life developed in Newark. As a direct outcome, the German-Jewish families that had controlled and led the Conference of Jewish Charities retreated from active involvement, unwilling and/or unable to make the necessary financial and time commitments. Dimond retired to Florida and the others became more involved with the Mountain Ridge Club. This paved the way for a new group of leaders, of whom the two most prominent were Michael A. Stavitsky and Samuel I. Kessler. It was they, along with Samuel Leber and Julius H. Cohn, who guided the Conference through the very difficult years of the 1930s.

Stavitsky was born in Russia and came to the U.S. at the age of eight. He possessed an unusual combination of credentials—an accounting degree from NYU and graduate studies in social work. This gave him the ability to deal with both financial and social issues as they emerged in the Jewish community. In fact, Stavitsky was, for a time, the national director of Field Work and Fund-Raising for the National Jewish Welfare Board. He also developed a disciplined approach to issues that was probably influenced to some degree by his stint in the army as a second lieutenant (he had attended officer's training school at Yale University).

In 1922, Stavitsky's career shifted from social work to business, mostly real estate and mortgage financing, where he became quite successful. As a community-oriented person, however, this was not enough to hold his interest and he became one of the most effective Jewish community leaders in the city's history. He was chairman of Newark's United Jewish Appeal, president of the Jewish Education Association, and president of Temple B'nai Abraham. As president of the Conference of Jewish Charities between 1931 and 1935, he presided over one of its most critical periods. Had he not taken firm control of the organization then, it is doubtful that it could have survived. Stavitsky believed in commitment to the Jewish community nationally and his involvement also extended beyond the Jewish sphere. The organizations in which he held important posts included the Council of Jewish Federations and Welfare Funds, the United Jewish Appeal, the Jewish Theological Seminary, the American Association for Jewish Education, which he founded, B'nai Brith Hillel Commission, Newark Public Housing Authority, and the United Service Organization. Perhaps the best statement summing up his achievements on behalf of Newark's Jewish community was made by Sidney Weinstein, who was president of the Federation between 1967 and 1970:

> Michael Stavitsky was a builder in the very finest sense of the word. A generation ago he took stock of the progress that had been made by the Jewish Community in Essex County, had the vision to perceive the achievements possible in the future, and together with a group of similarly dedicated leaders set himself to help realize our full communal potential. He laid the foundation for the developments in our community of which we are increasingly proud these days. His wise counsel, broad vision and warm compassion will be living and dynamic realities for us for many years to come.[9]

Of those who worked closely with him, Samuel I. Kessler had the greatest impact. Kessler had been an assistant U.S. attorney and had served as Democratic County chairman of Essex County. As a representative of important financial interests in the Jewish community he was admirably equipped to be treasurer of the Conference, a post he held from 1936 to 1938. In 1938, he became chairman of Newark's UJA, succeeding Stavitsky in that role. In 1941, he was elected president of the organization, serving in that capacity until October of 1944. A dominant and dynamic individual, he was president of the Y, a member of Beth Israel Hospital's Board, and the first president of the Jewish Education Association of Essex County.

In those years the Conference was not particularly strong organizationally. Indicative of that was that it made no move to join up, as did other older cities, with the Council of Jewish Federations and Welfare Funds when it was formed in 1932, waiting, instead, until 1944 to do so. Its weakness was its strength, however, because it was unable to sustain any real opposition to a merger of functions that came later and which ended up being the best approach.

Similarly, Newark's Community Chest was not considered to be overly generous when compared to community chests in other cities. While it did provide financial assistance, it could not, however, cover all of the community's perceived needs.[10] Moreover, there were certain areas that it felt were outside its mandate of communal assistance. It gave no money to combat anti-Semitism or to educate Jews about their traditions. While the Conference itself did not focus on such activities either, there were organizations, like the B'nai Brith or Young Judea, which did, and the Conference gave money to them and to many other like-minded groups. In 1934, to take a typical year, nineteen nonmember Jewish organizations received funding from the Conference. Many of these organizations, such as the American Jewish Committee, ORT, Mizrachi, and others, were branch offices. Because of their proximity to the national headquarters in New York City they tended to be weak in influence and were more dependent on the Conference than would have been the case had they been located in more self-contained communities like Detroit or St. Louis.

In general, Newark was affected by an organizational fragmentation that stemmed from its location. Although the city had a very clear identity, it was more difficult to maintain a unified structure because so many people commuted to their jobs in New York City or had business activities outside of Newark. Since their businesses were elsewhere, they felt obligated to support the Jewish organizations in the localities of their businesses. In addition, the move to the suburbs, which had already become prevalent by the 1920s, also contributed to divided loyalties. Awareness of this reality played a role in the decision to change the Conference's name, in 1940, to the Essex County Council of Jewish Agencies. Moreover, the Conference could not and did not ask or expect the Community Chest of Newark to financially support Jews who had left Newark, literally, for greener pastures. Yet, the Conference felt a responsibility to service its suburban coreligionists who could not maintain their own recreational and cultural facilities by themselves.

Besides the specialized needs of the Newark Jewish community and the shift to the suburbs, there was the fact that world Jewry had needs that the Jewish community wanted to address as well. Chief among these were the problems of poor and oppressed Jews in other countries and the struggle to establish a homeland in Palestine. Again, these problems were beyond the scope of the Newark Community Chest. Realizing that large amounts of capital would have to be raised to meet these challenges, the Jewish community decided to consolidate its efforts, to unite as one entity, to have combined campaigns and to avoid any unnecessary services and infrastructures. The beginnings of this process ushered in the next phase of organizational life for Newark's Jews. It was a process that was accelerated by the Depression, which weakened the community just as it did communities elsewhere in the U.S.

The Middle Period

The year 1939 was a pivotal one in the history of the Conference of Jewish Charities. Julius H. Cohn, then president, began talking to his Board about the need to unite under one umbrella as one elected council and about the importance of fund-raising. America was beginning to emerge from the Depression at the same time as a sense of urgency permeated a Jewish community increasingly worried about the fate of European Jewry and the future of Palestine. Cohn created an endowment fund, a new concept that eventually became central to the Federation's financial structure. Under his administration, the amount of money raised for the general campaign was triple that given just two years earlier.[11]

On April 30, 1940, the Conference was renamed the Essex County Council of Jewish Agencies, with the new name underscoring the fact that funds for the United Jewish Appeal were being solicited throughout the entire county. In 1941, at a May 5 board meeting, marked by festivities that included the singing of "Hatikvah" and the national anthem, incoming president Samuel Kessler bestowed service awards upon Michael Stavitsky and Julius Cohn.

Alas, the feeling of good will did not last long. The Council was about to enter a period of turbulence characterized by internal dissension. Joel Gross, a prominent attorney formerly from Jersey City, became active in the organization. Like Stavitsky and Kessler he was an activist but unlike them, he was not part of the establishment. In fact, he viewed them in much the same way they had perceived the earlier German-Jewish leadership, as "old guard." This is, of course, inevitable in organizations as new individuals seek to justify their activities in terms of pressing needs that are not, in their view, being addressed by those in power. There was substance to the position taken by the "young Turks," as they were known. One of their main themes was that the Council should become more involved with world Jewish affairs, namely the refugee crisis in Europe and the desire for a homeland in Palestine. The old guard, they claimed, was too parochial and too focused on local priorities. For their part, Stavitsky, Kessler, Cohn, Daniel Shiman, Herbert Hannoch, Ralph Wechsler, and other trustees felt that they had been devoted to the community and were now being unjustly attacked.

The Council's response was to try to turn Joel Gross into a player by making him a vice president. After all, Gross had been a successful fund raiser for the UJA and his talents in this area could be quite useful. In 1944, the Council of Jewish Federations and Welfare Funds (CJF) was engaged to evaluate the Council of Jewish Agencies and to come up with recommendations that would improve its operations. In addition, Kessler formed the Committee on Community Organization and asked it to prepare a plan that would democratize the Council by including more Zionist and fraternal organizations, and other constituencies under its aegis as well as suburban Jews in general. Joel Gross was named chairman and Alan Lowenstein, vice chairman.

Samuel Kessler's term ended in September and Dan Shiman succeeded him as president. Keenly disappointed that he had not been selected for the post, Joel Gross resigned from the Committee on Community Organization and soon threw in his lot with Israel Bonds, which was a direct competitor for funds with the Federation's national UJA. An intemperate letter to the Board by Jacob Shohan, a trustee and Gross ally, did not help matters. While Gross and Shohan were now gone, other, younger people remained on the Board. To appease them, Alan Lowenstein, then part of that group, was made chairman of the Committee on Community Organization and also a vice president of the Council of Jewish Agencies.

Lowenstein's committee worked hard on a restructuring plan, realizing that its conclusions could dramatically affect the future of the community. They spoke with many knowledgeable people active in communal life and carefully examined the models developed in cities around the country. What they came up with was unique—a framework that provided for organizational representation as well as for individual and geographic representation. The underlying philosophy was that Jewish organizational life should reflect the same democratic ideals expressed in American political life. To symbolize the far-reaching change in structure, the organization's name was changed once again, becoming the Jewish Community Council of Essex County on October 28, 1945. The way it worked was as follows.

Everyone who gave a minimum of $3.00 was a member of the Council. In addition, all member organizations, which now included synagogues, fraternal orders, women's organizations, national Jewish groups, educational associations, charitable organizations, service agencies, and so on, belonged to the Council. The individual Council members and organizations each elected delegates to represent them in another group called the General Assembly. The General Assembly, in turn, elected a Board of Trustees and the Board elected its own officers as well as a number of standing committees that dealt with allocations, community relations, fund raising and other related matters. At the time of its adoption, the broadness of representation was truly unique for a city of this size.[12] It went much further than the CJF recommendations, which had urged greater democratization and participation, but had not envisioned changes of this scope.[13] The model was eventually adopted by Los Angeles, San Francisco, Boston, Philadelphia, and many other cities.

The country soon learned of Newark's achievement, when its leaders addressed the fifteenth General Assembly of CJF at its Atlantic City Convention Meeting in February of 1947. The idea that the overseas and local organizations could be brought together made a deep and lasting impression on the delegates. Within a few short years Newark's Council had gone from a rather small and uninfluential organization to one that was creative, dynamic, highly professional, and on the cutting edge of change in American Jewish communal life. The difference can be clearly discerned from a look at its fund-raising success over the years. In 1938, about 8,000 donors gave a total of $100,000. In 1945, nine times that amount was raised from 22,000 individuals. Looking back, it seems also that, however bitter the antagonisms were, the lesson was that conflict can sometimes be healthy for a community by serving as an impetus for needed changes and new ways of approaching problems.[14]

These changes coincided with another extremely critical development in Newark—the recruitment of Herman Pekarsky to become the Community Council's new executive director. No other person, however important, was to have the impact that this man had on the community. The opportunity to appoint him came about because in April of 1944, Esther Jameson, who had been the Council's executive director since 1937, informed the Council of her impending retirement, thus necessitating a search for a replacement. Jameson was a very bright woman with degrees from London University, and an excellent public speaker. Before coming to the Conference she had been director of Women's Activities at the Y.[15] But she was not paid very well and that was in itself a reflection of the level at which she was expected to perform. While she had done a good job, the Board was now thinking in terms of someone who had a national reputation and who was highly innovative. As the magnitude of the European Jewish catastrophe became clearer with each passing week, and as the Board came under mounting criticism for not doing enough at either the national or local levels, finding the right person became a matter of the highest priority.

Pekarsky was one of two candidates for the position. The other was Jack Rich who had been the campaign director of the Jewish Community Council for seven years. Rich had been an excellent fund raiser and was a likeable man. He was favored by the Joel Gross group and his failure to be selected for the position was another reason for Gross' departure. Those who favored Rich felt that the Council's standing in general was due in large part to the fact that it had raised money. The establishment group, led by Kessler and Stavitsky, favored Pekarsky, however, and argued that, while Rich had garnered financial support for the community, this was the limit of his qualifications. They did not feel he understood the overall goals of the Jewish community and its philosophy as well as Pekarsky, though it was acknowledged that fund raising would not be Pekarsky's forte. They also wanted someone with direct experience as a manager.[16] And Lowenstein, who had originally sided with Gross, changed his mind and threw his support to Pekarsky's candidacy for the same reasons.

Who was Herman Pekarsky? Born in Poland, he was fluent in Yiddish and Hebrew and a graduate of the University of Michigan. He had begun his career as a social service caseworker, recruited by Harry Hopkins, and had rapidly progressed up the administrative ladder, becoming, eventually, under Governor Frank D. Murphy, supervisor of Michigan's assistance to the elderly program. Here, he developed the skills that were to serve him so well in Newark—supervising social service programs, accounting, statistics, personnel, with responsibility for an $18,000,000 annual budget. When the Council Personnel Committee recommended him for the job he was the executive director of the Council of Social Agencies of Detroit and had been assistant executive director of the Jewish Community Federation of Detroit. Although only thirty-seven years old, Pekarsky had already accumulated a great deal of experience and was unanimously recommended for the same position in Newark.

Pekarsky plunged into his new job with great enthusiasm and it was clear from the onset that he would be a force to be reckoned with. As Dan Shiman recalled:

Herbert Hannoch was an outstanding attorney. One time we had a meeting about something and Hannoch said it couldn't be done because there was no money to do it. Well, Pekarsky looked at me and said: "If it's the right thing, it's going to be done, whether or not we have the money." I thought: "He's a newcomer to the community and he talks up to Herbert Hannoch like that." But he knew what was right.[17]

Working together with the Committee on Community Organization, he set about disseminating information about the democratization plan and developing the mechanisms by which it would be implemented. With almost 400 delegates in attendance, the Jewish Community Council's General Assembly held its first meeting in January of 1946. From that day on, guided by Pekarsky's broad vision and dynamic personality, the Council began its transformation into one of the most successful Federations in the country.

Pekarsky also brought in some very good people to the Jewish Community Council and its agencies. Bert Gold was recruited from Pittsburgh to head the Y. Jacob Trobe, who had spent the war years working overseas for the Joint Distribution Committee, returned to the Jewish Child Care Service Association; Theodore Isenstadt became the top man at the Jewish Family Service Association, and Charles Miller came in from Cleveland to work as the Council's assistant executive director in social planning. At the same time, several local lay leaders were achieving recognition nationally. Herbert Abeles and Louis Stern were each elected president of the national CJF, further enhancing the reputation of Newark's Federation.

Adding to Newark's reputation was the fact that Pekarsky was highly regarded in professional circles around the country. His co-equals in other Federations knew who he was and saw him as a first-rate executive, especially in the area of planning. When he came to conventions he would meet and exchange ideas with other successful people like Harry Greenstein of Baltimore, Isidore Sobeloff of Detroit, Kurt Peiser of Philadelphia, and Cleveland's Henry Zucker. Each would learn from the other and return to their communities with new ideas. One of Pekarsky's key initiatives, according to Martin Fox, a past Federation president, was to encourage the Federation to control the real estate that the agencies were located on. This had the net effect of keeping the agencies within the Federation's orbit and was consistent with the Newark leadership's conviction that centralization was best for the community as a whole.[18]

Above all, Pekarsky was a man who could and did get things done. He founded the *Jewish News*, and was the driving force behind the decisions to build a new facility for the Daughters of Israel Home for the Aged, the Northfield Avenue Y, and the different social agencies as they moved out of the city. The ideas regarding social welfare in the community, the programming, and the priorities chosen, all reflected his thinking.

What made Pekarsky so unique was that he blended professionalism with intense personal commitment. Philip Bernstein, chief executive of national CJF for twenty-five years, knew Pekarsky well and described him in the following terms:

> Pekarsky was interested in the quality of Jewish life, ethics, and maintaining high standards. He was a strong person with real conviction. He could listen and was flexible, knowing that sometimes one has to adjust. He was not, however, an even-tempered person, but quite forceful. At the same time, he was not at all imperious with the lay people and not at all a manipulator. The people had complete confidence in his integrity and saw him as a very decent human being.[19]

These views were echoed by others in the community who worked closely with him throughout his eighteen year tenure in Newark. He was regarded as a change-agent who could see the big picture, a man who could get things done without sacrificing principles in the process. He did not suffer fools gladly but he worked hard to develop and encourage people whom he thought were talented. And while he was not a sentimentalist, he respected Jewish tradition in terms of its commitment to help others and better the world.

The involvement of men such as Pekarsky, Stavitsky, Kessler, and others like them emerges as a key factor in explaining the growth of Newark's organized Jewish community. Leaders need followers and Newark had a large Jewish community, relatively speaking. But followers need leaders to motivate and inspire them, and this too, Newark had in abundance.

The Later Period

It would require an entire book to detail all of the developments in the Federation and in Jewish organizational life from 1950 up to the present and this is not possible in a general introductory history of the community. Rather, what is being done here is a review of some of the highlights, leaving it to future historians to fill in the gaps.

Herbert Abeles, Jewish Community Council (JCC) president from 1947 to 1950, and Alan Lowenstein, president from 1950 until 1954, consolidated and expanded the Council's work. Various programs designed to aid the fledging Jewish state were supported, as were efforts to help Holocaust survivors adjust to life in their newly adopted homes. The Council increased its assistance to the poor, the elderly, the handicapped, and for Jewish education, as well as recreational, cultural, and social programming for all age groups. The lay leadership also fostered close professional and personal relationships with Herman Pekarsky. This was to stand it in good stead whenever crises emerged and close cooperation became essential. One especially painful period was the labor strife that occurred during Lowenstein's tenure.

In 1951, the Jewish Community Council (JCC) employees and those of its beneficiary agencies were represented by District 65. Upon learning, however, that the union had come under communist control, the Board decided not to negotiate with it, a policy decision already initiated by other area Jewish agencies. This was the McCarthy Era and Jews were anxious not to be seen as procommunist in any way. These concerns were heightened when the JCC learned that its offices and membership lists were being used by District 65 for recruitment and support of the Communist Party.

The union retaliated by organizing a strike on December 6, 1951. Pickets were set up at the various agencies and 1,000 protesters marched on Broad Street past Lowenstein's law firm's office. One of those who sought to break the picket lines at the JCC offices on Clinton Street, Charles Miller, was attacked and agency heads received telephone threats in the middle of the night. Even the police told of being "shocked" by the foul language of the protesters, men and women. There were internal divisions too, with some agency executives and lay people supporting the strikers and secretly reporting the JCC's strategy to the opposition. The strike ended on January 4, 1952 with the defeat of the union by an independent group, but the bitter feelings created by it took years to heal.

The Federation continued to grow and the agencies serving the people were highly thought of in the community. Of course, changes in the structure were also made from time to time. For example, a study of the General Assembly found that attendance at its meetings had declined and that interest was low. Some blamed the size of the group, others its procedures, and still others saw television as the villain. Whatever the reasons, new ways were found to increase direct representation.[20] All organizations require such "overhauls" periodically to avoid atrophying and becoming merely self-perpetuating.

Even though there was steady growth, some felt it was not enough, among them former Council president, Julius Cohn. In an editorial printed in the *Jewish News*, he wrote that the soul of a community:

is mainly measured by the degree of generosity exercised by its citizens for the maintenance and operation of programs and services . . .let us look at the amount raised in 1953 and the *average contribution*:

City	Number of Contributors	Amount Raised	Average Contribution
Cleveland	34,000	$4,327,000	$127.00
Detroit	29,000	$4,475,000	$154.00
NEWARK	31,000	$2,100,000	$67.70

Citing an article from a national marketing magazine, *Sales Management*, Cohn went on to note that the buying power of Newarkers was about the same as that of Detroit and Cleveland residents, leaving them with no excuse for their smaller donations. Charging that Newark's Jews "only have a 50 percent soul," he urged them to reexamine their consciences and priorities and open up their hearts by opening up their wallets.[21]

Several weeks later, another old-timer and respected leader, Sam Kessler, wrote an article for the *Jewish News* in which he asserted that the situation was even worse than Cohn had stated it to be. He pointed out that Cleveland and Detroit had a better record of giving even as they were raising millions of additional dollars in capital funds while Newark was not raising any capital funds. Defending Newark, others argued that Jews were moving from Newark to the suburbs but this was true of Detroit and Cleveland too.[22] Regardless, the net effect of this, as intended, was to spur greater giving, and, by 1955, the community was also in the midst of a building campaign, its first since 1923.[23]

The year 1956 was marked by an outpouring of financial and moral support because of the war between Israel and Egypt, otherwise known as "the Suez Campaign." Contributions increased by 63.6 percent.[24] Later on, in the same year, Newark's Jews came through again as communities across the land were asked to give on behalf of Jewish refugees from the 1956 Hungarian Uprising. Essex County took in families, gave them shelter and housing, found jobs for them, and helped them adjust socially to the new land. It was the second time in less than a decade that it had been called upon to help refugee brethren and the mechanisms were in place to do so.[25]

Throughout this period, Jews continued to move to the suburbs. While this did not affect giving as a whole, the distribution of gifts continued to shift heavily to those who resided in the suburbs. As a result, life in the inner city became increasing untenable for those who remained. Invariably there were those who could not afford to leave. The Federation did establish programs designed to foster better relations between blacks and Jews, but, as seen earlier, it was not enough to change the demographic trend. In 1963, Herman Pekarsky suffered a fatal heart attack and Saul Schwarz, who had succeeded Charles Miller in social planning, took over as acting executive director, performing ably, while a search for a successor was undertaken. The new person, Abe Sudran, came in 1964, with Schwarz serving as the number two man. Sudran was aggressive in terms of fund raising, turning off some people while stimulating others. The Federation lay leadership was also interested in social planning for local services, something that was becoming more and more important as the Jewish population became older and grew in terms of young families having children.

The agency-oriented nature of the community was crucial in another sense. It meant that when the Six Day War broke out in 1967, Essex County Jewry had a veritable army of volunteers. The Newark Federation's strength lay in its network of social programs. It was not as strong as some of the other Federations when it came to Israel. The war, however, caused it to come together and strengthened the commitment to Zionism by giving it a clear raison d'etre and a focus. It also gave new importance to Newark's Zionist organizations.

By the 1970s, the Jewish Community Council could accurately claim that it had adjusted to the suburban exodus. Although senior citizens' centers remained on Lyons Avenue and near the Seth Boyden Housing Development, the main Y was now located on Northfield Avenue in West Orange. The Jewish Counseling and Service Agency had moved to Millburn and the Jewish Vocational Service could be found in East Orange, with Theresa Grotta shifting to a West Orange location. The Federation was also moving in other areas. There was a greater commitment to education, with the Hillel Foundation at Rutgers, the Hebrew Youth Academy, and the Solomon Schechter Day School becoming beneficiary institutions. Significantly too, greater emphasis was being placed on developing more sophisticated endowment and bequest programs.

With the passage of time, the orbit of residential expansion widened. The new areas were no longer Livingston or West Orange, but Morristown, Newton, Parsippany, Dover, and other places in Morris and Sussex County. To accommodate to the changing demographic realities, a new Federation was established—the Morris-Sussex Jewish Federation. Dan Drench, one of the Federation presidents, explained what it was like in the early days:

> When we moved here at first, the only Jewish institutions were the synagogues. In 1974, we had a Y, but it was a Y without walls. We had an office in a basement and we rented camp facilities in a Catholic school. We had no gym. The first director, Mike Witkes, was a staff person from the Federation. We also built a day school, which was subsidized by Federation. We had no real infrastructure, but most of our money went overseas to Israel.[26]

The Morris-Sussex Federation was small compared to that of Essex County and while it lacked adequate resources, it had a certain pioneering spirit that can only happen when organizations are small and, as a result, tight-knit. Seymour Epstein, the owner of Epstein's Department Store, in Morristown and its first president, talked about his experiences at the helm in personal terms that demonstrate the depth of such feelings:

> I thought, I'll be busy; I'll have things to do at night and it was the greatest thing that ever happened to me. And I found in the glow of my new Jewish friends that it glowed more brightly for me. Jewish people have a warmth. I'm sure you've been to Jewish affairs in UJA where everybody's kissing and hugging. WASPs don't do that.[27]

In 1983, the Morris-Sussex Federation merged with the Jewish Community Federation of Metropolitan New Jersey, becoming the United Jewish Federation of MetroWest, a name it has retained until today. While the groundwork for the merger was laid during the administration of Horace Bier, the actual merger took place during Clarence Reisen's tenure, a man known for his rapport with the younger generation in the organization. The merger was desired by both parties but there were fears nonetheless. As Bier put it, "The Morris-Sussex people were sort of afraid of being swallowed up by the Essex big octopus."[28] And with good reason. In 1981, Morris-Sussex raised about $1,000,000 compared to about $12,000,000 for Essex County. The services provided by Morris-Sussex did not compare in any way to the extensive programs of the Metropolitan Federation.

The leaders of Metropolitan New Jersey felt that bringing the two communities together was in everybody's best interests, including, of course, their own. As past president, Jerome Waldor, put it, "I think the merger was a good and gutsy thing to do. Morris County is about 30 percent of our population and 10 percent of our fund raising." The reality was that the population growth was westward and the Campaign had become static at the time. It was clear that over the next quarter century the Jewish population center would continue in that direction. And although the first wave, consisting often of people unable to afford Livingston or Short Hills, was not as affluent, the next wave would almost certainly be better off as the areas became more developed and attractive.

The Morris-Sussex community stood to gain in equal measure. They did not have the infrastructure of agencies, recreational facilities, educational programs, and other services. It would probably have taken at least fifteen years to build it up to the level of Essex County's operation. They agreed to the merger provided three conditions were met— that the next community center would be built in the Morris County area and that this would become the center of the community in every sense of the word; that the Bohrer-Kaufman Hebrew Academy, the area's main Jewish educational institution, would be supported; and that the allocation for Israel would not be reduced for a fixed period of time. Metropolitan New Jersey met all of these requests and, in retrospect, nearly everyone agrees that the union was an excellent decision for both sides.

Still, there were some regrets, as noted by Judy May, the last president of Morris-Sussex before the merger:

Many of the people that were involved [with us] did not continue their involvement. What was lost was the feeling of touching one another. The merger had to happen but it wasn't done with enough sensitivity. We had wonderful programs on immigration, women studying and teaching the Talmud. We had Blu Greenberg one year, explaining how a Jewish woman makes a Jewish home, especially living in a non-Jewish area, and other topics. And we used to get 300–400 Jewish women and it was because people knew they would come away with something. When we merged, these lay people were left out.[29]

The Jewish Community Federation also had programs that were creative and which featured dynamic speakers. The problem, however, was the loss of solidarity and the feeling of being involved in something new with people one felt close to. That this is what troubles Judy May is apparent from the following observation:

> Today, there is a Hunterdon-Sussex Federation. I walked in and it was a flashback to our beginnings. I told them: "Don't look for mergers. Buy services and maintain your own character."[30]

This is the course of action that she felt should have been followed in their case. If there is any consolation in her mind, it is that the new agency directors are sensitive and often give services without compromising the identity or independence of those they serve. As examples, she cites Chaim Lauer of the Jewish Education Association and Max Kleinman the present executice vice president of the Federation.

As for the Metropolitan New Jersey side, some of those involved feel that they might have given away too much. The new Jewish Community Center (JCC), housed on the Federation campus, is beautiful but it does run at an annual $500,000 deficit. Stanley Strauss, another Federation past president, feels that the JCC should have been built thirty miles to the west, near Randolph, that is, closer to the true geographic center of the area's Jewish population. Strauss notes, "I have a niece who lives in Chester. She swims at the YMCA there. Why? Because it's much closer.[31] The Federation campus has had many programs for young people and the selection of the center as a Maccabiah Games site in the summer of 1996 gave it a tremendous boost. One of the largest events is the Israeli Independence Day celebration, with about 3,000 participants annually. Perhaps the best way to look at the location issue is Clarence Reisen's observation that the Jews of South Orange and Short Hills think it's too far west and those of Morris County believe that it's too far east. All of which suggests that it's probably in the right place.

Howard Charish became the executive vice president in 1982. He had followed Carmi Schwartz, Franklin Fogelson, and Donald Feldstein, and the merger happened on his watch. One of his key contributions was the recruitment of top-notch professionals. He also further solidified the organization's finances, making certain that things were done more efficiently. Important decisions were made with respect to the various agencies. On the one hand, the Jewish Family Service Association and the Jewish Vocational Service were not merged, as had been proposed, while the Developmentally Disabled Committee became a separate agency. Carmi Schwartz deserves special credit for ushering in a period of greater Jewish identification with tradition and Jewish education in a nonpartisan and nonconfrontational way. He was also a strong advocate of professionalization within the agency.

Why and How They Give

Looking at the minutes of the Federation meetings throughout its history, one element stands out—the organization's desire to centralize and thereby control fund raising in the community. Naturally, this is a reflection of the overall concept of American Jewish giving, namely that everyone gives to a large pot which is then distributed, hopefully, in an equitable fashion. In this way, no one gets special treatment. But not every Federation was as successful in maintaining party discipline. Even annual dinners of Hebrew day schools were subjected to scrutiny in this regard.[32] Sometimes organizations, realizing the importance of the concept to the Federation, were able to successfully manuever the Federation into granting them larger allocations. In 1945, for example, HIAS (Hebrew Immigrant Aid Society) threatened to conduct its own campaign if its funding was not increased. While decrying such pressure, the Council upped its contribution from $2,500 to $12,500.[33] In 1949, at the instigation of Herman Pekarsky, the Federation established a separate organization, the Jewish Community Foundation. Its purpose was to hold title to real estate owned by the Council and its agencies and to build an endowment for a rainy day. Today, the Foundation, whose board is named by the Federation Board, holds title to Federation and agency buildings and to substantial investment funds, totaling 73 million dollars.

In 1962, during the presidency of Martin Jelin, a study of the philanthropic habits of Essex County's Jews was carried out by the respected National Opinion Research Center. The findings were illuminating in a number of respects. Half of all donations came from first generation, American-born Jews, and about a quarter from foreign-born Jews. Of the biggest donors, one out of three were foreign born, compared to one out of five in the smallest givers category. This suggests that as Jews became more assimilated, their gifts became smaller. Loyalty to community also affected giving, with those who resided in Essex County the longest, contributing the most money. There was also a positive correlation between size of gifts and Jewish education and synagogue involvement. On the other hand, only 41 percent felt that charitable giving was "important" in terms of being a good Jew.[34]

Responding to the survey, Herman Pekarsky expressed doubt as to how good a job the Federation was doing in communicating with the Jewish community. The challenge was considerable because, unlike, say, food companies, the Jewish Community Council was selling "ideas, intangibles, good deeds, *mitzvoth*." Pekarsky also took note of the increasing secularization of the community. Perhaps, he mused, Jewish philanthropy should change its approach towards a community that seemed to emphasize the man-to-man dialogue more than one centered around a man-to-God relationship.[35]

Pekarsky's analysis was on the mark, but contrast the situation then with today's times. The overwhelmingly majority of contemporary Federation givers are second or third generation, but what is interesting is that they have become more involved with tradition than those who predominated in the 1950s and early 1960s. The reasons are many—the rise in ethnic pride generally, the search for greater personal meaning, the different relationship to Israel, fear of assimilation, and so on.

These differing factors necessitate a variety of approaches and MetroWest has done an excellent job of reacting to the situation. The desire for more Jewish tradition has been met by an intensification of programming in that area. Along the same lines, funding for Jewish education has been increased. Recognizing the needs of the more assimilated Jews in its catchment areas, especially the smaller Jewish communities of Morris and Sussex counties, MetroWest has developed programs that appeal to them, most notably devising special events and programs for those with little Jewish background and for intermarried couples and their children.

The methods of solicitation have been refined over the years too, though some have stayed pretty much the same. In 1955, Louis Stern, then president of the JCC, announced that there would be six area campaigns rather than one in order to increase identification with the appeals for funds. Moreover, making the approach more personal heightened the pressure to give because it meant that those who did not had to say no to people in their own communities who knew them.[36] Similar reasoning lay behind the grouping of donors according to professions such as the Liquor Wholesalers Division or the Manufacturing Division. Naming people heads of these divisions gave status to those individuals and made them feel more personally responsible for generating support. Crucial to the fund-raising apparatus was the Women's Division. In the words of Esther Kesselman, who was active from early on:

> Today they give big money but when we started we asked them to take a canister—ten cents a day for thirty-six days. After two years we realized that this was silly. We had to do something big, like a luncheon. There were women in Short Hills that were wearing expensive shoes. They could afford $100.00. I was chairman of the speakers bureau and I trained them how to speak.[37]

Today, these tasks are carried out by professionals, but, in the beginning, it was volunteers who generated the enthusiasm.

World events like wars in the Middle East were effective ways to tug at the heartstrings of local Jewry, but not all of them worked as well. The Eichmann trial, for instance, was used in appeals but it failed to attract significant giving. After all, it was more an alleviation of a threat than the emergence of one. Campaign leaders did not restrict their efforts to adults. Realizing that teenagers would one day take their place in the community as wage earners, they drafted them into service as well. In 1959, the local United Jewish Appeal Campaign appointed teenagers "captains," and held training sessions which featured lectures on how to obtain pledges from fellow teenagers. To drive the point home, they were to be shown a film on Romanian emigration.[38]

Today, the art of giving has been raised to a new level. Richard Slutzky, who was, until recently, MetroWest's assistant executive vice president and director of the Jewish Community Foundation, handled much of the gift solicitation, with considerable help from numerous lay leaders, such as Jerome Waldor. Aided by a booming stock market, he was kept quite busy by people looking for shelters, trusts, and philanthropic funds, and other ways to contribute. Aware of Slutzky's talents, CJF appointed him as national chair of its Endowment Directors Advisory Committee. The largest generator of endowment income for MetroWest has been the Lester Society, named after its founders, William and Betty Lester. In a 1996 interview, Martin Fox described how it works and the public's response to it:

> We saw people were passing away and we thought that if you're a person who gives $10,000 a year to the Federation, you should set up a $200,000 gift which

throws off $10,000 a year so that after you're gone your gift will continue. The response has been great. I guess you're buying a piece of immortality. Belonging to the Lester Society requires a minimum $100,000 endowment to the Society when you die. There are remainder trusts, charitable trusts, wills, insurance, different ways of doing it. We now have over 60 million dollars in funds. Other Federations are doing it too.[39]

All of the donations still go through MetroWest's Jewish Community Foundation, which is the largest Jewish foundation in the state. At last count, the Foundation administered over 400 funds and made annual grants totaling more than $8,100,000. In addition to the ways of giving enumerated by Fox, donors can also make gifts of property, including their own homes, State of Israel Bonds, zero coupon bonds, IRAs, and Lion of Judah Endowments, which are designed for women.

Giving in America has become huge. Hardly a day goes by without a publicized announcement of a major gift. Some give to universities, others to countries, or even the U.N. And the Jewish Federations of this country are very much a part of this trend. Perhaps the well will run dry one day, but, for now, it shows no sign of doing so.

Agencies and Institutions

While the Federation raises it own funds, it also receives money from the United Way of Essex and West Hudson. Since Jews, as well as Catholics and Protestants, all give to the United Way, and since there is no way of knowing just how much comes from each group, the United Way must give to all of the religious communities. True, the Jewish organizations are better at fund raising than the Catholics or the Protestants, but if the United Way were to use this argument as a reason for not giving to MetroWest, then Jews would probably stop giving to the United Way or give much less than they do now.

The Jewish Family Service Association is the main organization addressing the problems of families. It is the latest incarnation of twenty-eight or so mergers of groups over the years.[40] It helps people who are experiencing marital and psychological difficulties, counsels single parents, provides home care, aids in the resettlement of immigrants, and handles other related problems. Over the years, these agencies have coped with an incredible array of challenges. The majority have been typical maintenance and counseling issues. Every year, from the turn of the century, agencies took on the responsibility for hundreds, sometimes thousands, of cases. The following case history, as presented by the former executive director of the Child Guidance Bureau (a predecessor of the Jewish Family Service Association), Simon Doniger, gives us a sense of the problems dealt with:

> Larry was 3 1/2 years old when referred to us by Beth Israel Hospital because of his acute temper tantrums, biting and hitting of other children, and refusal to eat and feed himself. Our study of the family revealed a home with much conflict between mother and father and a child compensating for its lack of security through vicious, attention-getting mechanisms. The remarkable part of this picture was the total ignorance by the parents of the relationship between their own behavior and the symptoms displayed by their child.[41]

It was the unusual cases that took up an inordinate amount of time. For example, in 1930, there was the story of a rabbi who had requested assistance from United Charities, a beneficiary agency, for family support and to set up a combined synagogue and Jewish school. Upon further investigation, however, the agency found his ordination and general veracity to be highly suspect. Moreover, his wife had caught pneumonia in an apartment and the rabbi had refused to turn the heat on because of the Sabbath. Eventually she died on account of her illness. The rabbi did not attend the funeral, claiming illness, but was found by the agency to have been a malingerer. Two months after her death, according to United Hebrew Jewish Charities, the rabbi, a father of five, married a twenty-two-year-old-woman and had two more children with her. All of this is detailed in correspondence between the agency and the Conference of Charities. The Conference became involved in the case to the point where it asked a special committee "to study the matter." These events clearly demonstrate that social welfare could, indeed, be very complex and time consuming.[42]

Largely through the work begun by Pekarsky, there has been a consolidation process, so that people have a central address to go to when in need. Despite the plethora of organizations through the years, the needs have always been the same—family dislocation, refugees, employment and educational opportunities, and care of the sick. What it boils down to is a realization by the Jewish community that the larger society, no matter how hard it tries, is simply not equipped to provide the high levels of care for its citizens that the Jewish community wants to have for its own members.[43]

In addition to MetroWest's affiliated organizations, there are groups that function independently of MetroWest. This has always been the case, especially in the early years, when the Federation lacked the ability to control this aspect of communal life. Often these were attached to synagogues. A good case in point was the Jewish Day Nursery and Neighborhood House, a day-care center of sorts begun by a women's group affiliated with Temple B'nai Jeshurun. The reasons range from not being able to meet the standards of care established by the Federation, inability to pay at Federation salary scales, or simply a desire to be one's own boss. A good contemporary example of this phenomenon is JESPY House in South Orange, a boarding home for youngsters with learning disabilities. Operating on a budget of about $500,000, they are able to serve a population of eighteen to thirty students each year.[44] Although they are now a beneficiary of the Federation, they were initially independent. Another example of a separate agency is the Charles Bierman Home for the Aged.

One of the more important beneficiary institutions in the community is Daughters of Israel Geriatric Center. When it opened in 1906, it was the first Jewish home for the elderly in New Jersey. At first, led by Blume Hollander and several other dedicated women, it raised money the hard way—through linen showers, raffles, *pushka* drives, card games, rummage sales, food sales:"Sarah Reisberg contributed her delectable blintzes by the hundreds; golden challahs were baked and contributed by Sarah Friedman." And, in what is perhaps an organizational record, Rose Tepper was elected president of the home in 1918 and served in that capacity for twenty-eight years. Also, Esther Berlowe was executive director of the institution from 1949 to 1968. During that time the institution expanded to become a nursing home, in addition to a custodial residence.[45]

Daughters of Israel moved to a new home in West Orange in 1959. The land had been purchased by the Board through fund-raising drives and at the urging of Herman Pekarsky. Saul Schwarz, who was associate executive vice president of the Federation when he retired in 1980, remembers what the site looked like before construction began:

> Herman, myself, and Sidney Solomon went out and looked at the property, which was on a mountainside. And I said: "How are we going to build here?" And Herman said: "We'll carve out the mountain and we'll sell the dirt to the New Jersey Turnpike for its road." And that's how we did it. You see, dirt is expensive. With Pekarsky's involvement, we got more men involved and streamlined the organization.[46]

Schwarz also recalls several other homes during those days and his comments provide us with a better understanding of where and how Daughters of Israel stood out:

> There was the Hebrew Home for the Chronic Sick in Irvington. Mostly lower middle-class Eastern European Jews. They were afraid of being under Federation's control. We wanted to merge these two places under the chairmanship of Samuel Kessler. But they couldn't get together. This was in 1957. Kessler finally said: "I give you thirty days to get together. If you don't we'll start our own new home for the aged in West Orange." They couldn't do it and, after the thirty days, the Home for Chronic Sick said: "We withdraw and we're moving to Long Branch," which they did, before they ultimately closed.[47]

William Rothchild became the executive director of Daughters of Israel in 1972 and, together with the home's president, Arthur Schechner, made many innovations. Rothchild emphasized a holistic approach, stressing the integration of the physical, social, and emotional needs of the patient, rather than just the physical. Eventually, the home linked up with the various services offered by other community groups, thereby increasing the resources available to its residents.[48] Rothchild was succeeded by Larry Gelfand. Under his leadership, the Center continued to grow and significantly upgraded its facilities. Plans are currently underway to expand operations into Morris County.

An early example of what became commonplace was the JCC sponsored Council Club for the Elderly on Hawthorne Avenue which began functioning in the late 1940s. With its arts and crafts classes, cha cha lessons, plays, and community service projects, it gave the retired, but active elderly something to do with their free time. The Club received a good deal of assistance from volunteers brought in by the National Council of Jewish Women. The program was apparently considered so creative that delegations regularly visited it, coming from as far away as California.[49]

The elderly are also helped through the Jewish Community Housing Corporation, headed by Francine Klein, which provides housing in Federation Towers in Irvington, Federation Plaza in West Orange, Village Apartments in South Orange, and the South Orange B'nai Brith Federation House. Louis Stern and Saul Schwarz had taken a leading role in this as early as the 1960s, recommending different types of housing, special transportation programs for senior citizens, home care, homemaker service, neighborhood rehabilitation workshops and a geriatric multiservice center. In those days, progress was difficult because there was not nearly as much sympathy for integrating the elderly into the lives of the rest of the community. In fact, the Federation was compelled to engage in a legal battle, with Martin Kesselhaut as legal counsel, in order to achieve its goals.[50] In the end, however, it prevailed and, today, senior citizen programming is a major part of MetroWest's activities, as it is everywhere in the country.

Another agency that provides critical services for the community is the Jewish Vocational Service, headed by Ron Coun. Its primary role is job placement, vocational guidance, and rehabilitation workshops for the handicapped, difficult to place, and for those with special problems such as new immigrants. The rehabilitation workshops are designed to give the severely handicapped a chance to compile a satisfactory work record in a protected setting before applying for jobs in the private sector.

One of the most important institutions in the Jewish community and among Newarkers in general has been Beth Israel Hospital (see pp. 131–133). From its humble beginnings in 1902 in a small wooden frame structure, it grew, over the years, into a world-class hospital. While it has generally cooperated with the organized Jewish community, namely the Federation, relations were not always smooth. We see in the minutes of the Conference of Jewish Charities that the hospital resented what it regarded as efforts by the Conference to oversee its financial affairs. In fact, at one point, Abe Dimond threatened to resign over the hospital's attitude and criticisms. The hospital backed down.[51]

During the Depression, Beth Israel fell upon hard times. Money pledged within the Jewish community did not come through; nor did promised support from the Newark Welfare Federation.[52] As a result, the hospital was compelled to engage in a major fund raising drive, under the leadership of Abraham Lichtman, through a group called the Beth Israel Legion. The effort succeeded and Beth Israel survived the Depression.

By the late 1940s and the early fifties, relations between the Jewish Community Council and the hospital had improved, notwithstanding a disagreement over democratization of the hospital's governance system.[53] In 1950, the Council made available to the hospital a grant of $25,000, noting in its minutes that it recognized "the importance of the hospital as a community institution."[54] The changed attitude was due, in no small part, to the hospital's growing reputation as a first-rate medical facility. Today, of course, all of this is taken for granted. The "Born at the Beth" event held at the Newark Public Library several years ago attracted broad support from the community, including the African American part of it. Blacks, incidentally, did not always view Beth Israel so positively. As David Mallach, of the Federation, pointed out:

> Mayor Sharpe James told me that when he became a councilman in the early 1970s, he was absolutely convinced that Beth Israel was a blight on the community, was controlled solely by Jews, and must be eradicated. But gradually he learned that "The Beth" was the best thing for the community, with the commitment to the community.[55]

Another venerable institution was the Theresa Grotta Aid for Convalescents, a home for poor working women who were ill and needed post-acute hospital care. Founded in 1916, it was originally in West Caldwell, before moving to West Orange. Most recently, the property was sold, with the money used to create the Grotta Foundation for Senior Care. The Foundation awards grants to organizations that develop innovative programs relating to care of the elderly.[56]

One of the home's most unique aspects was the manner in which it was started. Theresa Grotta was born in Shoenwald, Bohemia in 1841. She immigrated to America, went to school in New York City, and, after marrying Heineman Grotta, lived with him in Wisconsin for a number of years before settling permanently in Newark. It was there that she achieved an enviable reputation as a selfless worker for the Jewish community and as a wonderful human being in general. As a member of the Hulda Lodge, she worked tirelessly on behalf of needy families, earning the gratitude of people throughout the city. She was also the founder of the Newark chapter of the National Council of Jewish Women. In addition to her communal activities she raised eleven children. As she neared her eightieth birthday her friends pondered what they might give her as a present. In the past she had received the usual—watches, household goods, and so on, but this time they wanted to to do something special. What could be more fitting, they decided, than to honor this fine woman's work with the ultimate gift—a home for the indigent named after her. And that's how the home began. As Saul Schwarz put it, "What do you give a woman who has everything?"

A major concern with respect to health in the early years was tuberculosis. In New Jersey, the problem was attended to by the Jewish

Anti-Tuberculosis League, which was organized in 1922, at the Progress Club. In the past, money for TB had been collected by individuals who often took for themselves up to half of the sums collected as fees for their efforts. Newark's most prominent Jewish leaders were heavily involved in this work, including Benjamin Hollander, Herman Kussy, Anton Kaufman, William S. Rich, Philip Schotland, and the leading rabbis of all the denominations. The League provided critical assistance over the years to thousands of Jews afflicted with the disease, arranging for care as well as transportation to sanatoriums in Denver, Colorado, Liberty, New York, Browns-Mills, New Jersey or elsewhere for those requiring it. Another group that made important contributions in this area was the Newark branch of the Deborah Consumptive Relief League. Most of its efforts were directed at supporting the Brown-Mills sanatorium.[57]

Jewish education had been a part of communal life from the very beginning, with a congregational school having been established in B'nai Jeshurun in 1863 and with the founding of the Plaut Memorial Hebrew Free School by the Hebrew Education Society in 1888.

Nevertheless, the Conference of Jewish Charities did not at first see Jewish education as falling within its purview. Complicating matters was the fact that the more traditional elements in the community felt that neither they nor this issue were being taken seriously. That changed in 1937, when the Conference, led by Samuel Kessler, Michael Stavitsky, and others, organized the Jewish Education Association (JEA), first headed by Sylvan H. Kohn. The change of heart was due to community pressure and to the gradual realization that Jewish education was important for Jewish survival.

Over the years, the JEA has operated as a sort of super board of Jewish education for all of the Jewish schools in the area. Among its functions have been licensing and supplying teachers, running conferences and programs, preparing curricula, in-service teacher training, establishing standards for the schools, and coordinating the activities of the different educational institutions. Through the JEA, MetroWest has given support to the Central Hebrew High School, to the expansion of Hebrew courses in public high schools, to the Rutgers Hillel, and to a host of other programs.

In 1943, the first major day school in the city, the Yeshiva of Newark, was founded. The Federation did not provide it with any assistance at first. Today, that could never happen because over the years the Federation has come to understand the centrality of Jewish learning for Jewish life. As a result, it has significantly increased its backing for day schools. Still, as the leadership acknowledges, there are problems that even the Federation cannot really solve. The views of James Schwarz, a past president of MetroWest, accurately reflect the frustrations inherent in this issue:

> One shift over the years has been that we give more money to Jewish education. But the amount that we give can't make a serious dent. If we give, say, $100,000 to Solomon Schechter, they could reduce tuition by perhaps $120 a child. There are no panaceas to Jewish identity. I dread the thought that my children might intermarry. Sending kids to Israel isn't an answer necessarily because there isn't much follow-up. We are no different than other communities in that there's so much lip service to Jewish education and so little funding, relatively speaking. Communities are fixed in their ways and don't change easily.[58]

Even as they assert these limitations, the Federation leaders indicate that they will continue their efforts because there is no alternative. Surely, the statistics indicate that they are both serious and active in supporting Jewish education. Today, more than 9,000 students at forty-five schools receive educational instruction in Morris, Sussex, and Essex Counties and there is a whole network of adult education courses. Nationally, there are some hopeful signs that leaders around the country are beginning to more fully appreciate the magnitude of the problem. In October of 1997, eleven well-known philanthropists, working with UJA-Federation of New York, unveiled a major 18 million dollar effort aimed at building and expanding Reform, Orthodox, and Conservative Jewish day schools around the United States. With a matching funds requirement, the program was actually a 36 million dollar undertaking. The very fact that the term "day school" now includes all of the denominations, highlights the rise in awareness about the subject and the amount of dollars committed underscores it. What it means in the long run remains to be seen.[59]

Larger Issues

Newark Jewry has a long history of support for Israel. While the Federation in Newark has tended to be more supportive of local community needs when compared to those of overseas Jews than some other communities, there is no question that the State of Israel has always been a priority, just as it is among Jews everywhere. Zionists were active in Newark well before the Conference on Jewish Charities was created, with numerous Zionist groups active in the city. The *Jewish Chronicle* reported in its December 23, 1921 issue on a visit to Newark by the president of the World-Wide Zionist Executive Committee and renowned Hebraic scholar, Nahum Sokolow. While there, he spoke at Krueger Auditorium as a guest of the Newark District Zionists. A few months earlier, Chaim Weizmann had also visited the city.

These, and other leaders traveled around the country visiting many communities, but it is clear that Newark was very much part of the lecture circuit. In that year, for instance, Newark had been apportioned the responsibility to raise $10,000 towards the total goal of $100,000 nationally. As it happened though, Sokolow noted in his address that he had never heard of Newark. Responding to Sokolow with tongue in cheek, Philip Schotland expressed his surprise at this since, twenty-one years earlier, Louis Aronson had won a $10,000 award offered by Belgium for his invention of a nonphosphorous match.[60]

Certainly, Palestine's Jewish leaders had no trouble recognizing Newark as the years went by. Already in 1922, one year later, the medical community raised another $10,000 toward establishing a medical school at Hebrew University. And in that same year, 8,000 Zionists paraded on Broad Street in support of the Palestine Mandate. In looking at accounts of those days it becomes apparent that Newark's Jews linked their activities on behalf of Palestine to what was happening to them in this country, good or bad. The *Jewish Chronicle* editorialized, in its piece on the parade, that although they were marching in support of their ancient homeland they "proudly bore the Stars and Stripes and the star and blue and white bars, denoting that America will always be remembered as the one great place of refuge for the persecuted Jew."[61]

On the other hand, Jews were not hesitant to criticize America for its failings. Announcing a trip by Jewish physicians from Newark, bound for Palestine, Dr. Nathan Ratnoff stated:

The establishment of the Hebrew University in Jerusalem which will become a fact with the founding of the medical faculty, will be one of the most effective answers that the Jews in defending their self-respect can give to the present agitation which started with Harvard University, to exclude Jews from American institutions of higher learning. I look forward to the time when the medical faculty of the Hebrew University in Jerusalem will make noteworthy contributions to the science of healing, from which all other universities, including Harvard, will derive great benefit.[62]

These two statements, on two different occasions, reflect the ambivalence of American Jewry that has continued to the present time—America is a great country but it is not perfect and if Jews truly feel uncomfortable here, there is always Israel.

Much of the support among Newark Jewry was spontaneous. German Jewry was more restrained in its backing when contrasted to that given by Eastern European Jewry. Nonetheless, it was favorably inclined, as can be seen from the minutes of the Conference of Jewish Charities which, in the 1920s, was controlled by Jews of German origin. For example, at its November 30, 1925 meeting, Rabbis Silberfeld (B'nai Abraham) and Hoffman (Oheb Shalom) and Nathan Kussy, requested permission to conduct a $10,000 drive towards the "erection of a synagogue center in Palestine." The money was to be raised at a dinner given "under the patronage of Albert Hollander and Meyer Kussy." Permission was given and the effort was endorsed by the members.[63]

Enthusiasm for Palestine-related causes declined in the 1930s because of the Depression, but in the 1940s, especially after the end of World War II, it increased greatly.[64] Moreover, the community understood that garnering support for statehood was not only an internal matter and set about making the case for a Jewish homeland among those outside the Jewish community. Typical of such efforts was a 1946 luncheon held for ninety-two Protestant ministers of Essex County, featuring a talk entitled, "Palestine—Fact and Fiction."[65]

Throughout this period, there were numerous struggles at the local and national level between organizations vying for control of the millions of dollars that were being raised for Israel. In 1945, the Newark leadership met in New York as part of a fourteen-city delegation and recommended that the National UJA be reconstructed and that local communities be given a greater say in the organization. In 1948, there were further conflicts between the Zionist Organization of America and the United Palestine Appeal (UPA) and the reverberations were felt among Newark's local leaders too. The battles were not only over money but centered around demands for greater democratization within the UPA.[66]

In 1948, Golda Meir (then known as Golda Myerson) visited Newark at the invitation of the UPA and made an impassioned fund raising plea to the Jewish Community Council. The Council responded generously, borrowing $500,000, which it then donated to Palestinian Jewry and recouped from the Campaign the following year. This pattern was repeated over the next few years. Once the situation stabilized in the 1950s, Newark Jewry raised millions of dollars as gifts to Israel and towards the purchase of Israel Bonds. In 1963, the year in which Jerome Fien chaired the Israel Bond drive, bonds were able to be redeemed for the first time, namely for those who had purchased them in 1951, the first year of the drive. Fien noted that during the twelve-year existence of the organization, twelve million dollars worth of Bonds had been sold in Essex County.[67] The amounts continued to grow and by the mid-1960s the goal had been doubled to $2,000,000 a year.

Another concern was the plight of Jews around the world. Ever since their arrival on these shores Jews had felt a sense of responsibility for their less fortunate brethren. In Newark, this took the form of rallies for oppressed Jews in Europe and elsewhere, appeals to American government officials for assistance to those overseas, and material aid, with the American Joint Distribution Committee, American Jewish Congress, American Jewish Committee, and the Jewish Labor Committee taking leading roles in the community. Many of these efforts were duly recorded in the Jewish newspapers. Typical was a notice in the October 14, 1921 "Social and Personal" column of the *Jewish Chronicle* regarding one of many "Bundle Days" to be held "when clothing and shoes will be gathered here for the children and other starving people here and in the Near East." In this case, the appeal was for the poor in general and in other cases it was made on behalf of Jewish communities, for example, survivors of the Kishinev pogrom.

The most direct and extensive involvement, however, was in the form of helping refugees who came to Newark. Here, the National Council of Jewish Women (NCJW), through its Bureau of Service to the Foreign Born, was in the forefront of such activities. The Newark Chapter was established in 1912, emphasizing in those days Americanization classes, preparation for citizenship, and legal assistance. In fact, one of the first all-year-round schools for immigrants was set up in Newark, with proficient students receiving prizes in the form of trips to other American cities.[68]

The passage of the Johnson Acts in 1921 and 1924 severely curtailed immigration to the U.S., but in the mid-1930s the rate increased when special allowances were made for German and Austrian Jews fleeing Nazi persecution. About 124,000 refugees came here, and Newark, as a city with a German Jewish population, proved attractive to a number of them. Since the influx occurred during Depression years, jobs were not always available, but the NCJW and the Federation made strong efforts to train and retrain the new arrivals in anticipation of better times.

An examination of the NCJW's Bureau of Service to the Foreign Born caseworker files reveals that the adaptation of most of these newcomers was both rapid and smooth. They were determined to do well and not be a burden on the community. Moreover, the caseworkers, while they saw them in stereotypical fashion, genuinely cared about the immigrants. The following description by a caseworker was typical:

> Hilde in office. Hilde is about five feet three inches tall, stocky, looks like a peasant girl. Has a large face, blue eyes. Wears her hair in a very old fashioned way. Wears unbecoming clothes. She graduated Gymnasium in Germany. Her marks are fairly good. She speaks little English.[69]

The caseworker developed a close relationship as seen from the following letter, dated July 24, 1938, and written to her by an appreciative and hopeful Hilde. It is reprinted here in full and exactly as written because it presents an excellent portrait of both the immigrant struggle and the personal nature of the contacts, thus revealing that those who worked with them did not necessarily see them as simply clients. The extent to which this was true is difficult to evaluate but many of the case histories demonstrated unusual commitment and concern towards the refugees:

> Dear Miss Rubin:
>   In my old, nothing-doing days, I pity you out of all my heart. Aren't you swimming on high sea already in your bungalow? I am so sorry that I couldn't come to see you out there, but, as you probably know, Deborah and I were laid off, and then I had my tonsils taken out.
>   The reason why I am writing is that I learned about a Jewish fund in New York that gives money to people who want to go to college. Do you know anything about that, the address, etc.? I thought, may-be they are interested giving me money, because I want to specialize in agricultural chemistry, and there are only such few Jews in that field. But I am afraid, it is too late to apply for anything like that now, or don't you think so? I think, I would need some money only for the very beginning to get a start. Then I hope, I can work my way through. I would like to see you personally about that. Do you have time during this week to come up for supper some day or shall I come up to the office?
>   If a job should happen to knock at your door, please remember me, but I can't work as waitress yet, since I lost ten pounds. I become more and more American.

Could you possibly call me up because of that fund? Thanks a lot.
>   A whole bunch of regards yours,
>   Hilde

Notice the self-confidence inherent in the invitation extended to the caseworker to come to her own home for a meal, as well as the desire to better oneself through college attendance and learning a profession, not to mention the general optimism and level of friendship. Most remarkably, the letter, in Hilde's own words, is extremely well-written for someone who had come to the U.S., as Hilde did, only two years earlier.[70]

With the outbreak of World War II, the situation became more critical. Refugee children began arriving to the U.S. in greater numbers. These had been the responsibility nationally of German Jewish Children's Aid but it was the NCJW that took financial responsibility for that organization between 1939 and 1943.[71] In Newark, Herbert Hannoch, outstanding attorney and community leader, redoubled his efforts to place the youngsters in the Jewish Children's Home, of which he was president, or in private homes. Jacob Trobe, the Home's director, described the initial reaction of of a group of young arrivals who came in June of 1941:

> All the youngsters were thrilled with ice cream sodas which they had not tasted in Europe. They were also startled when they saw the large number of motor cars on Pulaski highway. In France they were accustomed to seeing only a few cars used by military officers.[72]

Communities around the country varied in the degree of sympathy shown for the refugees.[73] Newark displayed considerable empathy, possibly because it was used to the idea of immigrants entering it and because of the example set by the Jewish leadership. Hannoch reported at a Board meeting on January 12, 1943, that he had received "confidential information" that thirty-five children were "on the high seas" and might be expected in Newark shortly. Newark accepted three of them (a more than respectable number for one city). Significantly, Leonard Shiman, brother of Federation president Daniel Shiman, offered to take a child and Michael Stavitsky offered to do the same for one of two brothers who had arrived on the S.S. Serpa Pinto if the home thought it a good idea to separate them.[74]

Jewish leaders from Newark also traveled to Europe to see what could be done. As a case in point, Joel Gross, then treasurer of the Essex

County Council of Jewish Agencies, was sent to the Middle East by the Joint Distribution Committee in 1943. His task was to help supervise in the distribution of aid to Polish Jewish refugees in Asiatic Russia and to be a liaison for the purpose of facilitating the immigration of refugees into Palestine. Jacob Trobe went to Europe on behalf of the Joint in November of 1944 and was the first representative of a Jewish relief agency to reach Bergen-Belsen. While in Germany, he oversaw a staff of sixty-five that fed, clothed, and retrained the survivors.

As the full picture emerged about the horrors and scope of what had happened to Europe's Jews, the Newark community sprang into action. The Bureau of Service to the Foreign Born had been helping refugees for decades and was admirably equipped to deal with such problems. As a result, it took the lead, working closely with the Federation's Jewish Family Service Association. Among those playing a prominent role in the Council's work were Mrs. Milton Lowenstein, Mrs. Martin Simon, Mrs. Fred Weiser, Mrs. David Josephson, Mrs. Gertrude Berger, and Mrs. William Weiser. In 1946, twenty-seven families received assistance in resettlement; a year later, the number had virtually tripled to seventy-seven, with expenditures of $55,500.[75] With the assistance of the Jewish Family Service Association, the refugees were resettled, placed in Americanization and citizenship classes, and given help in securing employment by the Jewish Vocational Service.

One of the immediate needs was family reunification. The Bureau of Service to the Foreign Born worked on 1,128 cases in Newark in 1947 alone, assisting Newark residents in their search for relatives and friends overseas. It was successful 158 times,[76] sometimes through its weekly feature in the *Jewish News*, "Is Your Name Here?" The Bureau's Port and Dock Volunteers unit welcomed the refugees when they came off the boats in both the blistering heat of summer and the freezing cold of winter, on Sundays and on holidays. These heroic individuals were the first contacts that the survivors had with this country and this made the dedication which they exhibited crucial in the adaptation process. In all this the Bureau cooperated closely with HIAS (Hebrew Immigrant Aid Society) and with the USNA (United Service for New Americans) in finding homes and communities for the newcomers. One especially successful program was the NCJW's Newark section's Ship-A-Box Program which sent clothes, candy, and toys to DPs in Europe. In 1946, the section was first among 176 sections nationwide in the amount it shipped, sending 732 parcels all over Europe.[77]

The NCJW did its best to make the immigrants feel at home as soon as possible. There were parties, dances, clubs, and trips. Council members and their husbands often hosted these events which sometimes coincided with Jewish holidays. In an attempt to link them up with the larger nation, the immigrants were invited to showings of films depicting the immigrant history of this country, such as Warner Brothers, *My Girl Tisa*, and *Passage to Nowhere* and MGM's, *The Search*, a film about displaced persons. NCJW volunteers participated in special seminars and listened to guest speakers describe the special needs of these latest immigrants who were unique in having endured years of starvation and torture in concentration camps or in hiding.[78]

Nationally, a $100,000,000 campaign was launched by UJA to meet the needs of Europe's homeless. Poignant ads were placed in Jewish newspapers around the country, similar to one in the *Jewish News* of May 10, 1946, which read, in part:

Dear Children: We Will Not Let you Die

Yes, we know that you are starved and frightened and ill—your eyes haunted with horror and your hearts torn with longing for parents you saw go into gas chambers and crematoria.

But dear children, you need no longer wish for death to rescue you. We in America have resolved that you shall live, that your broken bodies shall be mended, your broken lives made whole. We are determined that we will give you the chance to grow up as useful, decent citizens—strong and proud and free.

The ad concluded with an exhortation to give, referring to Newark's quota as determined by National UJA: "WE MUST RAISE $2,638,000."

Most of the DPs entered the U.S. after June 1948 when the Senate, by a vote of 63–13, passed the Displaced Persons Act, allowing up to 200,000 refugees into this country. While a vast improvement over the previous situation, the bill left much to be desired, clearly favoring Christian over Jewish DPs. Among the strongest voices urging passage of a more equitable law, was that of Senator H. Alexander Smith, Republican of New Jersey. A member of the Senate Foreign Relations Committee, Smith had visited the camps and was greatly moved by the suffering he witnessed there. On June 16, 1950, President Truman signed into law an amended version of the DP Act, expanding to 415,744 the number of refugees that could be admitted. As a result, more survivors were able to immigrate to America and to Newark. In

1951, the JCC's Jewish Family Service Association and the Bureau of Service to the Foreign Born, aided by Helen Gottlieb, sponsored a volunteer project to help survivors make claims for war reparations, which had then become available.

In 1956, when Hungarian Jewish refugees arrived in the U.S., the the Bureau and the Jewish Family Service were ready once again, as was Newark's organized Jewish community. At its meeting of January 29, 1957, the Jewish Community Council announced that it was providing assurances for thirty families who had fled in the aftermath of the Hungarian Revolution. According to Saul Schwarz, this group was different than those who came in the post-World War II period because its members found work and established themselves more quickly, usually within six to eight weeks.[79] They were also a healthier group largely because they had not come from concentration camps. Their adjustment was so good that, by 1958, the agencies who had been working with the refugees no longer had any contact with most of them. Further evidence of their success came from the fact that despite the existence of an economic recession at the time, few of the new-comers reported having been laid off from their jobs.[80]

Closer to home, there was the problem of domestic prejudice and this too was an important issue for Newarkers. The organized Jewish community was, of course, united in its opposition to anti-Semitism and discrimination, though its leaders and their constituencies did differ on how to combat it. On one side were those, like Rabbi Solomon Foster of Temple B'nai Jeshurun, who felt that America offered the Jews a great deal and that they should work quietly, and without public protest. As he put it in a 1938 interview given to the *Newark Evening News*:

> The Jewish people of the United States do not need to organize to defend our political and economic rights as long as we have a constitution, a Supreme Court, an Executive and a Congress, with state and municipal governments pledged to apply no religious tests to any person as to his status as a citizen.
> The political and economic rights that are accorded to Catholic, Protestant and other groups in America satisfy the Jewish people in fullest measure. It is untrue, unwise and unnecessary to suggest that the Jewish people in the United States require special safeguards to our economic and political rights.[81]

Given his viewpoint it was not surprising that Foster opposed a nationwide plebiscite called by the American Jewish Congress to protest anti-Semitism. The Congress felt that Jews faced great danger, both in America from the likes of Father Coughlin and from the hatred spewed forth by the *Dearborn Independent*, and abroad from the rise of Nazi Germany. While agreeing that anti-Semitism was a serious problem in Europe, Foster felt that Jews as a group were too weak to fight against governments and that they should rely instead on the United States and its allies to defend their rights.

Beneath all of this posturing for the public was a very real difference that made for a contentious atmosphere. Foster was anti-Zionist and Stephen S. Wise, head of the Congress, was a Zionist who had, in the past, attacked Foster for his views on Palestine. Responding to Foster's statements on the issue of holding a plebiscite, Wise minced no words:

> We as Jews, should be proud of our race, but apparently Rabbi Foster is not, because he objects to our organizing as a unit. All of the rabbis of Newark are present on this platform except one. The absence of that one shows, thank God, we are right in pushing the congress. I always wait to hear what the old lady scold emits, what rage and bitterness come from B'nai Jeshurun and then I take the other side and I know I am right.[82]

Aside from these pyrotechnics, Newark's Jews worked together, more or less. During the war, America's Jews tried, in a variety of ways, to draw attention to what was happening in Europe, notwithstanding the charges made later that they did not do enough. When synagogues were defaced or gravestones overturned, or people denied equal rights in employment or housing, the community spoke with one voice. This was particularly true after the Holocaust and the establishment of the State of Israel. By then, even assimilated Jews had come to realize that silence in the face of hatred only resulted in more hatred. While they might not favor an outspoken approach they did not actively oppose it either.

Other Activities

A Jewish newspaper is of critical importance to a community. To begin with, it becomes a repository of its history, without which it cannot have an identity. Second, it is a way of letting everyone know what of Jewish importance is happening. Without such information, Jewish life cannot function, for its activities, be they dinners, lectures, or parties, are inevitably group affairs. Third, a newspaper provides a forum for intellectual and spiritual views to be aired and debated. Absent that and the community becomes lifeless. Fourth, people need to be recognized for their achievements and the newspaper serves as a medium for expressions of both recognition and appreciation. Finally, forging a sense of solidarity among many Jews from different communities, is critical. That is what Herman Pekarsky had in mind when he involved the Federation in the purchase of the newspapers in 1947. For all of these reasons, it was imperative for Newark to have a viable and active Jewish press.

The earliest local news organs were Yiddish weeklies, namely the *Newarker Wochenblatt* and *Der Morgenshtern*.[83] Generally speaking, these newspapers contained both material of an intellectual nature and an emphasis on what was going on in Europe. This was a reflection of their audience which had not yet really crossed the bridge into American culture. It was left for the *Jewish Chronicle*, founded in 1921 by Anton Kaufman, to fulfill that goal. Kaufman was born in Hungary in 1882 and came to the U.S. in 1905. He was the publisher and editor of the *Chronicle* until his death on New Year's Day of 1943. The *Chronicle* was a mix of news, both local and national, as well as international, with a heavy dosage of communal events. Its advertisements are an anthropological gold mine, informing the reader of what movies and plays were "in," which camps Jewish children attended and what resorts their parents frequented. Social commentary was not its forte, although it did have a long-running column by Solomon Foster, rabbi of Kaufman's congregation.[84]

After Kaufman's death, Nathan Brodsky, son of Rabbi Hyman Brodsky, bought the *Newark Jewish Times* from a Rochester businessman in anticipation of the Jewish Community Council's impending establishment of its own paper. The newspaper tried to ride on the *Chronicle's* coattails by asserting in its inaugural issue that its sponsors had been good friends of Anton Kaufman, but this was not enough, however, to turn the paper into a success. Brodsky's real hope was to be bought out and that is precisely what happened. He soon sold the *Times* to the Council, which then absorbed it into its own effort, the *Jewish News*. In reality, the *Times* was floundering and there was no need to buy it. In fact, Pekarsky opposed the idea as a waste of community funds, arguing instead that the Federation should simply publish its own competing organ. This was opposed by others, who felt that if the relatively powerful Federation put the *Times* out of business it would be criticized as heavy-handed, and it was this view that prevailed. Shortly after receiving his money, Brodsky reneged on his agreement not to be involved with a competing newspaper and began writing a column for the privately owned *American Jewish Ledger*. He stopped doing so only after being threatened with a lawsuit by the Jewish Community Council.

The *Jewish News* was born on January 3, 1947. The primary moving forces behind the decision were Pekarsky, Daniel Shiman, Samuel Kessler, and Alan Lowenstein, all of whom felt that a good newspaper would be of enormous benefit to the community. It was a success from the start, picking up journalism awards in each of its first three years. Its reputation was marred, however, by the fact that its first editor was Allen Lesser, a man with decidedly anti-Zionist views. On the eve of the establishment of an independent Israel, such a position was intolerable. Lesser had been a staff member of the controversial and high-quality literary magazine, the *Menorah Journal*. It was, however, a magazine with Marxist leanings and perhaps the Board should have known better. But world-class scholars like Salo Baron and Jacob Rader Marcus had praised Lesser and it was probably too tempting for a fledgling newspaper to pass on such an obviously talented individual. The outcry from the community made the next move quite easy. Readers were deeply angered that a person with such views was at the helm and before long Lesser was gone.

He was replaced by the then managing editor, Harry Weingast, a native Newarker formerly with the *Newark Star-Ledger*. Weingast, incidentally, was annoyed with Lesser for another reason. He had discovered what was then a major news scoop—the existence of a direct relationship between the humanitarian efforts of Swedish diplomat Raoul Wallenberg and the U.S. Government. Alas, the story had been overshadowed by the whole brouhaha over Lesser's Jewish outlook. The new position somewhat mollified him and it was one he remained in for over thirty years. Weingast settled into his job and calmed the waters, so to speak. *The Jewish News*, while not very exciting in the eyes of some, became a predictable and quite decent house organ. Conrad Berke, also with the *News*, described it as follows:

There was a basic news style to it, a main format in terms of editorial content. Page one always had news of Israel; always had a Federation campaign story about money; always had a profile or interview with a major donor; there was usually a story on an agency; and there was a box with late-breaking news. It was a good mix.[85]

The "mix," which caused Jewish newspapers to be sarcastically referred to as "weaklies," was actually predetermined by larger forces. The spread of local newspapers to so many communities meant that, in terms of prestige, they could not attract the kinds of quality journalists that were eager to write for a national news organ, like, say, the *New York Times* or *Washington Post*. Moreover, the very fact that they were local made the editors gravitate towards community news. Then there were financial issues. Running a newspaper properly was simply too costly for private individuals and they were forced, invariably, to rely on the local Federations for support.[86] This not only resulted in issues that looked like public relations organs for the Federation and its donors but it also meant that they could not freely express themselves on many matters of concern to the Jewish community. Today, even independent newspapers like the *Long Island Jewish World*, while they do possess greater freedom of action, must still be mindful of the Jewish establishment if they want to maintain advertising revenues and have access to news sources.

Jonathan Sarna has pointed out that anti-Semitism, especially between the two World Wars, made Jewish newspapers afraid to cover controversial stories. There was a feeling that it might be best not to antagonize the forces in America that were not friendly to the Jews. An unfortunate by-product of that policy was that it made many Jews feel that they could not rely on their own ethnic press to give them a true picture of what was going on in this country when it came to their own communities and people. Naturally, what was detrimental for the Jewish press turned out to be a boon for the circulation of magazines like *Commentary* and *Midstream*, though they too had limits on what they could say because of their sponsors.[87]

Even so, there has been a definite trend in the last decade or two towards greater independence. The *Jewish News*, now called the *New Jersey Jewish News*, certainly falls into that category, having recruited David Twersky in 1993, himself formerly with the *Forward*, to run the paper. The change had actually begun in 1988, when David Frank took over from Charles Baumohl as editor in chief and revamped the paper. Under Twersky, the newspaper has continued its coverage of local events but it does not shy away from covering controversial topics. And its commentary on issues relating to religion or politics has been quite balanced. On occasion, people complain, like one Federation executive who said: "Yes, I know it's a Federation paper but what good is it? He [Twersky] doesn't listen to us anyway." In terms of genuine freedom of the press and Jewish communal life, that is probably a very good sign, for the *News*, for the Federation, and for the Jewish community.[88]

We know that Newark's Jews were charitable in supporting both their own and those in other parts of the world. The organizations that existed in the community—Israel Bonds, National Council of Jewish Women, Jewish Family Service Association, and so on, all had their counterparts in many cities with sizeable Jewish populations. And like other communities, Newark had loan societies, but one of them, the Hebrew Free Loan Association, founded by Rabbis Mordecai Radin and Hyman Brodsky at the beginning of the century, was rather unusual. In an article that appeared in the *Newark Sunday News* on November 26, 1950, reporter Max Weiner wrote:

> A "bank" which charges no fee or interest, which asks no questions as to why the applicant wants the money, which gambles on the notion that practically everybody is reasonably honest—that is the Hebrew Free Loan Association.[89]

The organization's rationale was that small merchants or poor parents unable to provide collateral for banks, were still entitled to help if they were honest and could pay back in small amounts over a long period of time. Sometimes, when applicants were unable to come up with endorsers, the Association's officer's signed.

The following story, recounted by Frank Slavitt, a central figure in the organization for many years, gives us an idea of the types of situations applicants faced: A peddler showed up at the Association one evening after it had closed. Only Slavitt was there. He explained that he had been trying everywhere to scrape together $200 (this was in the 1940s) to pay an overdue note and that the bank had threatened to take court action if it was not paid immediately. "Give me your address and go home and wait," Slavitt told him. "The safe is locked and I can't give you the money on my own authority, but I'll try to contact the others." The peddler thanked him, but did not believe anything would come of it. At midnight, to his amazement, Slavitt knocked on his door with the money in hand. That was the boost the peddler needed. He eventually opened up a store and became a devoted member of the Association.[90]

The Joint Chaplaincy Committee was another group dedicated to improving the lives of Essex County residents. The Committee was first set up in 1959 by Rabbis Zev Segal and Jeshaia Schnitzer, together with the then director of social planning, Saul Schwarz. The Committee appointed chaplains whose functions encompassed bedside prayers, religious services for the bedridden, distribution of religious literature, contacting the patient's rabbi, and pastoral counseling. At first, there was resistance to the idea, with some Federation officials taking the position that such matters ought to be arranged for by the local synagogues. But how quickly could they coordinate responses in times of crisis? What about those who had no temple affiliation, but were, nonetheless, identifying Jews? And wasn't this an opportunity to raise their level of Jewish consciousness? Realizing the merit in these arguments, the Jewish Community Council accepted the responsibility, one which it has maintained to this very day.[91]

Jewish Organizations

There were hundreds of Jewish organizations in Newark through the years. Some were branches of national entities, others were just local independent groups. These included, Hadassah, American Jewish Congress, B'nai Brith, American Jewish Committee, National Council of Jewish Women (discussed earlier), ORT, Jewish Labor Committee, Workmen's Circle, AMIT, Jewish Day Nursery and Neighborhood House, Vacation Home for Working Girls, and on and on. To provide the reader with a taste of this important feature of Newark's Jewish life, several of the more important ones will be described briefly. The full range of Jewish organizational life in the city still awaits its chronicler.

It is noteworthy that a local woman, Sarah Kussy, was involved with Henrietta Szold, when national Hadassah was founded in New York in 1912. Two years later, Kussy started the first Newark chapter at a meeting attended by twenty-seven women. At its high point, the chapter had about 5,000 members. Another prominent local leader in the group was Nettie Katchen, chapter president from 1928 to 1930. Katchen was the daughter of the Yiddish poet, Isaac Rabinovitch. The main focus of the organization has been on raising money for educational and health-related projects in Israel and organizing social functions.

B'nai Brith International has also been active in Essex County, and its South Mountain Lodge was one of the largest in the world. Philip Lax, a Maplewood resident and Newark native, gained international prominence in the organization as one of its vice presidents and also spearheaded a twenty-year campaign to build a center for the B'nai Brith Hillel at Rutgers University. The B'nai Brith/Anti Defamation League, along with the American Jewish Congress, American Jewish Committee, Jewish War Veterans, and the Jewish Labor Committee, all played an important role in Newark by fighting against anti-Semitism and prejudice in general. In addition, the Federation had its own Community Relations Committee that engaged in similar work. In 1944, they and the other organizations linked up with the National Jewish Community Relations Advisory Council, an organization headed at one time, by yet another community resident, Jacqueline Levine.[92]

Until 1944, the American Jewish Committee, founded in 1906, was national in its structure, without any representation at the local level. An effort to alter that, led by John Slawson, its executive director, went down to defeat, 60 to 4 at the executive committee level. One of the four voting in favor was Newark's Alan Lowenstein. When Jacob Blaustein became the AJC's president shortly thereafter, the policy changed. Chapters were established in the major Jewish population centers and, in 1947, one was set up in Newark, under the guidance of Julius Cohn and Alan Lowenstein.[93] Similarly, the American Jewish Congress established a presence in Newark with a delegation attending its national convention as early as 1919. Joachim Prinz, rabbi of Temple B'nai Abraham, served as the national president of the organization. One of the main issues on the agenda of the Congress through the years has been the need to maintain separation of church and state. Both groups were especially active during the civil rights movement in the 1960s. The Federation also reached out to non-Jewish groups, especially the black community, through its Community Relations Committee. The Committee has been equally involved with Jewish causes, among them Soviet Jewry and Holocaust education.

Was Newark's Federation really unique? Was there anything special about it? The answer to both questions is yes, particularly when one considers all of the distinguishing elements together. First and foremost, are the people of the community. The desire of Newark's early Jewish leaders to develop a separate and distinct identity for the community was of paramount importance. They could easily have succumbed to the temptation to let New York's organized community do the work for them, but they didn't. Instead, they built and nurtured their own communal institutions.

The decision to go this route may have been made, in part, because individuals had a need to be leaders and that option was not available in New York. This turned out to be the good fortune of Newark's Jews. As a result, strong organizations were formed in the city by dedicated people who developed the community into one better able to provide for its needs than would have been the case had it been dependent upon its larger neighbor. It is of interest that many of those who became leaders cited family members or close friends as role models whose actions propelled them into community service. The following quote from Sidney Weinstein, a past Federation president, is a good example of that pattern:

> My brother, Louis Weinstein, was a person who was president of the CJF and he was also Eisenhower's liaison to De Gaulle. I became involved in Federation because my family—my brother and father—were involved in Jewish communal affairs. My father was from Vilna. My mother's uncle or grand-uncle was the *Chofetz Chaim* [prominent European rabbi and talmudic scholar].[94]

A look at community leaders in Newark readily establishes that it is often a generational phenomenon, with children of leaders following in their parents' footsteps.

Further confirmation of the high degree of involvement came from Howard Charish, a past executive vice president of MetroWest, who is not a Newark native and who has worked in Federations elsewhere in the U.S. When asked how Newark's Jewish organizations were different, he answered:

> I will tell you that those who came from Newark have, in their lifeblood, the idea and practice of building Jewish agencies, working for the Campaign, building community and it's very obvious. It's not as much a part of other peoples' behavior patterns who move from, say, New York, where they skip over Route 287 into Morris County. Not that they're not capable of it, but they don't have generations of family members who worked in established agencies.[95]

A second characteristic of Newark's Federation is the strong degree of centralization. This can be traced back to the 1940s. The discord that existed then, even if only for a short time, was highly unpleasant and deeply affected the community's leaders. It seems to be human nature that, as a conflict recedes into the past, the particulars are often forgotten but what usually remains is a visceral abhorrence for the confict itself. Thus, people spoke about it as "a terrible time," as something to be avoided at all costs. The response was consolidation of authority with many different agencies and committees under one umbrella. One Federation official, David Mallach, observed that the creation of a united Federation in the form of MetroWest was by no means inevitable. There could have been separate units in Morris and Essex County, he noted, but the community regarded one unified place as a crucial objective.[96] In general, the Jews of the area do see MetroWest as a central address for them when it comes to matters Jewish.

A third critical factor is the quality of leadership and its level of commitment. Leaders come to meetings long after they have ceased to be active, even if they live far away. One example is past president Martin Fox, who travels to meetings from his vacation home in Massachusetts whenever they are held. Personalities play a major role too. It's not just a willingness to assume responsibility, but a readiness to submerge one's ego for the common good, that seems to typify the leadership. One person described it as: "a warm, welcoming, non-cliquey, place," a sentiment echoed by others. People do not, as a rule, leave the organization when they're displeased. They try to work things out. Richard Slutzky cites the case of one donor who insisted that funding for Israel go to communities beyond the "green line" that demarcates what is known as Judea and Samaria. Although he was a small donor and most people opposed the idea, a successful effort was made to reach a compromise.[97] It may well be that the strong positive feelings people have for each other also contributes to the tendency to be more community-oriented (as opposed to a national issues perspective) in the selection of projects and priorities. This tendency to be local has been noted by many observers as a hallmark of the MetroWest Federation.

The trend away from factionalization manifests itself at the denominational level as well. In many communities there are strong differences between the Orthodox and the Reform and Conservatives. The issues vary from one locale to another—keeping the Jewish Community Center closed on the Sabbath, supporting day schools, serving kosher food that meets everyone's standards, and so on. The change has taken place gradually, but is very noticeable and by no means cosmetic. Carmi Schwartz, a past executive vice president, was strictly Orthodox and others have had strong Orthodox backgrounds. Most significantly, the lay leadership, which is overwhelmingly non-Orthodox, recently elected Murray Laulicht, who is Modern Orthodox, as the MetroWest president. It is a tribute, not only to his capabilities, particularly in building consensus, but to the community's enlightened perspective. However, it could not have happened without the overall framework—namely a community whose members have learned to get along with each other and who take pride in that fact.

Notes

1. "Children's Home Sponsors Large Program," *Jewish Chronicle*, Fifteenth Anniversary Issue, April 24, 1936, 83.
2. Golda Och, "From Philanthropy to Community, The Organization of the Jewish Community of Newark." Paper for course given by Professor Ismar Schorsch, December 1977.
3. Subsequent changes were as follows: 1940—Essex County Council of Jewish Agencies; 1940—Jewish Community Council of Essex County; 1972—Jewish Community Federation of Metropolitan New Jersey; 1983—United Jewish Federation of MetroWest.
4. The others were: Hebrew Free Burial Society, Hebrew Ladies Immediate Relief Society, Hebrew Maternity Aid Society, Hebrew Sewing Circle, Jewish Anti-Tuberculosis League, Jewish Sisterhood, Ladies Guild of Newark Beth Israel Hospital, Newark Maternity Hospital, Women's Auxiliary to the Hebrew Orphan Asylum. New groups added in 1929 were: Neighborhood House, Jewish Child Guidance Bureau, Jewish Day Nursery and Neighborhood House, Jewish Social Service, Personal Service Association, Social Service Department, and West Side Ladies Relief Society. See Joseph A. Settanni, "Institutional Origins of the Conference of Jewish Charities of Newark: Initial Affiliated Agencies," July 12, 1995, Jewish Historical Society of MetroWest Archives.
5. Minutes of the Conference of Jewish Charities, Executive Committee Meeting, October 14, 1922. Until then, fund-raising was done individually. For example, wealthy Jewish individuals joined, in 1919, with other Jews elsewhere in the state to raise money to help "starving war sufferers." See "Leaders in New Jersey's Jewish Relief Drive," *Newark Star Eagle*, October 17, 1919 (no page given). The incorporators of the Conference were Fuld, Abraham Dimond, Frank Liveright, Nathan Bilder, Martin Goldsmith, and Leo Stein.
6. Minutes of the Conference of Jewish Charities, General Board Meeting, November 15, 1922.
7. Don Rubenoff, interview, August 20, 1996.
8. Minutes of the Conference of Jewish Charities, General Board Meeting, April 27, 1925.
9. "Michael A. Stavitsky, 72, Major Community Leader," *Jewish News*, February 24, 1967, 1.
10. Harry Lurie, *A Heritage Affirmed: The Jewish Federation Movement in America* (Philadelphia, Pa.: Jewish Publication Society, 1961), 288.
11. Och, "From Philanthropy to Community," 26–27.
12. Daniel Shiman, "Newark Sets Up Joint Council," *The Jewish Community*, January 1947, 5–7.; "Shiman Reviews History of Jewish Community Council," *Jewish News*, January 3, 1947, 7.

13. Correspondence from Harry L. Lurie, executive director of CJF to Samuel Kessler, February 24, 1944.
14. Lewis Coser, *The Functions of Social Conflict* (Glencoe, Ill.: The Free Press, 1956).
15. David Jameson, interview, April 1, 1996; "Mrs. Esther Jameson, 84; Former Agencies' Director," *Jewish News*, February 1, 1963, 16.
16. Minutes of the Essex County Council of Jewish Agencies, General Board Meeting, November 21, 1944.
17. Daniel Shiman, interview, November 30, 1994.
18. Martin Fox, interview, November 25, 1996. These professionals were already in contact in Newark years earlier. In 1937, the National Conference of Jewish Social Workers held a three day institute in Newark that attracted people from all over the country, including Harry Greenstein and Theodore Isenstadt. See "Jewish Social Workers to Confer in Newark," *Jewish Chronicle*, April 2, 1937, 2.
19. Philip Bernstein, interview, December 20, 1994. According to Judge Leo Yanoff, Pekarsky was also something of a "Rennaisance man, expert on wines, cigars, Bibles, on almost anything you could think of. See, Leo Yanoff, *Memoirs of Judge Leo Yanoff* (New Jersey, 1966), 97.
20. Jack J. Zurofsky, "General Assembly's Structure is Found to Have Deficiencies," *Jewish News*, December 26, 1952, 7.
21. Julius H. Cohn, "Are we a Community With a 50% Soul?" *Jewish News*, September 11, 1953, 1.
22. Samuel I. Kessler, "There is Only One Answer—From our Minds and Hearts," *Jewish News*, October 2, 1953, 7; Arno Herzberg, "Cites Trend in Population," *Jewish News*, October 2, 1953, 7.
23. "Building Fund Leaders Stress Debt to Old, Legacy to Young," *Jewish News*, January 7, 1955, 1.
24. "Record Gifts Launch National UJA Drive: Essex County Reports 63.6% Increase," *Jewish News*, March 2, 1956, 1.
25. Eugene W. Blum, "Hungarians Adjust Easily," *Jewish News*, September 26, 1958, 28.
26. Daniel Drench, interview, August 12, 1996.
27. Seymour Epstein, interview, August 12, 1996.
28. Horace Bier, Interview, December 2, 1996.
29. Judy May, interview, December 2, 1996.
30. Ibid.
31. Stanley Strauss, interview, November 25, 1996.
32. Minutes of the Jewish Community Council of Essex County, General Board Meeting, January 20, 1953.
33. Minutes of the Jewish Community Council of Essex County, Executive Committee Meeting, December 18, 1945.
34. "Jews in County Surveyed on Habits in Philanthropy," *Jewish News*, January 12, 1962, 1.
35. Herman N. Pekarsky, "Observations on Giving and Givers," *Jewish News*, January 19, 1962, 13.
36. Minutes of the Jewish Community Council of Essex County, General Board Meeting, October 25, 1955.
37. Esther Kesselman, interview, September 20, 1995, Jewish Historical Society of MetroWest.
38. Barbara Finkelstein, "Dates Give Way to Doorbells," *Jewish News*, April 10, 1959, 28.

39. Martin Fox, interview, November 25, 1996. The founding chairman of the Lester Society is Jerome Waldor.
40. Genealogy of the Jewish Family Service of MetroWest. Chart. Jewish Historical Society of MetroWest Archives.
41. Simon Doniger, "The Jewish Child Guidance Bureau," *Jewish News*, January 10, 1947, 8.
42. Correspondence from Ida G. Segal, executive director, United Hebrew Charities to Leah Frank Segal, executive director, Conference of Jewish Charities, January 6, 1930; Minutes of the Conference of Jewish Charities, Executive Committee Meeting, January 7, 1930.
43. For an excellent historical summary of Jewish social service in the MetroWest community, see Ronald L. Becker, "History of the Jewish Community in Newark, New Jersey," in William J. Dane & Charles F. Cummings (eds.), *Lasting Impressions: Greater Newark's Jewish Legacy*. (Newark, N.J.: The Newark Public Library, 1995), booklet, unpaged. Also, Jane Wallerstein, *Path of Service: A History of the Jewish Counseling and Service Agency of Essex County and its Predecessor Agencies 1861–1961* (Newark, N.J.: Hebrew Benevolent and Orphan Society, 1962), booklet. For the larger picture of social welfare see Warren Grover, *Relief in Newark, 1929–1933*. M.A. Thesis, New York University, 1962 and Saul Schwarz, *The Job of the Executive Director in Local Jewish Central Community Organization: An Occupational Monograph*. M.S.W. Thesis, New York School for Social Work, Columbia University, 1951.
44. Horace Bier, interview, December 2, 1996.
45. Sylvia Kramer, *Our First 75 Years Caring for the Elderly,* booklet(West Orange, N.J.: Daughters of Israel Pleasant Valley Home, 1982), 5–7.
46. Saul Schwarz, interview, December 6, 1994.
47. Ibid.
48. Sylvia Kramer, *Our First 75 Years*, 22–28.
49. Jo Bonomo, "Life Begins At—?" *Jewish News Supplement*, March 27, 1959, 26.
50. Speech by Saul Schwarz at *Annual Meeting of Jewish Community Housing Corporation*, West Orange, N.J., June 7, 1995.
51. Minutes of the Conference of Jewish Charities, Executive Committee Meeting, April 25, 1927.
52. Correspondence from Frank I. Liveright, President of Beth Israel Hospital, to Samuel F. Leber, President of the Conference of Jewish Charities, September 10, 1931; Minutes of the Administrative Committee Meeting of Beth Israel Hospital, September 10, 1931.
53. Minutes of the Jewish Community Council of Essex County, General Board Meeting, March 15, 1949.
54. Minutes of the Jewish Community Council of Essex County, Executive Committee Meeting, May 2, 1950.
55. David Mallach, interview, January 21, 1997. The person most responsible for Beth Israel's decision to remain in Newark was probably Alan Sagner.
56. Saul Schwarz, interview, December 6, 1994.
57. "Jewish Anti-Tuberculosis League, Organized Fourteen Years Ago, Has Furnished Relief for Thousands Afflicted With the Disease," *Jewish Chronicle*, April 24, 1936, 30.
58. James Schwarz, interview, December 2, 1996.
59. Steve Lipman, "Day Schools Get Financial Boost," *Jewish Week*, October 24, 1997, 1.

60. "Zionist Leaders Warmly Greeted on Newark Visit," *Jewish Chronicle*, December 23, 1921, 1.
61. "Newark's Zionists, 8,000 Strong, Stage Big Demonstration in Celebration of Ratification of Palestine Mandate," *Jewish Chronicle*, September 15, 1922, 1.
62. "Jewish Physicians Sail for Palestine," *Jewish Chronicle*, July 28, 1922, 1.
63. Minutes of the Conference of Jewish Charities, Executive Committee Meeting, November 30, 1925.
64. Correspondence from M.L. Lipis, Chairman of local American Palestine Campaign Steering Committee to Conference of Jewish Charities, March 16, 1931. In his letter, Lipis notes that, "due to the general economic condition, hardly any funds have been sent from this country to Palestine, during the year 1930."
65. Minutes of the Jewish Community Council of Essex County, General Board Meeting, December 17, 1946.
66. "United Palestine Appeal Battle Intensifies as Executives Quit," *Jewish News*, November 19, 1948, 1.
67. "Fien to be Chairman of Israel Bond Drive," *Jewish News*, January 4, 1963, 1.
68. "Newark Council Women in Front Rank of Organizational Service," *Jewish Chronicle*, May 29, 1931, 23.
69. Newark Collection: Jewish Family Service Files, Rutgers University, New Brunswick, New Jersey. The names of the parties involved have been changed.
70. Ibid.
71. Judith Tydor Baumel, *Unfulfilled Promise: Rescue and Resettlement of Jewish Refugee Children in the United States 1934–1945* (Juneau, Alaska: The Dinali Press, 1990), 50–70.
72. "Refugee Children Find Homes," *Jewish Chronicle*, June 27, 1941, 1. See also, "Herbert J. Hannoch Carries On in Guidance of Destiny of the Jewish Children's Home," *Jewish Chronicle*, Twentieth Anniversary Issue, June 20, 1941, 75.
73. William B. Helmreich, *Against All Odds: Holocaust Survivors and the Successful Lives they Made in America* (New York: Simon & Schuster, 1992), 33.
74. Minutes of the Essex County Council of Jewish Agencies, General Board Meetings, January 12, 1943 and February 9, 1943.
75. Memorandum from Theodore R. Isenstadt to Herman Pekarsky, November 14, 1947. Subject: "Expenditures for the Emigre Program by the Jewish Family Service Association of Essex County."
76. "Newark Bureau Locates Kin of Polish Refugees," *Newark Jewish Times*, December 28, 1945, 2.
77. "War Survivors Thank Newark Women," *Jewish News*, February 7, 1947, 2; "Newark's Ship-A-Box Tops the Nation; Makes Record Sending Parcels Overseas," *Jewish News*, June 27, 1947, 1.
78. "Service to Foreign Born," *Annual Report*, April 1948, 5–6.
79. Minutes of the Jewish Community Council of Essex County, General Board Meeting, January 29, 1957.
80. Eugene W. Blum, "Hungarians Adjust Easily," *Jewish News*, September 26, 1958, 28.
81. "Criticizes Plebiscite by Jews," *Newark Evening News*, May 8, 1938, 1.
82. "Wise Assails Rabbi Foster," *Newark Evening News*, June 10, 1938, 9.
83. Gershon Gelbart, Sylvan H. Kohn, and David Rudavsky, *The Essex Story: A History of the Jewish Community in Essex County, New Jersey*, booklet(East Orange, N.J.: Jewish Education Association, 1955), 51.
84. Other English language newspapers were the *Jewish Voice*, of which only a few

issues were published in 1924 and 1925 and which had a small Yiddish section too; the *Jewish Times* ,with only one known issue, July 19, 1946; and the *American Jewish Ledger*, published between 1946 and 1963 and, after that, intermittently until 1987.

85. As cited in Shammai Engelmayer, "The Birth of a Newspaper," *MetroWest Jewish News*, 50th Anniversary Edition, January 1997, 24. Charles Baumohl, who succeeded Weingast, followed the same approach, competent and effective, but not likely to strike out too far on his own. Technically speaking, the first editor, before Lesser, was Max Wiener, a reporter for the *Newark Evening News*, who edited a few trial issues in 1946.

86. For an excellent discussion of these points and other, related issues, see Jonathan D. Sarna, "The History of the Jewish Press in North America," in *The North American Jewish Press*, Waltham, Mass., Brandeis University, April 1995, 2–7, pamphlet.

87. Ibid., 6–7.

88. The frankness and self-criticism that characterize Engelmayer's piece in the 50th Anniversary Edition (pp. 12–28) are in itself a demonstration of the shift to greater openness.

89. Max Weiner, "This 'Bank' Lends From the Heart," *Newark Sunday News*, November 26, 1950, 66.

90. Ibid. Other individuals of note in the organization were "Pop" Ike Lillien, Jack Waldor, and Morris J. Savel.

91. Memorandum from Saul Schwarz to Rabbis Alvin Marcus and Jeshaia Schnitzer and Cecile Asekoff, August 28, 1996. Subject: Joint Chaplaincy Committee.

92. The Committee and the Anti Defamation League withdrew from NJCRAC in 1952, because of control issues, not returning until 1965–66.

93. The names of others active in the Committee can be found in "Building a Better World: 50th Anniversary." American Jewish Committee, pamphlet.

94. Sidney Weinstein, interview, November 25, 1996.

95. Howard Charish, interview, November 30, 1994.

96. David Mallach, interview, January 21, 1997.

97. Richard Slutzky, interview, January 21, 1997.

6

From Generation to Generation

Wherever they have been in their long history as a people, the two most important communal institutions for the Jews have always been the synagogue and the school. Both go back to Biblical times but their significance in ensuring Jewish survival became critical when the Jews went into exile. It was then that having a place where they could gather became essential.

In this capacity the synagogue fulfilled several functions. It was, first of all, a place where Jews could gather as a group and gain strength from the knowledge that they were not alone, that although they were now a people without a land, at the mercy of others, they had a collective memory and group consciousness that transcended such limitations. Moreover, the synagogue became the place where they could pour their hearts out and express their love for Israel and its cities, most notably Jerusalem, as well as their yearning for a return to that land. In more recent times, the synagogue, or, as it is also known, the temple, has become a center for community activities of all sorts. These are the ties that bind Jews to one another, and therefore an understanding of them is critical.

In the same vein, the school, known in earlier times as the "academy" or "yeshiva," also played a central role for Jews. It was there that the young were initiated into the laws, customs, and history of their people. In the synagogue they learned to pray but in school they learned about why they prayed. The synagogue was where the rabbi preached and taught, the yeshiva was where he learned how to preach and teach. Without the education provided by the schools the Jews could not have survived as a people, for culture that is not transmitted soon withers and dies.

As new immigrants to America Jews first turned their attention to the basics—securing food, shelter, and work. Once those matters were attended to they almost always set about establishing a place where they could worship. In this, they were no different from their gentile counterparts. The period between 1844 and 1860, when German Jews began arriving in Newark in significant numbers, was also a period of growth for Newark's Christian community. More than twenty-five houses of worship—Episcopalian, Methodist, Baptist, Catholic, Presbyterian, and Dutch Reformed, were built in those years. The construction of large and imposing edifices was already in full swing then. Churches like Grace Episcopal, the High Street Church, and Central Methodist, cost many thousands of dollars. The Jews, however, did not build temples on that scale until many years later.

Jewish immigrants were no strangers to oppression. They had come to America hoping to find greater tolerance and so they did. In fact, it was the Catholics who suffered the most in Newark in those days, particularly the Irish. Effigies of "St. Paddy" regularly appeared at various locations in Newark, and Catholics were the recipients of the same abuse that had swept the country at large wherever their coreligionists lived. The hatred culminated in a riot on September 5, 1854 at a parade held by the American Protestant Lodge Association of New Jersey. It began with stone-throwing and ended with marchers literally tearing up St. Mary's Church, located on William Street, breaking windows, smashing pews, making a shambles of the organ, and finally, attempting to set fire to the church itself.[1] Compared to this, the treatment given the Jews was positively benign, owing, in no small measure, to their own efforts at being unobtrusive and to the fact that their numbers were far smaller and hence, less threatening to the dominant Protestants.

Some think of the German Jews as perhaps less observant in the traditional sense, but it is clear from their writings that these early immigrants were deeply religious. As one early chronicler of the period wrote :

In our home a positive Judaism prevailed. We were taught little Hebrew prayers before we were able to articulate clearly; it didn't matter; we knew that we were praying to God . . . .And God was revealed to us clearly and early as the benign Creator of everything. Trees, flowers, singing birds, storm, lightning, thunder and rainbow, the heavenly bodies, the beauty of falling snow—all was pointed out to us by mother, as the creative miracle of a benevolent God . . . .It is perhaps due to this early influence that—confronted by some great natural phenomena as a storm at sea, the view from the summit of the Jungfrau, the brink of the Grand Canyon—a quotation from one of the great nature Psalms would spontaneously rise to my lips.[2]

The first three synagogues were B'nai Jeshurun, B'nai Abraham, and Oheb Shalom. B'nai Jeshurun was established in 1848 by German Jews, and while, like the others, it started out as a traditional congregation, it eventually became the first Reform temple in the city. In 1855, B'nai Abraham was founded by Jews from Posen (Poznan in Polish), and, in 1860, Oheb Shalom began functioning. Its founders, who had broken off from B'nai Jeshurun, were mostly of Bohemian origin. Both of them moved away from Orthodoxy after some years. They were followed, in 1875, by the first synagogue in Newark that remained Orthodox, Congregation Adas Israel and Mishnayes.

Bernard Drachman, who became the rabbi of Oheb Shalom for a short time in 1885, spoke in his memoirs of the general devotion to tradition, including dietary laws and Sabbath observance, of the German Jews of Newark. Drachman became a founding faculty member of the then newly established Jewish Theological Seminary. He also reluctantly resigned his post as Oheb Shalom's rabbi, most likely because he opposed its policy of mixed seating. In 1889, he was named dean of the Seminary. An ordained Orthodox rabbi, Drachman eventually left the Seminary because it had moved away from Orthodoxy, accepting instead a post at Yeshiva College.[3] Today, of course, these synagogues have long since departed Newark. B'nai Abraham is in Livingston, B'nai Jeshurun in Short Hills, and Oheb Shalom in South Orange. Yet all three still have members who are keenly aware of their congregations' rich and long heritage.

Jews as a group have always placed a premium on education and Newark was no exception. For the immigrant Jewish peddler, businessman, or factory worker, the dream was always to do for his children that which had been beyond his own reach. Thus, Jews were more likely than other groups to attend Newark's schools. They were more apt to complete their education and to do very well in their classes. From the start, they also viewed Jewish education as a priority and the early synagogues all had provisions for such instruction. Later on, in the 1880s, when Eastern European immigrants began arriving in large numbers, independent schools, most notably, the Plaut Memorial Hebrew Free School, were begun to serve their needs. In addition, there were small neighborhood *heders* where *melamdim* (teachers) taught. Other parents secured the services of individuals who came to their homes and provided instruction for the children after they returned from public school.

Surveys taken in the 1920s, 1930s, and 1940s, revealed that the percentage of Jewish youth receiving any Jewish education was usually between 30 and 40 percent.[4] The Federation's attitude in its early years toward such education was not positive. An early study pointing up to the need in this area was tabled for *fifteen* years. It was only when Michael Stavitsky became president of the Conference in 1936 that things began to change. Within one year, Stavitsky succeeded in creating the Jewish Education Association to take up the problems in this area. Even so, support remained weak. In his report on the subject, Stavitsky castigated the Conference of Jewish Charities, arguing that "the consequence of this niggardly attitude on the part of the community is obvious in the picture of inadequate facilities, poor organization, administration, and content in our present program of Jewish education."[5]

Perspective is important here. The attitude of Newark's Federation was no different than those of its counterparts elsewhere in the country. Still, Jewish schools proliferated in the country, especially in the post-World War II period. The Orthodox, who became more numerous in the U.S., regarded such schools as essential. They also benefited from changing attitudes in the U.S. towards ethnic identity.[6] Also, in the move to the suburbs, Jews found themselves forced to examine their own group identity by their encounters with Christian neighbors and this resulted in more of them sending their children to Jewish supplementary and day schools.[7]

Despite the greater need in the community, financial backing for the schools remained the responsibility of individuals who saw it as important, individual synagogues, and the religious movements to which they belonged. The Federations were finally taken to task on this when criticism of their position exploded into the open in 1969. Jewish students, led by Hillel Levine, then a Conservative rabbi and a graduate student at Harvard, protested their failure to support Jewish education.[8] And it was not until the 1980s that Federations began to set aside major funding for Jewish schools.

We begin our examination of this topic with a more in-depth analysis of Newark's synagogues. All told, in all their various incarnations, about 150 synagogues existed in the city from 1848 through the 1960s. We do not propose to present capsule histories of all of them and, in fact, information about them is readily available in the archives at Rutgers University and at the Jewish Historical Society of MetroWest. A more useful approach is to discuss the various aspects of the synagogues in order to demonstrate how they affected Newark's Jews in their general lives. Individual synagogues will only be brought into the discussion to serve that end. Nevertheless, some of the most important synagogues in Newark are worthy of special mention and we begin with a brief discussion of them.

B'nai Jeshurun

On August 20, 1848, thirteen men met in the home of Isaac S. Cohen and undertook to establish the first synagogue in Newark. Its name, B'nai Jeshurun (Sons of Righteousness), was meant to reflect a certain seriousness of purpose. They elected Isaac S. Cohen as president and Isaac Newman as their cantor. In the beginning, services were conducted in a former church on Harrison Street (now called Halsey Street). In 1851, the first permanent home was erected on Washington Street. The building, which cost $5,500, was followed, twelve years later, by a congregational day school for the children. In those early years, Orthodox ritual prevailed. There was a mikveh, an Orthodox service, no choir, and no organ.

July 19, 1868, marked the installation of Rabbi Joseph Leucht as B'nai Jeshurun's spiritual leader. He was to remain in that post for what may have been a record number of years, fifty-two, a time which saw the synagogue expand and grow into a leading Reform congregation in this country. That same year, the temple adopted a new constitution. Its preamble clearly indicated the direction it was heading in with the following words: "the discarding of antiquated forms and the preservation and adoption of such, whether old or new, as shall further the religion of enlightened Judaism."

Three years later B'nai Jeshurun dropped the Orthodox requirement for observing two days of holidays, like Passover and Tabernacles, and nine years after that, in 1880, the congregation abolished the requirement to wear a head covering inside the temple. By 1892, services were being conducted almost entirely in English. Compared to the Reform Movement as a whole, however, B'nai Jeshurun's members abandoned traditional Orthodoxy at a fairly slow pace. For example, the Reform prayer book was not introduced into B'nai Jeshurun until 1872.[9] This was due, in part, to the fact that its members came from modest backgrounds and were too busy earning a living to have much time for such matters. It was not until about 1892 that B'nai Jeshurun reached the same level of Reform that predominated in most parts of the U.S.

In 1902, Leucht was joined by Solomon Foster, who became associate rabbi of the temple. Foster was a dynamic individual and it was largely through the force of his personality, together with the leadership of several congregation presidents—Joseph Goetz, Leser Lehman, and Philip Lindeman, that sufficient funds were raised to build, in 1914, a new edifice on High Street. The cost was $300,000, a stupendous sum for those days. The synagogue school had hundreds of students, a good number of whom were not the offspring of temple members. Brotherhood was an important principle of the temple, as it was of Reform Judaism in general. In keeping with that spirit, the temple allowed the nearby First Baptist Church to worship in B'nai Jeshurun's quarters while its new structure, the Peddie Memorial Church on Broad Street, was being built. Over time, the temple acquired a reputation for being in the forefront of social causes and aid to the needy, such as the San Francisco earthquake, the Johnstown flood, and so on. These patterns of community involvement and social activism have continued to the present day.

It is a mark of the stability and continuity of B'nai Jeshurun that over a period of 100 years, only four individuals occupied the post of senior rabbi. Rabbi Foster was there for some forty years and he was followed by Rabbi David Wice, who served five years before leaving. While his stay was short, it was marked by a successful effort to enroll many new and younger members who were attracted by Rabbi Wice's personality.

Rabbi Ely Pilchik succeeded Rabbi Wice and it was during his tenure that B'nai Jeshurun, responding to the needs of its members, joined the exodus to the suburbs. In 1953, several of the temple's activities, including some religious classes were moved to a property it had bought in South Orange. Then, in 1968, a new and beautiful temple opened in Short Hills, New Jersey. Among those addressing the crowd at the dedication ceremonies were the composer, Aaron Copland, and the Chancellor of Brandeis University, Dr. Abram Sachar.[10] In 1971, B'nai Jeshurun hosted a giant Israel Fair, with over 20,000 people attending. It was one of the largest ever held in the U.S. In 1981, upon Rabbi Pilchik's retirement after thirty-four years, Rabbi Barry H. Greene assumed the duties of senior rabbi; he had previously served as B'nai Jeshurun's associate rabbi.[11]

B'nai Abraham

Most synagogues that use "Abraham" in their name, refer, of course, to the Biblical patriarch. That may have been in the minds of those who founded B'nai Abraham too, but the primary reason was one Abraham Newman. A founder of B'nai Jeshurun, Newman took an interest in a group of Jews who had come here, mostly from Posen, and who needed a place in which to worship, offering them the use of his home on Bank Street. Newman had also reportedly been involved in a dispute over ritual matters, which must have been a factor in his decision to link up with these new immigrants.[12]

It is unclear just how Polish or German these Jews were, but they apparently were not comfortable joining up with B'nai Jeshurun. As a further expression of generosity, Newman donated a Torah to the group, which reciprocated by naming its congregation after him—B'nai Abraham. On October 20, 1855, the synagogue, now located on Market Street, was incorporated and six years later, in 1861, Reverend Edward Rubin became its first spiritual leader. In that same year, the synagogue purchased and moved into the former home of the First Baptist Church. The following description of the dedication ceremony appeared in the October 19, 1861 edition of the *Newark Daily Advertiser*:

> The building was handsomely decorated with flowers and a large number of persons were present, including the mayor and other city officials. At the proper time, a procession, headed by the trustees bearing the Torah approached the synagogue from the street, singing in German. On reaching the door it was thrown open for their reception, displaying on either side of the entrance within the synagogue two rows of young ladies dressed in pure white and decorated with red, white, and blue ribbons, and burning red, white, and blue candles, indicative of the patriotism of the congregation.

Several observations can be made regarding these events. First, it is clear that the ceremony was seen as sufficiently important to attract the mayor and that may be an indication that Jews were favorably regarded in the community at large. Second, there appears to have been a good deal of contact between the Jewish community and the First Baptist Church since it was this same church that years later, took up temporary residence in B'nai Jeshurun while its new house of worship was under construction. Finally, if the founders of B'nai Abraham were Polish Jews, they seem to have adapted rather quickly, for here they are, singing in German, and, as indicated later on in the article, continuing in the same language as they moved into the temple and stood in front of the holy ark.

In subsequent years there were several splits in the congregation and it moved a number of times. Noteworthy during this period was the arrival to the synagogue, in 1870, of Rabbi Isidor Kalisch, father of the New Jersey Supreme Court Justice, Samuel Kalisch. The rabbi was the co-author, together with Isaac Mayer Wise, of the Reform movement's prayer book, *Minhag America*. It seems that his liberal views were not appreciated by a substantial segment of the membership and, as a result, he left for Nashville, Tennessee in 1872. Such disagreements, incidentially, were common during this period of growth and ferment in America. In fact, Kalisch had been involved in a similar dispute in Milwaukee, where he led a congregation between 1857 and 1860. Kalisch returned to Newark in 1875, devoting himself primarily to lecturing and to literary pursuits. He also conducted religious services on the holidays and on special occasions, as well as teaching the children, all this without payment. And the temple had certainly become more liberal over time, its use of an organ indicating its progress in that direction. At the same time, the eclecticism that was to be a distinctive trait of the synagogue, was symbolized by its adherence to the Orthodox prayer book. Two of the most important lay leaders during this period were Moritz Berla and William S. "Daddy" Rich.

In 1897, B'nai Abraham, now numbering 900 congregants, moved into new quarters at the corner of High Street and 13th Avenue. "Daddy" Rich officiated at the dedication. He served several terms as president of the congregation and was perhaps its most influential and revered lay leader. Rich was also active in many other organizations, including the Anti-Defamation League, Jewish Children's Home, and the socially prominent Progress Club. Known as a warm and charitable individual he was honored on his eightieth birthday at a banquet and presented with a $50,000 check, which he immediately turned over to the synagogue.[13]

Rabbi Julius Silberfeld became B'nai Abraham's rabbi in 1902, serving in that capacity until 1939. During his time and under the leadership of Philip J. Schottland and "Daddy" Rich (a term of affection), a successful building campaign was conducted. The new temple, an imposing, round-shaped structure in the Clinton Hill section at Clinton and Shanley Avenues, was dedicated in 1924. Besides the sanctuary and a large number of classrooms, the building also contained a gymnasium and a swimming pool.

Silberfeld was succeeded by the charismatic Rabbi Joachim Prinz. Within a short time Prinz acquired a national reputation as an orator and social activist and as he grew in stature so did B'nai Abraham. A long list of famous individuals from every walk of life graced its pulpit as speakers. Its adult learning program was one of the finest in the country. Led by Max Helfman, B'nai Abraham placed great importance on music. Although it never formally affiliated with any denomination, it was, for all intents and purposes, a liberal Conservative synagogue. Eventually, as life in a deteriorating Newark became untenable, the congregation was forced to move, taking up residence in a new home in nearby Livingston.

Oheb Shalom

Oheb Shalom was founded in 1860 by a dissident group that broke off from B'nai Jeshurun. Led by Rabbi Isaac Schwartz, it met, at first, in a nondescript wood frame building. Services were conducted in both German and Hebrew, the same as in the other synagogues. Several years later, the congregation's spiritual leader became Rabbi Ferdinand A. Sarner, who had the distinction of being one of the first Jewish U.S. Army chaplains and was also wounded in the Battle of Gettysburg. Unlike today, when many synagogues complain about their congregants' failure to attend services often enough, the early worshippers took their responsibilities as members quite seriously. As Sarah Kussy, whose father was a founder and president of Oheb Shalom, noted in a memoir about her family:

> We attended the synagogue on Saturday, as naturally and and regularly as we attended the public school during the week, only we went to the synagogue at a younger age . . ... Father was usually in his pew when the services began—Bertha, Nathan, Joe and I waited for mother. Father, however, begrudged us the extra hour of sleep, claiming that it was a *Harpe* and a *Bushah* (shame and disgrace) for a father to attend the service unaccompanied by his children.[14]

In 1884, the congregation dedicated a new brick building on Prince Street. Like the other temples in Newark, Oheb Shalom gradually moved away from Orthodoxy. An organ and a professional cantor were both introduced in that same year, with English becoming more predominant in the service as well. But Oheb Shalom did not go as far as B'nai Jeshurun, remaining in the Conservative orbit and relying on the Jastrow prayer book.

In 1906, Rabbi Charles I. Hoffman, a graduate of the Jewish Theological Seminary, accepted the pulpit. He was an enthusiastic proponent of Conservative Judaism, which was described then "as Jewish as the Torah and as American as apple pie."[15] Hoffman, who was to remain with the congregation for thirty-four years, profoundly influenced it. He was a nationally recognized leader, a president of the Rabbinical Assembly and a founder of the United Synagogue of America. Indeed, Rabbi Leon Lang, Rabbi Louis Levitsky, and Rabbi Alexander Shapiro, all of whom later became rabbis of Oheb Shalom, were also elected as heads of the Rabbinical Assembly. In general, Oheb Shalom was considered one of the top congregations in the movement, having been one of the seven charter members of the United Synagogue of America. Like B'nai Abraham and B'nai Jeshurun, Oheb Shalom had programs of high quality, a very active sisterhood, and an excellent children's school.

In 1911, Oheb Shalom's new home, a beautiful structure on High Street, was formally opened. It was to remain there until 1958. In fact, stability was a hallmark of the synagogue, not only in terms of how long the rabbis remained with the temple, but also in terms of family. Many of the founding families' descendants stayed on as members upon reaching adulthood. A good case in point was Roger Schwarz. The great-grandson of Rabbi Isaac Schwarz, little Roger was an usher at the synagogue's parting ceremony when it left High Street for its new home in South Orange. Symbolically, the door of the synagogue was closed with the same key with which it had been opened in 1911. Rabbi Levitsky, who had succeeded Rabbi Hoffman in 1940, stayed in his post until 1972, and was followed by Rabbi Shapiro, who led the community for the next two decades.

Other Synagogues

Mention has already been made of Congregation Adas Israel and Mishnayes. It is worth noting that, like other temples, it was reincarnated in the suburbs, in this instance, Springfield, where it is today known as Congregation Israel. The process of mergers that took place in many Newark synagogues over time was exemplified by Ahawas Achim/B'nai Jacob and David in West Orange, which absorbed many of Newark's smaller congregations as the inner city became less and less Jewish. Other important early temples were Anshe Russia (or, the "*Russiche Shul*"), Toras Emes, Estreich Hungary, Ahavath Zion, Adas Israel/Ein Yaakov (which later merged and became Knesseth Israel), Schley Street Shul, Ahavas Yisroel, Brisker Shul, Ahavas Achim/Anshe Varshaw and Linas Hatzedek.

Ahavas Achim/Anshe Varshaw, founded in 1898, which later merged with another synagogue in 1935 and was renamed Ahavas Achim/ B'nai Jacob, was built in a style typical of many of the medium-sized synagogues in the early twentieth century. The style was European, with a high ceiling. A large Jewish star adorned the white-painted building, which was covered by a slanted roof, and an iron fence ran around the structure. During the week, worshippers entered via a long alleyway off to the side. On the Sabbath, however, they walked up the stairs in the front and through the main entrance. Inside, the *bimah* was in the center of the temple with the seats around it and in the front. The women sat in an upstairs balcony that required no curtain because the men could see them only with great difficulty, if at all.

The larger synagogues, however, were much more ornate. There was, for example, Ahavath Zion, built in 1922 at a cost of $200,000. The style was Greco-Roman with a main entrance portico that rose majestically, with four columns upon a series of steps. The outside consisted of brick and a composite pinkish granite with terra-cotta trimmings. As opposed to Ahavas Achim, which seated perhaps 250 people, Ahavath Zion had room for 1,500 worshippers. Inside, the design featured finished walls made of stone and an ornamented ceiling.[16]

Another important synagogue was the Young Israel of Newark. At one time, with a membership of 400 families, it was probably the largest Orthodox congregation in the state of New Jersey. But it was also significant because it was part of a national movement of the same name, which, through its member synagogues, represented a modernizing trend within Orthodoxy. The Young Israel movement wanted to have more English in the Orthodox service while remaining strictly Orthodox, as well as greater decorum. It also attempted to attract young families to its synagogues. When it was founded in Newark, in 1922, it met in the basement of another synagogue. In 1942, it moved to Lyons Avenue where it remained during its heyday in Newark. Eventually, the Young Israel, whose long-time rabbi was Zev Segal, moved to Center Street in South Orange, and then, finally, to West Caldwell. Segal headed the congregation for over thirty years and exercised great influence over it during that period.

Although Newark was by no means a hasidic community, there were several rabbis who could be characterized as such. One such individual was the "Pittsburgher Rebbe," who built a large synagogue near the Young Israel, on Chancellor Avenue. For most who attended, the draw was not so much the daily hasidic lifestyle but more a desire to be in touch with one's roots in a way that they saw as more "real." After all, Newark's Eastern European Jews were but one or two generations removed from that way of life. The following vignette about a Newark youth of the fifties best sums up those yearnings:

> Joshua also found himself drawn to the Pittsburgher Rebbe's *shul*. And the Rebbe was interested in Joshua. Why, he thought, is a young man active in Young Israel coming to a *chassidishe shul*? "How long have you been wearing a *gartel* [a black rope tied around the waist]?" the Rebbe once asked Joshua. "For a year or so," Joshua answered. "What were your reasons?" the Rebbe gently inquired. "Probably not the correct ones," Joshua replied. "I think it has more to do with family tradition than religious conviction. My father wears a *gartel*, and so did his father. My maternal grandfather was a *chassidishe* rabbi in Poland, and he wore a *gartel*, too. It just seemed like the right thing for me to continue the practice, because I didn't want the tradition to die out." The Rebbe did not answer Joshua. He simply kissed him on the forehead.[17]

Some of Newark's synagogues, like B'nai Moshe and Beth David, stayed to the bitter end, but most did not. Two that still exist are Congregation Ahavas Shalom, at 145 Broadway, established in 1905, and Mount Sinai Congregation in the Ivy Hill apartment complex. All of Newark's suburbs with substantial Jewish populations had synagogues to meet the residents' spiritual and social needs. In Irvington, for example, there was Ahavas Achim/Bikur Cholim for the Orthodox and B'nai Israel for the Conservative community. Another major congregation was the Reform temple, Sharey Tefilo, in East Orange, which was founded in 1874 by Prussian immigrants. In 1949, a breakaway group started a new synagogue, called Temple Israel, in nearby South Orange. But then, in 1982, in an unusual move, it rejoined Sharey

Tefilo. South Orange is also graced by a prominent Conservative synagogue, Temple Beth El.

What was daily life like in the synagogues of Newark? Much more is known about the three major synagogues. For example, the minutes of B'nai Jeshurun's meetings in the 1850s and 1860s reveal that the congregation was occupied primarily with the mortgage, seats, repairs, with discussions of what kinds of business could be conducted at the meetings, and with starting a school. It was also apparently necessary to pressure people at times to fulfill their responsibilities. At one meeting, a rule was passed that in the event of a death, ten members of the congregation were to be "ordered to attend service." They were to follow in rotation and to appear in the house of mourning for services. Those who failed to do so were fined twenty-five cents.[18] Other interesting aspects emerge from the minutes as well. We see that on the day of his bar mitzvah, a boy read the Torah but the *Haftorah* was left to the rabbi or anyone else whom he might appoint. Seats were divided into five classes, with different prices for each grouping.[19]

To obtain a fuller picture of the community, however, it is equally important to understand how the other congregations, which served the majority of Newark's Jews, functioned as well. By examining the constitutions and minutes of one or two synagogues it becomes possible to obtain a better idea of how they functioned and what they considered important. Let's take a look first, at the 1903 Constitution of Congregation Linas Hatzedek, one of the city's oldest synagogues.

The congregation was sensitive to the needs of its impoverished members, realizing that they were often in need of help from the community. Provision was made for a carriage and all funeral expenses in the event that a member's child died before reaching the age of five. Furthermore, it also stipulated that any member who fell ill was to receive from the congregation five dollars a week for a period of twelve weeks.

Linas Hatzedek, like other synagogues of that era, had specific rules regarding the moral conduct of those who wished to be members in good standing. For example, article 13, number 10, stated: "If a member dies because of an immoral disease, God save us, he forfeits all benefits except the cemetery plot." Any member found guilty by the courts for a criminal offense such as theft, robbery, or murder, was expelled from the congregation. A similar fate awaited anyone who married a Christian. Religious behavior was also regulated. No member was permitted to enter the synagogue on the Sabbath carrying an umbrella or walking stick (a violation of the law against carrying between a private and public space.)

Office holders were subject to higher standards than members and the rules regarding their conduct were quite specific. If the president of the congregation was absent three times from meetings during his term, he was suspended from office. He was required to maintain order at the meeting, which included the injunction to "not permit two people to speak at the same time." If the president failed to attend a member's funeral (except by reason of being out of town) he was fined two dollars. Any congregational officers who arrived late to meetings or who failed to attend either Sabbath or holiday services were fined twenty-five cents for the first offense, fifty cents the second time, and seventy-five cents the third time. Fines were also levied against members who publicly insulted each other. Finally, a member who was called to the Torah and refused to accept the honor was punished by not being given an *aliyah* for three months. This may have been because people tried to get out of such honors, which carried with them an obligation to make a financial contribution.[20]

The minutes of the Young Israel are equally revealing. We see, first of all, through numerous instances, that the Young Israel, though a relatively small and not wealthy congregation, was charitable even to institutions outside of Newark. A 1950 meeting, for example, notes a donation of a hundred dollars to the Mirrer Yeshiva in Brooklyn and fifty dollars given to the yeshiva in Mt. Kisco.[21] Of even greater interest, when one considers the tendency today by Orthodoxy to draw inward, was the existence of cooperation with the Christian community on matters of common interest. In the minutes of one 1958 meeting, Rabbi Segal reports on discussions with the St. Charles Catholic Church. An overture had apparently been made that Protestants, Catholics, and the Young Israel as "the foremost congregation in Weequahic," work together to eradicate "the indecent literature prevalent in the candy stores in this area."[22] It is also interesting, along the same lines, that Rabbi Marius Ranson, spiritual leader of Sharey Tefilo, addressed the Young Israel Sisterhood in 1932. Not only was Ranson Reform, but he was in the left wing of his movement. People were not permitted to wear a *yarmulke* or *talis* in his temple. Imagine a Young Israel synagogue today tendering an invitation to such a rabbi!

The Young Israel also published a booklet, called, "Synagogue Eti-

quette and Procedure," that spelled out certain guidelines for synagogue behavior. The booklet is most revealing in terms of what the
members regarded as both important and in need of improvement. An
excerpt from one of the sections appears below:

Religious Services

Section One:
Do not take back seats. Come forward. You will find more inspiration in the
service.

Do not mumble . . . .Read unitedly and distinctly. Do not be afraid to sing out
in the congregational singing. Sincerity and enthusiasm, not necessarily trained
voices, make for effective singing of the hymns. It is customary to greet the rabbi
at the end of the service.

On Sabbath and Holidays, the display of pocketbooks, the jingling or open
display of money, chewing gum, reading of secular literature, and driving to the
synagogue, are indeed violations of good taste. Respect the traditions of our people
and of our sacred writings.

Proper dress ties, no sweaters, should be worn to the synagogue.[23]

Were these issues not a problem the admonitions would have been
unnecessary. Thus we see that proper decorum was a matter of concern as was the number of people who were not religiously observant.
In those days, it should be remembered, far more nonobservant Jews
belonged to Orthodox synagogues. They were, by and large, people
who had grown up Orthodox but had since ceased to adhere to the
rituals. Nevertheless, they felt most comfortable with an Orthodox
service that resembled that which they had grown up in. We also learn
from the above that the Young Israel believed that active participation
in the service greatly enhanced one's appreciation of the entire experience.

Did Newarkers view the synagogues any differently as they moved,
together with their communities, to the suburbs, or was it simply a
matter of going from one place to another? To discover the answer to
this question, Sylvan Kohn, head of the Jewish Education Association,
conducted a survey released in 1957. Twenty-nine out of fifty-four
congregations queried responded to a questionnaire asking them to
compare the situation at the time with what had existed in the past.

The results clearly pointed to a much higher level of involvement in
all areas. There was an increase in membership of 90 percent during
the period 1947–1957. Most of the congregations reported significant
increases in weekly attendance at services. Perhaps the most significant statistic was the 127 percent gain in synagogue school enroll-

ment, for this suggested that there would be continuity in the community, that the temple was not simply seen as a place where older people prayed on the Sabbath. In part, this was due to an increase in the birthrate during the postwar era. But the major reason was probably because suburban parents, living as they did in closer proximity to Christian neighbors whose children attended Sunday school, felt a similar need to do so. It was not, moreover, simply a question of "keeping up with the Joneses," but also a desire to retain their identity as Jews in a community that was now spread out and which seemed to emphasize homogeneity and materialism. In such an environment people felt that their children were missing something, that they needed to be anchored more securely in their traditions. All of these reasons were reflected in the responses to the survey.[24]

Rabbis and Cantors

One way of assessing a community is through its leaders and our task here is to do just that, as opposed to a series of biographies. Thus, the rabbis are important for our purposes primarily in terms of what they tell us about Newark's Jews as a whole. Newark had many rabbis in its 150 or so synagogues who performed nobly and ably and who were dedicated to their flocks. Unfortunately, space and the above considerations allow for only a brief discussion of them.

In general, the Jewish community of Newark was a remarkably cohesive one. Its leadership worked together and emphasized consensus as a basic principle. Whenever possible, the trend was to centralize. When there were differences of opinion, these were aired and discussed openly and, more often than not, resolved through compromise. Applying this model to the synagogues represented a challenge because they belonged to and were allied with movements that were opposed to one another on philosophical grounds. Simply put, there were many areas where Reform, Conservative, and Orthodox could not come to terms. In addition, the temples competed for members and the rabbis, by definition, were individuals with egos of their own.

It is, therefore, all the more remarkable that they were able to work together to the degree that they did. For example, kashruth supervision had been and continues to be a bone of contention in many communities. Standards cannot be uniform because criteria for kashruth and levels of observance do differ. That it was a sensitive area can be gleaned from a quick perusal of the local newspapers where kashruth scandals were regularly reported on, so much so that they were featured in the secular press too. For example, an article in the August 18, 1939, *Newark Evening News* noted that:

> Investigation of racketeering in the Kosher meat business in Newark, *often reported to the police* [emphasis added], is underway. *Complaints of long standing* [emphasis added]....Numerous cases of window smashing, throwing of stench bombs and other forms of violence have been reported to police the last two years by butchers not affiliated with the federation [of retail butchers].[25]

The charges of corruption were so serious that the rabbis of the community were forced to issue a statement denying any connection to the butchers' organization and emphasizing that they received no compensation for their certification of meat as kosher. Rather, they were simply performing a community service.

Problems with respect to kashruth supervision continued through the 1940s and 1950s too. Against this backdrop, it is noteworthy that the rabbis, when faced with problems over kashruth supervision, price wars between stores, and the like, banded together. In a communique to the Jewish Community Council in 1956, twenty rabbis signed a statement that said:

> The recent unpleasant events in the local Kashruth situation prompt us to reaffirm our support for community-wide concern and control in this area. We therefore urge that the Jewish Community Council take immediate action on the creation of a community board for the supervision of Kashruth in Essex County.[26]

What is significant is that the statement's signatories included the Reform rabbi, Herbert Weiner, the Conservative rabbis, Joachim Prinz and Morris Werb, and, several Orthodox rabbis, including Meyer Blumenfeld and Howard Singer. Today, rabbis of various denominations continue to work together on all sorts of committees in the community, many of them under the aegis of the MetroWest Federation. Naturally, they do not always agree and sometimes they even dislike one another, but the tendency is clearly in the direction of cooperation whenever possible. Such harmony in a community is unusual and demonstrates that a community vision, when clearly articulated and supported by its leadership, often has a broad ripple effect.

One of the most influential rabbis in the community was Solomon Foster, longtime spiritual leader of Congregation B'nai Jeshurun,

Newark's first synagogue. Foster was a true believer in the American ideal of separation of church and state and in the belief, also espoused by the Reform movement at large, that America was the promised land for the Jewish people. After all, they argued, the Jews were not a separate people but rather Americans of the Mosaic persuasion. He was born in Americus, Georgia in 1878 and his parents were also American-born.

Foster came to B'nai Jeshurun in 1902 and remained for thirty-seven years. During his tenure the congregation built a beautiful house of worship and Foster became a force among his fellow clergy and in the community, founding, among other organizations, the New Jersey Normal School for Jewish Teachers, a school which, at its height, had a student enrollment of over 600 pupils. But it was in articulating his philosophy of total integration into American society that Foster's influence was most felt. He advanced these views not only in his sermons but in public addresses everywhere—churches, business groups, literary clubs—and in the *Jewish Chronicle*. This was reflected by his membership in a host of non-Jewish groups and organizations in Newark, ranging from The Newark Museum and the Newark University Board of Trustees, to the Red Cross, the Salvation Army, and Traveler's Aid.[27]

Foster cut an imposing figure. He was a distinguished looking individual and people approached him with care. He was more than imposing, however. He was a lightning rod for antagonism and hostility when it came to the subject of Zionism. He was rabidly anti-Zionist, almost obsessively so. Once, when the noted Jewish writer, Maurice Samuel spoke at the Y on the subject, Foster reportedly stood up and said: "Stop right there. The good Lord above is expecting none of his children until the Messiah comes. " To which Samuel quipped: "Relax, Rabbi Foster. The good Lord is expecting no "foster" children."[28]

The most often told story on this topic, however, is the one about Rabbi Joachim Prinz's installation at Temple B'nai Abraham. Rabbi Stephen Wise, head of the American Jewish Congress and a noted Zionist with whom Foster had often tangled in print, was an invited guest to the event. Rabbi Wise entered the temple and strode to the front of the packed synagogue. As he stepped onto the raised area for the assembled dignitaries, Wise extended his hand and Foster simply refused to shake it. A collective gasp ensued from the crowd at this very public slight and those who were there have not forgotten it to this day. It was, as these things go, a community scandal.

Rabbi Foster was succeeded by Rabbi Wice in 1942 and there are some who believe he was brought in to "wean" the congregation away from Foster and his anti-Zionist views. Actually, it was not only his opinion about Israel that caused problems but it was his general stance towards any overt expression of Judaism. Apparently, Foster made a point of stating publicly on several occasions that the building of synagogues was the most important priority for American Jewry. Asked if helping the devastated European Jewish communities was not also a priority, Foster is said to have replied:

> There may be those of you who are wondering why I'm spending the money this way at this time. Well, the reason is, we are Americans,. We have nothing to do with the Jews of Europe.[29]

According to Janet Lowenstein, a long-time B'nai Abraham member who was present at the time:

> Wice got white as a sheet and the perspiration ran down his face. He finally staggered to the pulpit and said: "This is not only a house of meeting, but a house of worship as well and it's been desecrated. We cannot have a service here in this building. First, I want us to be thankful that the teachings of this man have not reached most of the people. We have good people in our congregation who have a heart. Second, I want to hope for a better future for all of us. Third, every member of the Board here will meet with me immediately." He met and he told them: "No discussion. Not a word. Either Rabbi Foster [by then, he had become rabbi emeritus] never mounts this temple again or I leave today. And I have no place to go to now, but I will leave and I will find a place." And Foster didn't speak again until Rabbi Pilchik came in 1947.[30]

Wice was not the only rabbi upset with Foster. Rabbi Julius Silberfeld had attacked him in print for his anti-Zionist views as early as 1922.[31]

In a very real sense, Foster was a victim of his environment. To understand this better, his attitude needs to be placed in a proper historical perspective. In 1885, the Reform movement had adopted a position at its Pittsburgh Conference which stated that they did not expect to ever return to Palestine. In 1937, this position was moderated at its Columbus, Ohio Conference when the movement adopted a position favoring the idea of a Jewish homeland, though it by no means called for an independent country. A bitter minority opposed this shift towards a more Zionist stance.[32] Foster was part of this group because his views had been shaped in an earlier era. But if he was constantly "looking over his shoulder" to see what non-Jews were thinking, he was no different than many Jews of his time and clearly he had broad support among his congregants who continued to favor him as their leader.[33]

Nor is the picture regarding Foster all bad. He was dedicated to his congregants and had his supporters. Apparently, Rabbi Joseph Konvitz, a prominent Orthodox rabbi, enjoyed a good relationship with him. On at least one occasion, Foster truly extended himself on behalf of a Jewish cause. It seems that a Jewish girl in Newark had been spirited away from her family by an evangelical Christian minister and secretly converted. The child's mother had been forced by reason of mental illness to enter a psychiatric institution for an extended period of time. Rabbi Foster intervened and energetically pursued the matter. He was primarily responsible for forcing the issue to be taken up by the courts. The account of his involvement is sharply divergent from his attitudes on such topics in general and demonstrates the complexity of the man and his views:

> Rabbi Foster . . .very frankly told Dr. Patterson [the minister] that he had taken advantage of Lillian's helplessness, inexperience, and tender age [she was sixteen] to convert her from Judaism to Christianity and that in the proper time and place, it was only right and just that every effort should be made to win the girl back to Judaism, the faith in which she was reared.[34]

Taken as a whole, these accounts of Foster and his interactions with other Newark individuals enable us to understand more clearly how these issues regarding Jewish identity in the 1920–1945 period were being played out in the larger Jewish community.

Rabbi Hoffman came to Oheb Shalom in 1906 and was there during the same period, roughly speaking, as Foster. A disciple of the great Conservative leader, Rabbi Solomon Schechter, Hoffman had blue chip credentials, having studied at the Jewish Theological Seminary, Cambridge University, and the University of Pennsylvania. Ideologically, he was quite different from Foster. In an interview with the *Jewish Chronicle*, Hoffman stated, "There ought to be intimate union among all those who are devoted to traditional Judaism and are loyal to the Torah. They ought to stand for Jewish observance, life and education." Such a statement, which could easily have been made by any Orthodox rabbi, illustrates how traditional Conservative Judaism was in those days. The move towards more tradition by some in the Conservative movement today is therefore not a new phenomenon.

Rather, it is a return to what the movement was like in its early days and Hoffman exemplified that. Unlike Foster, Hoffman belonged mostly to Jewish organizations, including the Talmud Torah, Zionist Organization of America, and B'nai Brith.[35]

Hoffman was apparently a somewhat distant figure in the eyes of those who knew him. Jerry Blum, a longtime member of Oheb Shalom, recalled his own experiences with the rabbi:

> Rabbi Hoffman was imposing, even scary. He used to stand and rock on his toes [when he spoke] . When you were confirmed, you had to go to Rabbi Hoffman's house for Friday night dinner. And he loved boiled fish, boiled potatoes, and boiled carrots. Just the blandest dinner. And everybody had to do it.[36]

Dore Schary remembered Hoffman as a quite formal individual who:

> had a black spade beard and a deep mellifluous voice that rolled out the ancient Hebrew prayers with awesome authority . . ..Rabbi Hoffman's ceremonies exuded dignity and a tone of solemnity, which was undoubtedly due in part to the rabbi's ministerial rather than patriarchal appearance.[37]

And Saul Schwarz remembers seeing him as he walked through the streets of Newark:

> My wife and I, when we lived on 636 High Street, could look out our window and see Rabbi Hoffman walking along, on a Saturday morning, wearing his black cutaway coat, high silk hat, and some leather-bound books under his arm. He was about 6'2 and I thought to myself: "That's what Abe Lincoln must have looked like, tall and thin."[38]

Others were less charitable in their assessments, with one member of the temple observing that Hoffman was "rigid and tyrannical," even with his own children.

Silberfeld, of Temple B'nai Abraham, was a different type from Foster and Hoffman, much more relaxed and informal. He was born in Oswiecim (Auschwitz), Poland in 1876 and came to the U.S. at the age of twelve. He was educated at City College of New York and received a private ordination. He became the rabbi at B'nai Abraham after serving briefly as assistant rabbi to Rabbi Leucht at B'nai Jeshurun. Schary's recollections, based largely upon his observations of these individuals' behavior in his family's catering hall, are again illuminating:

He wore no beard, only a mustache, which he assumed made him look older. His eyes had a gay and merry look. Silberfeld brought pace and warmth and intelligibility as well as religion to his ceremonies. So he thrived and soon earned the title of "The Marrying Rabbi." Silberfeld brought energy to his duties and a faster tempo more attuned to the times of his congregation. But he too had his critics, among them Zaida who didn't believe in a rabbi who didn't wear a beard. Also, Zaida believed that Silberfeld was making religion too easy. "It's not easy to be a Jew," argued Zaida. "It's hard. And if you make it too easy, you won't be a good Jew.[39]

Silberfeld certainly deserved the above-mentioned sobriquet. Over a twenty-five-year period, he reportedly officiated at 1,950 weddings, an average of almost eighty weddings a year![40]

Others thought of Silberfeld in a similar vein, not too serious, a great storyteller who was seen as "a regular guy," not at all pompous. He was also known as a man who enjoyed both a good drink and a good card game. In a sense, he was a fairly good fit to his congregation which saw itself as less stiff and Germanic than Oheb Shalom and B'nai Jeshurun. Politicians and even bootleggers probably preferred B'nai Abraham for the same reason—it seemed like a more freewheeling and spirited place. Nonetheless, in the larger sense, Silberfeld made important contributions to the Newark Jewish community and, in particular, to his synagogue. His ability to get along with people attracted many new members to the congregation which became a prominent institution during his tenure there. He was also a strong proponent of Zionism. The *Jewish News*, in an article shortly after his death, summed him up best in the following statement:

This nimble, industrious, ever-active man could be seen on the public platforms of city and state in the cause of justice and democracy, in the chambers of judges pleading for leniency, in the immigration offices in Washington arguing the case of a would-be immigrant. To untold people he was a father and a friend.[41]

Foster, Hoffman, and Silberfeld, all served during the same time frame, from around the turn of the century until, or a little bit into, the war years. After that, Leon Lang became the rabbi at Oheb Shalom for a short time and David Wice succeeded Foster for several years. But both of them left for greener pastures in Pennsylvania—Lang to Germantown and Wice to Philadelphia. Therefore, the next era at these three premier congregations was represented by Joachim Prinz at B'nai Abraham, Louis Levitsky at Oheb Shalom, and Ely Pilchik at B'nai Jeshurun. Of them, Prinz was the most influential.

Prinz was born in Germany and received his ordination from the Breslau Jewish Theological Seminary. He was arrested and expelled from Germany by the Gestapo. Adolf Eichmann had reportedly spied on one of his addresses to his congregation in Berlin and heard him announce his intention to emigrate. Eichmann cited this as proof of a New York-based, international Jewish conspiracy. In 1939, Prinz became the rabbi at B'nai Abraham and, in a Rosh Hashanah eve sermon, predicted the Holocaust, asserting that the Germans would eventually wipe out millions of Jews. In those days that was news. In fact, when Prinz first arrived in America he spoke at a Cleveland temple. The following day, the temple's rabbi called Stephen Wise, who had been instrumental in arranging Prinz's entry into the U.S., and asked him why he had sent "this rabble-rouser" to his congregation. He simply refused to accept what Prinz had told the audience about the Nazis' intentions.

Prinz made his mark as a humanist and as a social activist, not so much as a scholar. Under his leadership, B'nai Abraham's ties with the Conservative movement became more tenuous. While not an observant man, Prinz was, nevertheless, not really comfortable with the Reform movement either, and so he charted his own course. At the local level, he founded the B'nai Abraham Institute of Jewish Learning, which became known as one of the finest adult study programs of its kind in the U.S. Later on, when the Civil Rights movement emerged on the American scene, the temple created the B'nai Abraham Community Forum under whose auspices different speakers appeared, expounding on the great issues of the day in front of black and white, Jewish and Christian audiences. Prinz was at Reverend Martin Luther King's side during the 1963 Civil Rights March in Washington and spoke there. He was a close friend of King for many years. Prinz also sponsored and led memorable weekend retreats for his congregation, which featured lectures, skits, and other notable guest speakers in addition to the rabbi himself.

It was as a national leader, however, that Prinz became known to Jews throughout the country. In 1946, he was nominated to the Executive Board of the World Jewish Congress. Between 1958 and 1966, he was president of the American Jewish Congress. Then, in 1965, he was elected to the premier position in the Jewish establishment, chairman of the umbrella organization for the Jewish community, the Conference of Presidents of Major Jewish Organizations. There were those in Newark who criticized him for not paying enough attention to synagogue affairs, but, as Yehuda Hellman of the Conference once said: "Prinz was one of the few men who achieved greatness in two countries—Germany and the U.S."[42]

Prinz had great charm and charisma but he was not that approachable. Some were able to break through but most congregants were somewhat uneasy in his presence, largely because they were acutely aware of his stature. They knew he cared deeply about humanity, but they saw it as a more global quality. On the other hand, he had an excellent sense of humor and was able to reproach or chide people in a way that did not anger them. But his most important quality in terms of Newark was that, because of him, Newark's Jews stood taller. They derived great satisfaction from the fact that this man, who was known everywhere he went, was from Newark. No, he was not a native, but he was someone they chose and, moreover, were able to retain in their community.

Louis Levitsky of Oheb Shalom was a rabbi in the mold that had typified the congregation's spiritual leaders through the years. From the beginning, its rabbis had combined Jewish scholarship with a strong bent towards administration. Levitsky was not really the pastoral type who spent all of his time visiting congregants in hospitals and the like. Naturally, he fulfilled his duties, but his real strength lay in teaching. His Sunday morning Bible classes were usually packed and he taught a course at the Jewish Theological Seminary for many years.

Levitsky donated his letters and other personal materials to the Seminary and it is a very revealing collection, one that tells much about the man and the life of a rabbi in general. Of greatest value perhaps, is Levitsky's diary, penned in a neat script, in which he writes openly about his interactions with congregants and others in Newark's Jewish community. One entry deals with how he was asked to come at twelve noon to an affair. When he got there he learned that the musicians had been asked to show up at 12:30. "Rabbis never arrive on time, anyway," he was told. "That's why we tell them to come earlier." The following entry in Levitsky's diary provides a rare glimpse of how exasperated rabbis could feel at times and how they had to hide their feelings if they were to keep their jobs:

The Bore (Nudnick)
Those who attach themselves to the rabbis because he has to be courteous to everybody. They are of several kinds:

1. Mrs. _____ father, who once learned a few Hebrew phrases, attaches himself to me for the entire time I'm at the house and keeps on repeating these phrases, whether in place or not. You see, we're buddies, we're both talmidei chachamim [talmudic scholars]. And the family now establishes the rabbi's proper associations on this basis.

2. _____, who came one day with a problem he had with his summer home and I listened. He took it to mean that I was interested so he came to me regularly . . .and always walked in whenever he saw me in the office.

3._____, whom Hoffman consulted evidently, but away from me. I dare not show any sign of friendliness when I say good day to her, or else I'm parked for the day.

4. Generally, Yiddish-speaking people, who discover that I speak Yiddish, just make my office their parking bench, and I can't insult them either.[43]

Ely Pilchik, who succeeded Wice as Rabbi of B'nai Jeshurun, was, like Levitsky, a learned man. Born in Baranowicz, Poland, he came to the U.S. in 1920 and received his ordination from Hebrew Union College. He was more traditional than the typical Reform rabbi, thus giving rise to the following story told by Muriel Bloom, a longtime Newark resident:

There was a man in the community named Aaron Levinstone, who had Jewish learning. One day I was standing with my father and Levinstone before *Kol Nidre* [services]. And Levinstone said to my father: "You know, Joe, a remarkable miracle has happened in our community. Down in B'nai Jeshurun, Pilchik is making Jews out of *Goyim* and here, in our place, Prinz is making *Goyim* out of Jews." What he meant was that Prinz was not as interested in Jewish learning. People complained that he didn't pay enough attention to the Hebrew school. But he was a great human being.[44]

Pilchik was (and is) most definitely a scholar. He is the author of a number of books, including *Hillel* and *Maimonides' Creed*, and he served as president of the Jewish Book Council from 1954 to 1958.

A few years before Foster's ascension to his pulpit, another development occurred on Newark's religious scene. Hyman Brodsky became, in 1898, the rabbi of Congregation Anshe Russia, which was to become one of the city's most important Orthodox synagogues, due, in no small measure to his efforts. Brodsky was involved in many organizations, including Beth Israel Hospital, Daughters of Israel, and the Talmud Torah. He apparently had the respect of his non-Orthodox colleagues and was invited to preach in their temples as a guest lecturer on occasion.

A dignified looking man, with a long white beard, Brodsky was not only an orator but a scholar as well and wrote several works on the

Talmud. Born in Bialystok, Poland, Brodsky became known as a brilliant Talmud student at an early age, winning prizes for his knowledge. He was dedicated to education and helped organize yeshivas in several American cities before coming to Newark. Brodsky was considered the leader of the Orthodox community in his day. The quality that most endeared him to others was his tolerance. Though strictly Orthodox himself, Brodsky did not publicly criticize the Reform or Conservative movements, and was known as a consensus builder who used his considerable charm, affability, and self-effacing nature to bring people together.[45]

Brodsky was succeeded by Rabbi Joseph Konvitz, who became the spiritual leader of Anshe Russia in 1924. Konvitz, a great scholar, was born in Lithuania and was admitted to the famed yeshiva in Slabodka at the age of twelve, where he studied under the noted talmudist, Rabbi Natan Zvi Finkel. Later on, he became the communal rabbi for the ancient city of Safed, Israel. When he came to Newark, the city had about 70,000 Jews and perhaps sixty synagogues.

One of Konvitz's first achievements was to establish order in the field of kashruth supervision. He organized a council of Orthodox rabbis who made certain that all meat was properly inspected and certified. This was no easy task, for, as has already been noted, there was no shortage of dishonest butchers and even rabbis in this area. The extent of the problem is well portrayed by his son, Milton:

> Once a young man came to our home and confided to my father that he had been hired to attack him physically while he walked to his synagogue, but that, he went on to say, he really did not want to carry out the mission; would my father do himself, and the young man as well, the kindness to put some band-aids on his face for a day or two, so as to make it appear that he had been physically attacked? My father thanked the young man but said that he could not do what he had suggested and was prepared to take his chances. The man did not carry out his assignment, but for months we did not allow my father to go anywhere alone. No one outside the immediate family ever learned of this shameful incident.[46]

Konvitz was a gifted orator. The synagogue was packed with people who came to hear him, especially on the High Holidays, *Shabbat Shuvah* (the Sabbath of Repentance), and on *Shabbat Hagadol* (the major Sabbath, before Passover) the times when rabbis delivered their major sermons. Less well known is the fact that rabbis from New York frequently visited with Rabbi Konvitz between Rosh Hashanah and Yom Kippur, so that he could help them to prepare their Yom

Kippur sermons. Konvitz was also influential beyond the Newark community. In 1934, he was elected head of the Union of Orthodox Rabbis of the United States and Canada, which was then the largest organization of Orthodox rabbis in the world. In his role as head of the group, Konvitz established himself as an ardent Zionist, fighting hard against the anti-Zionist Agudah faction headed by Rabbi Eliezer Silver. He was also a strong supporter of the Mizrachi Organization of the United States.

Like his predecessor, Brodsky, Konvitz was lenient in what he asked of others, but strict when it came to his own level of observance. This played itself out in the larger community too, for Konvitz believed in working together, whenever possible, with Conservative and Reform leaders for the common good of Newark's Jews. As opposed to many of the Orthodox rabbis of his day who had studied in the great European yeshivas, Konvitz strongly favored secular studies and he enjoyed close relationships with Rabbis Bernard Revel and Samuel Belkin of Yeshiva University.

Even as he favored secular studies, however, he remained deeply committed to the study of Torah. As his son put it:

> For my father, the happiest hours were when he was alone in his study with his eyes concentrated on a sacred text, and we could hear his soft, melodious voice as he chanted the words on the page. At such moments he was supremely happy, the most fortunate of men . . . .So it was in my father's study: he only seemed to be reading printed words, while in fact he was immersed in a vision, in a view of "Glory beyond all glory ever seen." And the congregation, as they listened, shared in that glory.[47]

These comments tell us what was important in the life of most Orthodox rabbis. What they valued was not speeches, not organizational leadership, but the study of Torah. In their world, status was ultimately measured by textual erudition. The rabbis were seen in their communities as the most important transmitters of the tradition and those who could do it best received the greatest respect. It is telling that his son, Milton, a great legal and constitutional scholar, wrote in his memoir of his father that what he expects will most appropriately define his father's contribution to this world, is the two-volume work of his Jewish writings, arranged by Feldheim Publishers, *Divrei Yosef.*[48]

Other prominent Orthodox rabbis through the years included Chaim Glatzer, Mordechai Ehrenkrantz, Jacob Mendelson, Elias Singer, David Singer, Israel Turner, Herman Kahn, Zundel Levine, Louis Weller, and Meyer Blumenfeld. David Singer, the rabbi of Congregation Adas Israel and Mishnayes and Congregation Tifereth Zion, received his training at the Chofetz Chaim Yeshiva. He left Newark to head what was to become one of the most important congregations in the Borough Park section of Brooklyn, First Congregation Sefard, also known as the Sefardische Shul. Weller was ordained in Europe and, like Konvitz, was active in kashruth supervision. He was an active Zionist and was elected vice president of the Union of Orthodox Rabbis in 1963.

Another Newark congregation that merits some discussion is the Free Synagogue, which existed for a short time in the 1930s. Its rabbi was Lewis Browne, sent to Newark by Stephen Wise, founder of the Free Synagogue in New York City. Browne later became a prominent writer on American Jewish history and other topics and his book, *How Odd of God*, achieved best-seller status. As the name implies, the synagogue operated on the principle of freedom. There were no fixed dues, no assigned seats for members, anyone could speak from the pulpit, regardless of their ideological position, and the emphasis was on open and freewheeling discussions of the social problems that faced society at large.

The congregation had no permanent home and rented different halls in the area for its Friday evening services. Browne was a charming and charismatic man who dressed with flair, often sporting shirts with a long collar, along with wide ties. From the start, he was controversial, viewed by many as to the left of Reform and barely Jewish. The last straw apparently was a sermon he delivered at Schary Manor:

> What broke up the unity and harmony of the congregation was Rabbi Browne's second lecture, whose title was "The Life of Jesus." Even the most sophisticated of the congregants weren't ready for that. As Rabbi Browne started his surprise sermon there was a hushed but indignant murmur. A few of the congregation got up and walked out politely but hurriedly. The next interruption was neither polite nor hurried. A man rose and called out, "This is not the place for such a discussion. It's a disgrace in a temple. Either you stop it or I resign as vice-president."[49]

Browne continued with his talk and the vice president resigned on the spot. Not only that, but he lay in wait outside Schary Manor for Browne to come out and had to be forcibly restrained by two fellow congregants from physically attacking one of the good rabbi's supporters. The following week, there were fewer people in attendance as the rabbi judiciously and, not probably coincidentally, discussed the

Book of Job. Before long, Browne's support had dwindled to the point where there was no reason to continue and he departed, leaving behind him, as Schary put it, "a mixed but imperishable memory in the minds of many Newarkers."[50]

The surrounding communities of Newark were also home to a number of prominent rabbis. One of them was Max Gruenewald, Prinz's brother-in-law. Born in Germany, he served as rabbi of the city of Mannheim before coming to America. In 1944, he was appointed rabbi of the Conservative Congregation B'nai Israel in Millburn. He was very involved in the Leo Baeck Institute which he chaired for a time and was president of the Memorial Foundation for Jewish Culture. Gruenewald was a respected scholar and author and, as a result, the congregation was able to attract many well-known speakers to its lecture series over the years.

In nearby East Orange, the Reform temple, Sharey Tefilo, was headed by Rabbi Marius Ranson. Ordained at the Hebrew Union College, Ranson also studied at the University of Chicago and at Columbia University and was a member of the Central Conference of American Rabbis' Executive Committee. He was a gifted speaker and debater, best known in this area, for his debate with Clarence Darrow on the subject of "Can Religion Meet the Challenge of Modern Criticism?," an event that drew thousands of listeners. Ranson was particularly active in interfaith activities, speaking frequently in local churches.[51]

It is a typical pattern for breakaway groups to leave established synagogues and start new ones. This is what gave rise to the popular joke about the Jew who builds two synagogues on a desolate island. When asked why two houses of worship are needed for one person, he responds: "Oh, the other one is the synagogue I don't go to." People generally form new synagogues for a combination of reasons—a political fight involving a clash of personalities, accompanied by a desire to be one's own boss, and a feeling that something is lacking spiritually in the existing temple. The founding of Temple Israel, in 1949, is a perfect example of this phenomenon, one that was repeated over and over in the Newark area.

In addition to differences among individuals, the group that established Temple Israel felt that something was missing at Sharey Tefilo. Consequently, as mentioned earlier, they broke off from it. As Daniel Shiman, a past president of the Federation and a founder and first president of the synagogue, explained it:

I was in Sharey Tefilo, but I resigned because they didn't have enough Yiddishkeit. They [other congregants] said that Rabbi Ranson was only interested in Christian relations and they were probably right. So we started Temple Israel. The first year we had twenty-five families and Rabbi Herbert Weiner became our rabbi, a wonderful man. We had Rabbi Adin Steinsaltz as our scholar in residence for a year. Initially, we bought an old house on Scotland Road in South Orange. Eventually, we merged back again with Sharey Tefilo. The neighborhood around Prospect Avenue, in East Orange, where they were, had gotten really bad and we had built a beautiful building.[52]

Weiner was the opposite of Ranson, much more informal. His absent-mindedness and bent toward the mystical gave him a certain aura that attracted people who were looking for greater meaning in their lives. Unlike most Reform rabbis, he was deeply committed to Israel and had written a popular book on the country, called, *The Wild Goats of Ein Gedi*. In fact, when the Reform movement finally decided to establish a presence in Israel in 1962, Dr. Nelson Glueck, president of Hebrew Union College, selected Weiner to head its Israeli branch in Jerusalem. Weiner accepted and took a six-month leave of absence from his congregation to set things up.

Rabbis are by definition the central figures in houses of worship, but cantors are clearly important too. They beautify the services and inspire congregants to feel the power and majesty of the prayers. Newark was a city of many cantors. Recognition of this fact came as early as 1927 when the Jewish Ministers and Cantors Association of the United States and Canada held its national convention in the city. Among the many cantors who served Newark's Jewish community were Max Helfere, Moses Gann, Berele Chagy, Abraham Shapiro, Edgar Mills, and Eliezer Schulman.

Every cantor had his following and quite a few were marquee stars who could just as easily have had positions in New York's largest synagogues too. As opposed to, say, the Talmudic knowledge of a rabbi, everyone felt qualified to pass judgment on cantors because, after all, it was largely a question of how pleasant the voice was to the ear, a subjective matter. Nevertheless, other cantors were probably the best judges since they could evaluate a performer's technical skills in addition to the other, less objective, aspects. The following two evaluations impart a sense of what being a cantor meant to those around them and of the many considerations that went into making a judgment about a cantor. Eliezer Schulman, for a time the cantor at Anshe Russia, knew Berele Chagy and had heard him sing on many occasions. Chagy was the cantor at Congregation Adas Israel and Mishnayes, known as "the synagogue of cantors," because it hosted many famous cantors, including Yossele Rosenblatt, over the years. Here is what Schulman had to say about Chagy:

> Chagy ranks among the top-notch *chazzanim*. He gave his *probe* [tryout] saying *kinos* on Tisha Ba'av night. He had a very small voice compared to Koussevitzky or Kwartin. His greatness was his ability to interpret. He had a very soft and tender voice, but it carried. He had a *"gefeel"* [feeling or sensitivity in his voice.] You know what I mean? When Chagy *davened* [prayed] once a month with the choir the shul was jammed. He was a tenor with great sweetness and ability. If a man liked Chagy he was a *"Chagyische Yid"* [a Jew who was a real fan of Chagy]. If they liked him, Koussevitzky couldn't compare to him. When Chagy left Newark after ten years, he went to South Africa. How those people cried that *Shabbes*! They gave him *maftir* [the Haftorah portion read after the Torah reading] to say and he cried as he said it. And the people said: *Vus vaint er? Mir darfen vainen. Er fuhrt doch avec fun uns!* [Why is *he* crying? *We* should be crying. He's leaving *us*!] Years later, he came back and settled in Newark again. They had a concert in the old Metropolitan Opera. Chagy sang and they lowered the curtain and the guy who ran it said: 'I never had a case where they lowered the curtain in the middle of a performance." I, personally, didn't like his voice. I liked a hollerer, like Koussevitzky. But how he could interpret! He was also a very nice man.[53]

Lawrence Avery, who was, for many years, the cantor at the Beth-El Synagogue Center in New Rochelle, was similarly partisan towards Abraham Shapiro, who officiated at Newark's B'nai Abraham. Shapiro was said to have been admired by the great Enrico Caruso, and when Columbia Records issued a special recording of the ten greatest cantors in history, Shapiro was among those featured. Avery was a student of Shapiro at Hebrew Union College's School of Sacred Music and recalled him in the following terms:

> He was a glorious dramatic tenor. The first time I heard him I was blown away. It reminded me, oddly enough, of Caruso. There was something completely aristocratic about the way he turned a phrase. He had enormous flexibility and was extremely expressive. He sang very high, very elaborate. He was just a shade below Koussevitzky. There was a sweetness to his style. He was also creative. Much of what he sang was his own stuff.[54]

The cantors, it should be mentioned, were often accompanied by choirs, especially on the High Holidays. For example, Anshe Russia engaged the famous Machtenberg Choir, while Adas Israel was led by Oscar Julius with the renowned Leibele Waldman officiating. At B'nai Abraham, Max Helfman worked with the cantors for many years.

Special Occasions

As anyone who has ever spent time in a synagogue knows, the holidays were different from the weekly services. They were imbued with a special flavor and were awaited by the devout and even the not so devout, with keen anticipation. For those who had been raised in traditional homes but had lapsed somewhat, Yom Kippur was their opportunity to make it all good again. The description of the holiday by Benjamin Kluger, as it unfolded in his Down Neck neighborhood, is especially evocative:

> How they prayed, those transplanted Jews from the ghettoes of Vilna, Lodz, Kiev and Cracow, from the villages of Hungary, Rumania and Austria—for *parnussah* [success in business], for health, for luck, for peace, for life. With what wholeheartedness they believed, with what fervor they beat their hearts, with what devotion they swayed back and forth in their *tallism* [prayer shawls], with what awe and hope they listened to the weird, quivering notes of the *shofar!* "Their faith was their rock. It made sense out of everything, the inch by inch climb to better themselves, the setbacks, the disappointments, their tiny parcel of possessions amid the world's abundance, illness, death. Certainly it was a harsh, painful world, difficult, hazardous, but illuminating everything was the image of a just and caring God, and they were His Chosen. So they prayed in the morning and they prayed at night, and on Yom Kippur they punished themselves with fasting (passing the bottle of smelling salts from hand to hand as the day wore on). With the setting of the sun, they trudged back to their houses. The slate was wiped clean. The fast was broken. The lights in the stores went on again. They were bolstered and ready for whatever the year might bring.[55]

This description did not take into account that other segment of Newark Jewry, those who came out of some atavistic desire, or a feeling of obligation. Many of Newark's Jews were in the process of acculturating to life in America. In the struggle for daily bread, they had little time or room for religion. And yet, they could not completely break free from their ancestral moorings. Even so, such decisions were not always universally agreed upon within families. In *American Pastoral*, Philip Roth shows us how that played out in the clash between generations:

> I used to go on the High Holidays with my father, and I just never understood what they were getting at. Even seeing my father there never made sense. It wasn't him, it wasn't like him—he was bending to something that he didn't have to, something he didn't even understand. He was just bending to this because of my grandfather. I never understood what any of that stuff had to do with his being a man . . ..If he'd known as little about leather as he knew about God, the family would have wound up in the poorhouse.[56]

There is an edge to Roth's description, a disenchantment with faith, to say the least. Such sentiments were present in many Jews, just as the soaring flights of religious ecstasy marked the different road taken by others. For most, however, religion was something they enjoyed in moderation. When they appeared in temple on the holidays, it was to socialize, as much as to commune with the heavenly Father. A discussion about business, reminiscences with a childhood acquaintance about the old synagogue of their youth, or, perhaps, a political discussion, interrupted only occasionally by admonitions from an usher or a more seriously inclined worshipper in the pew ahead of them. It must be said that the High Holidays were not simply, or even primarily, religious events. Arthur Bernstein is a serious man, a prominent physician with a definite intellectual bent. Yet, when he describes one aspect of the holidays, there is a twinkle in his eye, a nod to the weaknesses and frailties of the human spirit, however well-intentioned:

> The rabbi of Adas Israel when I was growing up was Zundel Levine and he had a pretty daughter. On the Western Wall was a beautiful colored window so that when the sun was going down you got a rainbow of colors . . .and it was a very startling color. The rabbi's daughter came in once on a Yom Kippur afternoon when the sun was just hitting the area where she was. Her mother was sitting in the front, upstairs, and when she came in, the sun hit her gold, lame dress. The whole service stopped and everyone looked up there. It was really an amazing sight. She was about eighteen then and she knew what she was doing. That was the biggest Orthodox synagogue in the area.[57]

When Jews reflect on their youthful experiences with religion their thoughts most often turn to their bar or bat mitzvah. They may comment on its significance or insignificance, on how meaningful or meaningless it was for them, but, whatever the case, it is something they remember. The role of this ceremony in the life of Newark's youngsters did not differ substantially from that which prevailed in other communities. In a study done on three suburban communities near Newark, Morris Werb found that the desire to have a bar or bat mitzvah was one of the primary motivators in the decision by Jews to join synagogues. Almost 27 percent cited it as their *main* reason for doing so. By contrast, only 22 percent mentioned religion as the primary factor in their decision. For the synagogues it was an opportunity, not only to recruit members, but also a chance to fill their Hebrew schools by making school enrollment a precondition for having the ceremony take place in the temple.

What actually happened at the ceremony varied according to the denomination. The Reform required the least on the part of the youngsters, the Conservatives somewhat more, and the Orthodox, the most. Today, the emphasis is usually on the party. The huge garish shindig that took place in Miami's Orange Bowl was certainly the exception, but there are theme parties with lavish receptions, and hundreds of guests, every night of the week in New Jersey and this was the case from the post-World War II period on. Against this backdrop it is difficult for many Jews to grasp that in Europe the bar mitzvah (bat mitzvahs were unheard of) was a minor event that took place on a Monday or Thursday morning in a small synagogue with a few close relatives invited and with very little food served. One Orthodox Newark Jew reminisced about his bar mitzvah in 1933, a fairly typical affair for the Orthodox youth of his times:

> When I had my bar mitzvah, I did *shacharis* [morning service] and *mussaf* [additional service] and gave a speech. Afterwards, we had a hot *kiddush* with *chulent*. My mother would take the neck of a chicken and stuff it with the same ingredients you put in a *kishke* [called *helzle*] and she would put it in the *chulent*, not to serve, just to give it flavor.[58]

Auxiliary Groups

The functions of the synagogue were not only religious, they were social as well. After all, the synagogue, especially in the early years before Y's were built, functioned as a community center. To meet the needs of the community, "men's clubs" and "women's clubs" were formed. These clubs served two functions. First, they gave people an opportunity to do good works, be it gathering clothing for the poor, visiting the sick, or donating blood. Second, they were centers for social activities which were conducted under the temple's umbrella. Here, people held literary meetings to review books, presented fashion shows, formed bowling teams, sponsored lectures of all sorts, and so on. In fact, in every synagogue, there are people who are uninterested in its religious aspects, rarely attending services, but playing a major part in its social activities, and paying the same dues as those who attend weekly services.[59]

The following poem, translated from the German, was penned in 1920 by Oheb Shalom's Celia Lowenstein, on the occasion of the sixtieth year since the founding of the Miriam Auxiliary, the women's organization of the temple. The dedication and love that these women had for their synagogue clearly achieved its highest form of expression through the vehicle of this organization, not the temple services. And even though it was an organization devoted, in the main, to good works, the lyrical Biblical imagery of the poem makes it clear that they saw their work as the fulfillment of a divine calling:

Oheb Shalom's Jubilee Song

Come, oh sisters, women of Miriam
Join us in this Song of Joy
Let to Heaven, its sound travel
For 60 years we had a pact with God.
Fights and upsets could not rob us from our trust
In God's might, he helped us to achieve what
We set out to do, what we planned and worked for.
Our enemies have disappeared in the flow of time
Our pains, worries and wounds are gone with the wind.
Oh, Oheb Shalom, you sweet, you beautiful
You stand there majestically in the light
Daughters of Israel, you are now closely
Related to your God
Keep blooming and blooming
You beautiful flowers of Judah
God has blessed your toils, let's give to him today
Honor and Praise.[60]

Youth activities were of crucial importance to synagogues. No synagogue except, perhaps, a small *shtibl*, could hope to flourish without such a program. While the content of programs differed from one denomination to the next, the format was surprisingly similar. All had junior congregations, social clubs, and involvement with the adult congregation. For example, the Reform B'nai Jeshurun instituted "Girls' Day" and participated in "Boys' Week," a program in which all denominations took part. These programs consisted of messages, prayers, and responsive reading delivered in the main sanctuary. An almost identical program was run by the Orthodox Young Israel, called "Boys' Day in the Synagogue," with the only difference being that the service was more traditional.[61]

The temples realized that to succeed they had to work with other community youth groups. Thus, when Young Israel planned an event, organizations like Neighborhood House and the YMHA. Clubs were invited to the synagogue, with guest youngsters receiving honors during the service. Whenever possible, other youth groups were given space inside the synagogues. Temples often had branches of national organizations, such as Young Judea or the Boy Scouts, using their facilities, with the only restrictions being that they had to bring in kosher food or not allow activities contrary to Judaism. Obviously, these requirements varied from one place to another. One popular innovation in the Young Israel of Newark was the Oneg Shabbat program. There was a speaker and groups of children sang *zemirot* [songs traditionally sung on Friday night] and received refreshments. The evening ended with the singing of "Hatikvah."

What about the smaller synagogues? For those with only twenty or so participants, children were left to entertain themselves. This usually meant that once the Torah was taken out, they would gather in a corner of the synagogue, or, perhaps, out in the hallway, and play their own games, talk, or, as they would describe it later, in their adult years, "just run around." This kind of unorganized free play was probably more enjoyable than the structured junior congregation services that were the rule in the larger synagogues. Indeed, many remembered these "activities" fondly because they did not feel segregated from the adults and because it gave them a feeling of freedom.

The parents made sporadic efforts to hold the children's interest in the service. One method was to offer them a few pennies (payable after the Sabbath, of course) for every mistake they caught the Torah reader making as he read the weekly portion before the congregation from the parchment scroll. Medium-sized temples found other ways to involve the children, sometimes out of necessity. Esther Blaustein's father was the president of one such synagogue in Irvington, Congregation Beth David:

> The older grandchildren, Bernard and I, were used for odd jobs. When Poppa wrote numbers on laundry labels, we licked them and stuck them on the backs of the benches so everyone would know where his High Holiday seat was. We also were sent to pull men off the street if the congregation was short the required ten for a minyan. It wasn't hard. You just went up to any man walking by and asked, "Are you Jewish?" If he said, "Yes," you said, "Please come, we need you for a minyan." "If the man was very old, we often had to resort to *"Bist a Yeed"*? If he nodded his head affirmatively, or answered "Yuh," you said *"minyan"* and pointed

to the shul. We had to memorize this because although we understood everything, we really couldn't speak Yiddish.

We were also in charge of keeping the kids kind of quiet whenever we played outside during services. Poppa himself never came out and yelled at a kid. Even a crying infant, brought in for his adoring grandmother . . .never was asked to leave. Poppa always said, "Chase a child from shul, and he'll never come back."[62]

There were many Jews who rarely set foot inside a synagogue but who, nevertheless, were concerned about having their children relate positively to Jewish culture, if not religion. Recognizing this, synagogues sometimes worked together with other Jewish organizations to set up attractive programs. One of the most worrisome issues, as early as the 1950s, was intermarriage. In Newark, the Y hosted social get-togethers for Jewish youth. To take a case in point, an article in the *Jewish News* spoke of a local rabbi who expressed his appreciation to the Y's executive director, Manuel Batshaw, for his sponsorship of clubs, lounge activities, and dances, where young Jews could meet in a Jewish setting. Another article spoke of a panel on interfaith dating to be held at the Y.[63]

In keeping with the view that the synagogue was more than just a house of prayer, lay leaders and rabbis used it as a forum from which to advocate social action. Nor were the positions adopted always uniform. Newark had always been a stronghold of socialism and radical movements in general because of its many working-class Jews who toiled in its factories. But there was also opposition to those approaches. The *Jewish Chronicle* of May 7, 1926, printed an account of a talk given at Temple B'nai Jeshurun by Hermine Schwed, also known in the community as "the lady of the Constitution." In it, she excoriated communism and warned of the need to be vigilant. Tangible evidence of its dangers could be found, she asserted, in the "youth movements of the 'pink' variety."[64]

During the World War II years, activism took a different and more urgent form as the truth about the extent of the Holocaust became known. Many synagogues in Newark organized efforts to aid the refugees. Typical was the establishment, at a meeting held in Temple Beth Samuel, of a Newark branch of the American Federation of Polish Jews. The group was headed by Rabbi Meyer Blumenfeld.[65] And over at the Wainwright Street Synagogue, Rabbi Mordechai Ehrenkrantz spoke at the dedication of a Torah scroll in memory of the 6,000,000 Jews who had perished in the Nazi conflagration.[66]

The most lasting results of such efforts came in the form of lectures by well-known figures in Jewish intellectual life which were held at all of the major synagogues. For instance, in 1952, Oheb Shalom sponsored a series of lectures that brought first-rank scholars like Cecil Roth and Abraham Joshua Heschel to the synagogue. The temple also invited Orthodox speakers, like Leo Jung, to lecture. Over at B'nai Abraham, in 1954, Oscar Handlin, the noted Harvard historian, opened a lecture series, called "The Story of American Jewry." Other great scholars who presented their views there included Sidney Hook, Salo Baron, and Otto Klineberg. The net effect was to give Newark Jewry a clear sense of how they were part of a larger community of Jews, both in this land, and in the world as a whole. It also gave those who lacked a high level of formal education a way to learn about different ideas and to feel mentally stimulated. In a sense, these speakers, who traveled to many communities, were the intellectual glue that bound them together.

More than anyone else in Newark, Joachim Prinz embodied the belief, as stated in the Bible, that "all Jews are responsible for one another,"—and for others too. He was the social activist par excellence, but, unlike more assimilated Jews, he did what he did as a member of the Jewish people. Fittingly, when he became national president of the American Jewish Congress, Prinz observed that:

> A Jew interested solely in civil rights might join an organization like American Civil Liberties Union. Within AJCongress he must fight the civil rights battle as a Jew and not only as an American citizen.[67]

How ironic and sad, that Prinz, who wanted very badly to remain in Newark as long as possible, was forced to admit that the time had come to leave when he was mugged right in his own study.

When one thinks of recreation and relaxation, what comes to mind is the Y or Jewish Community Center of Newark. No doubt, most Jews availed themselves of whatever these institutions had to offer, but the synagogues were active in this area too, usually because they saw it as a way to draw new members into the fold. B'nai Abraham was the only synagogue which, at its Clinton Avenue location, had a gym and a swimming pool, but other synagogues had what to offer too. In those days, the Orthodox did not, as a rule, object to hearing the voice of a woman soloist. Thus, the Young Israel congregational newsletter reports on an evening of entertainment provided by one Frances Kogan, who is portrayed as "a well-known blues singer and

versatile Baby Clariss, who sang, danced, and played the accordian."[68]
There were annual dinners too, as recalled by Eliezer Schulman, who
belonged to Congregation Ahavas Achim/Anshei Varshaw:

> They used to have meetings during the week and they used to fight, fist fights.
> Uch, how they used to fight, with hollering. But then, once a year, they would have
> a membership dinner. And it was jammed. I remember my mother in the kitchen.
> And they used to cook and bake chicken, and gefilte fish and soup. And when they
> had the dinner the men would sit on one side and the women on the other, not
> because it was *frum* [religious]; that's just the way it was. It was a custom. The
> *chazzan* would sing and the rabbi would speak. And they didn't put out a journal.[69]

Synagogues also sponsored excursions and weekends. Prior to World
War I, for example, B'nai Abraham had its annual picnic at Bellwood
Park in Pennsylvania. The entire congregation took the Lehigh Valley
train to the Allentown area, a fifty-mile trip.[70] Other synagogues would
plan weekends in the Catskills or at the New Jersey shore. There were
bowling nights, evenings at the theater, and softball games. All of
these activities served to strengthen the bonds of solidarity that the
synagogue counted on to insure its financial and general survival. The
attendance at these events was an excellent barometer of their importance to members. One study of synagogue members found that almost 58 percent of those queried listed social, as opposed to religious,
reasons, as the main consideration in their decision to join a synagogue.[71] The temples knew that this was where "the action was" and
planned accordingly.

Supplementary Education

The interest among Newark's Jews in supplementary education was
by no means unique. It is worthwhile to dwell for a moment on how
other religious groupings in the city went about instructing their young
in the wisdom and lore of their heritage. This will make it clear that
Jews were not especially ethnocentric nor parochial in their pursuit of
this goal. In her general history of Essex County, Mary Travis Arny
writes that, in the 1700s:

> Children six years old struggled with Genesis, Exodus, the Psalms and the Prov-
> erbs and even with the Book of Job. They murmured prayers; they learned scrip-
> ture by heart; they learned the catechism; and it is sad to relate that according to
> Pastor Pierson's descendant, David, "It was not the God of love (who was) wor-
> shipped by the Puritans, but the God of fear."

The school was not "free public." Everyone who wanted his children or his servants taught, subscribed—usually at a cost of about two dollars per term per pupil . . ..The pupils may not have been scintillating. At least they were practical, to wit:

Schoolmaster John Catlin: "If John had four apples and father gave him nine more, how many would he have?"

Pupil: More'n two pocketsfull, sir."[72]

A century later, as German immigrants poured into Newark, schools were set up by the Christian community, with some instruction in German. There were two private, nonsectarian German day schools in the city at the time. While some Jews may have sent their children there, the majority were enthusiastic supporters of the public school system. They also believed in Jewish education and sent their children to the schools opened by the synagogues. The times of instruction were generally weekday afternoons and Sunday morning.

When one thinks of teachers literally whipping their charges into shape, what comes to mind is the *cheder* schools established by the Eastern Europeans. As the following description makes clear, the relatively poor quality of instruction was not confined to that group but existed, during the late nineteenth century, in the German-Jewish community as well:

There was but one classroom, and but one teacher for all the classes as well. While one group was being instructed, the others studied or played pranks. The teacher performed his duties with a book in one hand and a rattan switch in the other. When children were caught whispering during lessons, the teacher pounced upon them and beat a tattoo upon their hands or across their shoulders with his rattan switch. The culprit howled. The other children laughed gleefully.[73]

Besides the congregational schools, several other important afternoon schools were founded. One was the Plaut Memorial Hebrew Free School on Prince Street, which was sponsored by the Hebrew Education Society. The idea was the brainchild of German Jews who wanted to enlighten their newly arrived Eastern European brethren. A written appeal on behalf of the school, issued in 1889, a year after the school had been started, revealed both its goals and its biases:

To the Israelites of this City:

Will you stand aloof and see these little ones grow up without *any* religion? Will you allow them to fall a prey to the Conversionists, who try to allure them from their faith and become apostates to the religion of their fathers? Will you do nothing to prevent their becoming victims to the Anarchistic element which, alas, is also predominant among the Jewish immigrants from Russia? These anarchistic views, brought from the Empire of the Czar are to a great extent retained even here. It is a deplorable state of affairs, to continually fear lest the reputation, acquired by the Jews, of being a law-abiding, law-respecting people, be endangered by the fanaticism of a few wicked and stupid individuals, who cannot understand that America is not Russia, and that the freedom enjoyed in this country renders it a revolting crime to continue on these shores the blatant agitation for "human rights," however necessary it may be there.

To prevent the children of the Russian immigrants from growing up to be a menace to the community, and a burning shame to Judaism is the primary object of the Society . . .let us try to make the children of our poor Jewish immigrants intelligent, good, industrious and refined.[74]

Those who went to the school were exposed to a balanced program, one which emphasized Hebrew and traditional texts, but many were uncomfortable with attending a place that had been created out of a sense of noblesse oblige. They did not want to feel that someone was doing them any favors.

To address those sentiments, the Talmud Torah of Newark was established in 1899, in a store on Broome Street. It moved several times over the years, to Sterling Street, then to Morton Street, and, after that, to Osborne Terrace in the Weequahic section. One of its most influential principals was Charles Ehrenkrantz. Under his guidance, the school developed a rich and varied program combining Bible and prayer with modern Hebrew literature and stressing Hebrew language. This was all the more impressive because during his tenure, the 1920s, there was no board of Jewish education, no licensing procedures, and no set standards. Louis Halberstadter was another excellent principal who headed up the main school, while his brother, Joseph, led the then newly established Osborne Terrace branch. There was a definite need for quality programs. One story in the synagogue archives at Rutgers University concerns a small school visited by Alter Kriegel, a local rabbi. When asked by Kriegel who was the greatest Jew in history, one little fellow responded enthusiastically, "Jesus Christ." Dismayed, Kriegel turned to another youngster and asked: "Who was it that gave the Torah to our people?" "Harry Yeskel," was the answer. Indeed, Yeskel had presented a Torah scroll to the community at its synagogue dedication.[75]

A majority of the hundreds of students who attended the school came from stable, upwardly mobile families. But the school also had problem children and it apparently reached out to them. A series of articles that appeared in the mid-1930s in the *Jewish Chronicle*, focused on these cases. There was Morris, one of seven children, whose father was a junk peddler. Unable to pay for heat in their tenement flat, the family made do with overcoats for blankets, with newspapers thrown over them "for good measure." Then there were the three black children, whose impoverished father had converted to Judaism, become a scholar, and was the leader of a small synagogue on Broome Street. One of the children, eleven-year-old Norman, earned money by stoking furnaces and shining shoes. A third instance involved the child of an interfaith marriage whose parents had no money but whose non-Jewish parent begged the school to accept the child as a scholarship student. During World War II, the Talmud Torah took in, at no charge, a number of orphaned refugees.[76]

The Y also undertook to provide Jewish education in the form of the Herzliah School. A modern institution that concentrated on Hebrew as a language and on Palestine's history and culture, it was established in late 1929. Unfortunately, there were certain drawbacks, not the least of which was its location. It was hard for students who had been in public school all day to sit in class while all around them they could see sports activities, cultural events, and the like going on. Then, as Jews moved to Clinton Hill and Weequahic, transportation to High Street became a logistical problem. Added to that was the onset of the Depression which meant that many people could not afford to pay for a bus. These difficulties were insurmountable and, in August of 1932, Herzliah closed its doors.

Yet another effort was the Bet Yeled Jewish Folk School, a secular-socialist, Yiddish-speaking school organized, in 1950, by the Labor Zionist Organization. Among the founders were Jerry Ben-Asher, Herbert Gladstone, Israel Tumin, Joseph Cooper, and Leo Yanoff. The primary financial backing for the school came from Ralph Wechsler, an ardent Zionist leader and a friend of David Ben-Gurion. At its height it had approximately 350 students in a building on Chancellor Avenue that had been constructed at a cost of about $250,000. Eventually, the focus shifted from Yiddish to Hebrew with an emphasis on the works of I.L. Peretz and Sholom Aleichem and on Jewish history, but nothing in the area of religion.[77] With the move to the suburbs, the school lost much of its support and eventually closed. The demographic changes were accompanied by a general decline of interest in socialism as a movement, something that had been going on since the early 1930s.

In 1931, only about a quarter of Newark's Jewish children received Jewish education of any sort in the twenty or so schools in the city.[78]
It is fair to ask, perhaps, why the majority of parents did not send their children to the afternoon schools. First, there was the fact that many were unable to afford the tuition fees and were embarrassed to ask for financial assistance. Second, for many, anxious to acculturate to America, Judaism was relatively unimportant. In part this was because, once the gates to America were locked by the Johnson Immigration Acts of 1921 and 1924, there was no longer the steady infusion of Jewish life and culture that had been part of the immigrants' cultural baggage. The restrictions on immigration also reflected a change that had been taking place in American life and culture generally, namely a downgrading in the desirability of maintaining one's culture. Instead, the emphasis was on "becoming an American," and attending a Jewish school was not seen as fitting in with that viewpoint.

Most problematic was the quality of the schools themselves. Those who ran them tried, but funds were often lacking and, as a result, both the facilities and the staff were often second rate. Many in the organized Jewish community, at least until the 1940s, did not feel that supplemental education was a priority and were reluctant to invest in these schools. The educational shortcomings would not, of course, have been noted in any histories written by the schools themselves, but the students served as a rich lode of information about the conditions that prevailed in them. In his autobiographical account, *The Facts*, Philip Roth contrasts the Talmud Torah with public school and, in so doing, clarifies why youngsters both disliked and liked it:

In those after-school hours at the dingy Hebrew School—when I would have given anything to have been outdoors playing ball until suppertime—I sensed underlying everything a turbulence that I didn't at all associate with the airy, orderly public school where I was a bright American boy from nine to three, a bubbling, energetic unruliness that conflicted head-on with all the exacting ritual laws that I was now being asked to obey devoutly. In the clash between the anguished solemnity communicated to us by the mysterious bee-buzz of synagogue prayer and the irreverence implicit in the spirit of animated mischievousness that manifested itself almost daily in the little upstairs classrooms of the *shul*, I recognized something far more "Jewish" than I ever did in the never-never-land stories of Jewish tents in Jewish deserts inhabited by Jews conspicuously lacking local last names like Ginsky, Nusbaum, and Strulowitz. Despite everything that we Jews couldn't eat—except at the Chinese restaurant, where the pork came stowed away in the egg roll, and at the Jersey shore, where the clams skulked unseen in the depths of the chowder—despite all our taboos and prohibitions and our vaunted self-denial, a nervous forcefulness decidedly *irrepressible* pulsated through our daily life, converting even the agonizing annoyance of having to go to Hebrew School, when you could have been "up the field" playing left end or first base, into unpredictably paradoxical theater.

What I still can recall from my Hebrew School education is that whatever else it may have been for my generation to grow up Jewish in America, it was usually entertaining. I don't think that an English Jewish child would necessarily have felt that way and, of course, for millions of Jewish children east of England, to grow up Jewish was tragic. And that we seemed to understand without even needing to be told.[79]

Most of those who attended these schools were, as Roth implies, resentful that, while others, including most Jewish kids, were out playing ball, they had to troop off to a school where they were taught by mostly uninspired and uninspiring pedagogues for whom this was almost always a second job. It was hard for these teachers to recognize that Biblical stories meant nothing to children for whom any kind of reinforcing Jewish culture was often absent in the home. The "irrepressible" behavior that Roth speaks of is not necessarily Jewish, in this writer's view; it is the response that children of *any* religion would have. What makes it Jewish is that it was tolerated to the degree which it was by indulgent parents who, when receiving reports of what these miscreants had done, rebuked them only mildly if at all and often with a wink or two. After all, had they not gone to such schools themselves and had they not acted out in much the same way?

Roth informs us that, if nothing else, these places were "entertaining," and that is definitely true. But they were not entertaining because of any design on the part of those who administrated them. Rather, it was that children are marvelously adaptable and were able to turn a negative experience into a positive one for them by engaging in mischief and sometimes, even mayhem. Harold Eppston, in a letter to the *Jewish Chronicle*, reminiscing about the Talmud Torah, writes about the *shammes* (sexton), a man "who had a long red nose and was a bewhiskered dwarfish Rip Van Winkle [who] was forever chasing, like the ad on Old Dutch Cleanser, some *"tachshit:* [troublemaker] who had plucked a whisker just for the merriment of the chase."[80] Still, it would be fair to say that deep down, most youngsters knew it was wrong, even if deliciously so. Again, Roth's description, this time in his short story, "The Conversion of the Jews," is most helpful. In it, the Hebrew School teacher explains that Jesus' father could not have been God because, "The only way a woman can have a baby is to have intercourse with a man." Upon hearing that, a student asks, in what is clearly a mix of sincerity and a desire to provoke:

> How, if He [God] could create the heaven and earth in six days, and make all the animals and the fish and the light in six days . . .and He could pick the six days He wanted right out of nowhere, why couldn't he let a woman have a baby without having intercourse . . . .What Ozzie wanted to know was always different. The first time he had wanted to know how Rabbi Binder could call the Jews "The Chosen People" if the Declaration of Independence claimed all men to be created equal . . . .That was the first time his mother had come.[81]

Another, often neglected aspect of the whole experience was what it taught Jewish children about their place in the larger scheme of things. Attending Hebrew School entailed certain dangers, namely the risk of being attacked by locals who had imbibed anti-Semitism in their mother's milk, as it were. Some ran, while others stood their ground. Clearly, the former are more reluctant to speak, and they may have been more profoundly affected by what happened than those who stood up to the bullies. The latter, however, speak freely and, hopefully, do not exaggerate:

> [But] new thrills came when a continuous and unremitting war developed with the Italian boys around South Orange Avenue and Howard Street. The ammunitions were stones, coal, and even rocks, brickbats and what-not coupled with a "tzitzis" under one's shirt just for luck! The charm worked too, for there were few of us permanently maimed though there were scarcely any of us who couldn't show a scar or two to mark the barbarity of those momentous days.[82]

Evidently, Jews in public school were transformed in the eyes of their classmates once they showed their Jewishness. Jerry Lehman, who grew up in the Third Ward near Bergen Street, tells us how and why:

> JL: "I studied in the rabbi's house 3–5:30 twice a week. And I had to walk through a horrible neighborhood. These guys who started up with me were the same nice guys in school. But once they got out of school, they saw me coming. Every month or so I had to buy a *siddur* because I was always banging it over someone's head."
> WH" You were a strong guy."
> JL: "Yeah."
> WH:"But what would you do if there were five of them?"
> JL: "Run faster. The next day they'd see me in school and they'd say, 'That hurt.' And I'd say, 'What hurt?' And they'd say, 'You hit me over the head with that book of yours.' And I'd say, 'Watch out; next time it might be a bat.' You'd be surprised—hitting somebody across the face with a book . . .You see they were getting all this crap about Jews from their parents."[83]

Despite all of the disadvantages associated with the schools, they not only remained in the Jewish community in the trek to the sub-urbs—they flourished. Contact with Gentiles in their new neighbor-hoods exposed the Jews to the importance of ethnic identification. It was also a sign of the changing times. The postwar period marked the beginning of America's love affair with cultural pluralism, the idea that you could and should identify with your people so long as that identification posed no threat to the national interest. Moreover, life in suburbia revolved around children. Raising and educating them was a primary topic for these middle-class, second and third generation par-ents, whose Jewish roots included a strong affinity for the family. Here, all of the synagogues had schools and enrolling in them was the key that opened the door to a synagogue bar or bat mitzvah celebra-tion, and all for the same price of membership. Besides, it was differ-ent than in the old days:

> My son has been attending only about three years. The amount of knowledge he has obtained surprises me. The new methods and the modern system used today is far from the type of Jewish education I received. I grew to dislike it. I believe it even carried over with me for many years. My son, however, seems to enjoy his Hebrew school. He seems to be growing up as a happy Jew.[84]

This was a far cry from what had been the case a generation earlier. Greater financial support was an important factor in this transforma-tion. It meant that better teachers could be hired. The new breed of teacher was younger and therefore better able to relate to the children. He or she was also licensed and better trained, largely because of the work of the Jewish Education Association.[85] And the effect on the family was often profound. Armed with greater knowledge, children told their parents that they wanted more Jewish observance at home—a Chanukah party, a Passover *seder* with songs and stories, not just a nice meal. The decision by the parents to shift the responsibility for cultural transmission came back to either haunt or energize them, de-pending on how they viewed themselves as Jews.

Day Schools and High Schools

In a national study of Jewish education in this country, reported on in 1959, the noted educators, Alexander Dushkin and and Uriah Z. Engelman, had written that "American Jewish schooling is like a shal-low river, 'a mile wide and an inch deep.'"[86] In the early part of the twentieth century, Jewish education in Newark was even less developed. Indicative of this was the fact that, aside from a small day school, which existed for a few years under the auspices of Temple B'nai Jeshurun, starting in 1863, Newark had no day school of significant size until 1943. In a June 26, 1925 editorial that reflected the sentiments of many in the community, the *Jewish Chronicle* editorialized:

> First, it [the day school] is unnecessary for the preservation of our religion as long as we maintain good religious schools for our youth. We are not afraid of sending our boys and girls to the grammar and high schools of our community. We are satisfied with the secular education as it is taught in our public schools and we know that we could not improve on it . . .we do not feel that we need to segregate our children in Parochial Schools in order to safeguard our Jewish heritage. We realize that by so doing, when there is no vital need prompting it, we would invite sectarian strife and creedal controversy that would affect our political life for generations to come.
>
> Nor are we doing our share to keep our America true to her course toward the attainment of perfect tolerance and good will among the different religious groups. If we turn against this theory by establishing our own secular institutions, we would be morally bound to permit the zealots in our midst to do what they pleased with the public schools, to make them accessories to the Protestant churches and to see the classrooms become missionary centers."[87]

These words have a rather distant ring to them today, a time when not only are day schools flourishing in America, but ideas like granting tuition tax credits for those who send their children to them are routinely discussed. In 1925, however, the position taken by the *Chronicle*, was certainly not unusual. There were very few day schools, almost all of them in New York City, and Jews felt far less secure in their newly adopted home. Furthermore, the Orthodox, who were the impetus behind the day school movement when it began growing in the post-World War II period, were a negligible presence in America then.[88]

There was an attempt, not well known, to start a day school, a year later, in 1926. The name of the school was Rambam (Maimonides) and the guiding force behind it was Dr. H.L. Gordon, who had lived in Palestine and held advanced degrees in philosophy and Semitic languages. Gordon was also the principal of the Talmud Torah afternoon school at the time and this effort was an offshoot of the larger enterprise. An article about the school appeared in November of 1929 in the *Morgen Journal*. In it, the writer praised the yeshiva's staff and students, calling it "the pride of Newark." Another article about the school had been published earlier, in 1927, in the Hebrew language weekly, *Hadoar*.[89] At its peak, Rambam had about fifty students. Unfortunately, Gordon, who was apparently a gifted, well-trained, and progressive educator, left Rambam, probably in 1930, because of a dispute with the Talmud Torah Board over cutbacks in his program. Shortly afterwards, the day school, rudderless without its founder, closed. As for Gordon, he returned to college to pursue a career in psychology.[90]

In 1943, a new day school opened, the Yeshiva of Newark. It was not a sound school academically, however, and, in 1948, it merged with the Talmud Torah, which was a good school, but which was teetering on the edge of bankruptcy. The merger was brought about by Samuel Klein, a successful accountant and attorney, and Jewish community leader, and the school was renamed the Hebrew Academy of Essex County, with Louis Halberstadter as the principal. Klein became president of the day school and served with distinction in that capacity for thirty years, an incredibly long period for a school president. During his tenure, in 1962, the school merged with another yeshiva, the Hebrew Youth Institute, and was again renamed, this time as the Hebrew Youth Academy. At that time it had about 300 students.[91] Today, the yeshiva, which has also opened a high school, is known as the Joseph Kushner Hebrew Academy and has 560 students. It is situated on a beautiful thirty-acre campus with state-of-the-art facilities for its students—soccer fields, tennis courts, a college-size gym, and 120 new computers.

There were also sporadic efforts, during the 1940s and 1950s, by Rabbi Sholom Ber Gordon, a disciple of the Lubavitcher Rebbe at the time, Joseph Isaac Schneerson, to set up an elementary school. The school, Yeshiva Achei Temimim, was not successful on the whole, and never attracted more than a dozen or so students at any one time. There was also an afternoon school attached to the yeshiva and Rabbi Gordon did succeed in turning on one student to Talmud study who became very prominent in the Orthodox world—Rabbi Nosson Scherman. Scherman heads the hugely successful ArtScroll Publishing Company.[92]

In 1959, the Lubavitcher movement opened an advanced, post-high school yeshiva, with ten students as its nucleus. It was founded by Rabbis Gershon Mendel Gorelig and Label Raskin and located on Grumman Avenue. There was also a short-lived high school with a ninth and tenth grade in the building, in 1961 and 1962, but it did not pan out. As a result, it was decided to concentrate more on developing the advanced yeshiva, called the Rabbinical College of America. In 1971, the school, under the leadership of Rabbi Moshe Herson, purchased a fifteen-acre site in Morristown and relocated there.[93]

The Conservatives were also active in Jewish education, beginning in the mid-1960s. A study by Professor Nathan Winter and Horace Bier demonstrated that there was a real need for more intensive Jewish education that would appeal to the non-Orthodox. These two individuals, who were responsible for most of the Solomon Schechter day schools founded in New Jersey, started such a school in nearby Union. The school attracted children from Essex County as well. Eventually, in 1991, a new home was built in West Orange for the Solomon Schechter Middle and High School.

Winter asked for and received the blessings of Rabbi Pinchas Teitz, before embarking on this venture. He was concerned that Teitz, who headed a large day school in nearby Elizabeth, might view the new school as a threat, but he did not. Reflecting on the whole matter, Winter said:

> The Solomon Schechter schools made day school education quite kosher for the non-observant. They also made more of the Orthodox send their children to yeshivas, which they didn't do so readily in the earlier years. The reason was that if a yeshiva education was good enough for the Conservatives, then it was *very good* for the Orthodox.[94]

Until very recently, no all day Hebrew high schools of any substance were begun in Essex County. In part, this was due to the fact that such schools were established in nearby Union and Bergen Counties, to meet the demand for this type of education. There, were, on the other hand, part-time programs, such as the one begun by the Y in 1930. Classes met twice a week there and studied Bible, Hebrew literature, and Jewish history.[95] Some teenagers even traveled to New York City on Sundays, to attend high school level classes. Bernard Bloom remembers taking the train with a group of friends in 1927 to a school on Stuyvesant Place, in Manhattan, where he studied together with students from different parts of New York City.[96] The most important effort has been the Central Hebrew High School, run by the Jewish Education Association, with branches in different parts of the MetroWest area. And, naturally, there are adult study programs of all sorts available in the various temples and at the Jewish Community Center.

Zionism

It seems fitting to conclude a chapter devoted to how tradition was passed from generation to generation with some discussion of Zionism, for it was the memory of its ancient homeland together with the practice of religion, that kept the Jewish people alive spiritually through the centuries. Newark was a center for Zionist activity from the beginning. Some of the early organizations in the city were the Sons and Daughters of Zion, the Brandeis and Herzl Zionist Societies, Hatehiya, Poale Tzion, Young Judea, the Zionist Organization of America, Mizrachi, local branches of the various national Jewish youth organizations, and, of course, Hadassah and the Jewish National Fund.[97]

Most of these groups were established in the first decade of the twentieth century and they were indicative of what was to come, for, in the next twenty years, Newark Jewry was to express its support very volubly in a variety of ways. There were rallies, meetings, parades, and demonstrations, and Newark was a favorite stopping-off point of those pleading the cause. Typical was an ad that appeared in the *Jewish Chronicle* of December 2, 1921. It announced a forthcoming reception at Krueger Auditorium to greet Nahum Sokolow, Vladimir Jabotinsky, and Otto Warburg. When Chaim Weizmann visited Newark, two years later, in 1923. thousands turned out to welcome him and $50,000 was raised in one evening.[98]

Support for Israel generally, increased tremendously after the Holocaust and Newark's Jews joined in the national effort to establish a state. Several young men from Newark volunteered to assist Israel and one of them, Jack Rothman, from Maplewood, was killed while in the country, in 1948. Parents undertook to raise the consciousness of their children about the new country. Every year, youngsters gathered by the thousands to celebrate Israeli Independence Day, both in Newark and in New York City, where they performed at festivals with other schools.[99]

After the creation of the state, Newark's Zionists continued to be active. Essex County typified the national split between the Labor and Revisionist Zionists. In Newark, the Labor Zionists, led by Morris Palevsky, and with the involvement of people like Leo Yanoff and Ralph Wechsler, developed programs in support of Zionist education and also donated money to Israel. There was a chapter within the organization for the younger people, called Dorot Zion. Ralph Goldman, a member of Dorot, directed a program supported by the Truman administration to send talented people in the arts to Israel to help the country. The Revisionists, led by Nathan Brodsky, Frances Nusbaum, and a number of other people, engaged in similar activities on behalf of their organization. They remained closely allied with the Zionist Organization of America, which had moved to the right over the years.[100]

The portrait sketched here is that of a Jewishly vibrant community. Newark's Jews built synagogues and community centers that would stand up very well when measured against other communities. The afternoon school system was begun early and, with all its faults, trained thousands of young children to be committed Jews, even if they were not especially observant. Unlike neighboring New York, Newark did not have a powerful Orthodox presence but, then again, no city could compare to New York in that respect, not even Chicago. What Newark did have though, was a community that was proud of its ethnic identity, one that lived together in distinct neighborhoods whose very Jewishness was embedded in its daily life—restaurants, clubs, friendship circles, and formal organizations. That is what gave it life and culture and a sense of a shared history.

Notes

1. John T. Cunningham, *Newark* (Newark, N.J.: The New Jersey Historical Society), 135–37.
2. Sarah S. Kussy, *The Story of Gustav and Bella Kussy of Newark, N.J.: A Family Chronicle*, booklet, n.d., 18.
3. Bernard Drachman, *The Unfailing Light* (New York: Rabbinical Council of America, 1948), 168–75, 182–85.
4. Leon S. Lang, "Prospects for Jewish Education in Newark," *Jewish Chronicle*, May 29, 1931, 18.
5. Michael A. Stavitsky, *New Trends in Community Programs for Jewish Education*, unpublished report, 7.
6. William B. Helmreich, *The World of the Yeshiva: An Intimate Portrait of Orthodox Jewry* (New York: The Free Press, 1982), 302–310.
7. Morris R. Werb, *Jewish Suburbia: An Historical and Comparative Study of the Jewish Communities in Three New Jersey Suburbs*, Ph.D. dissertation, New York University, 1959, 222, 230.
8. Charles E. Silberman, *A Certain People* (New York: Summit Books, 1985), 207. Levine is currently a sociology professor at Boston University.
9. Actually, the prayer book adopted at the Cleveland Conference was Isaac M. Wise's, *Minhag America*, while the one eventually adopted by B'nai Jeshurun was the more radical Reform prayer book of David Einhorn. Regardless, the

point is that the introduction of a Reform version came later to B'nai Jeshurun than was the case in other American Reform communities.

10. For detailed descriptions of the temple from an architectural standpoint, see Margaret A. Vance, "Reform Jews to Dedicate New Temple in Short Hills," *Newark Evening News*, September 3, 1968, 21; "New Temple Structure: A Merger of Beauty, Simplicity," *Jewish News*, September 13, 1968, 18.

11. Most of the discussion in this section is based on the following sources: "B'nai Jeshurun Oldest Congregation in State," *Jewish Chronicle*, Fifteenth Anniversary Issue, April 24, 1936, 69; *B'nai Jeshurun Temple, Manuscript Minute Book of Congregation Meetings*, Newark, N.J., August 20, 1848 - April 30, 1871. American Jewish Archives, Manuscript Collection, Waltham, Massachusetts; "B'nai Jeshurun Boasts Colorful History," *Jewish Chronicle*, Twentieth Anniversary Issue, June 20, 1941, 66; Gustav P. Heller, A Century of Temple B'nai Jeshurun, unpublished paper, n.d.; "A Concise History of B'nai Jeshurun," *Jewish News*, September 13, 1968, 20; Barry Hewitt Greene, *Our One Hundred Fortieth Year: Tracing the History of Congregation B'nai Jeshurun*, booklet.

12. Abner R. Gold, "Pilgrims in a New Land," *Jewish News*, June 24, 1949, 12.

13. Abner R. Gold, "Pilgrims in a New Land," *Jewish News*, August 19, 1949, 9.

14. Sarah S. Kussy, *The Story of Gustav and Bella Kussy*, 19.

15. See, Oheb Shalom, *135th Anniversary: An Evening of Song and Celebration*, booklet.

16. "Dedicate Ahavath Zion's Beautiful New Synagogue Sunday Before Notables." *Jewish Chronicle*, May 25, 1922, 1.

17. Sidney R. Lewitter, *American Dreams: The Story of a Jewish Immigrant Family* (Lakewood, N.J.: Bristol, Rhein & Englander, 1994), 223. Actually, the Czerhowitz Rebbe. There was also, during the 1950s, an Agudath Israel-style synagogue, known as the Hebrew Youth Institute, located on Pomona Avenue. Another important synagogue in the Weequahic section was the Schley Street Synagogue. See "Schley Street Synagogue is Pioneer Congregation in Weequahic Section," *Jewish Chronicle*, Twentieth Anniversary Issue, June 20, 1941, 103.

18. Minutes of Congregation B'nai Jeshurun meeting, April 28, 1864. American Jewish Archives, Hebrew Union College, Cincinnati, Ohio.

19. Ibid., April 23, 1868.

20. "Linas Hatzedek Constitution": Special Collections and University Archives, Synagogue Collection, Rutgers University Libraries.

21. "Young Israel": Minutes of Young Israel of Newark, meeting, January 11, 1950. Special Collections and University Archives, Synagogue Collection, Rutgers University Libraries.

22. Ibid., June 12, 1958.

23. "Young Israel": Synagogue Etiquette and Procedure. Special Collections and University Archives, Synagogue Collection, Rutgers University Libraries.

24. Sylvan H. Kohn, "Aspects of Congregational Life in Essex County: Synagogue Activities are on Marked Upswing," *Jewish News*, June 21, 1957, 14; See, also, Louis M. Levitsky, "Defends Suburban Synagogue," *Jewish News*, October 13, 1961, 19.

25. "Kosher Butchers are Being Probed," *Newark Evening News*, August 18, 1939, 1. See also "Rabbi Defines Kosher Duties," *Newark Evening News*, 6.

26. "Essex Board of Rabbis Asks Community Kashruth Control," *Jewish News*, June 1, 1956, 3. See also Jose Ann Steinbock, "Butchers Federation Sues Seroffs for Libel," *Jewish News*, July 13, 1956, 1.

27. "A Biographical Background," *Jewish News*, January 7, 1927, 1

28. Janet Lowenstein, interview, December 13, 1994.

29. The respondent requested anonymity.

30. Janet Lowenstein, interview, December 13, 1994.

31. "Protests Attack on Jewish Body as Unwarranted," *Jewish Chronicle*, Letter to the Editor, April 7, 1922, 4. Foster often lashed out against his critics. See, for example, "Majority of Jews are Anti-Zionists, Says Rabbi Foster," *Jewish Chronicle*, August 14, 1925, 1.

32. Nathan Glazer, *American Judaism* (Chicago: University of Chicago Press, second edition, revised, 1972), 41–42; 103.

33. One respondent, who did not wish to be named, tells another story about Foster's concerns in this area. "When B'nai Jeshurun put on its 100th Anniversary exhibit at the Newark Museum in 1948, Foster wanted it to be like a Protestant exhibit. Here was a chance to bring Judaism to the greater Newark community, but he wanted it to be more like a Christian exhibit. Rabbi Foster was shocked at the Jewish content: "What will the Gentiles think?" he said. The Protestants came in droves. And Foster was there every day to see what the Gentiles were thinking. Finally, he said: "The Gentiles love it."

34. "Court Asked to Allow Jewish Mother her Child Alienated from her Faith by Strangers," *Jewish Chronicle*, December 16, 1921, 1.

35. "Dr. Hoffman Seeks to Keep Traditional Judaism Alive," *Jewish Chronicle*, March 20, 1931, 1. Milton Konvitz recalls how: "When my father [Rabbi Joseph Konvitz] first came to Newark, Rabbi Hoffman paid him a visit and he had a handkerchief wrapped around his wrist because he was a *shomer Shabbes* [Sabbath observer]," interview, April 8, 1997.

36. Jerry Blum, interview, August 8, 1996.

37. Dore Schary, *For Special Occasions* (New York: Random House, 1961), 147.

38. Saul Schwarz, interview, December 6, 1994.

39. Schary, *For Special Occasions*, 147–48.

40. "Intimate Views of Rabbi Silberfeld," *Jewish Chronicle*, February 25, 1927, 1.

41. "Rabbi Julius Silberfeld," *Jewish News*, Editorial, January 3, 1958, 8.

42. Howard Levine, interview, August 29, 1996. One of the people he had a profound influence on was Jacqueline Levine, former President of the National Community Relations Advisory Council. Levine, who also marched for Civil Rights in the South, described Prinz as "a deep personal friend . . . a father figure . . . my inspiration." See Edith K. Schapiro,'"Jackie Wins Prinz Award for 'Exemplary Leadership,'" *Jewish News*, September 14, 1978, 1.

43. *Papers and Correspondence of Louis Levitsky*. Jewish Theological Seminary Archives, New York City.

44. Muriel Bloom, interview, August 5, 1996.

45. "Community Mourns Death of Brodsky," *Jewish Chronicle*, March 5, 1937, 1; Anton Kaufman, "Rabbi Hyman Brodsky," *Jewish Chronicle*. Editorial, March 5, 1937, 1.

46. Milton R. Konvitz, "Rabbi Joseph Konvitz: A Son's Memoir," forthcoming, in *Torah U'maddah*, Volume 8, 1998., 27 (in manuscript).

47. Ibid., 53.

48. Ibid., 50.

49. Dore Schary, *For Special Occasions*, 150–54.

50. Ibid., 154.

51. "Temple Sharey Tefilo's Rise Traced to Rabbi Ranson," *Jewish Chronicle*, Twentieth Anniversary Issue, June 20, 1941, 63.

52. Dan Shiman, interview, November 30, 1994.

53. Eliezer Schulman, interview, December 25, 1996.
54. Lawrence Avery, interview, November 9, 1997.
55. Benjamin Kluger, "Growing Up in Newark," *Jewish News*, September 8, 1977, B2.
56. Philip Roth, *American Pastoral* (New York:Houghton Mifflin Company, 1997), 314.
57. Arthur Bernstein, interview, October 27, 1994.
58. Eliezer Schulman, interview, December 25, 1996.
59. For a description of a typical sisterhood, see Sarah Slater, "The Sisterhood of Young Israel," *Jewish Chronicle*. Young Israel Supplement, February 28, 1936, 4. One can see how far to the right things have moved today by the activities listed, such as the annual "Purim Ball." There are almost no Young Israel synagogues left that allow social dancing.
60. Celia Lowenstein, "Poem," in *60th Anniversary Issue of Oheb Shalom*, 1920.
61. "Observe Girls' Day at Temple," *Jewish Chronicle*, May 7, 1926, 1; "Young Israel Synagogue of 'Y' to Conduct Services at Talmud Torah," *Jewish Chronicle*, April 24, 1925, 1.
62. Esther Blaustein, *When Momma was the Landlord* (New York: Harper & Row, 1972), 110–11.
63. "All Ages at Newark Y Find 'Boy Meets Girl' Important," *Jewish News*, April 8, 1960, 55; "Panel to Discuss Interfaith Dating," *Jewish News*, January 29, 1960, 31.
64. "Pink Propaganda Threatens Youth," *Jewish Chronicle*, May 7, 1926, 1.
65. "Newark Group Organizes to Aid Jewish Group in Poland," *Newark Evening News*, December 26, 1940, 9.
66. "Scroll Will Honor Victims of Nazis," *Newark Evening News*, April 12, 1947, 6.
67. Eugene W. Blum, "New AJCongress President Stresses Jewish Survival," *Jewish News*, May 23, 1958, 7.
68. Irving Laskowitz, "Our Installation and Dinner Dance," *Young Israel Review*, Vol. 1, No. 1, 5.
69. Eliezer Schulman, interview, December 25, 1996.
70. Jane Grotta, interview, August 29, 1996.
71. Morris Werb, *Jewish Suburbia*, 160.
72. Mary Travis Arny, *Red Lion Rampant: An Informal History of Essex County, New Jersey* (no publisher, 1965), 12.
73. *Oheb Shalom, Seventy Fifth Anniversary: The Story of a Congregation*, booklet, 17.
74. Joseph Leucht, Wolff Willner, and Isaac Schwartz, "Appeal in Behalf of the Hebrew Education Society of Newark, N.J.," flier, November 21, 1989.
75. David Rudavsky, *Report and Survey of Verona Jewish Community*, Synagogue Archives, Rutgers University.
76. "Why the Talmud Torah?," *Jewish Chronicle*, December 4, 1936, 1; "Why the Talmud Torah?," *Jewish Chronicle*, December 25, 1936, 1; "Why the Talmud Torah?" *Jewish Chronicle*, January 8, 1937, 1; "Talmud Torah Portraits . . .," *Jewish Chronicle*, February 13, 1942, 1.
77. Jerry Ben-Asher, interview, May 26, 1997.
78. Leon S. Lang, "Prospects for Jewish Education in Newark," 18.
79. Philip Roth, *The Facts: A Novelist's Autobiography* (New York: Farrar, Straus & Giroux, 1988), 121–22.
80. Harold A. Eppston, "Memories of the Talmud Torah," *Jewish Chronicle*, letter to the editor, January 23, 1942, 5.
81. Philip Roth, "The Conversion of the Jews," in *Goodbye Columbus* (New York: Bantam, 1963), 101–02.

82. Harold Eppston, "Memories of the Talmud Torah," 5.

83. Jerry Lehman, interview, June 27, 1996.

84. Morris Werb, *Jewish Suburbia*, 222.

85. David Rudavsky, "A Unifying Force in Jewish Education," *Jewish News*, June 14, 1957, 50. Judah Pilch was President of the JEA between 1948 and 1949, before becoming head of the American Association for Jewish Education. The Chayil Society, organized by the JEA, gave recognition to the accomplishments of outstanding students in the various Jewish schools. For more on this, see Correspondence from David Schechner to Joseph A. Settanni, archivist, January 16, 1996. Available at the Jewish Historical Society of MetroWest. The New Jersey Normal School, founded in 1926, also set standards and provided training for teachers, but it was limited to the Reform movement.

86. As cited in Milton Konvitz, "Rabbi Joseph Konvitz," 28.

87. "The Parochial School Idea," *Jewish Chronicle*, editorial, June 26, 1925, 4.

88. William Helmreich, *The World of the Yeshiva*, 18–51.

89. As cited in Gail Schaffer, *Memoirs of an American Sabra Hebrew Teacher* (North Miami, Fla.: Renaissance Booksetters, 1977), 51, 55, 57. The *Morgen Journal* published a Newark edition, distinguished by a special column, in which this discussion appeared, called "Newark News." The *Hadoar* article appeared on January 21, 1927.

90. Ibid., 78.

91. "Hebrew Youth Academy Formed," *Jewish News*, September 7, 1962, 1.

92. Sholom Ber Gordon, interview, November 20, 1997.

93. "Young Israel," Young Israel Records, Box 6, Folder 29. Special Collections and University Archives, Synagogue Collection, Rutgers University Libraries; Moshe Herson, interview, November 20, 1997.

94. Nathan Winter, interview, November 11, 1997.

95. "Hebrew High is Organized Under Auspices of 'Y,'" *Jewish Chronicle*, November 21, 1930, 1.

96. Bernard Bloom, interview, August 5, 1996. Some of the more Orthodox students attended post-high school yeshivas. For example, Rabbi Dr. Morris Charner, long-time principal of the Dov Revel Yeshiva in Queens, New York, and rabbi of the school's congregation, and currently a professor at Yeshiva University, attended Mesivta Tifereth Jerusalem (MTJ) on New York City's Lower East Side, after graduating from South Side High School. He studied there during the week while attending City College of New York in the evening. Others from Newark who also studied at MTJ included, Rabbi Theodore Charner, former Principal at Hebrew Academy of Nassau County, the Nulman brothers, Macy, Louis, and Seymour, all cantors, Rabbi David Singer, and Samuel Adelman, who was raised in Irvington.

97. Gershon Gelbart, Sylvan H. Kohn, and David Rudavsky, *The Essex Story: A History of the Jewish Community in Essex County, New Jersey*, booklet (Newark, N.J.: Jewish Education Association of Essex County, 1955), 54–55.

98. "In Upbuilding of Palestine we are Deadly in Earnest," Weizmann Declares at Dinner Here—Raise $50,000 for Fund," *Jewish Chronicle*, June 15, 1923, 1.

99. "Eleven Hundred Essex Children Join in Israel Anniversary Fete," *Jewish News*, May 13, 1949, 1.

100. Leo Yanoff, interview, November 24, 1996.

7

The Past, the Present, and the Future

Looking at Newark, we see a community that was once a major center of Jewish life and which had a great impact on both its residents and beyond. In its gradual demise, Newark followed the pattern of many major cities, Atlanta, St. Louis, Detroit, and Cleveland, all of which watched helplessly as their inner cores became urban wastelands and those who made up the tax base fled to the suburbs.

The migration out of Newark was essentially a westward one and Jews settled in many different communities. The challenge posed by that decision was how to create a sense of community that could unify the villages and towns that dotted the suburban landscape. How could these places develop a shared sense of values and goals? The concept of MetroWest was a way to do it organizationally, but it did not translate into reality. After all, the average resident of Essex or Morris Counties did not list it anywhere as a real address nor did they think of it as an all-encompassing community. When people from, say, Newton, meet people from Verona, they do not say to each other: "Oh, you're from MetroWest."

Nevertheless, there is a common identity. It manifests itself when the talk shifts to things Jewish—religious education, the community center, an interfaith couples program, a joint synagogue effort. It is here that the linkages, both geographical and psychosocial, emerge from the tapestry that makes up human existence. We begin our discussion, therefore, with a look at the type of community that MetroWest is today.

MetroWest Today

It is important to keep in mind at the onset that MetroWest's Jewish population consists of three groups—those who came from Newark and its environs, those who came from elsewhere, be it other parts of the state or New York, or beyond; and those who grew up in the suburbs of the area. The amalgam that resulted is what MetroWest is all about. MetroWest consists of Essex, Morris, Sussex, Warren, and portions of Somerset, Hudson, and Union Counties. In terms of being a community, MetroWest cannot be viewed as if it were a country with borders. There is spillover into neighboring counties, with people from Passaic or Union counties taking advantage of its offerings. There is fluidity at the Federation level too. MetroWest services Springfield, even though that community is located in Union County. Bernardsville, Basking Ridge, and Bedminster (known to insiders as "the three Bs"), are part of Union County's Federation even though these communities are in Somerset County. It should be kept in mind that Jews who left Newark did not move only to the MetroWest area; they went to Hudson, Bergen, and other nearby counties.

Close to half of MetroWest's Jews live in traditional households, namely two parents with one or more children, a higher percentage than is the case nationally. The intermarriage rate is somewhat lower than the national average, but not by much. In 1985–86, the Federation sponsored a survey of the community and the information that follows is based on that. Whatever changes have occurred since then have been in the direction of greater growth and expansion into the outlying areas beyond Essex and Morris Counties. At the time, Essex County had 78,300 residents and Morris/Sussex had 42,600 for a total Jewish population of 120,900. A more recent development has been the arrival of Russian-Jewish emigres, many of whom have found permanent homes in Springfield and Bloomfield and in the newer community of Budd Lake.

Of those interviewed then, 34 percent said they were Reform, 38 percent Conservative, and 6 percent Orthodox. Another 13 percent responded that they were "just Jewish" and the remainder identified themselves as "other." About half have joined synagogues, with those between the ages of thirty-five and fifty-four exceeding 60 percent and those between twenty-five and thirty-four at 37 percent. This pattern reflects the fact that as people become older their interest in religion increases and that those raising children often join temples for reasons such as bar or bat mitzvahs, play groups, and other child-centered activities. Joining and being active are two different things. Only 13 percent attend services on a regular basis. About one in five buys kosher meat but the majority still observe Passover and the High Holidays in some form. Finally, about three-quarters of those children between the ages of six and thirteen receive some type of Jewish education, a percentage which drops to about one-quarter for those ages fourteen and seventeen.[1]

The majority of the Jewish population still resides in Essex County and most of the funds for the community are raised there, but more and more young couples are moving into Morris, Sussex, and Warren, and these counties grew the most in the 1980s and 1990s. Indeed, the majority of those who have joined the Jewish Community Center in Whippany come from places like Morristown, Randolph, Parsippany, and Montville. It would be impossible to examine all of these communities but a look at some of them can tell us much about life in the area in general.

A good starting point is Cedar Grove, which is technically in Essex County, but quite close to Morris County. A predominantly Italian Catholic community, Cedar Grove has about 100 Jewish families. Its Reform temple, with over 500 families, draws from the wider area. The problems in such communities are different than in the more densely populated towns. When a community has to limit itself to one denominational affiliation there will always be those who are not happy. The majority in Cedar Grove opted for Reform, in part because those who were Conservative could attend services in nearby Verona's, Congregation Beth Ahm. But, as a concession to such sentiments, the temple decided to have two days of services for Rosh Hashanah, instead of only one.[2]

The largest of the communities in the western areas is Morristown. Henry and Rosena Sire settled there before the Civil War. And when the war came, Henry did a thriving business selling horses to the Union cavalry. His son, Benjamin, was, in 1860, probably the first Jewish child born in Morristown.[3] The major growth in the community began in the 1890s when immigrants from Russia and Poland settled there, some of whom first stopped off in nearby Plainfield before moving on. By the 1930s, Morristown had grown to the point where it had a beautiful temple with a large Moorish dome, that came to be a landmark in the area.[4] Another landmark of a different sort was Epstein's Department Store, founded in 1918. Although it faces stiff competition from larger stores in nearby malls, it still does about $15,000,000 worth of business a year.

During the 1930s, the synagogue, called the Morristown Jewish Center, was the hub for virtually all community activities, ranging from Scout programs, sports, and social events, to symphony orchestras and, of course, religious services. For a time, during the 1950s, the Jewish Center was home to Orthodox, Conservative, and Reform congregations. Today, it is aligned with the Conservative movement. But to see what life was like there, growing up, we need to listen to the words of Elaine Menkes:

> In 1945, the theater in Morristown, which was built by Walter Reade, was the showcase of the area. People used to get in their cars and come here from the surrounding area. The lines stretched around the block and down the hill. There was also an ice cream parlor in Morristown where people hung out, called Thode's, a *real* old-fashioned ice cream parlor. It was a real town, a wonderful town. If you were rich and you had a house in New York or in Newport, you might also have a big house in Morristown for the summer.[5]

Seymour Epstein remembers Morristown as a friendly and warm place, embodying all of the values traditionally associated with smaller towns. His circle of friends was Jewish, but not because of anti-Semitism, which, he says, was almost nonexistent. As he put it: "We weren't a large enough community to have been much of a threat."[6] It would seem he is correct. In 1978, seven men marched through the town dressed in brown shirts, black boots, and sporting swastikas. They were quickly denounced by the community, with the mayor declaring the goals of the group, the National Socialist White People's Party, "un-American." In fact, only one of the marchers, one Thomas Vetere, Jr., was a Morristown resident.[7] Efforts by organizations of this sort are, however, endemic to small towns throughout America, where the Jewish community is small.

One of the most important groups in Morristown's Jewish community is the Rabbinical College of America, an advanced yeshiva under the auspices of the Lubavitcher movement. Its board is an eclectic group of people, including both Orthodox and non-Orthodox Jews and numbering among them quite a few prominent and successful Holocaust survivors. The school came to Morris Township in 1971 from Newark and has been there ever since. It prepares male students to be rabbis, teachers, and communal leaders. Its New Directions program offers college students an opportunity to study with rabbinic students.

The students celebrate the holidays and build community-oriented programs around them,. For example, each year they distribute 50,000 Purim gift packages to Jews throughout the State of New Jersey. They have also had an annual fair on their campus for the past nineteen years that draws thousands of visitors to see the performances and exhibits on display there.[8] Their reception in the community has been mostly positive though some are put off by what they see as the Lubavitchers' aggressiveness in propagating their views. One Morristown resident put it somewhat bluntly:

> In the beginning Lubavitch in Morristown was very aggressive. You know—Are you Jewish?; Did you light candles? And the townspeople resented it because what right did they have to come up to people right in the middle of the street? That was in the 1970s. But now they're very effective. They were able to put up this menorah, this forty-foot-high monstrosity. You know, it's in every town. They have to allow it because they have a creche in every corner.

But others disagree, expressing admiration for the commitment of the Lubavitchers. Rabbi Moshe Herson, the college's dean, was mentioned favorably by a number of people for the study programs he has instituted in the community at large. In an address at the school's dinner on November 16, 1997, Governor Christine Todd Whitman said:

> And next month we will light the candle on the menorah that graces the state house. . . . It's a tradition that the Lubavitch movement can take great pride in bringing to our State. . . . And building a strong educational system—as exemplified by the Rabbinical College—cements all that we work so hard for, every day. . . . Only twenty-five years ago, the College was located in a one family house in Newark. Today, it's an eighty-two-acre campus with students from more than twenty-four states and a dozen countries.

Does Lubavitch really have a role to play in the suburbs? Are they not somewhat out of place amid the rolling hills of western New Jersey? To be sure, the hasidic lifestyle is more commonly associated with urban settings or in what are essentially self-contained small towns like Monroe or New Square, New York. Nevertheless, they do seem to fill a need for what many feel is a spiritual void or emptiness in their lives. That is why they are able to attract people who are assimilated and who do not belong to a temple. They function outside the orbit of the Federation and the people they reach are often unreachable by any other way.

Throughout the history of America, there have been Jewish farming communities. Some examples are Danielson, Connecticut; Vineland, New Jersey; and Petaluma, California. In Morris County, there was Pine Brook, located near Montville Township and founded more than 100 years ago by Jewish farmers, some of whom had received grants from the Baron De Hirsch Fund. The Baron believed that Russian Jews would best improve themselves if they engaged in productive agricultural work and he gave money to anyone who immigrated to the U.S. or Palestine and wanted to purchase farmland.

In 1896, Josef Konner became the first president of Chevra Agudas Achim Anshe Pine Brook. Konner was a farmer who, like Jennie Grossinger of Catskills fame, transformed his farmhouse into a boarding house. Called the Sunrise Hotel, it became a popular resort for Orthodox honeymooners from New York as well as for vacationers from Newark. By all accounts, the Jews got along quite well with the Dutch farmers who predominated in the area. The following story, related by Helen Stiel, is a good example of how the two groups viewed each other:

> The Dutch Reform Church was having a big dinner. But there was a problem with their kitchen, and they couldn't use it. The church women asked Mrs. Konner if they could use her kitchen [in the Sunrise Hotel]. She said "sure," but she told them her kitchen was kosher. Fortunately there was [a] *shohet* in the community; he quickly slaughtered chickens for the first Dutch Reform kosher dinner!"[9]

In the 1960s, the community in the Montville area experienced significant growth as developers built housing on land they had bought from the farmers. Dr. Asher Krief, an Orthodox rabbi, became the head of the congregation, which joined the Conservative Movement in an attempt to attract more young families who were buying homes in Montville Township. In 1995, the Pine Brook synagogue merged with nearby Lake Hiawatha Jewish Center and became a 500–member congregation. Another important nearby congregation is Agudath Israel in Caldwell, whose rabbi, Alan Silverstein, is a recent past president of the Rabbinical Assembly.[10]

Another community with a substantial Jewish population is White Meadow Lake, in Rockaway Township. It began in the 1940s as a summer community that attracted Jews who were not welcome in the nearby communities of Mountain Lakes and Lake Arrowhead. Sanford Hollander remembers those days well:

We played Mountain Lakes, which discriminated residentially against Jews, in football. We were up by twenty points and we won. It was about 1946. We showered together after the game and I was the only circumcised guy there. Well, this one kid makes a remark and my black teammate was so uptight that he took a swing at him and said: "I'm a Yom Kippur too." Then the fight ended; there was just a lot of slipping and sliding."[11]

White Meadow Lake Temple was established in 1953. Two years later, Rabbi Jacob Weitman became its spiritual leader and stayed on for thirty-four years. Despite its being a relatively new community, it is home today to more than 2,300 families. The religious groups in the community include both the Conservative congregation, which counts women in its *minyan*, as well as a Lubavitch-led Orthodox synagogue and Jewish center. Jews from the surrounding communities of Boonton, Mount Olive, and Mountain Lakes also participate in White Meadow Lake's activities.[12]

One of the oldest Jewish communities in Morris County is Mount Freedom, famed as a summer resort, whose hotels and bungalows were popular with Newark residents looking for a vacation spot in the area. When the first Jew, Yetta Levine, arrived there, before the turn of the century, Mount Freedom was a farming community. The early settlers of Mount Freedom worshipped in private homes but eventually, a synagogue, the Hebrew Congregation of Mount Freedom, was established. In its heyday, Mount Freedom could vie successfully with Lakewood, Atlantic City, Bradley Beach, and other resort areas. There is still a Jewish presence there, but for most young people moving out to the area, the center of activity has shifted to the nearby towns of Randolph and Parsippany. In large part, Mount Freedom continues to be viable because it is surrounded by Randolph, which has proven attractive to young Jewish families.

Dover was not so fortunate, however. Its organized Jewish life began around 1902 and its permanent temple building was completed in 1935. It was a close-knit community and, at its height, had about 250 families. As the years went by, the community "aged out," so to speak and the older generation moved away. At the same time, there was no influx of younger people. The older homes did not appeal to them and there was no community like Randolph immediately adjacent to Dover. Seeing no future for their community, those who were left decided to merge with a Boonton temple, Beth Shalom, which had a young population but no room for its members. The two synagogues joined forces and built a new temple in Parsippany called Adath Shalom, whose rabbi is Eliseo Rozenwasser.

Further west, but still in Morris County, is Temple Shalom in Succasunna, led by Rabbi Joel Soffin. It has a membership of more than 500 families and draws widely from neighboring communities. Soffin and his congregants are very active in social action projects. Several years ago, he led a group of Jews on a trip sponsored by Habitat for Humanity and helped to build homes for poor people in Kentucky. To the southeast, between Morristown and Bernardsville, lies the small and well-to-do community of New Vernon (residentially zoned for three acres), which is also beginning to attract Jewish families.

Out in Sussex County, the little town of Newton began attracting Jews around the turn of the century, with the first family arriving there in 1890. By the 1920s, there was a small Jewish congregation called Reuben Shimon, in memory of the father of Nathan and Solomon Fogelson. In 1951, the name was changed to the Jewish Center of Sussex County and a permanent rabbi hired. Today, the temple has a membership of about 100 families.[13]

Anti-Semitism showed its ugly face in Newton too. It was a center of Klan activity and, in 1923, a Jewish boy was tarred and feathered there. In 1941, a Nazi Bund camp was set up six miles away, in Lake Iliff. Fritz Kuhn, head of the German-American Bund, was a regular visitor there, and the organization held rallies and marched in Newton, until the sheriff, Denton Quick, arrested the members and ran them out of town.[14] While today there is no overt prejudice against Jews, many of whom interact socially with the gentile residents, there is still, at times, a lack of sensitivity, that seems based more on ignorance than anything else. Rabbi Michal Shekel, a past president of the Newton Area Clergy Association, wanted to start a local Habitat for Humanity group in his temple. Before he could do so, however, the local Habitat organization incorporated itself "according to the gospel of Jesus." According to Shekel, his Christian colleagues expressed bewilderment that doing so made Shekel feel he couldn't join the organization.[15]

Being Jewish in the area is harder than it would be in larger communities, but it is not simply a matter of size. Clearly, when people make decisions on where to move, they investigate and those who moved to Sussex County a decade or two ago were probably not that concerned with leading an actively Jewish life, thus weakening the potential for Jewish growth there. As one resident put it: "Years and years ago, a lot of Jewish families moved to Sussex County to get away from being Jews, and a lot of the families were [already] intermarried." This appears to have changed in recent years and there is now an upsurge of interest in being Jewish, although getting a minyan together, or finding kosher food locally, is still not that easy.[16]

Myron and Paulette Katz both grew up in families that identified strongly as Jews. Myron's parents were Newarkers. For a time, he lived on Hunterdon Street and Myron still has warm memories of the delicious chicken his grandmother cooked for the Sabbath. Paulette was born in the Bronx and moved to Newark as a youngster where she attended Weequahic High School. Five years ago, they purchased a waterfront home on Lake Hopatcong. They still belong to Temple B'nai Jeshurun in Short Hills, but their involvement in things Jewish seems more centered around the area in which they now reside. Myron's description of the form that this has taken highlights the realities of living in Sussex County as opposed to, say, an established Jewish town like Livingston or West Orange. Basically, one has to take one's Judaism from wherever one can find it. More often than not this involves a willingness to travel to other communities, even outside the county, if necessary, and to accept an eclectic mix of Jewish culture from different denominations:

> We partake in Sparta as a group. We meet in a church and in peoples' homes. It's a younger group. We went to a Friday night service in a church. Then there's the temple in Newton, where we have Hebrew classes. We're also active with the Lubavitcher in White Meadow Lake. I got a flier from them that said, "All Jews are welcome." Now where did you ever see that from an Orthodox organization? We go to the Picattiny Arsenal, where the Lubavitcher have a "Lunch and Learn" every Friday.[17]

The Sparta group that Katz refers to is actually B'nai Emet, a Conservative congregation that is housed in a space rented from a church and is run by Lucy and David Katzen.

There are places even further removed from Jewish life, such as Washington Township in neighboring Warren County, home to the area's only synagogue, the Jewish Center of Northwest New Jersey. At last count, there were eighty-five member families, many of whom come from towns surrounding the township such as Clinton, Hackettstown, Long Valley, and Belvidere. In 1996, the synagogue, now headed by Rabbi Ellen Jay Lewis, celebrated its fiftieth anniversary. It is a warm and welcoming community that does not even charge admission for High Holiday services. It meets every other week, but, as opposed to many larger synagogues, more than half the members attend regularly. In fact, the Sunday school is staffed entirely by congregation members. As Rabbi Lewis explained, "They [the congregants] are fully aware that the survival of the congregation is on them. They don't expect that the rabbi's job is to keep them alive."[18]

Can an ethnic group forge a common identity when it is spread out over six counties? It is actually a statewide problem, caused, in part, by the fact that New Jersey lacks a large city center like Los Angeles or Denver or Miami. The noted political scientist, Daniel Elazar, has referred to the proliferation of small towns, mixed in with a few medium-sized cities, as "the Balkanization of New Jersey." Those who planned the services and programs for the area's Jews were acutely aware of the challenge that faced them in doing so. Howard Charish, MetroWest's former executive vice president, was involved with this issue from the onset and his description demonstrates both the creativity and hard work that went into finding a solution:

> We have succeeded in that the man in the street confirms that this is MetroWest. We tried several names. One I liked a lot was *"Emes"*[Truth]—Essex, Morris and Sussex. We closed the door and Clarence Reisen [a past Federation president] said, "We're not leaving till we have a name." The "M" and the "W" were both capitalized, so that no part was greater than the other. The other important part is there's no space between "Metro" and "West." Now there's a supervisory board of kashruth of MetroWest. Other people will tell you they're from MetroWest. That's something we could never have anticipated. No one who is not Jewish who lives here uses it. Framingham, Massachusetts decided on the same name at one point because their transportation system was called by that name. And we fought that decision. It was ridiculous. But they didn't listen to us. However, the Boston Federation solved that problem. They merged with them.[19]

It is true, as Charish notes, that gentiles have no idea that there is such a place. The story is told of the Israelis who landed at Kennedy Airport and instructed the cab driver to take them to "MetroWest" and insisted that it was a well-known city in New Jersey, even as he searched fruitlessly for it on his map of the state. The contrast with Newark, which did succeed in developing its own identity, is brought into sharp relief by the recent campaign to support the exhibit of Jewish Newark in the Library, called "Born at the Beth [Israel Hospital]."

The idea for the program had grown out of a discussion in 1993, initiated by Ruth Fien, then president of the Jewish Historical Society, and Charles Cummings and Bill Dane of the Newark Library. Working with staff members of Beth Israel, these three individuals did the major work on the project in order to insure its success. The effort generated 3,000 responses, an incredible demonstration of the local drawing power of nostalgia. With 8,000 to 10,000 people attending, the show was probably the most successful ever put on by the library. Those who work in community organization realize the importance for the future of building such connections today and that is why they work so hard at it.

Much of the success in doing so depends on the people who live in each town or village. Their Jewishness, their professions, and their group values, often determine the outcome. Richard Slutzky, a past administrator at MetroWest, compared two communities in this regard:

> People in Montclair, for instance, are Big-Applecentric. They don't think of themselves as living in New Jersey, but as New Yorkers living in a suburb. They see New York as their cultural hub. This is not as true in Millburn or in Short Hills. Many of the people in Montclair are writers, editors, and work in New York. In Maplewood [on the other hand] there is a history of involvement in the Jewish community. In Montclair you don't have that tradition.[20]

Fortunately, the demographics favor MetroWest. The Federation survey found that only one person in seven from the area commutes to work in New York. Those who do, tend to be younger and it is reasonable to expect that as their families grow larger, so will their communal responsibilities with respect to school, PTA, temple, and the like and they will seek the convenience of employment closer to home. At that point the ball shifts to MetroWest's court in terms of designing programs and activities that will attract them.

Jewish Programs and Activities

As in real estate, location is crucial for effective programming. In today's society, with so many people fulfilling multiple professional, familial, and communal roles, having a place that is easily accessible is critical. Moreover, to borrow a phrase from the business world, "A good deal is one where no one is really happy." Both of these factors were admirably combined in MetroWest's Whippany site:

> As Martin Fox said, the Jewish community's center should be in a place that is surrounded 360 degrees by Jews. When we were in East Orange, you had about

355 degrees behind us. Clarence Reisen tells the story of how the Jews of South Orange and Short Hills think it's too far west and the Jews of Morris County think it's too far east. That's why it's the perfect location. What we succeeded in doing was distributing the inconvenience of travel equally. The infrastructure of Interstate 287 and Route 10 was also good.[21]

The staff of the Federation tends to be young, smart, and innovative, but it is also balanced by middle-aged and older people in key positions whose experience meshes well with the excitement and enthusiasm of the young. This combination of talents, knowledge, and energy has resulted in an incredible array of programs that takes in just about every interest and age group in the community. In both its daily functioning and in its long-range goals, MetroWest's philosophy reflects the changing trends in the larger Jewish community as well.

Forty or fifty years ago Federations addressed themselves primarily to the basic needs of the poor, the immigrants, and the socially dislocated. Today, Jews are well off and not so much in need of basic services. The needs of physical and economic survival have been replaced by psychological and spiritual needs. This is a change of watershed proportions and both personnel and programming must respond to it. Developing activities for divorcees, singles, and interfaith couples is easier than increasing and deepening the spiritual content of programs. This is because Federation professionals have the necessary backgrounds in social work and psychology to deal with these issues. What they lack, more often, is the religio-spiritual training that is required to help Jews fill what they see as a spiritual emptiness in their lives. Fortunately, MetroWest's executive vice president, Max Kleinman, has a strong background in both areas and this puts him on the cutting edge of the priorities of the nineties.

This trend, incidentally, is also quite noticeable in the synagogues, where all of the denominations are responding to the desire of many congregants to have a more traditional approach on both the ritual and spiritual levels. This in itself can be traced to a variety of factors of which the most important one is a feeling of isolation and loss of individuality stemming from the nature of our increasingly computerized and technologically advanced world.

Added to this is the general approach in MetroWest of working together to overcome differences of opinion and even conflict. Contrast this with the national picture which has been marked by vociferous disagreements between the Orthodox community and the rest of

American Jewry and between those who support and those who oppose the current Israeli government. Emblematic of this is the breakup of the Synagogue Council of America. The Council was the only organization that represented Orthodox, Reform, and Conservative Jewry. It was also its representative to other non-Jewish religious organizations. What led to its demise was not money or individual personalities, but rather a lack of will to work together, with the outcome being that the extremists on both sides emerged victorious.

In MetroWest, the opposite is the case. Through the Joint Chaplaincy Project, rabbis of all denominations work together, thus making it one of the only communities where a rabbi from the Lubavitch community cooperates in certain areas with a female Reform rabbi. There is a culture of civility that predominates. A recent article in the *New Jersey Jewish News* focused on new outreach programs to the unaffiliated that have been started by seven new MetroWest area rabbis, ranging from Reconstructionist to Orthodox. Not one of them made a single, even slightly negative comment about other Jewish denominations. The leitmotif behind these efforts was succinctly summed up by one of the participants, Isaac Jeret, spiritual leader of the Conservative Congregation Beth Ahm of West Essex in Verona: "We are all Jews. None of us has the whole truth. The closest all of us can get to that truth is when all of us get together." Daniel Alter, assistant rabbi at the Orthodox temple in West Orange, Ahawas Achim B'nai Jacob and David, echoes Jeret's view. In his opinion, unity is "what's needed more than anything today."[22] Although they may be new, the stances adopted by these leaders fit in perfectly with the long-standing emphasis on consensus that has always characterized MetroWest.

One of the hardest groups to reach is teenagers. With this in mind, Jack Boeko, former executive vice president of the Jewish Community Center of MetroWest, developed what is generally thought of as one of the best and largest teen programs anywhere. Currently, there are more than 3,000 youths in the program, many of whom would undoubtedly be spending their time in malls and movie theaters were it not for the JCC program. An additional 4,000 to 5,000 youngsters participate on an occasional basis. Among the projects are charity programs, lobbying efforts in Washington, and fund raising. A large part of the enthusiasm is generated by the latitude given the teenagers to "run their own show." It is a model that has been copied in many communities throughout the U.S.[23]

Addressing the needs of singles is another daunting challenge. MetroWest's Singles Professionals Division, a committee of its Young Leadership Division, enables singles to become both socially and Jewishly involved at the same time. The group has singles *Shabbats, Oneg Shabbats* (Sabbath parties), fund-raisers, and social action projects, and it is seen as a place where successful people can meet each other. As Michael Lowenthal, a Morristown resident, put it:

> I enjoy the YLD [Young Leadership Division] crowd because these people are committed to something. I date only Jewish women, but being Jewish isn't enough. We go to these other singles events and what do we have? A bunch of Jewish singles.[24]

Another community offering is "MetroMatch," a new confidential service where responses to ads are phoned into a voice "mailbox" 900–number at the newspaper instead of someone's home. From there they can be easily retrieved and screened. This idea, which exists in various forms elsewhere provides a practical solution for singles who often have a hectic lifestyle.

Another program, which originated in Detroit in the 1980s, is JEFF—Jewish Experiences for Families. Run by MetroWest's Jewish Education Association (JEA) and adapted to the unique needs of the community, it creates opportunities for family to celebrate Jewish life together. Working with area synagogues, JEFF sponsors events such as "The Great *Afikomen* Adventure," or the "*Shana Tova* Choo Choo" in which entire families do things that are both spiritually and culturally enriching and also fun. The "Choo Choo" event drew over 1,100 participants from sixty-six communities who discovered, among other things, eighteen ways to celebrate the New Year. The net effect is to strengthen the Jewish family as a cohesive unit.[25] Another successful event was "*Simcha* 95." Families entered eight rooms at the Aidekman Campus and experienced Chanukah in eight different cities from Minsk, to Istanbul, to Beit She'an, Israel. More than 100 children and parents laid down ceramic tiles which formed a menorah. The previous year the focus had been on *shtetl* culture.[26]

There was a sense by professional leaders that the standard bar and bat mitzvah programs weren't doing enough in terms of fostering a true sense of Jewish identity. With that in mind a congregation for youth was established at the Aidekman Campus, and a curriculum centered around thirteen core mitzvoth was prepared. The afternoon schools got involved in the programs and brought their students out. The J. Crew Company was persuaded to donate heavy-duty T-shirts with a logo design that said *"Mitzvoth* in MetroWest." Each religious school did a textile panel on the mitzvoth that they had focused on.[27]

A key program has been Pathways, a program for the children of interfaith couples that allows them to learn about Judaism in a nonjudgmental setting. Various events for both children and parents are sponsored and, in 1995, Brian Barkauskas became the first Pathways participant to have a bar mitzvah, which he celebrated in a synagogue. Brian, who had considered himself a Catholic, admitted to having certain stereotypes about Jews. "Pathways took some of the mystery [of being Jewish] away from me," he said. In 1995, the program could count fifty participants, of whom about half had joined a synagogue.[28] Related to Pathways is the Outreach to Intermarried Families Program which runs workshops and discussion groups for those interested in understanding the issues and challenges facing intermarried couples and their families.

Of equal significance is MetroWest's Connections program, under the aegis of the JEA, catering to unaffiliated families. Organized by Judy Beck of MetroWest, it offers a broad range of activities, ranging from play groups, theater trips, book discussion groups, and hayrides, to *Oneg Shabbats*, holiday programs and parenting workshops. The stated goal of Connections is to "get Jews to affiliate to overcome the alienation, unfamiliarity, or whatever stands in the way of involvement."[29] For Peter Waldman, a physician who recalls having been "a major discipline problem in Hebrew school," Connections is a non-threatening way of linking up again with the Jewish community:

> We joined Connections when it started, four years ago. We were definitely not ready to join a synagogue. We felt this would be a way to connect with something Jewish without being too religious, because neither one of us are very religious, especially me.[30]

Paradoxically, the program appeals to people searching for the opposite too. Lisa Monday became interested in Connections because she was looking for more religious content. She participated in a *"sukkah raising"* and found it "educational without being painful." *Sukkah* raisings, incidentally, were held in three communities in 1997—Essex Fells, Randolph, and Long Valley. Contrasting Connections with what she saw as an empty exposure to ritual in Hebrew school devoid of any real meaning, she said:

I think a lot of people now hesitate to say the "J" word, it's almost as if they don't want to deal with the ritualistic end of Judaism. They don't want to know about "why." For me, the ritualistic stuff is what binds me to my mother and grandmother and great-grandmother, and all the generations before her. That's the essence of who my people are.[31]

Connections, which seems to have something for everyone, has been studied as a model by 300 other Jewish communities.

Education is one of the main building blocks for Jewish continuity and MetroWest is very active in this area. The MetroWest region has five day schools—the Joseph Kushner Hebrew Academy, the Solomon Schechter Day School of Essex and Union, the Nathan Bohrer-Abraham Kaufman Hebrew Academy of Morris County, which is affiliated with the Solomon Schechter system, and the Cheder Lubavitch Elementary and Junior High School, and Hebrew Academy of Morris County. The Kushner Academy has also started a new Orthodox yeshiva high school called, Yeshivat Bet Yosef-Kushner Yeshiva High School. In its first year of operation, 1997, the school attracted over 120 applicants for its 1998 entering class. Part-time studies at the high school level are available through the Central Hebrew High School and the Morris County High School for Jewish Studies, which is directed by Rabbi Stuart Warner. All of the latter are run by the JEA. Congregation B'nai Israel in Millburn also has a school called, the Community Hebrew High School. Finally, there is an independent, nonprofit institution, the Suburban Jewish School, in Summit, which focuses on a secular-humanistic approach to Jewish studies.

At the adult level there is the JEA/Midrasha, directed by Dr. Wallace Greene, a well-known educator, which runs many courses that are held in dozens of locations throughout MetroWest's communities. In 1997, there were courses on a cornucopia of topics, including Hebrew, Holocaust, environment, character development, black-Jewish relations, film, the Haggadah, Jewish-Christian relations, Jewish identity, legends, Ethiopian Jews, ethics, and a great deal more. The Community Lectures Series featured a symposium on German reparations, a talk about Jewish gold in Swiss banks, and an evening commemorating Kristallnacht. Through its Open Door Program for New Americans, the JEA also sponsored education courses geared to those newly arrived in this country. There is also a resource center called MERKAZ, whose staff helps people find and use educational materials and which conducts workshops relating to Jewish education. The JEA also administers the Waldor Memorial Library which has an extensive collection of books on Judaica.

The JEA has its own Web Site page, and, under the leadership of its Executive Director, Chaim Lauer, it continues to develop new programs, upgrade existing ones, and to insure, via its licensing programs for educators, that the highest standards are maintained in all of the Jewish education efforts sponsored in the MetroWest area. The JEA is involved in far more endeavors than can be listed here. Some of them, like the program on the Jews of India, are one-time events; others, like The March of the Living, involve participation with international organizations on an annual basis; and still others, like the Fatherhood Project and the Jewish Baby Loss and Miscarriage Support Group, run by Judy Beck, are ongoing.[32] The Chaverim (Friends) and Yaldeinu (Our Children) projects minister to the needs of developmentally disabled children. All together, the programs of the JEA are among the most extensive of any such organization in the country. Another important organization that works with adults who have learning disabilities is JESPY House, in South Orange.

Jews have survived as a group, in large measure, because they have transmitted their history in written form to those who have followed after them. At the local level in MetroWest, this task has been, and continues to be achieved, by the Jewish Historical Society of MetroWest, one of the finest such groups in the country. The importance of such an organization was first envisioned by Herman Pekarsky and, over the years, several efforts were made to start one, but, for one reason or another, they did not get very far. Finally, in 1989, Ruth and Jerome Fien asked Saul Schwarz, who had long been the chief proponent for a historical society, to join them in creating one. With the strong support of Howard Charish, a proposal was submitted in February of 1990 to the Federation's Board of Trustee's, which approved the concept to fund the Society. Subsequent to that, the Jewish Community Foundation provided the seed money for the organization.

The Society's primary goal is to ensure that the community's history will not be forgotten. In this way it enhances Jewish awareness, identity, and pride. The organization serves as the official repository of the historical records and memorabilia of the MetroWest Jewish community. It possesses a state-of-the-art archival vault and enters the data it receives in its computer base. In addition to this primary function, the Society presents seminars and lectures, joint conferences with like-minded groups, exhibits, tours of historic sites, and responds to research inquiries. It also publishes material related to the community's history and plays an important role in advising others who undertake efforts to write about MetroWest and its past.

MetroWest also sponsors a variety of summer camps for children. There are day camps in Flanders and Whippany, which also has a separate All-Star Clinic where campers can improve their skills in basketball, soccer, and in-line hockey. Round Lake Camp, near Lake Como, Pennsylvania is for children with learning disabilities. And, of course, MetroWest youngsters attend the New Jersey Y Camps.

Different, but related programs are those that are not necessarily Jewish but are devoted to assisting members of the Jewish community. While they may not have specific Jewish content, recipients develop a stronger relationship with Judaism simply because they know that the organization providing the services is Jewish. A good case in point is the METRO Ride for Seniors Program. In a community as geographically dispersed as MetroWest, this fulfills a basic need. Another project is CareLink, developed by Julian F. Reichman, former president of the Jewish Family Service Association (JFS) and Rueben Romirowsky, executive director of JFS, which brings people together for community-wide, one-time efforts, such as its program to provide kosher meals for Passover.[33]

Then there is the decision by the Daughters of Israel Geriatric Center, a MetroWest beneficiary, to become the first nursing home in New Jersey to officially affiliate with a hospice care program. Housing is another crucial issue. The organized Jewish community has built housing for senior citizens and the disabled and has sometimes had to overcome local opposition to its efforts from residents, both Jewish and non-Jewish. A good example of Jewish community efforts in the face of objections by local residents, was the construction of apartments for the elderly poor in West and South Orange. The struggle to do so was led by Alan Sagner, with Arthur Schechner chairing the board that ultimately ran the apartments in West Orange, known as Federation Plaza.[34]

The Jewish Vocational Service, headed by Ron Coun, has a long history in the community. It continues to provide job and career counseling. It also runs the Jewish Employment Network program together with area synagogues. Similarly, the Jewish Family Service counsels and offers support to families in trouble. Its Rachel Coalition extends help, on a twenty-four-hour basis, to victims of domestic violence. It provides adoption services and otherwise helps children with various problems, especially school learning. Finally, it acts as the local agency for the resettlement and acculturation of new arrivals to the U.S., working together with Federation's Committee on Absorption and Resettlement of Emigres (CARE). In this capacity it has helped hundreds of Russian immigrants attain American citizenship. Other agencies that service emigres and which are also represented on the CARE Committee are JVS, JEA, and the Jewish Community Center.

In another area, MetroWest, through its Jewish Family Service, has formed a gay and lesbian task force to help them connect with the Jewish community. One of its main challenges has been to sensitize the community to the special problems still faced by gays and lesbians. The task force was created in response to requests from gays and lesbians "seeking authentication by the general Jewish community." As one gay man observed: "I don't necessarily feel a need to be catered to . . . I just don't want to be excluded."[35] There is also a Community AIDS Task Force, coordinated by the Community Relations Committee, that seeks to increase awareness about AIDS and to provide various types of support for those who have the disease.

A different type of issue, but one which also faces the problem of insensitivity by some, is the twin problems of alcoholism and drug addiction. Slowly but surely, Jews have come to recognize that these ills can strike in their own communities, but there is still a considerable amount of denial. Locally, a branch of a national organization, Jewish Alcoholics, Chemically Dependent Persons and Significant Others, has been meeting for some years in Temple Beth Shalom in Livingston to provide support for those affected.[36] The Hebrew Free Loan Society, reestablished in 1995 and administered by Martin Kesselhaut, Jerome Fien, and Arthur Schechner, has maintained a long-standing tradition in the MetroWest community of providing interest-free loans to the needy, with very few questions asked. The loans are available only to MetroWest residents and only those who have been refused by a bank are eligible.[37]

When Newark Beth Israel Hospital was sold to the St. Barnabas Health System, the proceeds totaled over $125 million. The money was used by Lester Z. Lieberman to create a new foundation, the Newark Beth Israel Healthcare Foundation. Besides funding medical research, the Foundation also assists the MetroWest Jewish Community on a variety of projects, one example of which is its support for MetroWest's current demographic study of the Jewish community. The foundation's assets have now grown to $150 million, making it one of the largest charitable foundations in the state. Another linkage between the past and the present is the establishment of the Jewish Heritage Concert Foundation/Jewish Community Foundation, headed by Edward Zinberg. It funds an annual concert at the New Jersey Performing Arts Center as well as cultural events in the Jewish community. Yet another initiative is the building of 180 residential units for senior citizens right on the Aidekman Campus, called Lester Senior Citizen Housing.

Senator Frank Lautenberg has been and continues to be actively involved in the MetroWest Jewish community. He has given generously over the years to the community and the Lautenberg Jewish Community Center is perhaps the most visible symbol of his largesse. But he has also helped New Jersey's Jews in other ways. He is a strong supporter of Israel and of issues deemed important by the Jewish community. One very important outcome of that support has been the Lautenberg Amendment, which has allowed refugees, including Russian Jews, to come to the United States.

Beyond the borders of New Jersey, MetroWest has been active in Israel and it has a coordinating office on its campus devoted to this area called, the Israel Program Center. Like other Jewish communities in the U.S. it has, through UJA's Project Renewal Program, twinned with Israeli cities, in this case Ra'anana and Ramat Eliyahu, which is part of the city of Rishon leTzion. In Ra'anana, there is MetroWest High School, the only such school in Israel named after an American community. The city was the site for an innovative absorption program involving Russian immigrants and has become a model for others. According to some, the Federation raised millions of dollars by taking prospective donors to the program site in Ra'anana. The State of New Jersey opened a trade office in Ra'nana in 1995 and there is also a MetroWest-Israel Think Tank which meets to thrash out the challenges of Israel-Diaspora relationships. The Ramat Eliyahu location has been host to various exchange programs between young people and youths from there also visit MetroWest as part of various programs.[38]

More recently, MetroWest has, together with the Bergen County/North Hudson Federation become involved with Ofakim, a city in

Israel's Negev region. The project, under the guidance of the Federation's Partnership 2000, helps communities that are considered economic priorities by the Israeli government.[39] The community was also actively supportive of Operations Moses and Exodus, which together raised close to $20 million. In another area, but still related to Israel, MetroWest has begun an association with AMCHA, a support center for Holocaust survivors and their children, that is based in Israel. The goal is to have programs in this country that address the needs of survivors living here. In the fund-raising area, both the Jewish National Fund in Springfield and State of Israel Bonds, operating out of Livingston, maintain an active presence here. Finally, the New Jersey-Israel Chamber of Commerce has generated millions of dollars as a result of trade between New Jersey and Israeli-based companies.

Other organizations besides MetroWest itself also have programs of Jewish interest. They are too numerous to fully identify, but some examples should give the reader an idea of the range of activities available in the community. The American Jewish Committee concentrates on building coalitions with other groups and on educational programs. In 1992, it initiated the Stamp Out Hate Coalition, now consisting of twenty-three different ethnic and religious groups. Like the American Jewish Congress, it is especially interested in fostering black-Jewish dialogue and in fact-finding and educational missions to other countries. The Congress promotes and conducts special tours of Israel and advocates on behalf of the liberties of all Americans. This last function is also the central goal of the Anti-Defamation League, which focuses its energies on combating anti-Semitism. All three organizations have offices in Essex County.

There are several Jewish War Veterans' branches, with posts in Morristown, Dover, and other communities. The women's organizations of AMIT, Hadassah, Brandeis University National Women's Committee, Jewish Women International, the National Council of Jewish Women, ORT, and the Women's League for Conservative Judaism, are all represented in the area. The NCJW also sponsors a Holocaust education program aimed at junior high school students. Finally, many of the synagogues have all sorts of social action and cultural programs open to both their members and to the general community.[40]

Cooperation exists with non-Jewish groups too. For example, MetroWest's Community Relations Committee, directed by David Mallach, works with Hispanics to improve relations between them and the Jewish community. An organization called the Latino Jewish Collaboration tries to find common ground in the area of building economic self-sufficiency among Latinos by utilizing the business know-how of the Jewish community. In February of 1997, in conjunction with the Jewish Reconstructionist Foundation, the Community Relations Committee sent twenty-seven volunteers to Millen, Georgia to help rebuild a Baptist church that had been burned to the ground, a fire in which arson was suspected.[41] Philip Lax, a prominent Jewish businessman in the area and a top leader of B'nai Brith International, played a major role in the long campaign to have the U.N. rescind its infamous "Zionism is racism," resolution. Lax also worked with former Chrysler chairman, Lee Iacocca, the comedian, Bob Hope, and others on restoring Ellis Island. In 1982, he was appointed to the Ellis Island-Statue of Liberty Commission by then President Ronald Reagan and was instrumental in raising millions of dollars to refurbish both sites.[42]

What about the future? here is a community whose seeds have sprouted everywhere. Many of those who make their homes in these little towns are not enamored of bureaucracy even as they admit that Jewry must have a central address. MetroWest must address their needs and to do so it must find out what they are. Looking at the programs they are doing and the participation in them it seems they have succeeded to a degree, although there are thousands of Jews in these counties who have not been reached and, in fact, may not want to be reached. In a sense, Jews are victims of their own success. The prospects and dilemmas are thoughtfully and insightfully addressed by Stanley Strauss, past president of MetroWest:

> We sold America an idea and America sold it back to us: Jews are the same as other Americans; we all worship the same God. So if we're all the same, why be Jewish?
>
> But there is no "all the same." There is no Judeo-Christian ethic. That's a *bubbe meyseh* [old wife's tale]. Now the problem we face is to develop a constructive, creative Jewish life in America.
>
> As a Federation, we want to take care of Jews in need, wherever they may be. Second, we want to help make this a better world for all people everywhere. . . . We've been around for 4,000 years. If we want to survive we will.[43]

Strauss's analysis is, in large measure, correct. Jews are different but they need to be given a positive reason to identify. And at the rate things are going, one can question whether most Jews will relate to Israel ten years from now, not to mention a hundred. The problem is that the great amorphous middle that used to make up American Jewry, the one to which Conservative Judaism most appealed, is fast disappearing. In its place a bifurcated community is growing, one in which Jews are either highly identified or not at all. For the former group, MetroWest has plenty. It is to the latter group that the Federation must address itself, however. This is because without their involvement, the Jewish community is in grave danger of becoming so small that it will not have the critical mass it needs to sustain itself in a viable manner.

Murray Laulicht, MetroWest's current president, is given high marks by people in the community for articulating a vision for the future that addresses the broader needs of its population. As he put it:

> I am a strong proponent of pluralism because the beauty of the concept is that it means people care about being Jewish. The priority today is one of satisfying communal and spiritual needs. We are working hard towards these goals by stressing the importance of Jewish identity and education. Our scholar in residence, Eugene Korn, has developed a leadership learning program where people study together to find out what thirty-five centuries of learning can teach us about Jewish leadership. We are also working hard to improve the Federation's relationships with the synagogues through a variety of programs. On another, but equally important, level, the budget process has been restructured to allow for more cutting-edge programs.[44]

There are real teeth to these statements. MetroWest recently facilitated a $250,000 grant from the Harrison Trust to help rebuild a Reform congregation in Israel that had been firebombed, emphasizing that it did so out of a desire to reinstate the congregation's programs on diversity and tolerance. It is also the first Federation in the U.S. to fund religious pluralism projects in Israel, allocating an additional $250,000 for that purpose. Finally, it has publicly endorsed the efforts of the Ne'eman Committee to find a solution to the conversion problem in Israel.

Laulicht worries about the fragmentation within the larger Jewish community, both here and in Israel. He feels that the divisions have a negative impact on the ability to provide for basic needs such as financial help for Ethiopian Jews. American Jews are withholding contributions out of anger at the Israeli government, he says. He does not feel it has become a major problem but is concerned that it could. In the meantime, however, he is satisfied that the MetroWest leadership has continued to work together despite different viewpoints and sees that as a central feature of the community's essential character.

Newark Today and Tomorrow

Newark today certainly has its share of problems. Its mayor, Sharpe James, has been in the news on several occasions, accused of repeatedly violating state election laws by turning a personal charity he started, into a fund-raising arm of his political machine. Around the same time, former U.S. Attorney Michael Chertoff signed on with the new Essex County Executive, Republican James W. Treffinger, to investigate corruption in that office, previously occupied by a Democrat convicted of extortion.[45] Then again, Mayor Ellenstein's record in terms of political rectitude was not unblemished either.

The schools, however, are another matter. From a system that had achieved a national reputation for excellence, educational standards had plummeted to record low levels by the 1990s. A 1995 article in the *New York Times* revealed that even after a decade of monitoring by the State Board of Education, only 25 percent of high school seniors in one recent year had passed the exams required for graduation, a far cry from the glory days of Weequahic and South Side High. The final embarrassment came in July of 1995, when state officials ousted Newark's school officials and took direct control of the school system.[46]

In 1997, yet another article in the *Times*, this time on the front page, commemorated the thirtieth anniversary of the riots by publishing a historical retrospective on the city and how it has fared since then. In it, the black nationalist poet, Amiri Baraka, told a reporter what things were like today as he sat on the porch of his home in a well-maintained, west-central Newark neighborhood: "If you go two blocks in either direction you are in some of the worst slums imaginable."[47] The portrayal of today's Newark by Philip Roth, in his novel, *Zuckerman Unbound*, supports that description and also conveys the bitterness felt by Jews at what happened to the city they once loved and inhabited:

> Newark is bankruptcy! Newark is ashes! Newark is rubble and filth! Own a car in Newark and then you'll find out what Newark's all about! Then you can write *ten* books about Newark! They'll slit your throat for your radial tires![48]

And then, on a visit to the old neighborhood, Roth writes of an old apartment building there:

> Had there been a canopy? If so, it was gone. The building's front door was also gone, torn from its hinges, and, to either side of the missing door, the large windows

looking into the foyer had lost their glass and were boarded over. There was exposed wiring where once there had been two lamps to light your way in, and the entryway itself was unswept and littered with trash. The building had become a slum.[49]

That these descriptions are accurate is not in question, but there is also another, more hopeful side to Newark. Not far from poverty-stricken streets stands the new $180 million New Jersey Performing Arts Center. Nearby can be found Society Hill, a new development of reasonably priced townhouses and more are constantly being built. Most of those moving in are black, middle-class professionals. And nearby are spanking-new office tower buildings, with shiny glass windows and brick or marble facings that would look at home in any modern American city. A new shopping mall is being built nearby and several major urban universities have joined in the building boomlet now taking place there. The city is planning a $22 million stadium for its minor league baseball team, the newly reestablished Newark Bears,

Even amidst the squalor and misery that typifies many of Newark's residential neighborhoods, there are sections of the city that are still vibrant. More than 30,000 Portuguese make their home in the old Ironbound, or Down Neck, section of Newark. A nighttime walk down the neighborhood's main commercial thoroughfare, Ferry Street, inspires no fear or sense of danger. "In Portugal, everybody knows about Newark," says Tony Oliveira, who has lived in the area since 1967 and who, like many of his countrymen, works in construction.[50] And the Ironbound is not the only part of town that has maintained itself. North Newark and Roseville, in particular, is still a viable community, as is Vailsburg.

Newark is probably too important a city to die. As the administrative and judicial nerve center for New Jersey and as a center for federal government, it is the unofficial capital of the state. There are five universities in the city, not to mention the largest museum and library in the state, and the New Jersey Historical Society. There is the Seton Hall Law School and Rutgers University gave the city a vote of confidence when it broke ground for a new $55 million law school in downtown Newark. It is, from a transportation standpoint, an extremely well-situated city. The New Jersey Turnpike and the Garden State Parkway are very close by, as are Interstates 78 and 280. There is a train to New York City, which is only minutes away, and, of course, Newark Airport.

The main problem facing Newark is how to shake off the image of a crime-ridden, decaying city. People are willing to work there during the day, but at night they scurry home to the safety of their suburban enclaves. The Performing Arts Center, with its concert hall, theater, and food concessions, represents the greatest hope (and investment) in Newark's future. Its promoters offer easy access to the Center by day or night and ticket sales are brisk; the question is, will the Center succeed in attracting enough shops to transform the entire area into a place where people will feel comfortable spending time? And will the nearby areas become sufficiently gentrified to attract the dry cleaning stores, upscale food markets, beauty parlors, and other businesses that make an urban space liveable and even desirable? Or will it go the way of the bankrupt Newark Renaissance Mall, whose developer, Harry Grant, pledged a 121–story building to Newark more than ten years ago before fading from public view? Will it be a magnet for an urban center or will it become simply an arts center? No one knows the answers to these questions, but a start has certainly been made and only time will tell whether the financial gamble taken by both government and business will pay off.[51]

While an impressive achievement, the Performing Arts Center makes it easy to forget that Newark's core problems still remain unsolved. These are a very weak fiscal base, crime, a poor educational system, and political corruption. True, the recent gentrification in parts of the city has brought in middle-class residents, but they are overwhelmingly black. For the city's fortunes to truly change it will be necessary for it to become home to a multiethnic population, something like New York City's Upper West Side. The resulting transformation into a safe and worthwhile environment will require great imagination by a leadership committed to a democratic and inclusive vision of Newark.

If Newark revives as a city, it will bear little resemblance to the Newark that its Jewish population identified with. After all, B'nai Jeshurun is now the Hopewell Baptist Church, Anshei Russia is today home to the Abyssinian Baptist Church, and the Y that was a second home for thousands of Jews, became, for a time, the abode of the Citadel of Hope Miracle Temple, now defunct. Perhaps Jewish yuppies will come, perhaps not, but the Newark of old will not even have the cachet of nostalgia for them unless their parents happened to have grown up there. Still, there are small pockets of hope that, while they may not portend anything for the future, illustrate the connections that can sometimes be made.

Take, for instance, Ahavath Shalom, one of Newark's last remaining synagogues. Benjamin Arons tells of how a small group of young people, led by Robert Steinbaum, a Montclair resident who publishes the *New Jersey Law Journal*, saved it from extinction. Something resonated in their hearts, something made them feel that it was important to to do this. But this is the exception, not the norm. Realistically speaking, Jews are not likely to return in any numbers to Newark. Nor is the cluster of senior citizens, living in the Ivy Hill section, likely to serve as the prototype for any revival.[52]

For Jews who grew up there, Newark is really a state of mind. It is part of their life experience. When they think of it what usually comes to mind is a life rich with meaning and a sense of something that cannot, by definition, be replicated. The interviews conducted here and the written material of Jews from Newark make it clear that it was a place they truly enjoyed living in. Not surprisingly, given human nature, the glow of nostalgia frequently causes them to minimize the disappointments and hardships they endured as a part of growing up in those years.

Charles Cummings, an astute historian who is an expert on Newark, once observed that just as a river goes through stages in its life cycle, so does a city. He made those comments with reference to his belief that Newark might be on the verge of a rebirth. For those who have grown old, however, there is no second chance. They can think only of what once was. And it is fair to say that when they think of the Newark that was, they think also of who they themselves once were. They pine for their youth and may even confuse that yearning with a yearning for the city itself. For this reason it is fitting to close our story with a paean of praise from the pen of Benjamin Kluger, a lifelong Newark resident, written in 1977, that embodies both the Newark that once was and the young man he once was:

> All you who scoff at Newark, all you who see only a scarred relic, picture it as it looked to a youth emerging at sunset into Washington Park . . . fringed by gracious Town Houses, tall buildings, the Newark Museum; turning out into the panoramas of Broad Street, past Trinity Cathedral, the central meadow of Military Park, threading among throngs of people shopping at Hahne's, Kresge's, Goerke's, Bamberger's, socializing at its hotels, the Robert Treat, the Douglas, the Essex House, the Riviera . . .
>
> O youth, youth, lost, golden irretrievable youth! If youth's fire and dreams can irradiate the meanest streets, think how memory lights up a vanished Newark in which all of us were young, with the beloved dead restored to life, the stilled voices rising into the music of living words."[53]

Notes

1. Much of this information is drawn from Ron Meier, Ruth Greenfield, and Gary A. Tobin, *A Population Study of the Jewish Community of MetroWest, New Jersey*, report, Fall, 1988.
2. Alison Imbriaco, "Jewish Population at Home in Cedar Grove," *MetroWest Jewish News*, September 7, 1995, 10.
3. Carl B. Scherzer, "Early Jewish History in Morristown," unpublished paper, 3. This is the most thorough account of Morristown's Jewish community. Available at Jewish Historical Society of MetroWest Archives.
4. Betty Chafetz, "Once Upon a Time, in 1893," *Morris Sussex Jewish News*, September, 1975, 19.
5. Elaine Menkes, interview, August 5, 1996.
6. Seymour Epstein, interview, August 12, 1996.
7. "Morristown to Nazis: Keep Out," *Morris Sussex Jewish News*, August, 1978, 5.
8. Tony Borelli, "Festival of Fun Drawing Thousands," *Daily Record, Morris County, N.J.*, September 2, 1996, A3.
9. Alison Imbriaco, "Pine Brook Jewish Center Celebrates 100 Years in Morris County," *MetroWest Jewish News*, January 11, 1996, 8.
10. Alia Ramer, "Jewish Farmers of Pine Brook Planted Seeds for Montville Community," *MetroWest Jewish News*, August 8, 1996, 13.
11. Sanford Hollander, interview, November 24, 1996.
12. Alison Imbriaco, "White Meadow Lake Described as Close-Knit Community," *MetroWest Jewish News*, February 23, 1995, 9.
13. *Yearbook of the Jewish Community Center of Sussex County, 1996–97*, 1. The discussion of these smaller communities benefited considerably from interviews with the following individuals: Laurie Levy, Eleanor Cohen, and Sheila Moller. All were conducted on December 1, 1997.
14. Sanford Hollander, interview, November 24, 1996.
15. Miriam Jacobs, "Newton—Small Town With a Haimisch Touch," *MetroWest Jewish News*, May 18, 1995, 16.
16. Ibid., 17.
17. Myron and Paulette Katz, interview, August 5, 1996.
18. Alia C. Ramer, "Synagogue Central to Washington Township's Community," *MetroWest Jewish News*, June 26, 1997, 12.
19. Howard Charish, interview, November 30, 1994.
20. Richard Slutzky, interview, January 21, 1997.
21. Howard Charish, interview, November 30, 1994.
22. Lori Silberman Brauner, "New Area Rabbis Look Toward Outreach, Unity," *New Jersey Jewish News*, October 23, 1997, 8.
23. Cheryl L. Kornfeld, "As he Retires, Boeko Cited as Visionary," *New Jersey Jewish News*, June 19, 1997, 14.
24. Sherri Umansky, "Single in Metrowest: Is There Life Beyond Marriage?," *METRO Source: A Guide to Jewish Living*, 1993–94, 17.
25. Arnold Dashefsky and Alyson Bacon, "*'WHO'S JEFF? WHAT'S JEFF?' A Formative Evaluation of the 'Jewish Experiences for Families' (JEFF) Program in MetroWest, New Jersey*," report. Storrs, Conn.: Center for Judaic Studies and Contemporary Jewish Life, 1997.
26. Shari Berke, "Simcha '95 a Mix of Jewish Cultures," *MetroWest Jewish News*, December 14, 1995, 18.

27. Howard Charish, interview, November 30, 1994.
28. Alison Imbriaco, "Bar-Mitzvah Boy a First for Pathways," *MetroWest Jewish News*, September 14, 1995, 11.
29. Ellen Forman Muraskin, "Creating Community," *METRO Source: A Guide to Jewish Living, 1993–94*, 25.
30. Ibid.
31. Ibid.
32. Alison Imbriaco, "Fatherhood Project Casts Spotlight on Business of Daddyhood," *MetroWest Jewish News*, December 14, 1995, 14; Cheryl L. Kornfeld, "Parents Experiencing Baby Loss Seek Jewish Response in JEA Group," *MetroWest Jewish News*, November 30, 1995, 8–9.
33. Miriam W. Jacobs, "S. Orange Septuagenarian Force Behind Community Volunteer Effort," *MetroWest Jewish News*, February 20, 1997, 11.
34. Correspondence from Arthur Schechner, chairman, Housing Committee to Jerome Fien, January 9, 1996.
35. Donna Ezor, "JFS Helping Gays Find Place in Community," *MetroWest Jewish News*, July 20, 1995, 9.
36. Carrie Mattison, "JACS Combating Jewish Denial About Alcohol, Drug Addiction," *MetroWest Jewish News*, June 26, 1997, 14.
37. The opposite seems to be the case in many other communities. See, Jon G. Auerbach, "Jewish Loan Societies Rethink the Tradition of Helping All Comers," *Wall Street Journal*, September 11, 1997, 1.
38. David Twersky, "Think Tankers Seek to Expand Ra'anana Ties," *MetroWest Jewish News*, March 2, 1995, 8; Shari Berke, "Past and Present Come Together in MW's Sister City," *MetroWest Jewish News*, June 29, 1995, 5.
39. Alia C. Ramer, "UJF of MetroWest Has New Israeli Partnerships in the Negev," *MetroWest Jewish News*, January 2, 1997, 8.
40. For a full listing of the most recent Jewish programs, see *METROSOURCE: A Guide to Jewish Living*, 1997–98.
41. Andrew Frank, "Helping to Rebuild the World—Shingle by Shingle," *MetroWest Jewish News*, March 6, 1997, 16.
42. Frederick W. Byrd, "Jerseyan Will Help 'Polish' Symbols of America," *Newark Star Ledger*, May 23, 1982, 39.
43. Stanley Strauss, interview, November 25, 1996.
44. Murray Laulicht, interview, January 9, 1998.
45. Clifford J. Levy, "Newark Mayor Accused of Violations," *New York Times*, February 22, 1995, B5; Clifford J. Levy, "From Convictions to Code of Ethics," *New York Times*, May 26, 1995, B1.
46. Neil MacFarquhar, "Newark School Takeover Is Seen as Early as July," *New York Times*, May 20, 1995, A28; Neil MacFarquhar, "Taking Control, State Ousts Newark's School Officials," *New York Times*, July 13, 1995, B6.
47. Ronald Smothers, "In Riots' Shadow, a City Stumbles On," *New York Times*, July 14, 1997, A1.
48. Philip Roth, *Zuckerman Unbound* (New York, Farrar, Straus & Giroux, 1981), 156.
49. Ibid., 222.
50. Clifford J. Levy, "From the Old Country: A Portuguese Village in Newark," *New York Times*, October 6, 1995, C1.
51. Ralph Blumenthal, "Newark Hopes for Revival Far Beyond Arts Center," *New York Times*, October 15, 1997, 1A; Judith Miller, "A Self-Made Man Takes on Newark," *New York Times*, October 14, 1997, B1; David W. Dunlap, "In Newark,

Prologue to an Arts Center," *New York Times*, January 1, 1995; Ronald Smothers, "As Newark Bounces Back, So Does Mayor," *New York Times,* January 31, 1998, B1; Abby Goodnough, "Newark is Practical (and Symbolic) Answer to Logistical Puzzle," *New York Times,* January 21, 1998, B5.

52. Felice Maranz, "Life Among the Ruins," *The Jerusalem Report*, March 25, 1993, 32–33. For an account of Ahavas Shalom from its beginnings to the present, see Rachel Nierenberg, "Congregation Ahavas Shalom: A Continued Presence. An Important Legacy," paper written for course in *American Jewish Social History, 5531x* at Jewish Theological Seminary, November 1997.

53. Benjamin Kluger, "Growing Up in Newark," *Jewish News*, September 8, 1977, B4.

Bibliography

"A. Hollander & Son—Industrial Leader." *Jewish Chronicle*, Fifteenth Anniversary Issue, April 24, 1936, 25.

"A. Hollander and Son's Splendid Record Marks Triumph of Great Perseverance." *Jewish Chronicle*, Twentieth Anniversary Issue, June 20, 1941, 83.

"Abraham J. Dimond, at 76, Philanthropist, Civic Leader." *Jewish News*, August 10, 1956, 3.

"Activities of Organizations, Clubs and Fraternal Groups." *Newark Jewish Times*, October 13, 1944, 3.

"Activities of Organizations, Clubs and Fraternal Groups." *Newark Jewish Times*, October 27, 1944, 3.

"Aged Home Nears Four Decades of Service." *Jewish Chronicle*, Twentieth Anniversary Issue, June 20, 1941, 92.

"Agencies Here Serving in Aftermath of Disturbance." *Jewish News*, August 4, 1967, 1.

"All Ages at Newark Y Find 'Boy Meets Girl' Important." *Jewish News,* April 8, 1960, 55.

Alt, Herschel and Herbert H. Aptekar, *A Study of Jewish Case Work Agencies in Essex County*, mimeograph. Newark New Jersey. The Jewish Community Council, 1946 (Newark: Jewish Community Council, 1946).

"Amelia Earhart will Lecture at Y.M.H.A. Monday." *Jewish Chronicle*, January 3, 1936, 1.

"America Only For Young, Rabbi Brodsky to Warn." *Newark Evening News*. March 20, 1920, 5.

"Americanization Classes to Be Open to All Newcomers." *Jewish News*, July 1, 1949, 1.

"Anthropologist in Address to JFSA." *Jewish News,* November 28, 1947, 2.

"Anti-Tuberculosis Society in Session at Progress Club." *Jewish Chronicle*, April 6, 1923, 1.

"Anti-Tuberculosis Workers Organize." *Jewish Chronicle*, July 21, 1922, 1.

"Appointees of New City Hall Regime." *Newark Star-Eagle*, May 18, 1937, 3.

Arny, Mary Travis, *Red Lion Rampant: An Informal History of Essex County, New Jersey*, 1965.

"Around Town With the Women." *Jewish Chronicle*, column, April 18, 1941, 7.

"Artist in Silver was Color-Blind." *Newark Star Ledger*, March 9, 1958, 32.

"Ask Newarkers Adopt Orphans." *Jewish Chronicle*, November 4, 1921, 1.

"Asserts Hebrew Academy has 'Achieved Outstanding Record.'" *Jewish News*, December 17, 1954, 5.

"Aver Andrews's Attitude on Wine Won't Affect Jewish Rites Here." *Newark Evening News*, October 30, 1925, 17.

Baglivo, Angelo, "Pledge Given to 'Clean House,'" *Newark Evening News*, July 1, 1954, 1.

Bahrenberg, Bruce, "Ghetto Audience Thrills to Symphony Orchestra." *Newark News*, July 15, 1968, 1.

Louis Bamberger, 1855–1944, Honorary President of the Newark Museum: A Tribute to his Memory by his Fellow Trustees, pamphlet (New York: Newark Museum, 1944).

"Bamberger to Mark 80th Birthday." *Jewish Chronicle*, May 10, 1935, 1.

"Bans on Immigration of Jews are Denounced." *Newark Evening News*, November 24, 1924, 18.

"Bards of 'Beat' Generation 'Immature' to Rutgers Poet." *Jewish News*, October 2, 1959, 57.

Baron, Steve, "Thanks, Dad—For Memories of a House in Millburn." *MetroWest Jewish News*, June 12, 1997, 5.

Batshaw, Manuel G. "'The Y Drew us Like a Magnet.'" *Jewish News*, June 14, 1957, 55.

Baum, Charlotte, Paula Hyman, and Sonya Michel, *The Jewish Woman in America* (New York: The Dial Press, 1974).

Becker, Ronald L., "History of the Jewish Community in Newark, New Jersey," in William J. Dane and Charles F. Cummings (eds.), *Lasting Impressions: Greater Newark's Jewish Legacy,* booklet (Newark, N.J.: The Newark Public Library, 1995).

Behrman, I.E. "Beth Israel, 10 Years of Achievement." *Jewish News*, June 14, 1957, 36.

Berke, Shari, "Dover—Once a Thriving Jewish Area." *Metrowest Jewish News*, October 5, 1995, 10.

———, "Past and present Come Together in MW's Sister City." *MetroWest Jewish News*, June 29, 1995, 5.

———, "Simcha '95 a Mix of Jewish Cultures." *MetroWest Jewish News*, December 14, 1995, 18.

"Beth Israel Treated Many Victims of Riot." *Jewish News*, July 21, 1967, 1.

"Bible Bill Faces Wastebasket End from Opposition." *Jewish Chronicle*, March 17, 1922, 1.

"Bilder Distinguished Member of Bar and Banking." *Jewish Chronicle*, Twentieth Anniversary Issue, June 20, 1941, 87.

"'Bits of Hits' Draws Applause." *Jewish Chronicle*, January 22, 1926, 1.

"'Bits of Hits' is Offering to be Given by the 'Y's'." *Jewish Chronicle*, December 9, 1921, 1.

Blaustein, Esther, *When Momma was the Landlord* (New York: Harper & Row, 1972).

"B'nai Abraham Institute of Jewish Learning Opens New Program on October 21st." *Jewish Chronicle*, September 26, 1941, 6.

"B'nai Abraham Schedules Its Institute of Jewish Learning." *Jewish News*, November 17, 1961, 14.

B'nai Jeshurun Congregational Guide, 1985–86, pamphlet.

Blum, Eugene W. "New AJCongress President Stresses Jewish Survival." *Jewish News*, May 23, 1958, 7.

———, "Hungarians Adjust Easily." *Jewish News*, September 26, 1958, 28.

Blumenfeld, Ralph, "Newark Hopes for Revival Far Beyond Arts Center." *New York Times*, October 15, 1997, 1A.

"B'nai Abraham Institute Program is Extraordinary, Studded with Big Names." *Jewish Chronicle*, September 26, 1941, 4.

B'nai Abraham Temple: Yesterday, Today, Tomorrow, Newark, N.J., 1969.

B'nai Abraham Temple: Our 125th Anniversary, Livingston, N.J., 1978.

"B'nai Brith Ball Was Gala Affair." *Jewish Chronicle*, November 11, 1921, 1.

"B'nai Jeshurun Boasts Colorful History." *Jewish Chronicle*, Twentieth Anniversary Issue, June 20, 1941, 66.

"B'nai Jeshurun Oldest Congregation in State." *Jewish Chronicle*, Fifteenth Anniversary Issue, April 24, 1936, 69.

B'nai Jeshurun Temple, The Ninetieth Anniversary Celebration of Congregation B'nai Jeshurun, Newark, N.J., 1938.

B'nai Jeshurun Temple, Manuscript Minute Book of Congregation Meetings, Newark, N.J., August 20, 1848–April 30,1871. American Jewish Archives, Manuscript Collection.

"Board to Appeal Raubinger Decision on Fired Teachers." *Jewish News*, June 1, 1956, 6.

Bodner, Allen, *When Boxing was a Jewish Sport* (New York: Praeger Publishers, 1997).

"Bomber is Gift of Oheb Shalom." *Newark Jewish Times*, September 17, 1943, 1.

Bonomo, Jo, "Life Begins At—?" *Jewish News*, Supplement, March 27, 1959, 26.

"Book of Newarker is Blamed." *Newark Evening News*, September 8, 1941, 4.

Borelli, Tony, "Festival of Fun Drawing Thousands." *Daily Record, Morris County, N.J.*, September 2, 1996, A3.

Boroff, David, "The Jewish Student in the Midwest." *Jewish News*, August 7, 1959, 10.

Braun, Robert, "School Peace Talks May Resume Today." *Newark Star-Ledger*, February 3, 1971, 1.

Brauner, Lori Silberman, "New Area Rabbis Look Toward Outreach." *New Jersey Jewish News*, October 23, 1997, 8.

"Breaking Ground." *Workmen's Circle Lyceum*, Newark, N.J., June 1926 (n.p.).

"Brilliant Future is Predicted for New Institution." *Jewish Chronicle*, October 8, 1926, 1.

Broad National Bancorporation, 1985 Annual Report, booklet.

Brody, Ed. "Mother's Shtetl." unpublished manuscript, 9 pp.

———, "The Neighborhood Merchants Associations in Newark, N.J.: A Personal Recollection." August 30, 1995, 1–30, unpublished manuscript.

Brody, Jeffrey H. "Bergen Street Ten Years After the Newark Riot." M.A. thesis (Columbia University School of Journalism, 1977).

Brody, Seymour, *Jewish Heroes in America* (New York: Shapolsky Publishers, 1991).

Brotherhood of Painters, Decorators, and Paperhangers of America, Local 777, 50th Anniversary Issue 1902–52, 1952.

Brown, Herman, "Cooperative Roles Discussed by Rabbis, Social Workers." *Jewish News*, November 3, 1961, 15.

"Building a Better World: 50th Anniversary." American Jewish Committee, pamphlet.

"Building Fund Leaders Stress Debt to Old, Legacy to Young." *Jewish News*, January 7, 1955, 1.

Burack, Molly, *Memoirs: Reminiscences from the Older Adult Creative Writing Class* (Whippany, N.J.: Jewish Historical Society of MetroWest, 1991).

Byrd, Frederick W. "Jerseyan Will Help 'Polish' Symbols of America." *Newark Star-Ledger*, May 23, 1982, 39.

"Camp Activities Largest in History." *Jewish Chronicle*, July 3, 1931, 8.

"Capacity Enrollment Expected for Weequahic's Home Camp." *Jewish News*, May 12, 1954, 23.

"Celebrating 85 Years of Caring." leaflet, Daughters of Israel Geriatric Center: 1991–1992 Annual Report, 1–5.

Chafetz, Betty, "Once Upon a Time, in 1893." *Morris Sussex Jewish News*, September, 1975, 19.

"Chagy is One of America's Great Cantors." *Jewish Chronicle*, August 25, 1922, 1.

"Cheerless Rooms for Churlish People." *Jewish Chronicle*, editorial, March 17, 1922, 4.

"Cheers Acclaim Lindeman Boom for City Office." *Jewish Chronicle*, November 18, 1921, 1.

"Children's Home Sponsors Large Program." *Jewish Chronicle*, Fifteenth Anniversary Issue, April 24, 1936, 83.

"Clark Will Speak Here." *Jewish News*, January 7, 1966, 2.

Cohn, Julius H. "Are we a Community With a 50% Soul?" *Jewish News*, September 11, 1953, 1.

"Community Chest is Discussed by Jewish Charities." *Jewish Chronicle*, October 13, 1922, 1.

"Community Mourns Chronicle Publisher's Passing." *Jewish Chronicle*, January 8, 1943, 1.

"Community Mourns Death of Brodsky." *Jewish Chronicle*, March 5, 1937, 1.

"Conference Sends Girls to Camp." *Jewish Chronicle*, August 8, 1930, 1.

"Congregation Ahavas Sholom Engages Rabbi Solomon as its Spiritual Leader." *Jewish Chronicle*, September 5, 1941, 1.

Congregation B'nai Abraham, pamphlet, 1935.

Congregation B'nai Israel History (Millburn), pamphlet, undated.

"Congregation B'nai Jeshurun, Past and Present." *Jewish Chronicle*, Section III, December 7, 1923, 1.

Congregation Shomrei Emunah 50th Anniversary Journal, (Montclair).

Congregational History of Congregation Ahavas Achim & B'nai Jacob David (West Orange), pamphlet.

"Conspicuous City Posts Awarded to Thirteen Jews." *Newark Jewish Times*, May 25, 1945, 2.

Constitution of Congregtion Anshei Sfard-Linas Hazedek. In Rutgers University Synagogue Collection.

"Court Asked to Allow Jewish Mother her Child Alienated From her Faith by Strangers." *Jewish Chronicle*, December 16, 1921, 1.

Crisp, Allan, "Belleville's Historical Past: The Hendricks Family: Copper For America 1755–1939." Belleville Historical Society, Belleville Public Library, undated.

———, "Founding of New Jersey: History of Belleville." Belleville Historical Society, Belleville Public Library, undated.

"Criticizes Plebiscite by Jews." *Newark Evening News*, May 8, 1938, 11.

Darling, Anne M. "Helping the Foreign Born." *Jewish News*, June 14, 1957, 38.

Dashefsky, Arnold and Alyson Bacon, "'WHO'S JEFF? WHAT'S JEFF?': A Formative Evaluation of the 'Jewish Experiences for Families'" (JEFF) Program in MetroWest, New Jersey, report. Storrs, CT.: Center for Judaic Studies and Contemporary Jewish Life, 1997.

Dawidoff, Nicholas, *The Catcher was a Spy: The Mysterious Life of Moe Berg* (New York: Pantheon, 1994).

"Deborah Gets Shipment of Books from Newark's Library for Circulation." *Newark Jewish Times*, August 24, 1945, 1.

"Deborah Shows Remarkable Progress." *Jewish Chronicle*, Fifteenth Anniversary Issue, April 24, 1936, 74.

"Dedicate Ahavath Zion's Beautiful New Synagogue Sunday, Before Notables." *Jewish Chronicle*, May 25, 1922, 1.

"Dedication and Service." *Jewish News*, editorial, May 11, 1962, 10.

"Defends Suburban Synagogue." *Jewish News*, October 13, 1961, 19.

DePalma, Anthony, "Exodus." *New Jersey Monthly*, September 1985, 64–96.

"Development of Medical Profession." *Jewish Chronicle*, Fifteenth Anniversary Issue, April 24, 1936, 49.

"Dick Savitt Wins Place on American Davis Cup Squad." *Jewish News*, August 11, 1950, 1.

Die Colonistim (play about Zionism, by Celia Lowenstein).

"Dimes and Quarters Built Beth Israel Hospital." *Jewish Chronicle*, April 18, 1924, 2.

Doniger, Simon, "The Jewish Child Guidance Bureau." *Jewish News*, January 10, 1947, 8.

"Dr. A. E. Parsonnet Adds Lustre to Able Career With Many Avocations." *Jewish Chronicle*, Fifteenth Anniversary Issue, April 24, 1936, 81.

"Dr. Abraham Heschel to Give Next Lecture at Oheb Shalom." *Jewish News*, February 29, 1952, 24.

"Dr. Alex S. Wiesel New Leader of B'nai Zion Congregation." *Jewish Chronicle*, August 29, 1941, 1.

"Dr. Cecil Roth Will Lecture at Oheb Shalom Wednesday." *Jewish News*, March 21, 1952, 32.

"Dr. Danzis has Proven Builder of Jewish Role in Progress of Medicine." *Jewish Chronicle*, Fifteenth Anniversary Issue, April 24, 1936, 81.

"Dr. Danzis, Rabbi Prinz, Head Russian War Aid Holiday Campaign Here." *Newark Jewish Times*, December 8, 1944, 1.

"Dr. Hoffman Seeks to Keep Traditional Judaism Alive." *Jewish Chronicle,* March 20, 1931, 1.

"Dr. Shuster and Dr. Jung Will Speak at Oheb Shalom Forum." *Jewish Chronicle*, March 6, 1942, 1.

Drachman, Bernard, *The Unfailing Light* (New York: Rabbinical Council of America, 1948), 169–185.

Dressler, Joachim, "Express Gratitude." *Jewish News*, letter to the editor, April 25, 1947, 4.

Drogin, Linda M. "Growing Up in Newark: Friendships Cemented in Fraternal Clubs Survive with Memories of a Simpler Time." *Jewish News*, September 20, 1984, 11.

Dumas, Lynne S. *Elephants in My Backyard: Alex Aidekman's Own Story of Founding the Pathmark Supermarket Powerhouse* (New York: Vantage Press, 1988).

Dunlap, David W. "In Newark, Prologue to an Arts Center." *New York Times*, January 1, 1995.

Dunn, Bruce, "The Jews of Newark, 1955–1970." Paper written for Newark history class at New Jersey Institute of Technology.

"Eastern Capitalists and Western Farmers Clash in Newark Film." *Jewish Chronicle,* January 22, 1926, 7.

"Eleven Hundred Essex Children Join in Israel Anniversary Fete." *Jewish News*, May 13, 1949, 1.

"Elizabeth Blume," in *The Municipalities of Essex County, New Jersey, 1666–1924,* Vol. III (New York: Lewis Historical Publishing Company, 1925), 106–107.

Engelmayer, Shammai, "The Birth of a Newspaper," in *MetroWest Jewish News 50th Anniversary Edition,* January 1997, 12–28.

Eppston, Harold A. "Memories of the Talmud Torah." *Jewish Chronicle*, January 23, 1942, 5.

Epstein, Phyllis J. "First Councilwoman Follows Pattern of Life-Long Service." *Jewish News*, March 8, 1957, 1.

"Erection of New Beth Israel is Outstanding Achievement of City Jews During Past Ten Years." *Jewish Chronicle*, May 29, 1931, 17.

"Essex Board of Rabbis Asks Community Kashruth Control." *Jewish News*, June 1, 1956, 3.

"Essex Jews Jubilant." *Newark Evening News,* November 30, 1947, 1.

The Essex Story: A History of the Jewish Community in Essex County, New Jersey, booklet. East Orange, N.J.: Jewish Education Association, 1955.

"Essexites Mourn Death of Councilman Samuel Cooper." *Jewish News*, January 25, 1957, 5.

"Evening of Sports to Feature Stars." *Jewish News*, November 17, 1950, 19.

"Extensive Program Offered." *Jewish News*, September 26, 1958, 27.

Ezor, Donna, "Roseland's Jewish Minority Has Grown Throughout the Years." *MetroWest Jewish News*, June 15, 1995, 14.

———, "JFS Helping Gays Find Place in Community." *MetroWest Jewish News*, July 20, 1995, 9.

———, "MetroWest Responds to Need: HIV/AIDS Support Group Forming." *MetroWest Jewish News*, September 5,1996, 8.

"Facts and Figures." Information Bulletin of the UJA of Essex County, March 1949.

Faust, Elie, "Social Change, Negro Held Factors in Jewish Exodus." *Jewish News*, February 2, 1961, 1.

———, "Beth Israel Marks Advances in Heart, Cancer Research." *Jewish News*, August 11, 1961, 5.

———, "Nuptials Held by Hasidim." *Jewish News*, June 22, 1962, 17.

"Felix Fuld Earned Leading Place Among Country's Jews in Brilliant, Helpful Life." *Jewish Chronicle*, Twentieth Anniversary Issue, June 20, 1941, 81.

"Felix Fuld Reports $425,000 Sent to Aid European Jews." *Jewish Chronicle*, July 28, 1922, 1.

"Felix Fuld Scaled Greatest Heights, Earned Respect Over Entire Nation, During his Brilliant, Helpful Life." *Jewish Chronicle*, Fifteenth Anniversary Issue, April 24, 1936, 38.

"Feldman to Lead Israel Bond Drive." *Jewish News*, January 14, 1966, 1.

"Fien to be Chairman of Israel Bond Drive." *Jewish News*, January 4, 1963, 1.

Finkelstein, Barbara, "Dates Give Way to Doorbells." *Jewish News*, April 10, 1959, 28.

Finley, Charles Q. "A Tremendous Need: Symphony's New President Tackles its Fiscal Woes." *Newark Star-Ledger*, November 28, 1971, 34.

Fischer, Sophia M. "MetroWest: Where We Live, Where We're Moving." *METRO Source: A Guide to Jewish Living, 1993–94*, 19–23.

"For Domestic Tranquility." *Jewish News*, Editorial, July 21, 1967, 10.

"Forgotten Jews." *Jewish Chronicle*, editorial, May 1, 1936, 4.

"Form Education Association Here." *Jewish Chronicle*, March 12, 1937, 1.

"Former Temple Youth Leader is Combat Casualty in Korea." *Jewish News*, September 22, 1950, 1.

"Fortieth Annual Ball of the Workmen's Circle." *City Central Committee and Branches of Newark, N.J.*, January 27, 1942 (n.p.).

"Forty-nine Graduate From Normal School; Tributes Paid Foster." *Jewish Chronicle*, June 8, 1928, 1.

"Forum of Jewish Christian Laity Acclaimed; 500 Hear Inspiring Talks at Good Will Meet." *Jewish Chronicle*, March 20, 1936, 1.

"Foster and Hoffman Speak at Cornerstone Laying of Ahavas Sholem's Synagogue." *Jewish Chronicle*, September 22, 1922, 1.

"Forum of Jewish Christian Laity Acclaimed; 500 Hear Inspiring Talks at Good Will Meet." *Jewish Chronicle*, March 20, 1936, 1.

Foster, Solomon. *The Workingman and the Synagogue* (Newark, N.J., n.p., n.d.).

———, *Papers*, Newark, N.J., c. 1900–1940s. Manuscript Group #1350, New Jersey Historical Society. (Foster was the rabbi from 1902–41).

———, *Spiritual Trails to Happiness*. New York: Bookman Associates, 1953.

"Fox, Goldman are Leaders of UJA's Suburban Division." *Jewish News*, February 5, 1965, 5.

Fox, Martin, *A Message From the President*, pamphlet. Jewish Community Council of Essex County, December 3, 1972.

Frank, Andrew, "Helping to Rebuild the World—Shingle by Shingle." *MetroWest Jewish News*, March 6, 1997, 16.

The Free Synagogue Monthly Bulletin, Vol. 4, No. 10, February 1925.

"Free Synagogue of Newark" in *Synagogues Uncatalogued*, American Jewish Historical Society Archives, Waltham, Massachusetts.

"Freeman Condemns Plebiscite." *Newark Evening News*, May 11, 1938, 5.

Freund, Michael, *et al.*, *Jewish Community Organization in Newark and Essex County*. Report, Survey Committee, Jewish Community Council, 1945.

Fried, Albert, *The Rise and Fall of the Jewish Gangster in America* (New York: Holt, Rinehart & Winston, 1980, 119–121).

Friedman, Gordon David, "Issues, Partisanship and Political Subcultures: A Study of Voting in Statewide Referenda in New Jersey, 1944–1966," Ph.D. thesis (University of North Carolina, Chapel Hill, 1971).

Friedenberg, Albert M., *The Jews of New Jersey From the Earliest Times to 1850*, (Baltimore, Md.: American Jewish Historical Society, 1908 or 1909), No. 17, 33–43.

"Functions of Young Israel Outlined." *Jewish Chronicle*, Fifteenth Anniversary Issue, April 24, 1936, 28.

"Future Home of Workmen's Circle." *Jewish Chronicle*, October 23, 1945, 7.

"Future of World Democracy Topic of Town Hall Meeting in Mosque Wednesday Nite." *Jewish Chronicle,* October 25, 1940, 1.

Garten, Steven, *A Statistical Analysis of Jewish Occupations in Four Major New Jersey Communities Between 1850 and 1860*, unpublished paper. Hebrew Union College, Cincinnati, Ohio, May 16, 1972. In American Jewish Archives, Manuscript Collection.

Gelbart, Gershon, Sylvan H. Kohn, and David Rudavsky, *The Essex Story: A History of the Jewish Community in Essex County, New Jersey* (Newark, N. J.: Jewish Education Association of Essex County, 1955).

Geltman, Max, *The Confrontation: Black Power, Anti-Semitism, and the Myth of Integration* (Englewood Cliffs, N.J.: Prentice-Hall, 1970).

"Genealogy of the Jewish Family Service of MetroWest," chart. Available at Jewish Historical Society of MetroWest.

"Ghetto Rite Will Hear Prinz." *Jewish News*, April 30, 1965, 48.

"Goal for Third Successive Year Reached by United Appeals." *Jewish News*, December 3, 1954, 1.

Gold, Abner R. "Pilgrims in a New Land." *Jewish News*, May 13, 1949, 12.

———, "Pilgrims in a New Land." *Jewish News*, June 24, 1949, 12.

———, "Pilgrims in a New Land." *Jewish News*, July 15, 1949, 12.

———, "Pilgrims in a New Land." *Jewish News*, July 22, 1949, 12.

———, "Pilgrims in a New Land." *Jewish News*, August 19, 1949, 9.

———, "Named as First Jewish Police Captain in History of Newark." *Jewish News*, May 26, 1950, 1.

———, "Good Progress is Made by Fledgling Jewish Community." *Jewish News*, August 10, 1951, 12.

———, "Abeles, Lowenstein Cited for Services." *Jewish News*, February 6, 1953, 1.

———, "JVS' 'Mr. 5,000' is Typical in Desire to Earn Own Living." *Jewish News*, February 12, 1954, 20.

"Golda Hollander Schwartz Endowment Foundation Dedicated to Memory of Woman Who Devoted her Life to Bring Relief, Soothe Pains of Those in Need." *Jewish Chronicle*, Fifteenth Anniversary Issue, April 24, 1936, 74.

Goldberg, Isaac, "B'nai Abraham Unfolds Picturesque History." *Jewish Chronicle*, Fifteenth Anniversary Issue, April 24, 1936, 53.

Goldstein, Stanley J. "Synagogues, Suburbs and Symbolism." *Jewish News*, June 14, 1957, 48.

"Golf Tournament Successful." *Jewish News*, July 4, 1958, 1.

Goodnough, Abby, "Newark is Practical (and Symbolic) Answer to Logistical Puzzle." *New York Times,* January 21, 1998, B5.

Gordon, Abraham Julius, Scrapbook, 1917–18 of military man and prisoner of war experiences of a hospital administrator. First president of Martland Medical Center in Newark.

"To Graduate 50 Students at Normal School Here." *Jewish Chronicle*, May 18, 1927, 1.

"Greek War Not a Thriller, Young Newark Cadet Finds." *Jewish News*, July 29, 1949, 12.

Greene, Barry. *Our 140th Year: Tracing the History of Congregation B'nai Jeshurun.*

"Greetings from Our President." *Jewish Chronicle*, South End Club of Newark Supplement, April 18, 1941, 1.

"Mrs. Griffith, Civic Leader, Directed Music Foundation." *Jewish News*, December 16, 1960, 8.

Grossman, Barbara W. *Funny Woman: The Life and Times of Fanny Brice.* (Bloomington: Indiana University Press, 1991).

"Mrs. Grotta Dies, Thousands Mourn." *Jewish Chronicle*, January 27, 1922, 1.

Grover, Warren, "Relief in Newark, 1929–1933," M.A. thesis (New York University, 1962).

"Growth of Oheb Shalom School Reported at Annual Meeting." *Jewish Chronicle*, May 2, 1930, 1.

Gurock, Jeffrey S. "From Exception to Role Model: Bernard Drachman and the Evolution of Jewish Religious Life in America, 1880–1920." *American Jewish History,* Vol. 76, No. 4, June 1987, 457.

Guyot, Dorothy M. "Newark: Crime and Politics in a Declining City." in Anne Heinz, Herbert Jacob, and Robert L. Lineberry (eds), *Crime in City Politics*, (New York: Longman, 1983), 23–93.

Haberman, Joshua O. *The Jews in New Jersey.* Unpublished manuscript of talk presented at the Institute of American Jewry, Estes Park, Colorado, June 21, 1953. In Special Collections and University Archives, Rutgers University Libraries.

Halberstadter, Louis, "Dedicated to Hebrew Education." *Jewish News*, September 27, 1957, 42.

Halperin, Abe, "Dear Linda,. . . .Love, Abe." *MetroWest Jewish News*, January 9, 1992, 25.

Hannoch, Isador, "One Year's History: Dedicated to The Elks" (n.p., 1882). Available at Jewish Historical Society of MetroWest.

"Hannoch Picked as President of Children's Home." *Jewish Chronicle*, November 8, 1940.

"Hannoch Tells of OSE's Work." *Jewish Chronicle*, May 30, 1941, 1.

Hannoch Scrapbook, 1877–1898. At JHS.

Harris, Alexander, "As I Knew Him." *Jewish Chronicle*, December 6, 1940, 4.

"Hebrew Academy Enrollment Expected to Reach New High." *Jewish News*, January 14, 1955, 4.

"Hebrew High is Organized Under Auspices of 'Y.'" *Jewish Chronicle*, November 21, 1930, 1.

"The Hebrew Orphanage and Sheltering Home." *Jewish News*, January 24, 1947, 9.

"Hebrew Youth Academy Formed." *Jewish News*, September 7, 1962, 1.

Hebrew Youth Academy, Newark and South Orange, N.J., *Records, 1953–1981*. In Young Israel South Orange Jewish Center *Records*, Special Collections and University Archives, Rutgers University Libraries, Manuscript Collection #902.

Heller, Gustav P. *A Century of Temple B'nai Jeshurun*, unpublished paper.

Hendricks Papers, Box 19, File Folder "Newark Property," at New York Historical Society.

"Herbert J. Hannoch Carries On in Guidance of Destiny of the Jewish Children's Home." *Jewish Chronicle*, Twentieth Anniversary Issue, June 20, 1941, 75.

Hershkowitz, Leo, "Wills of Early New York Jews (1704–1799)." *Studies in American Jewish History, No. 4, 1967.*

Herzberg, Arno, "Cites Trend in Population." *Jewish News*, October 2, 1953, 7.

Hirschhorn, Isidor, "Recollections," unpublished, undated paper.

"Historical Record of Roseville and East Orange Hebrew Association." *Jewish Chronicle*, October 30, 1936, 1.

"History of the Brith Abraham." *Jewish Chronicle*, Fifteenth Anniversary Issue, April 24, 1936, 82.

"History of the Brith Sholom." *Jewish Chronicle*, Fifteenth Anniversary Issue, April 24, 1936, 88.

History of Conference of Jewish Charities." *Jewish Chronicle*, Section 4, September 26, 1924, 1.

"History of Order Sons of Zion." *Jewish Chronicle*, Fifteenth Anniversary Issue, April 24, 1936, 84.

"Hold 'Graduation' in City Thursday for German-Jews." *Jewish Chronicle*, June 21, 1935, 1.

"Holidays, Events, Weddings, and Social Programs." *Jewish Chronicle*, column, April 11, 1941, 8.

"Hollander Again Choice as Leader of Talmud Torah." *Jewish Chronicle*, February 24, 1922, 1.

"Home's Recreation Program Cheers Days of Elderly Folk." *Jewish News*, March 12, 1954, 24.

"Hood Reminisces on Growth of City." *Jewish Chronicle*, Fifteenth Anniversary Issue, April 24, 1936, 78.

"Howe Will Lecture in Livingston." *Jewish News,* April 2, 1965, 24.

Imbriaco, Alison, "White Meadow Lake Described as Close-Knit Community." *MetroWest Jewish News*, February 23, 1995, 9.

———, "Jewish Population at Home in Cedar Grove." *MetroWest Jewish News*, September 7, 1995, 10.

———, "Bar-Mitzva Boy a First for Pathways." *MetroWest Jewish News*, September 14, 1995, 11.

———, "Fatherhood Project Casts Spotlight on Business of Daddyhood." *MetroWest Jewish News*, December 14, 1995, 14

———, "Pine Brook Jewish Center Celebrates 100 Years in Morris County." *MetroWest Jewish News*, January 11, 1996, 8.

"'In Upbuilding of Palestine We are Deadly in Earnest,' Weizman Declares at Dinner Here—Raise $50,000 for Fund." *Jewish Chronicle*, June 15, 1923, 1.

"An Interesting History of B'nai Abraham." *Jewish Chronicle*, Twentieth Anniversary Issue, June 20, 1941, 82.

"Intermarriage: Rabbi Calls it Dissolution, Not Solution, For Jews." *Newark Evening News*, September 20, 1939, 8.

"Irvington's First Jewish Edifice: B'nai Israel Dedication to Conclude Sunday." *Jewish Chronicle*, February 12, 1926, 1.

"Is your Name Here?" *Jewish News*, April 25, 1947, 2.

"Isaac Lowenstein, Veteran School Official, to End 58 Years Service." *Jewish Chronicle*, February 6, 1942, 3.

"Israel Philharmonic to Play in Mosque Theater January 9th." *Jewish News*, September 22, 1950, 1.

Isserman, Alexander, "Aaron Levinstone: In Honor of his 25th Anniversary of Communal Work." *Jewish Chronicle*, November 28, 1941, 5.

"It Was in the Best Tradition of America" (on the March on Washington). *Jewish News*, September 6, 1963, 1.

"JCC N.J. Y Camps Attendance Up." *MetroWest Jewish News*, August 21, 1997, 8.

"J.L. Newman, Former County Prosecutor, Temple President." *Jewish News*, January 29, 1960, 28.

"JVS' 'Employer of the Year' Award Presented to S. Klein." *Jewish News*, November 6, 1959, 7.

Jacobs, Miriam, "Newton—Small Town With a Haimisch Touch." *MetroWest Jewish News*, May 18, 1995, 16.

"Jersey Boy Wins Harvard Honors." *Jewish Chronicle*, June 23, 1922, 1.

"Jew Will Head Fraternal Order of Eagles." *Jewish Chronicle*, August 11, 1922, 1.

"Jewish Anti-Tuberculosis League, Organized Fourteen Years Ago, Has Furnished Relief for Thousands Afflicted With the Disease." *Jewish Chronicle*, April 24, 1936, 30.

"Jewish Affairs Luncheon to Hear Talk by Noted Writer." Jewish News, February 12, 1954, 2.

"Jewish Anti-Tuberculosis League Plans Sanatorium." *Jewish Chronicle*, February 5, 1926, 1.

"The Jewish Children's Home." *Jewish News*, January 17, 1947, 6.

"Jewish Children's Home Subject to Modern Innovations From Viewpoint of Health, Spirit and Education." *Jewish Chronicle*, May 29, 1931, 14.

"Jewish Citizens Chosen for Important Municipal Posts." *Jewish Chronicle,* May 21, 1937, 1.

Jewish Community Blue Book, Newark, New Jersey (Newark, N.J.: Jewish Community Blue Book Publishing Company, 1924).

Jewish Community Council of Essex County, *For Your Information: The Record of Our Life, in Our Time, in Our Community*, pamphlet. Newark, 1948.

Jewish Community Council Memorandum on Capital Needs, January 10, 1951. At JHS.

Jewish Counseling and Service Agency of Essex County, *Records, 1920–1961.* In Special Collections and University Archives, Rutgers University Libraries, Manuscript Collection #2366. (Contains archives of the Jewish Family Service Association of Essex County and the Jewish Child Care Association, which merged in 1961 to form the Jewish Counseling and Service Agency of Essex County.)

"Jewish Court Has First Case to Try." *Jewish Chronicle*, May 6, 1927, 1.

"Jewish Day Nursery and Neighborhood House." January 16, 1931, 1.

"Jewish Educators Take New Posts." *Jewish News*, September 2, 1949, 1.

"Jewish Girl Takes Veil as Nun of Cloistered Catholic Order." *Newark Evening News*, May 3, 1926, 5.

"Jewish Guidance Bureau Aiming to Aid Delinquents in Early Youth." *Jewish Chronicle*, May 29, 1931, 19.

"Jewish Home for Chronic Sick, Only Institution of its Kind in New Jersey, Serves Noble Purpose." *Jewish Chronicle*, Twentieth Anniversary Issue, June 20, 1941, 88.

"The Jewish Immigration Into Newark." in *A History of the City of Newark, New Jersey,* Volume 2 (New York & Chicago: Lewis Historical Publishing Company, 1913). Chapter Seven, unpaged.

"Jewish Officers Helped Advance of Newark University." *Jewish Chronicle*, Twentieth Anniversary Issue, June 20, 1941, 5.

"Jewish Physicians Sail for Palestine." *Jewish Chronicle*, July 28, 1922, 1.

"Jewish Pioneers in Educational Field." *Jewish Chronicle*, Twentieth Anniversary Issue, June 20, 1941, 94.

"Jewish Social Workers to Confer in Newark." *Jewish Chronicle*, April 2, 1937, 2.

"Jewish Teachers Organize Alumni." *Jewish Chronicle*, July 6, 1928, 1.

Jewish Vocational Service of Metrowest, Minutes, January 17, 1939; February 27, 1939; December 1, 1939.

———, *First Annual Report*, Community Employment Service of Essex County, December 1940.

"Jewry at Seth Boyden Housing Project Establishing Own Center, JEA Reports." *Jewish Chronicle,* April 4, 1941, 1.

"Jews in Protest of Olympic Grant." *Newark Evening News*, July 7, 1936, 1.

"Jews in County Surveyed on Habits in Philanthropy." *Jewish News*, January 12, 1962, 1.

"Jews' Gifts to America." *Newark Evening News*, December 3, 1946, 27.

"Jews Here to Hold Protest Gathering." *Newark Evening News*, September 11, 1929, 2.

"Jews in Protest of Olympic Grant." *Newark Evening News*, July 7, 1936, 1.

"Jews Will Strive to Raise $3,000 Daily in Campaign." *Newark Evening News*, June 6, 1923, 6.

"J.N.F. 'News' Cites Newark for Record 'Flower Day' Sum." *Jewish Chronicle*, July 31, 1931, 1.

"Joel Gross Heads '42 UJA Campaign." *Jewish Chronicle*, November 28, 1941, 1.

Johnston, Richard J.H. "Teachers Beaten in Newark Strike." *New York Times*, February 3, 1971, 1.

"Judge Voids Newark Layoffs." *The Daily News*, January 13, 1979, 1.

"Judge Untermann, Long Active in Children's Aid, Dies Suddenly." *Newark Jewish Times*, February 11, 1944, 1.

"Jumping Jack Judaism." *Jewish Chronicle*, editorial, March 31, 1922, 4.

"Jungen Maenner Wohlthaetigkeits Gesellschaft." *Protocoll Buch*, Newark, 1861–76. Available at Jewish Historical Society of MetroWest.

Kahn, Elaine, "Jews and Blacks Seen as Continuing to Drift Apart." *MetroWest Jewish News*, January 11, 1996, 8.

———, "Marcus Stresses Duty to Go Beyond Denominational Differences." *Jewish News,* February 20, 1997, 8.

Kasen, Louis. *Love is not a Potato: An Autobiography*, self-published book.

Kasinetz, Moshe, "Introductory Message," in *Anniversary Dinner Journal* (Livingston), February 9, 1986.

Katkov, Norman, *The Fabulous Fanny: The Story of Fanny Brice* (New York: Alfred A. Knopf, 1952).

Katz, Rose D., *Golden Memories* (n.p., n.d.), available at Newark Public Library.

Katzler, William von, "The Germans in Newark," in Frank J. Urquhart, *A History of the City of Newark, New Jersey,* three volumes, (New York: Lewis Historical Publishing Company, 1913) Volume II, 1065–70.

Kaufman, Anton (ed.), *Jewish Community Blue Book of Newark.* Newark, 1926.

———, "Kessler Logical Head for Educational Body." *Jewish Chronicle,* editorial, March 12, 1937, 1.

———, "Joseph Wolber's Record: It Speaks for Itself." *Jewish Chronicle,* editorial, May 11, 1934, 1.

———, "Rabbi Hyman Brodsky." *Jewish Chronicle,* editorial, March 5, 1937, 1.

———, "Real Caution—and Real Criticism." *Jewish Chronicle,* editorial, April 9, 1937, 1.

———, "When Wise Counsel and Cool Heads Prevail." *Jewish Chronicle,* editorial, June 7, 1935, 1.

Kaufman, Louis, *Moe Berg: Athlete, Scholar, Spy* (New York: Little, Brown, 1974).

Kaye, Lauren, "Keeping your Jewish Commitment on Campus." *Metrowest Jewish News,* August 10, 1995, S-3.

Keshen, Milton, "Ellenstein Remembered," letters to the editor, *New Jersey Jewish News,* July 10, 1997, 7.

"Kessler Denounces 'Political Jews.'" *Jewish Chronicle,* April 9, 1937, 1.

Kessler, Samuel I. "There is Only One Answer—From Our Minds and Hearts." *Jewish News,* October 2, 1953, 7.

Klein, Gary M. "A Study of the Economic Activity of the Jewish Community of Newark, New Jersey, 1861–1875," unpublished paper, Hebrew Union College, Cincinnati, Ohio, May 15, 1972. In American Jewish Archives, Manuscript Collection.

Kluger, Benjamin, "Growing Up in Newark." *Jewish News-New Jersey,* September 8, 1977, B1–B10.

Koch, Edward I., with Daniel Paisner, *Citizen Koch: An Autobiography* (New York: St. Martin's Press, 1992), 1–25.

Kohn, Sylvan H. "Aspects of Congregational Life in Essex County." *Jewish News,* June 21, 1957, 14.

Konvitz, Milton R. "Rabbi Joseph Konvitz: A Son's Memoir." forthcoming. *Torah U'Maddah Journal.*

Kordova, Shoshana, "Newark's Only Jewish Mayor Feted." *MetroWest Jewish News,* June 19, 1997, 18–19.

Kornfeld, Cheryl L. "Jewish Community's Diversity Called 'Tribute to Springfield's Pluralism,'" *MetroWest Jewish News,* March 23, 1995, 9.

———, "One Hundred Candles—and Russian Immigrant Knows No Trick to Longevity." *MetroWest Jewish News,* June 15, 1995, 15.

———, "Parents Experiencing Baby Loss Seek Jewish Response in JEA Group." *MetroWest Jewish News,* November 30, 1995, 8–9.

———, "Beth Israel Sale Won't Affect Jewish Commitment, Say Leaders." *MetroWest Jewish News,* December 14, 1995, 8.

———, "Sale to St. Barnabas Could Affect NBIMC Relationship With MetroWest Federation." *MetroWest Jewish News,* December 14, 1995, 11.

———, "Conference in MetroWest Aims to Awaken the Jewish Heart to AIDS." *MetroWest Jewish News,* February 29, 1996, 8.

———, "As He Retires, Boeko Cited as Visionary." *MetroWest Jewish News,* June 19,1997, 14.

"'Kosher Kitty Kelly' Comes to Broad." *Jewish Chronicle,* January 22, 1926, 7.

"Kosher Butchers are Being Probed." *Newark Evening News*, August 18, 1939, 1.

Koshetz, Herbert, "Emigrant Builds Zipper Business to Second Largest in the World." *New York Times*, Section 3, December 28, 1952, 54.

Kramer, Sylvia, "Our First 75 Years Caring For the Elderly," booklet. Daughters of Israel Pleasant Valley Home, West Orange, New Jersey, 1982.

Kramer, Sylvia and Peter Ortner, *Images of MetroWest 1985,* booklet (West Orange, N.J.: YM-YWHA, 1985).

"Krantztohr Will Head Fund Campaign of Kessler Institute." *Jewish News*, September 28, 1951, 13.

"Kresge Store Ranks Among Best in Country." *Jewish Chronicle*, Fifteenth Anniversary Issue, April 24, 1936, 39.

"Kresge's to Aid Ruth Kohn Home in Two-Day Drive." *Jewish Chronicle*, October 18, 1940, 5.

"Kresge's to Distribute Tickets to Schools for Byrd Lecture." *Jewish Chronicle*, October 10, 1930, 1.

Kriegel, Alter, "Combatting Intermarrriage." *Jewish News*, March 28, 1947, 4.

Kuntz, William, *Once There was a Synagogue: A Study of Newark's Synagogue-Church Transformations.* (n.p., N.J.).

Kurman, Louis A. "Study of the Development of Jewish Community Organization in Essex County, New Jersey, 1922–1946." M.S. thesis (New York School of Social Work, Columbia University), December 1946.

Kussy, Nathan, "Early History of the Jews of Newark." in *The Jewish Community Blue Book of Newark*, (Newark, N.J.: Jewish Community Blue Book Publishing Company, 1925).

———, "Marching On With the Y.M.—Y.W.H.A." *Jewish Chronicle*, Fifteenth Anniversary Issue, April 24, 1936, 9.

———, "Early Jewish Settlers Helped Build Newark." *Jewish Chronicle,* Twentieth Anniversary Issue, June 20, 1941, 25.

Kussy, Sarah S. "Diary Kept During War with Spain, April-August, 1898." in Manuscript Collection #P-, *Sarah Kussy Papers*, American Jewish Historical Society Archives, Waltham, Massachusetts.

———, "Ladies Patriotic Relief Society." in Manuscript Collection #P-, *Sarah Kussy Papers,* American Jewish Historical Society Archives, Waltham, Massachusetts.

———, "Minutes of Miriam Auxiliary, Newark, N.J., 1898–1955. in Manuscript Collection #P-, *Sarah Kussy Papers,* American Jewish Historical Society Archives, Waltham, Massachusetts.

———, "Reminiscences of Jewish Life in Newark, N.J." *Yivo Bletter* 29 (1947).

———, *The Story of Gustav & Bella Kussy of Newark, N.J.: A Family Chronicle,* booklet, n.d.

———, "The Story of Miriam Auxiliary of Oheb Shalom. "Sixty Five Years in Retrospect." in Manuscript Collection, *Sarah Kussy Papers*, American Jewish Historical Society Archives, Waltham, Massachusetts.

Kwartler, Marion, "Synagogue Central Address for Bloomfield Jews." *MetroWest Jewish News*, April 20, 1995, 16.

"L. Simon Plaut, Store Executive, Passes Away." *Jewish Chronicle*, April 24, 1942, 1.

"L.V. Aronson Entertains Civic Leaders Aboard his Yacht." *Jewish Chronicle*, July 30, 1931, 2.

"L.V. Aronson—Newark's Civic Leader." *Jewish Chronicle*, Fifteenth Anniversary Issue, April 24, 1936, 54.

"Lakewood's Most Prominent Hotel." *Jewish Chronicle*, December 16, 1921, 5.

Lang, Leon S. "Prospects for Jewish Education in Newark." *Jewish Chronicle*, May 29, 1931, 18.

"Large Attendance at Refugee Dance." *Jewish Chronicle*, March 27, 1936, 3.

Laskowitz, Irving, "Our Installation and Dinner Dance." *Young Israel Review*, Vol. 1, No. 1, 5.

"Lauds A.H. Puder Creed as Best in American Tradition." *Jewish News*, May 11, 1962, 4.

"Lawyer's Club to Close Season by Annual Dinner." *Jewish Chronicle*, April 6, 1923, 1.

"Leaders in New Jersey's Jewish Relief Drive." *Newark Star Eagle*, October 17, 1919.

"Leadership and Popularity Mark Civic, Professional Career of Dr. Joseph Kussy." *Jewish Chronicle*, Twentieth Anniversary Issue, June 20, 1941, 104.

"Leaves Congregation Because of Drift From Orthodoxy." *Jewish Voice*, November 27, 1925, 1.

Lefson, Leon, "Aspects of the Community Organization Process in the Evaluation of a Social Agency." M.S. thesis (New York School of Social Work, Columbia University, 1948)

Lerner, Marvin G. "A Study of the Relationship Between Jewish Family Service Association of Essex County and the Newark Department of Public Welfare," M.A. thesis (New York, Columbia University School of Social Welfare, 1949).

"Let's Go to the Tavern." *New Jersey Business*, April 1959, 30–31.

"Letters on 'Newark and the Suburbs,'" editorial. *Jewish News*, September 26, 1958, 11.

"Letters on 'Newark and the Suburbs,'" editorial. *Jewish News*, October 3, 1958, 11.

Leucht, Joseph, Wolff Willner, and Isaac Schwartz, "Appeal in Behalf of the Hebrew Education Society of Newark, N.J." flyer, November 21, 1989.

Levy, Clifford J. "Newark Mayor Accused of Violations." *New York Times*, February 22, 1995, B5.

———, "From Convictions to Code of Ethics: Ex- Prosecutor Tackles Essex County Graft in Counsel Role." *New York Times*, May 26, 1995, B1.

———, "From the Old Country: A Portuguese Village in Newark." *New York Times*, October 6, 1995, C1.

Lewitter, Sidney R. *American Dreams: The Story of a Jewish Immigrant Family* (Lakewood, N.J.: Bristol, Rhein & Englander, 1994).

"Liberty Young Men's Association to Celebrate." *Jewish Chronicle*, October 13, 1922, 1.

"Lindeman Chosen Director of Freeholder Board." *Jewish Chronicle*, December 28, 1934, 1.

"Lindeman, Siegler, Ellenstein and Mones Nominated." *Jewish Chronicle*, September 28, 1923, 1.

Linden, Rose, "A Study of the First Year Adjustment of 25 Refugee Families," M.A. thesis (New York, Columbia University School of Social Work, 1948).

"Listings." *METRO Source: A Guide to Jewish Living*, 1993–94, 47–101.

Littman, Annette, "A Narrative History," in *The Shaarei Tefilo Story*, pamphlet.

"Local Jewry to Mark Herzl Birth at Rally Monday." *Jewish Chronicle*, May 10, 1935, 1.

"Local Men Invited to Parley on Jews' Back-to-Land Move." *Newark Evening News*, September 3, 1925, 8.

"Local Youth is Princeton Grad of Fine Record." *Jewish Chronicle*, July 13, 1923, 1.

"Louis Plaut Passes Away in Los Angeles at Age of 82." *Jewish Chronicle*, January 8, 1943, 7.

"Louis Schlesinger Has Cure for City's Problems." *Jewish Chronicle*, Twentieth Anniversary Issue, June 20, 1941, 61.

"Louis V. Aronson Heads Drive of Salvation Army." *Jewish Chronicle*, April 20, 1923, 1.

"Louis Weller is Dead at 68; Was Kehilath Israel's Rabbi." *Jewish News*, July 14, 1967, 9.

Lowenstein, Alan V. "Who is a Community Leader?" *The Jewish Community*, Vol. 3, No. 4, December 1948, 10–11.

———, *Eulogy for Herman M. Pekarsky*, Delivered on September 18, 1963.

———, *The Challenges of a Professional Career: The Autobiography of a Twentieth Century New Jersey Lawyer*, manuscript in progress.

Lowenstein, Amy, *One Hundred Years of the "Y", 1877–1977: History and Guide for the "Y" Centennial Exhibition*, September 18 to November 28, 1977 (West Orange, New Jersey: YM-YWHA of Metropolitan New Jersey, 1977).

Lowenstein, Celia, "Poem" in *60th Anniversary Issue of Oheb Shalom*, 1920. Available at Jewish Historical Society of MetroWest.

"Lowenstein Elected President of Jewish Community Council." *Jewish News*, January 20, 1950, 1.

"Lowenstein Named 'Volunteer of Year.'" *Newark Star-Ledger*, June 16, 1960.

MacFarquhar, Neil, "Newark School Takeover is Seen as Early as July." *New York Times*, May 20, 1995, 28.

———, "New Jersey Sends Team to Manage Newark Schools." *New York Times*, July 6, 1995, 1.

———, "A Battle on the Waterfront: Conflicting Visions for the Renewal of the Passaic River." *New York Times*, July 11, 1995, B1.

———, "Taking Control, State Ousts Newark's School Officials." *New York Times*, July 13, 1995, B6.

———, "Downtown Newark Gambles on the Arts." *New York Times*, January 14, 1997, B1.

"Majority of Jews are Anti-Zionists, Says Rabbi Foster." *Jewish Chronicle*, August 14, 1925, 1.

Mandelbaum, Morris B. "I Remember Well my Father's Newark Friends." *MetroWest Jewish News*, January 9, 1992, 24.

Mann, Cynthia and Shammai Engelmayer, "UJA-CJF Partnership Plan Gets Mixed Reviews at MetroWest." *Jewish News*, February 20, 1997, 8.

"Many Endorsing New Sanatorium." *Jewish Chronicle*, February 12, 1926, 1.

Maranz, Felice, "Life Among the Ruins." *Jerusalem Report*, March 25, 1993, 32–33.

Marks, Paulina Konoff, "Alexander Konoff," unpublished paper. Jewish Historical Society of MetroWest.

Maske, Monica, "Preparing for Passover." *Newark Star-Ledger*, April 19, 1989, 69.

Mattison, Carrie, "JACS Combating Jewish Denial About Alcohol Drug Addiction." *MetroWest Jewish News*, June 26, 1997, 14.

"Mayor Murphy Pledges Aid Towards 'Commonwealth' Aim in Platform." *Newark Jewish Times*, July 21, 1944, 1.

McCarter, Robert H., *Memoirs of a Half Century* (n.d.,n.p.), 95–99.

McLarin, Kimberly, "An Educator Who Passionately Believes the Poor can Succeed." *New York Times*, July 6, 1995, 1.

"Meeting Religious Needs of Jewry in Housing Project." *Jewish Chronicle,* April 4, 1941, 1.

"Meeting Thursday to Protest Great Britain's White Paper; New York Rally on Sunday." *Jewish Chronicle*, October 31, 1930 1.

Meier, Ron, Ruth Greenfield, Gary A. Tobin, *A Population Study of Study of the Jewish Community of MetroWest New Jersey*, report(United Jewish Federation of MetroWest, 1988).

Memoirs, unpublished, undated. Available at Jewish Historical Society of MetroWest.

METROSOURCE: A Guide to Jewish Living, 1997–98.

"Metrowest and Israeli Twin Communities Share Unique Relationship." *MetroWest Jewish News*, April 27, 1995, 5–6.

Miller, Judith, "A Self-Made Man Takes on Newark." *New York Times*, October 14, 1997, B1.

Minutes of the Conference of Jewish Charities from 1922 to the present.

"Miss Blume First Jersey Girl to Act as Murder Counsel." *Newark Morning Ledger*, April 29, 1918, 1.

""Miss America" Visits New Plaut Store in Newark." *Jewish Chronicle*, October 8, 1926, 1.

"Morristown Jewish Community Center, " unpublished pamphlet, undated.

"Morristown Jewish Personalities." *Morristown Daily Record*, August 30, 1938, 1.

"Morristown to Nazis: Keep Out." *Morris Sussex Jewish News*, August, 1978, 5.

"Motherless Kiddies Join Fathers Here After Years of Weary Toil and Hardships in Ukrainian Fields." *Jewish Chronicle*, December 23, 1921.

"Mrs. Esther Jameson, 84; Former Agencies' Director." *Jewish News*, February 1, 1963, 16.

"Mrs. Griffith, Civic Leader, Directed Music Foundation." *Jewish News*, December 16, 1960, 8.

"Mrs. Meyer Kussy Eulogized: 'Exemplified Finest Virtues.'" *Jewish News*, January 14, 1955, 3.

"Mrs. Parsonnet is Named President of Women Voters." *Jewish Chronicle*, January 27, 1927, 1.

Muraskin, Ellen Forman, "Creating Community." *METRO Source: A Guide to Jewish Living*, 1993–94, 25–27, 36.

"Music Festival Set at Newark 'Y'." *Jewish News*, February 5, 1965, 1.

"Name 7 Trade Chairmen for UJA Manufacturing Division." *Jewish News*, March 15, 1957, 9.

Namkin, Sidney, "Helping Others to Help Themselves." *Jewish News*, September 27, 1957, 38.

"Nathan Kussy a Novelist and Dramatist and Active in Jewish Affairs Besides Being a Successful Attorney." *Jewish Chronicle*, Twentieth Anniversary Issue, June 20, 1941, 90.

Nathan, Robert, *Report on Newark*. United Jewish Appeal, 1946. Available at Jewish Historical Society of MetroWest.

"The National Convention of Cantors." editorial, *Jewish Chronicle*, May 13, 1927, 4.

"Nazi Attacks on Jews Draw Protest Here." *Newark Evening News*, March 28, 1933, 1.

"Negro Held Vital Factor in Jewish Urban Exodus." *Newark Evening News*, January 26, 1962, 21.

"Neighborliness Lauded by Rabbi." *Jewish News*, January 16, 1959, 4.

"The New Newark." *TIME*, October 21, 1957, 27.

"New Religious Summer School of Council to Close First Term Thursday; Report Plan Success." *Jewish Chronicle*, August 10, 1928, 1.

"New Sessions at Normal to Begin on October 2nd." *Jewish Chronicle*, July 27, 1928, 1.

"New Temple Structure: A Merger of Beauty, Simplicity." *Jewish News*, September 13, 1968, 18.

"Newark." *Universal Jewish Encyclopedia*, 206–209.

"Newark Beth Israel Elects Sagner at Annual Meeting." *Jewish News*, April 29, 1966, 5.

"Newark Bureau Locates Kin of Polish Refugees." *Newark Jewish Times*, December 28, 1945, 2.

"Newark is Cited in Survey On Anti-Poverty Programs." *Jewish News*, January 7, 1966, 4.

"Newark Council Women in Front Rank of Organizational Service." *Jewish Chronicle*, May 29, 1931, 23.

"Newark GI Wins Bronze Star for Courage, Devotion to Duty." *Jewish News*, June 27, 1952, 1.

"Newark Group Organizes to Aid Jews in Poland." *Newark Evening News*, December 26, 1940, 9.

"Newark Jews Have Inferiority Complex, Claims Rabbi Wise." *Jewish Chronicle*, January 8, 1932, 1.

"Newark Jews Parade in Protest of Massacres." *Newark Evening News*, May 22, 1919, 9 (about the Pinsk pogrom in which 56 Jews were killed.)

"Newark Museum Schedules Exhibit on 'Art in Judaism.'" *Jewish News*, March 15, 1957, 5.

Newark Ozeraner Society, *8th Anniversary and Victory Banquet*

"Newark Soldier, Killed in Bitter Fighting at Taegu." *Jewish News*, October 6, 1950, 1.

"Newark and the Suburbs," editorial. *Jewish News*, September 5, 1958, 10.

The Newark Y.M. & Y.W.H.A.: A History. 20th Anniversary Celebration, 1924–1944, pamphlet.

"Newark Y Activities Scattered in Various Spots Throughout City." *Jewish News*, December 31, 1954, 3.

"Newark of Yesterday, Today, and Tomorrow, With the Stamp of Morris Rachlin, Master Builder, Indelibly Printed on Each Phase." *Jewish Chronicle*, September 23, 1927, 1.

"Newark's Ship-A-Box Tops the Nation; Makes Record Sending Parcels Overseas." *Jewish News*, June 27, 1947, 1.

"Newark's Zionists, 8,000 Strong, Stage Big Demonstration in Celebration of Ratification of Palestine Mandate." *Jewish Chronicle*, September 15, 1922, 1.

Nierenberg, Rachel, "Congregation Ahavas Shalom: A Continued Presence. An Important Legacy," paper written for course in *American Jewish Social History*, given at Jewish Theological Seminary, November 1997.

———, "Joachim Prinz: Political-Religionist Rabbi," paper written for course in *Methodologies in Jewish History*, given at Jewish Theological Seminary, May 1997.

Nieves, Evelyn, "Police Anger Unsettles City Already Edgy." *New York Times*, June 19, 1997, B1.

"No Anti-Semitism Evident in Rioting." *Jewish News*, July 21, 1967, 3.

"Normal School Heads Plan Celebration of Tenth Anniversary." *Jewish Chronicle*, November 22, 1935, 1.

"The Normal School for Jewish Teachers," editorial. *Jewish Chronicle*, October 8, 1926, 4.

"Normal School Officials Plan Social Service Study Program." *Jewish Chronicle*, June 15, 1928, 1.

"Notables Pay Final Respects to Louis V. Aronson, Noted Philanthropist and Inventor." *Jewish Chronicle*, November 8, 1940, 1.

"Noted Leader to Lecture at Sharey Tefilo." *Jewish News*, May 5, 1961, 24.

Novak, William, "A Conversation with Arthur Green." *Kerem*, Spring 1995, 30–52.

Novich, Max M. "Letters From Readers: A Journey Filled With Nostalgia for Columnist." *Jewish News*, February 8, 1979, 46.

————, "A Recent Visit Revives Old Memories of a Legendary Jewish Community." *Jewish News*, June 7, 1979, 31.

Nutley: Yesterday-Today, Ann A. Troy (ed.), (Nutley, N.J.: Nutley Historical Society, 1961), 174–75.

"Observe Girls' Day at Temple." *Jewish Chronicle*, May 7, 1926, 1.

Och, Golda, "From Philanthropy to Community: The Organization of the Jewish Community of Newark," paper for course given by Professor Ismar Schorsch, December 1977.

O'Connor, John E. and Charles F. Cummings, "Bamberger's Department Store, *Charm Magazine*, and the Culture of Consumption in New Jersey, 1924–1932." *New Jersey History* 102 nos. 3–4 (Fall/Winter, 1984, 1–33).

"Oheb Shalom, B'nai Abraham Announce Program to Merge All their Suburban Activities." *Jewish News*, June 27, 1947, 1.

Oheb Shalom Congregation, 125th Anniversary of Oheb Shalom, South Orange, N.J., 1985.

Oheb Shalom Congregation Records, Box 1, Folder 3, *Board of Trustees Minutes*, February 10, 1948.

————, April 23, 1953.

————, July 21, 1953.

————, March 29, 1956.

————, March 4, 1959.

————, September 15, 1959.

————, November 3, 1959.

————, June 16, 1977.

Oheb Shalom, Seventy Fifth Anniversary: The Story of a Congregation, booklet.

"Oheb Shalom Synagogue Burns Up Its Mortgage of $40,000 at Banquet to Celebrate 70th Anniversary." *Jewish Chronicle*, May 2, 1930, 1.

"Opportunity Corner." *Jewish News*, July 28, 1950, 5.

The Origin and Growth of Temple B'nai Israel (Irvington), pamphlet, May 1, 1983.

"Orphanage Has Gained Wide Recognition." *Jewish Chronicle*, Twentieth Anniversary Issue, June 20, 1941, 99.

"Orphan's Home Among Leading Institutions." *Jewish Chronicle*, Fifteenth Anniversary Issue, April 24, 1936, 71.

"Our Life in Our Time," pamphlet. Essex County Council of Jewish Agencies, 1948.

"Our Young Artists are a Gifted Lot." *Jewish News*, June 14, 1957, 58.

"Overseas Post to Joel Gross." *Newark Evening News*, June 10, 1943, 21.

"Panel to Discuss Interfaith Dating." *Jewish News*, January 29, 1960, 31.

Papers and Correspondence of Louis Levitsky. Available in Rare Manuscript Room, Jewish Theological Seminary.

"The Parochial School Idea," editorial. *Jewish Chronicle*, June 26, 1925, 4.

Patt, Ruth M. *The Workman's (sic) Circle: Its New Jersey Story* (Somerset, N.J.: Jewish Historical Society of Central Jersey, 1989).

Paul, Sylvia Wiederhorn, "East Orange—My Own Home Town." *MetroWest Jewish News*, January 9, 1992, 24.

Pekarsky, Herman M. "Building Our House Together," report, 1948.

————, "New Developments in Jewish Community Organization." *Jewish Social Service Quarterly*, 24, No. 1, September 1947, 6–15.

————, "Observations on Giving and Givers." *Jewish News*, January 19, 1962, 13.

————, "Observations on Giving and Givers." *Jewish News*, January 26, 1962, 13.

————, "Organizing the Community," in *Building the Successful Campaign* (New York: Council of Jewish Federations and Welfare Funds, 1948), 1–6.

"Permanent Body to Assist in Newcomers' Search for Jobs." *Jewish News*, July 28, 1950, 1.

"Peter R. Nehemkis, Jr., Newark Product, One of Leading Figures in Defense Program." *Jewish Chronicle*, Twentieth Anniversary Issue, June 20, 1941, 73.

"Pfc. Louis Schleifer, Who Died Firing Revolver at Jap Aircraft in Pearl Harbor Attack, is Extolled at Ceremonies Dedicating Park, Memorial in his Name." *Jewish Chronicle*, December 11, 1942, 1.

"Philip Lindeman's Career Reads Like Excerpts from Book Romance." *Jewish Chronicle*, Fifteenth Anniversary Issue, April 24, 1936, 31.

Pierson, David Lawrence, *History of the Oranges to 1921,* Vol. 3, (New York: Lewis Historical Publishing Company, 1933), 635. Lists names of early synagogues in South Orange/Maplewood.

Pilchik, Ely E. "One Hundred and Twenty-Five: Notes for a History," pamphlet, undated (about B'nai Jeshurun). American Jewish Archives, Congregation B'nai Jeshurun.

"Pink Propaganda Threatens Youth." *Jewish Chronicle*, May 7, 1926 1.

"Plan Protest Rally Against Polish, Nazi Outrages on Jewry." *Jewish Chronicle*, May 1, 1936, 1.

"Plaut Store, Long on Broad Street, Passes into Hands of S.S. Kresge in Big Deal Involving $17,000,000." *Jewish Chronicle*, August 3, 1923, 1.

"Police Find Cemetery Vandals." *Jewish News*, May 30, 1958, 3.

Pool, David De Sola, *Portraits Etched in Stone: Early Jewish* Settlers, 1682–1831 (New York: Columbia University Press, 1952), 319, 432, 476.

———, *An Old Faith in the New World: Portraits of Shearith Israel, 1654–1954* (New York: Columbia University Press, 1955), 329, 433, 435.

Porter, Laura Smith, "From Intellectual Sanctuary to Social Responsibility: The Founding of the Institute for Advanced Study, 1930–1933." Ph.D. thesis (Princeton University, 1988).

"Predicts Jews Will Shun Reich." *Newark Evening News*, March 24, 1945, 7.

"President of West Side Trust Company Recalls Great Ability of Meyer Kussy." *Jewish Chronicle*, Fifteenth Anniversary Issue, April 24, 1936, 40.

Price, Clement, "Blacks and Jews in the City of Opportunity: Newark, New Jersey, 1900–1967," paper presented at the meeting of the Jewish Historical Society of MetroWest, Whippany, New Jersey, June, 1994.

Price, Samuel, "Diary, Newark, N.J., 1913." in Manuscript Collection, #P-95, *Samuel Price Papers*, American Jewish Historical Society Archives, Waltham, Massachusetts.

Prinz, Joachim, *The Dilemma of the Modern Jew* (Boston: Little Brown, 1962).

Pristin, Terry, "Former Aide in Newark is Sentenced for Bribery." *New York Times*, July 15, 1997, B4.

"Probe Sought in Shule Vandalism." *Newark Jewish Times*, May 7, 1943, 1.

"Problem Child Home Under Consideration by Guidance Bureau." *Jewish Chronicle*, March 27, 1931, 1.

"Professor Handlin Will Inaugurate Series of Lectures at Temple." *Jewish News*, January 8, 1954, 3.

"Progress Club's Long History is Monument of Achievements That Stand Aloft in Splendor." *Jewish Chronicle*, January 27, 1922, 1.

"Progress Club Ranks with Foremost of Kind in Country." *Jewish Chronicle*, Fifteenth Anniversary Issue, April 24, 1936, 77.

"Prominent Headliners of Stage, Screen, Radio to Appear Here on April 19th." *Jewish Chronicle*, March 20, 1936, 1.

"Protest Reading New Testament in Public School." *Jewish Chronicle*, March 3, 1922, 3.

"Rabbi Criticizes Plan to Teach Religion in West Orange Schools." *Jewish Chronicle*, June 8, 1928, 1.

"Rabbi David Wice Assumes Duties at Temple B'nai Jeshurun Monday." *Jewish Chronicle*, August 29, 1941, 1.

"Rabbi Defines Kosher Duties." *Newark Evening News*, August 21, 1939, 6.

"Rabbi Foster Declares Zionism Opposed Here." *Newark Evening News*, January 25, 1919, 8.

"Rabbi Julius Silberfeld," editorial. *Jewish News*, January 3, 1958, 8.

"Rabbi Weiner Named Head of HUC-JIR School in Israel." *Jewish News*, June 22, 1962, 4.

"Rabbis Urge No Absenteeism on Holidays." *Newark Jewish Times*, April 16, 1943, 1.

Raff, Lisa, "Haberdasheries to Epstein's, Morristown's Jewish Roots in Retail." *MetroWest Jewish News*, July 27, 1995, 8.

———, "MetroWest Rejects Request to Fund West Bank Settlements." *MetroWest Jewish News*, February 15, 1996, 8.

———, "JWV—100 Years of Dispelling the Myth That Jews Didn't Serve their Country." *MetroWest Jewish News*, March 14, 1996, 12.

Ramer, Alia, "Jewish Farmers of Pine Brook Planted Seeds for Montville Community." *MetroWest Jewish News*, August 8, 1996, 13.

———, "UJF of MetroWest Has New Israeli Partnerships in the Negev." *MetroWest Jewish News*, January 2,1997, 8.

Ravitz, Abraham Noah, "A History of Events and Activities of Congregation Anshei Russia," unpublished manuscript in Yiddish, 1910, English translation, Harry M. Rosenthal. American Jewish Archives, Manuscript Collection.

"Reasons Why you Should Shop on Springfield Avenue." *Jewish Chronicle*, March 26, 1926, 7.

"Recall Beginnings of B'nai Abraham." *Jewish News*, January 13, 1950, 2.

"Record Gifts Launch National UJA Drive: Essex County Reports 63.6% Increase." *Jewish News*, March 2, 1956, 1.

"Record Number Gets Malbish Arumim Gifts." *Jewish Chronicle*, September 19, 1930, 1.

"Refugee Children Find Homes." *Jewish Chronicle*, June 27, 1941, 1.

"Reinfeld, Striar to Be Honorary Leaders of 1965 UJA Campaign." *Jewish News*, January 8, 1965, 1.

"Renaissance vs. Hebrews Sunday." *Jewish Chronicle*, November 29, 1935, 2.

"Reveals 20% Increase in Jewish School Registration." *Jewish News*, August 4, 1950, 5.

Richer, Jack C. *Papers*, Newark, N.J., 1917–1919. New Jersey Historical Society, Manuscript Group #1082 (letters between Richer and his family in Newark during his naval service in Europe, Yiddish and English).

Robinson, Sophia M. *The Jewish Population of Essex County*, Report, Jewish Community Council, 1948.

Rockaway, Robert A. *BUT—He Was Good to His Mother: The Lives and Crimes of Jewish Gangsters* (Gefen: Jerusalem, 1993), 24–29, 30–31, 166–70, 188–91, 207, 211–13, 222–24, 228–29, 236–38.

Romm, Jacob. *History of Jewish Community of Kearny and North Arlington* (covers 1889–1961 with some correspondence; about 100 pages long).

"Rossini and Gershwin Captivate Audience in a Newark Slum." *New York Times*, July 15, 1968.

Roth, Ben and Eva H. Robinson. *Beth David in Review*, pamphlet (Vailsburg and Sanford Heights communities).

"Roth Lodge Has Splendid Growth." *Jewish Chronicle*, November 4, 1921, 1.

Roth, Philip, *Goodbye Columbus* (New York: Bantam Books, 1963).

———, *Portnoy's Complaint* (New York: Random House, 1969).

———, *Zuckerman Unbound* (New York: Farrar, Straus & Giroux, 1981).

———, *The Facts: A Novelist's Autobiography* (New York: Farrar, Straus & Giroux, 1988).

———, *Patrimony* (New York: Touchstone, 1991).

———, *American Pastoral* (New York: Houghton Mifflin Company, 1997).

Rothseid, Doris, "The Requests of Refugees and How they are Met by a Family Agency," M.S. thesis (Smith College School for Social Work, 1946).

"Rube Goldberg Sees His Own Characters Prance at Cotillion." *Jewish Chronicle* February 4, 1922, 1.

Rudavsky, David, "A Unifying Force in Jewish Education." *Jewish News*, June 14, 1957, 50.

———, "Report and Survey of Verona Jewish Community," unpublished Report in Synagogue Archives at Rutgers University.

Rudolph, Robert, *The Boys from New Jersey: How the Mob Beat the Feds* (New York: William Morrow & Co., 1996).

Russem, Louise, "A Family Agency's Activities in Raising Public Welfare Standards," MSS thesis (Smith College School for Social Work, 1946).

Salzman, Ruth, "Unfair to B'nai B'rith," letter to the editor, *Jewish News*, February 14, 1947, 4.

"Samuel I. Kessler—Prominent Member of Bar and Outstanding Leader of State Jewry." *Jewish Chronicle*, Twentieth Anniversary Issue, June 20, 1941, 91.

"Samuel Kessler is Appointed as Prosecutor." *Jewish Chronicle*, March 2, 1923, 1.

"Samuel L. La Pidus Wrote Success Story in Dramatic Rise of Firm." *Jewish Chronicle*, Twentieth Anniversary Issue, June 20, 1941, 54.

Scarr, Jacob, *Listen, My Children: A Grandfather's Legacy* (Philadelphia, Pa.: Dorrance, 1972).

Schaffer, Gail. *Memoirs of an American Sabra Hebrew Teacher* (North Miami, Fla.: Renaissance Booksetters, 1977).

Schapiro, Edith K. "'Jackie' Wins Prinz Award for 'Exemplary Leadership.'" *Jewish News*, September 14, 1978, 1.

Schary, Dore, *For Special Occasions* (New York: Random House, 1961).

———, *Heyday* (Boston: Little, Brown & Co., 1979).

Scher, Rhoda, "Meet the Presidents." *Jewish News*, May 13, 1949, 13.

———, "Discovers Mrs. Ben-Gurion was his Student at 'Beth.'" *Jewish News*, June 24, 1949, 1.

———, "Meet the Presidents." *Jewish News*, July 8, 1949, 12.

Scherzer, Carl B. "Early Jewish History in Morristown," unpublished paper.

"Schleifer Cited for Bravery and Gallantry." *Jewish Chronicle,* December 4, 1942, 1.

"Schley Street Synagogue is Pioneer Congregation in Weequahic Section." *Jewish Chronicle*, Twentieth Anniversary Issue, June 20, 1941, 103.

"Schwarz Drug Stores Have Been in Business Almost Half of Century." *Jewish Chronicle*, Twentieth Anniversary Issue, June 20, 1941, 96.

Schwarz, Saul, "Building Jewish Community Along 'the Turnpike': The Unique Difficulties of a Populous Region," paper presented at the Meetings of the Mid-Atlantic Region of the Association of Jewish Community Organization Personnel, New Brunswick, New Jersey, June, 1984.

Schwarz, Saul, "The Job of the Executive Director in Local Jewish Central Community Organization, An Occupational Monograph," MSW thesis (New York School of Social Work, Columbia University, 1951).

Schwarz, Saul, Paper presented at workshop for professional social planners, St. Louis, May 1956. Available at Jewish Historical Society of MetroWest.

Schwarz, Saul and Martin Fox, "Jews Are Not To Blame for the Decline of the City of Newark." *MetroWest Jewish News*, April 12, 1990, 21, 29.

"Scroll Will Honor Victims of Nazis." *Newark Evening News*, April 12, 1947, 6.

Septee, Moe, "Experiencing Boom," letter, *Jewish News*, October 17, 1958, 10.

"Service to Foreign Born." *Annual Report*, April 1948.

"Service for War Brides: Bureau in Newark Which Aids Refugees Now Flooded with Appeals from GIs." *Newark Evening News*, January 14, 1946, 9.

"Set Newark Rally for Bus Riders." *Jewish News*, July 7, 1961, 13.

Settanni, Joseph A. *Initial Historical Chronologies of the United Jewish Federation of MetroWest's Major Administrative Officers*, pamphlet. Jewish Historical Society of MetroWest Archives, July 11, 1995.

————, *Institutional Origins of the Conference of Jewish Charities of Newark: Initial Affiliated Agencies*, pamphlet. Jewish Historical Society of MetroWest Archives, July 12, 1995.

"Seventeen Hundred at Huge Meeting Here Hail Life Work of Dr. Theodore Herzl." *Jewish Chronicle*, May 17, 1935, 1.

Shearith Israel Congregation Papers, minutes of January 17, 1847; Minutes of July 1, 1898.

Shapiro, Edward S., "The Jews of New Jersey," in Barbara Cunningham (ed.), *The New Jersey Ethnic Experience* (Union City, N.J.: William H. Wire and Co., 1977), 294–313.

Shiman, Daniel, "Newark Sets Up Joint Council." *The Jewish Community*, January 1947, 5–7.

"Shiman Reviews History of Jewish Community Council." *Jewish News*, January 3, 1947, 7.

Silberfeld, Julius, "This is a Sorry Sight." February 7, 1947, 4.

Silver, Helen P. "Newcomers Aid Each Other in Problems of Adjustment." *Jewish News*, July 21, 1950, 12.

————, "Newcomers' Classes Stress Vocabulary Needed for Jobs." *Jewish News*, July 28, 1950, 8.

————, "Retiring Principal is Leaving Just One of his Many Jobs." *Jewish News*, June 1, 1951, 7.

"Silverstein, Aide to Mayor, is in Newspaper Work for 19 Years." *Jewish Chronicle*, Twentieth Anniversary Issue, June 20, 1941, 89.

Silverstein, Elizabeth Blume, Papers, Newark, NJ. New Jersey Historical Society, Manuscript Group #1320 (correspondence of a N.J. attorney 1893–1991).

Sinnott, Arthur J. "Is Newark a Suburb of New York?:An Answer to a Question Often Asked." *The Newarker*, June 15, 1936, 2.

"Six Hundred Soldiers Acclaim 'Y' Annual Revue." *Jewish Chronicle*, May 30, 1941, 1.

Slater, Sarah, "The Sisterhood of Young Israel." *Jewish Chronicle*, Young Israel Supplement. February 28, 1936, 4.

Smith, Sylvia, "The Cause of Immigrants in Newark Ably Championed by Intensive Work of Mrs. Max Danzis, Once One of Them." *Jewish Chronicle*, September 23, 1927, 6.

Smothers, Ronald, "In Riots' Shadow, a City Stumbles On." *New York Times*, July 14, 1997, 1.

———, "As Newark Bounces Back, So Does Mayor." *New York Times,* January 31, 1998, B1.

"Social and Personal." *Jewish Chronicle,* October 14, 1921, 5.

"Social and Personal." *Jewish Chronicle,* October 21, 1921, 5.

"Social and Personal Activities: Social Activities." *Jewish Chronicle,* September 26, 1930, 6.

"Social and Personal Activities: Some of Newark's New Female Barristers." *Jewish Chronicle,* August 8, 1930, 6.

Sokobin, Samuel to Jacob R. Marcus, typescript letter, December 29, 1964 (reminiscences of Cong. Eyn Yakkov and other Newark memories, 1899–1964). American Jewish Archives, Miscellaneous Near Print Collection.

"Some of Newark's New Female Barristers." *Jewish Chronicle,* August 8, 1930, 6.

"State Groups Will Meet Tuesday to Sift Discrimination Charges at Rutgers; Allegations Denied." *Jewish Chronicle,* October 17, 1930, 1.

Stavitsky, Michael A. "New Trends in Community Programs for Jewish Education," unpublished report. Available at Jewish Historical Society of MetroWest.

Steinbock, Jose Ann, "Butchers Federation Sues Seroffs for Libel." *Jewish News,* July 13, 1956, 1.

———, "Gangs Can Become Clubs." *Jewish News,* May 16, 1958, 36.

Stellhorn, Paul, "Champion of the City: The Political Career of Meyer C. Ellenstein," paper presented at annual meeting of the Jewish Historical Society of MetroWest, June 9, 1997.

Sterling, Guy, "Hail of Bullets Polished Legend of Dutch Schultz." *Newark Star-Ledger,* 31.

"The Story of Temple B'nai Israel," undated, unsigned report.

Stuart, Mark, *Gangster #2: Longy Zwillman, The Man Who Invented Organized Crime* (Secaucus, N.J.: Lyle Stuart, 1985).

"Survey Newark Population Shift." *Jewish News,* April 10, 1959, 14

Susswein, Jane, "No Task was Too Menial or Too Small in Church Rebuilding." *MetroWest Jewish News,* March 6, 1997, 16.

Synagogue Etiquette and Procedure of Young Israel of Newark, pamphlet.

"Synagogue Hecklers Severely Beaten." *Jewish Chronicle,* October 11, 1940, 3.

"Talmud Torah is Helping Educate Children Through Scholarships." *Jewish Chronicle,* Twentieth Anniversary Issue, June 20, 1941, 97.

"Talmud Torah Portraits . . ." *Jewish Chronicle,* February 13, 1942, 1.

"Talmud Torah's Inspiring Leader." *Jewish Chronicle,* Twentieth Anniversary Issue, June 20, 1941, 80 (about Israel Fishman).

"Teen-Age Activities for UJA are Moving into High Gear." *Jewish News,* March 12, 1954, 23.

Temple B'nai Abraham Dedication Journal, undated.

Temple Sholom of West Essex: A Handbook for our Members, pamphlet, undated.

"Ten Thousand Hear Byrd Lecture on Flight." *Jewish Chronicle,* October 31, 1930, 1.

"Thirteen North Jersey Lodges to Launch $1,000,000 Campaign for U.S. War Bonds Sale Tonight." *Newark Jewish Times,* April 2, 1943, 1.

Thorndike, Thelma, "Growth of Temple Sharey Tefilo Reviewed." *Jewish Chronicle,* Fifteenth Anniversary Issue, April 24, 1936, 8.

———, "Temple Sharey Tefilo's Rise Traced to Rabbi Ranson." *Jewish Chronicle,* Twentieth Anniversary Issue, June 20, 1941, 63.

"Three Jews to Get Important Posts in New Jersey Assembly." *Jewish Chronicle,* December 18, 1931, 1.

"Throng Laughs at Big 'Y' Show." *Jewish Chronicle,* January 13, 1922, 1.

"To Aid Inquiry on Insurance." *Newark Evening News*, November 4, 1938, 2.

"To Graduate 50 Students at Normal School Here." *Jewish Chronicle,* May 18, 1927, 1.

Troy, Ann A. (ed.), *Nutley: Yesterday-Today* (Nutley, N.J.: Nutley Historical Society, 1961), 174–75.

"Twenty-Two Graduated at Normal School." *Jewish Chronicle*, June 13, 1930, 1.

Twersky, David, "Think Tankers Seek to Expand Ra'anana Ties." *MetroWest Jewish News*, March 2, 1995, 8.

"Twin Distinction Won by Joel Gross." *Jewish Chronicle*, May 29, 1942, 1.

Umansky, Sherri, "Single in Metrowest: Is There Life Beyond Marriage?" *METRO Source: A Guide to Jewish Living, 1993–94,* 17, 32–34.

Union of American Hebrew Congregations, *Statistical Analysis of Jewish Communities in New Jersey for the Year Ending September 18, 1876*, Philadelphia, Pa. In American Jewish Archives, Manuscript Collection.

"United Hebrew Association to Celebrate 35th Year; Has Done Notable Work." *Jewish Chronicle*, Twentieth Anniversary Issue, June 20, 1941, 10.

United Jewish Federation of MetroWest, *Records of the Federation and Affiliated Agencies and Individuals*, Whippany, N.J., c. 1850– to the present.

"United Palestine Appeal Battle Intensifies as Executives Quit." *Jewish News*, November 19, 1948, 1.

Unterman, Isaac, *Newark Jewry: A History of the Jews of Newark, Their Institutions, and Leading Personalities,* 2 volumes, Newark, N.J., *Newarker Morgenshtern*, 1939 (Yiddish).

"Untermann, Silverstein, Parsonnet, Schotland, Gansler Among Jewish Appointees to City Posts." *Jewish Chronicle*, May 23, 1941, 1.

"Urge More Help in Effort to Have Jewish Homeland." *Newark Evening News*, June 5, 1923, 7.

"Vailsburg Bank Opening Creates Wide Interest." *Jewish Chronicle*, April 6, 1923, 1.

Van Gelder, Lawrence, "David Lasser, 94, a Space and a Social Visionary." *New York Times*, May 7, 1996.

Vance, Margaret, "Reform Jews to Dedicate New Temple in Short Hills." *Newark Evening News*, September 3, 1968, 21.

"Vandals Hit Local Cemeteries." *Jewish News*, May 23, 1958, 3.

"Vandals Invade Local Cemeteries." *Jewish News*, September 5, 1958, 3.

"Venerable Newarker Has Notable Legal Career." *Jewish Chronicle*, Fifteenth Anniversary Issue, April 24, 1936, 86.

Verosub, Vera, *The Way it Was*, (n.p.,1992).

"Vote to Support Jewish Plebiscite." *Newark Evening News*, May 5, 1938, 15.

Wagner, Richard, *The Jewish Education Association and You: The First Fifty Years, Jubilee Album*, booklet (Newark, N.J.: MetroWest Federation Department of Public Information, 1987,).

Wallerstein, Jane, *Path of Service: A History of the Jewish Counseling and Service Agency of Essex County and Its Predecessor Agencies 1861–1961*, booklet (Newark, N.J.: Hebrew Benevolent and Orphan Society, 1962).

"War Survivors Thank Newark Women." *Jewish News*, February 7, 1947, 2.

"War Veterans Lead Fight for Principles." *Jewish Chronicle*, Fifteenth Anniversary Issue, April 24, 1936, 73.

Waxman, Henrietta Konner, "Looking Back to the Sunrise," booklet.

"We Scan the History of the Chronicle." *Jewish Chronicle*, May 29, 1931, 2.

"Weequahic Jews Face Rift Due to Talmud Torah Site." *Jewish Chronicle*, July 24, 1931, 1.

"Weequahic School Meeting Tuesday." *Jewish Chronicle*, September 7, 1928, 1.

Weiner, Max, "This Bank Lends From the Heart." *Newark Sunday (Evening) News*, November 26, 1950, 66.

Weissman-Joselit, Jenna, *Our Gang: Jewish Crime and the New York Jewish Community*, 1900–1940 (Bloomington: Indiana University Press, 1983), 97, 190.

Werb, Morris R. "Jewish Suburbia: An Historical and Comparative Study of Jewish Communities in Three New Jersey Suburbs," Ph.D. thesis (New York University, 1959).

"What Women's Organizations are Doing." *Jewish Chronicle*, column, May 25, 1934, 6.

———, *Jewish Chronicle,* column, June 1, 1934.

Whiteman, Max, *Copper For America*, (New Brunswick, N.J.: Rutgers University Press, 1971), 4, 112, 142–145, 232–233, 285.

"Why the Talmud Torah?" *Jewish Chronicle.*" December 4, 1936, 1.

"Why the Talmud Torah?" *Jewish Chronicle*, December 18, 1936, 1.

"Why the Talmud Torah?" *Jewish Chronicle*, December 25, 1936, 1.

"Why the Talmud Torah?" *Jewish Chronicle*, January 1, 1937, 1.

"Why the Talmud Torah?" *Jewish Chronicle*, January 8, 1937, 1.

"Why the Talmud Torah?" *Jewish Chronicle*, January 15, 1937, 1

"Will Honor Golda Myerson at Special Gifts Dinner for UJA." *Jewish News*, May 27, 1949, 1.

"Will Raise Fund of $100,000 for Medical School." *Jewish Chronicle*, June 23, 1922, 1.

"William Schiffenhaus' Passing is Mourned by Whole Community." *Jewish Chronicle*, April 25, 1941, 1.

"Wise Assails Rabbi Foster." *Newark Evening News*, June 10, 1938, 9.

Wolf, Edwin and Maxwell Whiteman, *History of the Jews of Philadelphia from Colonial Times to the Age of Jackson* (Philadelphia, Pa.: Jewish Publication Society, 1957).

"Women Praised at Dedication of Ward for Kiddies." *Jewish Chronicle*, November 25, 1921, 1.

"Women's Association Bazaar Opens in Temple B'nai Jeshurun November 29th." *Jewish Chronicle*, November 17, 1922, 1.

"Women's Organizations." *Jewish Chronicle*, February 6, 1931, 8.

"'Y' to Mark End of First Year in New Building With Elaborate Week's Program." *Jewish Chronicle*, May 15, 1925, 1.

"'Y' Summer Camp Plans Completed." *Jewish Chronicle*, June 19, 1925, 1.

Yanoff, Leo. *Memoirs of Judge Leo Yanoff* (New Jersey: n.p., 1996).

Yearbook of the Jewish Community Center of Sussex County, 1996–97.

"Years of Service Capped by Promotion to Fire Captaincy." *Jewish News*, September 21, 1951, 17.

"You and Your Community: A Plan For a Jewish Community Council." Essex County Council of Jewish Agencies, 1945.

"Young Israel of Newark." *Jewish Chronicle Supplement*, February 28, 1936.

"Young Israel of Newark." *Jewish Chronicle* Supplement, March 11, 1938.

Young Israel South Orange Jewish Center, Records, 1926–1981. In Special Collections and University Archives, Rutgers University Libraries, Manuscript Collection #902.

"Young Israel Synagogue of 'Y' to Conduct Services at Talmud Torah." *Jewish Chronicle*, April 24, 1925, 1.

"Young Men's Welfare Society." *Minute Books, January 2, 1861– January 28, 1877* (Newark, N.J.: Jewish Community of Essex County, 1961). In American Jewish Archives, Histories File.

"Zionism Seen as Move Back to Judaism by Nathan Kussy." *Jewish Chronicle*, February 1, 1924, 1.

"Zionist Leaders Warmly Greeted on Newark Visit." *Jewish Chronicle*, December 23, 1921, 1.

"Zionists Hit B'nai Brith." *Jewish News*, February 7, 1947, 2.

Zurofsky, Jack J., "'Send These, the Homeless Tempest-Tossed, to me.'" *Jewish News*, December 19, 1947, 9.

———, "General Assembly's Structure is Found to Have Deficiencies." *Jewish News*, December 26, 1952, 7.

General Works about Newark:

Bruni, Frank, "In Fleeting Moments, Pope Vitalizes Streets of Newark." *New York Times*, October 5, 1995, A1.

———, "Archbishop is a Man in Motion for His Newark Flock." *New York Times*, October 5, 1995, B4.

Cummings, Charles F. & John E. O'Connor, *Newark: An American City,* Newark, N.J.: Newark Bicentennial Commission, 1979), booklet.

Cunningham, John T.. *Newark* (Newark, N.J.: The New Jersey Historical Society, 1988, revised ed.).

——— and Charles F. Cummings, *Remembering Essex: A Pictorial History of Essex County, New Jersey.* (The Donning Company:Virginia Beach, Virginia, 1995).

Folsom, Joseph F. (ed), *The Municipalities of Essex County, New Jersey, 1666–1924* (New York & Chicago: Lewis Historical Publishing Company, 1925), 106–07.

Galishoff, Stuart, *Newark, the Nation's Unhealthiest City, 1832–1895* (New Brunswick, N.J.: Rutgers University Press).

Hayden, Tom, *Rebellion in Newark: Official Violence and Ghetto Response.* (New York: Vintage, 1967).

Jordan, George E. "Developer Puts Great Store in Plan for Newark Future: Family Proposes $4.7 Million to Renovate Macy's Building." *Newark Sunday Star Ledger*, August 18, 1996, 1.

Levy, Clifford J., "U.S. Investigates Newark Group as a Possible Political Slush Fund." *New York Times*, December 9, 1994, B1.

———, "Newark Mayor Accused of Violations." *New York Times*, February 22, 1995, B5.

———, "A Portuguese Village in Newark." *New York Times*, October 6, 1995, C1.

Lipton, Barbara, "Newark Long Ago: 19th Century Photographs From the Museum's Collections." *Newark Museum Quarterly*, 26, No. 4 (Fall 1975), 1–28.

Nieves, Evelyn, "Touring the Glories of Newark." *New York Times*, April 18, 1995 , B5.

Rippon, F.F.C., *Survey of the Boys of Newark, New Jersey* (Newark, New Jersey: Baker Printing Company, 1928).

Siegel, Fred, "The Mental Ruins of the Newark Riot." *New York Post*, July 27, 1997, 47.

Stout, David, "On Newark's Highest Hill, Faith and Joy Overflow." *New York Times*, October 5, 1995, B4.

Urquhart, Frank J., *A Short History of Newark* (Newark, New Jersey: Baker Printing Company, 1910).

General Works About New Jersey:

Brandes, Joseph, *Immigrants to Freedom: Jewish Communities in Rural New Jersey Since 1882* (Philadelphia: University of Pennsylvania Press, 1971.

"New Jersey at a Crossroads, 1845: A Look Back." in *New Jersey Historical Society News*, January-April 1995, 3.

Rudolph, Robert, *The Boys From New Jersey: How the Mob Beat the Feds* (New York: William Morrow, 1992).

Vecoli, Rudolph J. *The People of New Jersey* (Princeton, N.J.: D. Van Nostrand Company, 1965).

Related Interest:

Abu-Lughod, Janet L. *Changing Cities: Urban Sociology* (New York: Harper-Collins, 1991).

Auerbach, Jon G. "Jewish Loan Societies Rethink the Tradition of Helping All Comers." *Wall Street Journal*, September 11, 1997, 1.

Baumel, Judith Tydor, *Unfulfilled Promise: Rescue and Resettlement of Jewish Refugee Children in the United States 1934–1945* (Juneau, Alaska: The Dinali Press, 1990).

Bernstein, Philip, *To Dwell in Unity: The Jewish Federation in America Since 1960*. (Philadelphia: Jewish Publication Society, 1983).

Birmingham, Stephen, *The Grandees: America's Sephardic Elite* (New York: Harper & Row, 1971).

Block, Alan, *East Side-West Side: Organizing Crime in New York, 1930–1950*. (New Brunswick, N.J.: Transaction Books, 1995).

Coser, Lewis, *The Functions of Social Conflict* (Glencoe, Ill.: The Free Press, 1956).

Endelman, Judith E., *The Jewish Community of Indianapolis: 1849 to the Present* (Bloomington, Ind.: Indiana University Press, 1984).

Gartner, Lloyd P., *History of the Jews of Cleveland* (Cranbury, N.J.: Associated University Presses, 1987, revised ed.).

Glazer, Nathan, *American Judaism*, (Chicago: University of Chicago Press, second edition, revised, 1972).

Gettinger, Max C., *Coming of Age: The Atlanta Jewish Federation, 1962–1982* (Hoboken, N.J.: KTAV, 1994).

Helmreich, William B., "Jewish Marginality and the Struggle for Equality." *Journal of Intergroup Relations*, 5, No. 3, 1976, 37–40.

———, *The Things they Say Behind your Back: Stereotypes and the Myths Behind Them* (New York: Doubleday, 1982).

———, *The World of the Yeshiva: An Intimate Portrait of Orthodox Jewry* (New York: The Free Press, 1982).

———, *Against All Odds: Holocaust Survivors and the Successful Lives they Made in America* (New York: Simon & Schuster, 1993).

Howe, Irving, *World of our Fathers: The Journey of the East European Jews to America and the Life they Found and Made* (New York: Harcourt, Brace & Jovanovich, 1976).

Kochman, Thomas, "Toward an Ethnography of Black American Speech Behavior," in Norman E. Whitten Jr. & John F. Szwed, *Afro- American Anthropology: Contemporary Perspectives* (New York: The Free Press, 1970), 145–62.

Kraft, Louis, *A Century of the Jewish Community Center Movement, 1854–1954*, New York: Jewish Community Center Centennial Committee, 1953. Booklet.

Levine, Hillel & Lawrence Harmon, *The Death of an American Jewish Community: A Tragedy of Good Intentions* (New York: The Free Press, 1992).

Lipman, Steve, "Day Schools Get Financial Boost." *Jewish Week*, October 24, 1997, 1.

Lurie, Harry, *A Heritage Affirmed: The Jewish Federation Movement in America* (Philadelphia: Jewish Publication Society, 1961).

Moore, Deborah Dash, *To the Golden Cities: Pursuing the American Jewish Dream in Miami and L.A.* (New York: The Free Press, 1994).

Myrdal, Gunnar, *An American Dilemma: The Negro Population and Modern Democracy*, Volume One, (New York: Harper & Row, 1944), 191–197.

Reider, Jonathan, *Canarsie: The Jews and Italians of Brooklyn Against Liberalism* (London: Cambridge University Press, 1985).

Rischin, Moses, *The Promised City: New York's Jews 1870–1914* (New York: Harper Torchbooks edition, 1970).

Rockaway, Robert A. *The Jews of Detroit: From the Beginning, 1762–1914.* (Detroit, MI: Wayne State University Press, 1986).

Rybczynski, Witold, *City Life: Urban Expectations in a New World.* (New York: Scribner, 1995).

Sarna D. Jonathan, "The History of the Jewish Press in North America." in *The North American Jewish Press*, Waltham, Mass.: Brandeis University, April, 1995, 2–7. Pamphlet.

Sklare, Marshall & Joseph Greenblum, *Jewish Identity on the Suburban Frontier: A Study of Group Survival in the Open Society* (New York: Basic Books, 1967).

Smith, Judith E. *Family Connections: A History of Italian & Jewish Immigrant Lives in Providence, Rhode Island, 1900– 1940* (State University of New York Press, 1985).

Swichkow, Louis J. & Lloyd P. Gartner, *The History of the Jews of Milwaukee*, (Philadelphia: Jewish Publication Society, 1963).

Vorspan, Max & Lloyd P. Gartner, *History of the Jews of Los Angeles* (Huntington, CA: The Huntington Library & Jewish Publication Society, 1970).

Ward, David, *Cities and Immigrants: A Geography of Change in Nineteenth-Century America* (New York: Oxford University Press, 1971).

Weisbord, Robert G. & Arthur Stein, *Bittersweet Encounter: The Afro-American and the American Jew* (New York: Schocken, 1970).

Weissman-Joselit, Jenna, *Our Gang: Jewish Crime and the New York Jewish Community, 1900–1940* (Bloomington, Indiana: Indiana University Press, 1983).

Wright, Richard, *Black Boy* (New York: Harper & Row edn., 1966).

Name Index

Subject Index

357